Process Tracing

Advances in qualitative methods and recent developments in the philosophy of science have led to an emphasis on explanation via reference to causal mechanisms. This book argues that the method known as process tracing is particularly well suited to developing and assessing theories about such mechanisms. The editors begin by establishing a philosophical basis for process tracing – one that captures mainstream uses while simultaneously being open to applications by interpretive scholars. Equally important, they go on to establish best practices for individual process-tracing accounts – how micro to go, when to start (and stop), and how to deal with the problem of equifinality. The contributors then explore the application of process tracing across a range of subfields and theories in political science. This is an applied methods book which seeks to shrink the gap between the broad assertion that "process tracing is good" and the precise claim "this is an instance of good process tracing."

Andrew Bennett is Professor of Government at Georgetown University. He is also President of the Consortium on Qualitative Research Methods, which sponsors the annual Institute on Qualitative and Multi-Method Research at Syracuse University. He is the co-author, with Alexander L. George, of *Case Studies and Theory Development* (2005), which won the Giovanni Sartori Prize in 2005 for the best book on qualitative methods.

Jeffrey T. Checkel is Professor of International Studies and Simons Chair in International Law and Human Security at Simon Fraser University. He is also a Global Research Fellow at the Peace Research Institute Oslo. He has published extensively in leading European and North American journals, and is the author of *Ideas and International Political Change: Soviet/Russian Behavior and the End of the Cold War* (1997), editor of *International Institutions and Socialization in Europe* (Cambridge University Press, 2007), co-editor (with Peter J. Katzenstein) of *European Identity* (Cambridge University Press, 2009), and editor of *Transnational Dynamics of Civil War* (Cambridge University Press, 2013).

Strategies for Social Inquiry

Process Tracing: From Metaphor to Analytic Tool

Editors
Colin Elman, Maxwell School of Syracuse University
John Gerring, Boston University
James Mahoney, Northwestern University

Editorial board
Bear Braumoeller, David Collier, Francesco Guala, Peter Hedström,
Theodore Hopf, Uskali Maki, Rose McDermott, Charles Ragin, Theda Skocpol,
Peter Spiegler, David Waldner, Lisa Wedeen, Christopher Winship

This new book series presents texts on a wide range of issues bearing upon the practice
of social inquiry. Strategies are construed broadly to embrace the full spectrum of
approaches to analysis, as well as relevant issues in philosophy of social science.

Published titles
John Gerring, *Social Science Methodology: A Unified Framework, 2nd edition*
Michael Coppedge, *Democratization and Research Methods*
Thad Dunning, *Natural Experiments in the Social Sciences: A Design-Based Approach*
Carsten Q. Schneider and Claudius Wagemann, *Set-Theoretic Methods for the Social
    Sciences: A Guide to Qualitative Comparative Analysis*
Nicholas Weller and Jeb Barnes, *Finding Pathways: Mixed-Method Research for
    Studying Causal Mechanisms*

Forthcoming titles
Diana Kapiszewski, Lauren M. MacLean and Benjamin L. Read, *Field Research in
    Political Science: Practices and Principles*
Jason Seawright, *Multi-Method Social Science: Combining Qualitative and
    Quantitative Tools*
Peter Spiegler, *A Constructive Critique of Economic Modeling*

Process Tracing

From Metaphor to Analytic Tool

Edited by

Andrew Bennett

Georgetown University

Jeffrey T. Checkel

Simon Fraser University

CAMBRIDGE
UNIVERSITY PRESS

CAMBRIDGE
UNIVERSITY PRESS

University Printing House, Cambridge CB2 8BS, United Kingdom

Cambridge University Press is part of the University of Cambridge.

It furthers the University's mission by disseminating knowledge in the pursuit of
education, learning and research at the highest international levels of excellence.

www.cambridge.org
Information on this title: www.cambridge.org/9781107686373

© Cambridge University Press 2015

First published 2015
Reprinted 2015

Printed in the United Kingdom by Clays, St Ives plc

A catalogue record for this publication is available from the British Library

Library of Congress Cataloging-in-Publication Data
Process tracing : from metaphor to analytic tool / edited by Andrew Bennett, Georgetown University,
Jeffrey T. Checkel, Simon Fraser University.
    pages   cm. – (Strategies for social inquiry)
ISBN 978-1-107-04452-4 (hardback) – ISBN 978-1-107-68637-3 (paperback)
1. Political science – Methodology.   2. Causation.   3. Case method.   4. Qualitative
research.   5. Social sciences – Methodology.   I. Bennett, Andrew, 1960– editor.   II. Checkel,
Jeffrey T., 1959– editor.
JA71.P756   2015
320.01–dc23
                                                                            2014021292

ISBN 978-1-107-04452-4 Hardback
ISBN 978-1-107-68637-3 Paperback

Contents

Figures

Tables

Contributors

Andrew Bennett, Professor, Department of Government, Georgetown University

Jeffrey T. Checkel, Professor and Simons Chair, School for International Studies, Simon Fraser University, and Global Research Fellow, Peace Research Institute Oslo

Thad Dunning, Robson Professor of Political Science, Department of Political Science, University of California, Berkeley

Matthew Evangelista, President White Professor of History and Political Science, Department of Government, Cornell University

Alan M. Jacobs, Associate Professor, Department of Political Science, University of British Columbia

Jason Lyall, Associate Professor, Department of Political Science, Yale University

Vincent Pouliot, Associate Professor and William Dawson Scholar, Department of Political Science, McGill University

Frank Schimmelfennig, Professor of European Politics, Swiss Federal Institute of Technology, Zürich

David Waldner, Associate Professor, Woodrow Wilson Department of Politics, University of Virginia

Preface

When the editors of the Strategies for Social Inquiry Series at Cambridge University Press first approached us to write a book on process tracing, our response was "yes, but . . ." That is, we absolutely agreed there was a need for such a book, but, at the same time, we were leery – hence that "but" – of writing a standard methods text. Of course, process tracing is a method, so there was no getting around writing a methodology book.

Yet, from our own experience – be it working with Ph.D. students, reviewing manuscripts and journal articles, or giving seminars – we sensed a need, indeed a hunger, for a slightly different book, one that showed, in a grounded, operational way, how to do process tracing well. After discussions (and negotiations!) with the series editors, the result is the volume before you. We view it as an applied methods book, where the aim is to show how process tracing works in practice, using and critiquing prominent research examples from several subfields and research programs within political science. If the last fifteen years have seen the publication of key texts setting the state of the art for case studies, then our volume is a logical follow-on, providing clear guidance for what is perhaps the central within-case method – process tracing.

All chapters have been through numerous rounds of revision. The broad outlines of Chapter 1 were first presented to the Research Group on Qualitative and Multi-Method Analysis, Syracuse University, in June 2010, where we received critical but constructive feedback from some of the sharpest methodological minds in the business. A fully revised version of the first chapter together with drafts of most of the others were then critiqued at a workshop held at Georgetown University in March 2012. During this meeting, Peter Hall and Jack Snyder – in their role as "über-discussants" – gave indispensable help, assessing the project as a whole, but also providing trenchant criticisms and constructive suggestions on individual chapters. At this same workshop, we also received valuable feedback from Colin Elman and the Georgetown scholarly community, especially Kate McNamara and

Dan Nexon. In the summer of 2012, three anonymous reviewers for Cambridge University Press evaluated key parts of the manuscript. Their comments were invaluable in helping us (re)frame the project, but also – and more specifically – in pushing us to rethink and justify key arguments we lay out in the opening chapter.

We owe thanks to many people and institutions, with the most important intellectual debt to our authors. Throughout, they rose to our challenge – "to make process tracing real!" – while diligently responding to multiple rounds of requests for changes and improvements in their chapters and providing insightful feedback on our own. For helpful comments on various parts of the manuscript, we thank – in addition to those already named – Derek Beach, Aaron Boesenecker, Jim Caporaso, Marty Finnemore, Lise Howard, Macartan Humphreys, and Ingo Rohlfing, as well as seminar audiences at the Freie Universität Berlin, Graduate Institute of International and Development Studies, Geneva, and the Massachusetts Institute of Technology. In addition, we received excellent feedback from what is perhaps our main target audience – Ph.D. students – in courses and workshops at Georgetown University, Goethe-Universität Frankfurt, the Institute for Qualitative and Multi-Method Research, Syracuse University, the Massachusetts Institute of Technology, the Research School on Peace and Conflict, Peace Research Institute Oslo, and the Oslo Summer School in Comparative Social Science Studies.

The academic editors of the series – Colin Elman, John Gerring, and Jim Mahoney – are owed a special thank you. From the beginning, they pushed us to produce the best possible book. We often agreed with their criticisms; when we did not, their help made us more aware about our central aim.

Checkel also thanks the Kolleg-Forschergruppe "The Transformative Power of Europe," Freie Universität Berlin and its directors – Tanja Börzel and Thomas Risse – for providing a stimulating and collegial setting during the book's final write-up.

Last and certainly not least, we owe a debt of gratitude to Damian Penfold, who carefully – and cheerfully – copy-edited and formatted the entire initial manuscript, and to Barbara Salmon for preparation of the index. At Cambridge University Press, we thank John Haslam for organizing an efficient and rigorous review process, and Carrie Parkinson and Ed Robinson for overseeing the production of the book.

For administrative and logistical assistance, we thank Ellen Yap at the School for International Studies, Simon Fraser University, and Eva Zamarripa of the Mortara Center at Georgetown University. Financial support was provided by the Simons International Endowment at Simon Fraser

University, and by the School of Foreign Service and Mortara Center, both at Georgetown University.

One issue that can arise for readers who seek to interpret any co-authored text is the division of labor among the authors or editors. This book was a joint effort from the start, with equal contributions from the two editors. Bennett wrote the first draft of Chapter 1, while Checkel did the same for Chapter 10, and we each revised the other's draft, so the results are truly collaborative. In addition, both editors provided feedback to each of the contributing authors. It is thus not fair to list one editor's name first, but we have followed alphabetical convention in doing so to avoid any impression that our partnership was unequal, and we have listed the authorship of our co-authored chapters to reflect which of us wrote the first draft of each.

The two of us each have a special relation to rock. If one – Bennett – relishes the challenge of climbing straight up cliffs and rock faces around North America, the other – Checkel – enjoys the thrill of climbing iced-up rock ridges at 4,200 meters in the Swiss Alps. For all their differences, these passions are united by a common thread. It is called a rope – or, for Checkel, a *Seil* – and, without it, we are in grave peril. After four intense years working on this project, we are happy to report that neither of us dreams of secretly cutting the other's rope. In fact, it is the opposite. We now better appreciate the intellectual core of that rope we have never shared when climbing – a joint commitment to empirically rich, rigorous, but pluralistic knowledge production. It is our hope that this book contributes to that goal.

AB and JTC
Washington, DC and Vancouver

Part I

Introduction

1 Process tracing
From philosophical roots to best practices

Andrew Bennett and Jeffrey T. Checkel

Introduction

Why did the Cold War end peacefully, without a shot being fired? Why did some European democracies survive the interwar period while others were replaced by fascist dictatorships? In the post-Cold War world, civil conflicts have replaced interstate war as the dominant form of organized political violence, with rebel groups – instead of intercontinental ballistic missiles (ICBMs) – as a key focus of both policy and scholarship. Yet what makes such groups tick? Why do some engage in wanton killing and sexual violence while others do not? The European Union is a unique experiment in governance "beyond the nation state," but how are its supranational governance structures being crafted and with what effect on the ordinary citizens of Europe?

Contemporary political science has converged on the view that these puzzles, and many more on the scholarly and policy agendas, demand answers that combine social and institutional structure and context with individual agency and decision-making. This view, together with recent developments in the philosophy of science, has led to an increasing emphasis on causal explanation via reference to hypothesized causal mechanisms. Yet this development begs the questions of how to define such mechanisms, how to measure them in action, and how to test competing explanations that invoke different mechanisms.

This book argues that techniques falling under the label of process tracing are particularly well suited for measuring and testing hypothesized causal

Earlier versions of this chapter were presented at a workshop on "Process Tracing in the Social Sciences," Georgetown University, March 2012; a panel on "Process Tracing," American Political Science Association Annual Convention, Seattle, WA, September 2011; and to the Research Group on Qualitative and Multi-Method Analysis, Syracuse University, June 2010. We thank participants at those meetings, as well as Derek Beach, Jim Caporaso, Colin Elman, Matt Evangelista, John Gerring, Peter Hall, Jim Mahoney, Jack Snyder, and three anonymous reviewers at Cambridge University Press for helpful comments.

mechanisms. Indeed, a growing number of political scientists now invoke the term. Despite or perhaps because of this fact, a buzzword problem has arisen, where process tracing is mentioned, but often with little thought or explication of how it works in practice. As one sharp observer has noted, proponents of qualitative methods draw upon various debates – over mechanisms and causation, say – to argue that process tracing is necessary and good. Yet, they have done much less work to articulate the criteria for determining whether a particular piece of research counts as good process tracing (Waldner 2012: 65–68). Put differently, "there is substantial distance between the broad claim that 'process tracing is good' and the precise claim 'this is an instance of good process tracing'" (Waldner 2011: 7).

Should be obvious

This volume addresses such concerns, and does so along several dimensions. Meta-theoretically, it establishes a philosophical basis for process tracing – one that captures mainstream uses while simultaneously being open to applications by interpretive scholars. Conceptually, contributors explore the relation of process tracing to mechanism-based understandings of causation. Most importantly, we articulate best practices for individual process-tracing accounts – for example, criteria for how micro to go and how to deal with the problem of equifinality (the possibility that there may be multiple pathways leading to the same outcome).

Ours is an applied methods book – and not a standard methodology text – where the aim is to show how process tracing works in practice. If Van Evera (1997), George and Bennett (2005), Gerring (2007a), and Rohlfing (2012) set the state of the art for case studies, then our volume is a logical follow-on, providing clear guidance for what is perhaps the central within-case method – process tracing.

Despite all the recent attention, process tracing – or the use of evidence from within a case to make inferences about causal explanations of that case – has in fact been around for thousands of years. Related forms of analysis date back to the Greek historian Thucydides and perhaps even to the origins of human language and society. It is nearly impossible to avoid historical explanations and causal inferences from historical cases in any purposive human discourse or activity.

Although social science methodologists have debated and elaborated on formal approaches to inference such as statistical analysis for over a hundred years, they have only recently coined the term "process tracing" or attempted to explicate its procedures in a systematic way. Perhaps this is because drawing causal inferences from historical cases is a more intuitive practice than statistical analysis and one that individuals carry out in their everyday lives.

(margin note: read carefully)

Yet, the seemingly intuitive nature of process tracing obscures that its unsystematic use is fraught with potential inferential errors; it is thus important to utilize rigorous methodological safeguards to reduce such risks.

The goal of this book is therefore to explain the philosophical foundations, specific techniques, common evidentiary sources, and best practices of process tracing to reduce the risks of making inferential errors in the analysis of historical and contemporary cases. This introductory chapter first defines process tracing and discusses its foundations in the philosophy of social science. We then address its techniques and evidentiary sources, and advance ten best-practice criteria for judging the quality of process tracing in empirical research. The chapter concludes with an analysis of the methodological issues specific to process tracing on general categories of theories, including structural-institutional, cognitive-psychological, and sociological. Subsequent chapters take up this last issue in greater detail and assess the contributions of process tracing in particular research programs or bodies of theory.

Defining process tracing

The term "process tracing" originated in the field of cognitive psychology in the United States in the late 1960s or early 1970s.[1] As used in psychology, process tracing refers to techniques for examining the intermediate steps in cognitive mental processes to understand better the heuristics through which humans make decisions. In 1979, the Stanford University political scientist Alexander L. George appropriated the term to describe the use of evidence from within case studies to make inferences about historical explanations (George 1979).

Because much of George's own research was in political psychology, and because the term "process tracing" originated in cognitive psychology, it has sometimes been viewed as applying mostly or only to analyses of individual level decision-making. Although process tracing does apply well to the individual level and cognitive theories (see Jacobs, this volume, Chapter 2), George made clear in subsequent writings that it can also be used to make inferences on structural or macro-level explanations (George and Bennett 2005: 142, 214; see also Waldner, this volume, Chapter 5). For example, many economic theories hypothesize relationships and sequences among macroeconomic

(margin note: in what way can original micro study explain macro trends?)

---

[1] The very first usage of the term remains unclear; the earliest relevant citation on Google Scholar is Hobarth 1972, a Ph.D. thesis at the University of Chicago.

variables that can be tested through process tracing at the macro level as well as that at the micro or individual level.

Similarly, because of its origins in cognitive psychology and because many of its early practitioners in that field went on to explore the errors that individuals make and the biases they exhibit in their decision-making, process tracing is sometimes viewed as incompatible with rational choice theories. We concur, however, with the many prominent rational choice theorists who argue that their hypotheses should bear some correspondence with the actual processes through which individuals make decisions, and that they should therefore be amenable to process tracing (Bates *et al.* 1998; see also Schimmelfennig, this volume, Chapter 4).

The essential meaning retained by the term "process tracing" from its origins in cognitive psychology is that it refers to the examination of inter-mediate steps in a process to make inferences about hypotheses on how that process took place and whether and how it generated the outcome of interest. In previous work together with George, one of us defined process tracing as the use of "histories, archival documents, interview transcripts, and other sources to see whether the causal process a theory hypothesizes or implies in a case is in fact evident in the sequence and values of the intervening variables in that case" (George and Bennett 2005: 6). We added that "the process-tracing method attempts to identify the intervening causal process – the causal chain and causal mechanism – between an independent variable (or variables) and the outcome of the dependent variable" (ibid.: 206).

The authors then used a metaphor to expand on this definition. If one had a row of fifty dominoes lying on the table after they had previously been standing, how could one make inferences about whether the first domino caused the last to fall through a domino process, or whether wind, a bump of the table, or some other force caused the dominoes to fall? The answer, George and Bennett argued, was to use evidence on the intervening processes posited by each of the alternative explanations. Did anyone hear a succession of dominoes? Do the positions of the fallen dominoes shed light on how they fell? And so on.

While we feel this definition is still an excellent starting point, it is necessary to point out a weakness in both it and the accompanying metaphor. The term "intervening variable" opens the door for potential confusion because social scientists are accustomed to thinking of variables as either causal (independent) or caused (dependent). However, both the term and the metaphor of dominoes falling suggest that an intervening variable is both fully caused by the independent variable(s) that preceded it, and that it transmits this causal force, without adding to it, subtracting from it, or altering it, to subsequent intervening variables and ultimately through them to the dependent variable.

When the observable events that intercede between hypothesized causes and observed effects have this character, they constitute "diagnostic evidence," not "variables." Diagnostic evidence indicates the kind of process taking place, but does not transmit any independent effects to the dependent variable. This is analogous to a diagnostic medical test, such as a dye injected into a patient to enhance a CAT scan of blood flow. Ideally, the dye does not transmit any noteworthy side-effects to the patient, but it provides evidence on the processes taking place in the patient. Similarly, in social and political life, the ways in which actors privately frame or explain their actions may provide diagnostic evidence on their motives without independently affecting the outcomes of interest.

Quite often, however, the events that lie temporally and/or spatially between the independent variable and the dependent variable are *not* fully determined by the specified independent variables and these events *do* have independent effects on the nature, timing, or magnitude of the dependent variable. In such instances, researchers have to make theory-building choices. Are they going to model these intervening events as variables? If so, should they treat them as exogenous, complementary, or endogenous to the theory or explanation of interest? Exogenous variables are those excluded from a model because they are either not powerful or frequent enough, or too complex or unpredictable, to be brought into the theory. Complementary variables are those that add to or subtract from the effects of the main variables of interest, but do so independently, or without interaction effects related to the main variables. When such variables are sufficiently simple to be theorized, they can be added to a model without changing the main variables or mechanisms of interest. Additional variables that interact with the independent variables of interest in more complex ways need to be either brought into the model (endogenized) or identified but set aside from the model (exogenized) for the sake of simplicity. Methodologically, whatever way additional variables are brought into or set aside from the theory that aims to explain the case, this modification can be tested through additional process tracing.

We thus drop the term "intervening variable" and define process tracing as the analysis of evidence on processes, sequences, and conjunctures of events within a case for the purposes of either developing or testing hypotheses about causal mechanisms that might causally explain the case. Put another way, the deductive theory-testing side of process tracing examines the observable implications of hypothesized causal mechanisms within a case to test whether a theory on these mechanisms explains the case (Schimmelfennig, this volume, Chapter 4, emphasizes such a procedure). The inductive, theory development side of process tracing uses evidence from within a case to develop hypotheses that might explain the case; the latter hypotheses may, in turn, generate additional testable implications in the case or in other cases (Pouliot, this volume, Chapter 9, stresses inductive research procedures).[2]

It is important as well to define "case" and "within a case" as we use them. Following George and Bennett, we define a case as "an instance of a class of events" (George and Bennett 2005: 17). This definition recognizes that classes of events – revolutions, democracies, capitalist economies, wars, and so on – are the social constructions of both political actors and the social scientists who study and define political categories. They are not simply given to us by history, but defined by our concepts, and much contestation in interpreting the results of case-study research concerns disagreements over which "cases" should or should not be included in a defined population.

We define within-case evidence as evidence from within the temporal, spatial, or topical domain defined as a case. This can include a great deal of evidence on contextual or background factors that influence how we measure and interpret the variables within a case. Henry Brady and David Collier provide a useful distinction here between data-set observations and causal-process observations (see also Dunning, this volume, Chapter 8). Data-set observations are "an array of scores on specific variables for a designated sample of cases," and these observations provide the basis for statistical analyses. Causal-process observations are "observations on context, process, or mechanism" and are used in within-case analyses such as process tracing (Brady and Collier 2010: 12).

With these definitions in hand, we note that process tracing is closely related to historical explanation, as that term is used by the historian Clayton Roberts. In Roberts's view, an historical explanation is not simply a detailed description of a sequence of events; rather, it draws on theories to explain each important step that contributes to causing the outcome. Roberts distinguishes between macro-correlation and micro-correlation, the latter of which is quite similar to process tracing. Macro-correlation involves an attempt to explain historical cases at a high level of generality through universalistic theories, similar to Hempel's notion of theories as covering laws.

---

[2] Beach and Pedersen 2013a suggest three different types of process tracing: theory testing, theory building, and outcome explaining. The first is primarily deductive, the second more inductive, and the third uses both kinds of logic with the goal of causally explaining an individual case.

Roberts argues that historical events are too complex to fit easily under exception-less covering laws, and efforts to explain history in this way "have met with little success" (Roberts 1996: 15). He urges instead that researchers should use micro-correlation, which involves "the minute tracing of the explanatory narrative to the point where the events to be explained are microscopic and the covering laws correspondingly more certain" (ibid.: 66).

One difference between Roberts's approach to process tracing and our own is that Roberts felt that – at the micro-correlational level – the theories underlying an historical explanation would be "platitudinous." Historians, he thus argues, rarely reference them explicitly because to do so would "hopelessly clog the narrative" (ibid.: 66–67, 87–88). We emphasize instead the importance of making explicit the hypotheses about underlying causal mechanisms that are theorized to have caused an outcome so that these can be rigorously assessed, even if this results in political science narratives that are more clogged – and alas, less likely to become best-sellers – than those of historians (see also Evangelista, this volume, Chapter 6, for analysis of works that focus their process tracing as much on explaining an important historical case as on developing and testing general theories).

Yet, these disciplinary differences need not be viewed in zero-sum terms. That is, it is possible to have an application of process tracing that is simultaneously rigorous, explicit, and transparent, and that also reads well – say, by placing the process tracing tests in an appendix separate from the main narrative (Fairfield 2013 provides an excellent example).

Our concept of process tracing differs even more sharply with time series cross-sectional analysis, which involves the correlational study of data across a variety of units (often, annual data across a range of countries). Although this form of analysis might be confused with process tracing because it involves temporal data from within cases over time, it is still a form of cross-case and correlational inference, rather than the study of hypothesized processes within individual cases, and it is thus fundamentally different from process tracing (see also the discussions and examples in Lyall, Chapter 7; and Dunning, Chapter 8, both this volume).

In sum, process tracing is a key technique for capturing causal mechanisms in action. It is not simply glorified historiography, nor does it proceed by the logic of frequentist statistics. And – as we argue below – there are metrics and best practices that allow one to distinguish good process tracing from bad. However, since standards flow from underlying philosophical positions, it is important first to clarify the meta-theory of process tracing.

Philosophy of social science and process tracing

On a philosophical and epistemological level, process tracing is closely related to the turn toward social science explanations based on reference to causal mechanisms (Elster 1998; Gerring 2007b; Mayntz 2004), or the underlying entities that generate observed processes and outcomes. Much of the thinking about causality and causal explanation over the last 200 years has been strongly influenced by David Hume's argument that constant conjunction – the frequent conjoint occurrence of variables A and B – is the essence of causal inference. More recent work by pragmatist (Johnson 2006) and scientific realist (Wight 2006) philosophers of science, however, provides a meta-theoretical foundation more amenable to thinking in terms of mechanisms. Indeed, for these scholars, a causal explanation is built around contiguity and sequencing of events – concepts that Hume mentioned, but gave insufficient attention. These open a methodological space for process tracing.

One difficulty in making use of contemporary discussions in the philosophy of science is that there are at least a half-dozen variants of scientific realism (Chernoff 2002) and even more different definitions of causal mechanisms (Mahoney 2001; see also Hedström and Ylikoski 2010). While a full discussion of scientific realism is beyond our present purposes, we concur with the emphasis it places on causal processes and causal mechanisms as central elements of causal explanation.

More important for this volume is the task of sorting out the competing definitions of causal mechanisms. These divide along three fundamental issues: (1) Are causal mechanisms in some sense unobservable? (2) Does explanation via reference to causal mechanisms involve a commitment to methodological individualism, or beyond that, to explaining human behavior by neuroscience and ultimately by sub-atomic physics? (3) Are causal mechanisms sufficient to explain outcomes in specified circumstances or contexts, or might mechanisms be inherently probabilistic or stochastic?

On the first issue, most discussions of mechanisms place them on the ontological level. This means we make hypotheses or theories about how such ontological entities as mechanisms might work, and we test the observable implications of these hypotheses, but we do not observe causal mechanisms directly. Some proponents of mechanisms take a different view, arguing that they are at least somewhat observable. Hedström and Ylikoski, for example, critique Mahoney for the view that mechanisms are unobservable, and draw an analogy to our ability to observe the inner workings of an auto engine (Hedström and Ylikoski 2010: 50–51; Mahoney 2001).

Such critiques, however, miss the more fundamental point that causal mechanisms are in some sense ultimately unobservable. We do not get to observe causality – we make inferences about it. We cannot unproblematically observe many mechanisms at lower levels of analysis – brain waves, neurons, atoms, etc. Rather, we rely on potentially fallible instruments of observation (brain scans, microscopes) and theories about how they work. We may be able to push back the borders of the unobservable world by developing instruments of observation in which we have great confidence, but there will always be some still finer level of detail that we cannot observe.

The boundary between the observable and unobservable worlds is like the horizon. We can push this border back as our instruments of observation improve, but it also recedes as we move toward it, and some part of the universe always remains beyond the horizon and thus unobservable. Even if brain scans are beginning to reveal some of the inner workings of the brain, we do not have these in real time for actual social actors in real world settings, we cannot scan brain activity from the past, and there will still be additional micro-level brain processes that we cannot observe.

This raises the second issue concerning methodological individualism and the degree to which mechanism-based explanations have to go to minute levels of detail, tiny increments of time, and temporally distant causes of events. In our view, explanations need not always go to the individual level of analysis (or beyond); it is possible to do process tracing on hypothesized causal mechanisms at the macro level (Waldner, this volume, Chapter 5; see also Pouliot, this volume, Chapter 9). In principle, mechanism-based explanations have to be consistent with the finest level of detail we observe; however, in practice, this does not mean we must always go to this level to have confidence that one explanation is more likely to be true than the alternatives.

The controversy surrounding this issue has led some critics to argue that explanations built on causal mechanisms – and, thus, process tracing – involve a potentially infinite regress to look at steps between steps in a hypothesized process at ever-smaller increments of time and more detailed levels of analysis (King *et al.* 1994: 85–87). It is true that a commitment to explanation via mechanisms means the former are always incomplete and provisional, and that every explanation can be called into question if it can be shown that its hypothesized processes are not evident at a lower level of analysis. It is also true that there is no infallible way of deciding how far down, or how far back, to go in explaining an event. As we argue below, however, researchers can and do make defensible decisions about when and where to begin and stop in constructing and testing explanations (see also Hedström and Ylikoski 2010: 52).

The issue of when to stop is related to the third controversy of whether causal mechanisms involve relations of sufficiency or probabilism. Mahoney (2001: 580) defines mechanisms as being sufficient in specified circumstances to generate the outcome of interest, while Hedström and Ylikoski (2010: 51) argue that mechanisms could be inherently stochastic. This is a thorny issue, as stochastic relations – like those posited by quantum theory – have some aspects of causal explanation, but lack others (Salmon 1990: 120).

The core problem is that even if the world is deterministic, we observe it as probabilistic because of measurement error and specification error, including the omission of important variables from our models. We cannot tell with 100 percent confidence whether we are witnessing a probabilistic world or a deterministic one, or whether some processes are deterministic or nearly so, while others are inherently stochastic. The most that can be said here with any confidence is that researchers implicitly make choices on this issue in deciding when to stop trying to reduce or explain the "error term," or unexplained variation.

In sum, on the key issues in the definitional debates about causal mechanisms, we argue the following. Causal mechanisms are ontological entities and processes in the world, and theories or hypotheses are in our heads; we theorize about mechanisms. Such mechanisms are ultimately unobservable, but our hypotheses about them generate observable and testable implications. Explanation via reference to causal mechanisms, unlike that via reference to covering laws, involves a commitment in principle to being consistent with the lowest level of analysis and finest degree of detail observable. We can never know with certainty whether the world in general or a particular mechanism that we hypothesize is deterministic or nearly so under specified circumstances or whether the world or a mechanism is stochastic. We thus define causal mechanisms as (see also George and Bennett 2005: 137):

ultimately unobservable physical, social, or psychological processes through which agents with causal capacities operate, but only in specific contexts or conditions, to transfer energy, information, or matter to other entities. In doing so, the causal agent changes the affected entities' characteristics, capacities, or propensities in ways that persist until subsequent causal mechanisms act upon them. If we are able to measure changes in the entity being acted upon after the intervention of the causal mechanism and in temporal or spatial isolation from other mechanisms, then the causal mechanism may be said to have generated the observed change in the entity.

The challenge, then, is to develop theories about causal mechanisms in which we can place some confidence, and understandings of the scope conditions in which they operate. Process tracing is one powerful method of addressing these challenges.[3] Before turning to the nuts and bolts of how to do it well, however, three additional issues demand attention: the relationship of process tracing to generalization, to interpretive social science, and to Bayesian inference.

Generalizability and process tracing

Because causal mechanisms are operationalized in specific cases, and process tracing is a within-case method of analysis, generalization can be problematic. Case-study methodologists have argued that a hypothesis is strongly affirmed and might be generalizable if it explains a tough test case or a case that, a priori, it looked least likely to explain. Conversely, the failure of a hypothesis to explain a most likely case strongly reduces our confidence in it.[4] It has always been rather ambiguous, however, whether these inferences should apply only to the case being studied, to cases very similar to the one studied, or to a broader range of more diverse cases.

The use of process tracing to test and refine hypotheses about causal mechanisms can clarify the scope conditions under which a hypothesis is generalizable. A researcher cannot have a very clear idea of whether, how, and to which populations an explanation of a case might generalize until they have a clear theory about the workings of the mechanisms involved in the case (see also Jacobs, this volume, Chapter 2; Schimmelfennig, this volume, Chapter 4). To some degree, this theory can evolve inductively from close study of the case itself.

Indeed, a theory or explanation derived inductively from a case does not necessarily need to be tested against a different case for us to have confidence in the theory; rather, it can be tested against different and independent evidence in the case from which it was derived (Mahoney 2012: 587). Often, this is a kind of evidence that the researcher had not thought to look for or did not recognize as relevant prior to developing the new explanation. Detectives,

---

[3] However, it is not the only one. See Checkel and Bennett, this volume, Chapter 10.

[4] As Rohlfing (2012: 194–196) points out, there has been some ambiguity on what constitutes a "least likely" or "most likely" case. As he notes, if this term applies only to the prior probability attached to the likelihood a theory is true, then this prior will not necessarily be updated sharply even when a theory fits a least likely case or fails in a most likely one. As argued elsewhere in this volume, process tracing tests result in the sharpest updating of priors when the likelihood ratio constitutes a strong failed hoop test, passed smoking-gun test, or doubly decisive test (Bennett, this volume, Appendix).

medical doctors, and case-study researchers in many sciences and professions frequently make this move.

For example, in a study of international socialization in Europe, Checkel and collaborators theorized three mechanisms of socialization, two of which were partly derived from their own case material. The careful application of process tracing to additional, independent evidence from the cases was then used to specify better the scope conditions of each mechanism. The result and central finding was that the theory was limited in its application to the – albeit crucially important – case of contemporary Europe (Checkel 2007: chapters 7–8).

Conversely, a researcher focusing on one or a few cases might uncover a new hypothesis that is broadly applicable, as when Charles Darwin's study of a few species led to his theory of evolution. In short, we may uncover hypothesized mechanisms through process tracing that may be either very generalizable or unique to one or a few cases, but it is almost impossible to know prior to researching a case the degree to which any inductively derived explanations will be one or the other.

The general point – one we address in more detail in Chapter 10 – is that process tracing on causal mechanisms raises issues of generalizability and theory development that have received insufficient attention. For many epistemologies – and certainly the scientific-realist one espoused here – theory is more than lists of causal mechanisms that cumulate in no real sense; yet, all too often, this is the result of case studies employing process tracing (see also Checkel, this volume, Chapter 3).

Interpretivism and process tracing

Another important issue is the relation between process tracing and interpretivism, or more specifically, between process tracing and constructivism. Recall our earlier discussion, where we argued that scientific realism provides a possible meta-theoretical basis for process tracing. With its stress on cause, objectivity, the consideration of alternative explanations and the like, scientific realism is closer to positivism in its various guises than to interpretivism (Wight 2002: 35–36). What (meta-theoretical) space does this then leave for interpretive process tracing?

One difficulty here is that scholars have embraced many different kinds of interpretivism and constructivism.[5] Most constructivists agree that structures or institutions are social as well as material, and that agents and structures are

---

[5] We will use these terms interchangeably in the following.

mutually constitutive; however, they differ on important epistemological issues (Adler 2013). One common typology that we find useful distinguishes among conventional, interpretive, and radical or post-modern views of social life. In this schema, conventional constructivists still aspire to causal explanation and believe that there are standards for assessing some interpretations of social life to be superior to others. Alexander Wendt, a leading constructivist in international relations who has espoused scientific realism and a role for causal mechanisms, fits into this school of thought (Wendt 1999). Not surprisingly, process tracing figures prominently in the work of many conventional constructivists (Risse et al., 1999, 2013, for example).

It is more challenging to reconcile the technique with a second, interpretive view, although some scholars are attempting to do so (Autesserre 2009; Hopf 2002, 2007, 2012; Pouliot 2007). Here, agents and structures are so inherently mutually constitutive that it is impossible to separate events into discrete moves in which either the agent or the structure is primarily driving the process. If indeed mutual constitution is completely continuous at all levels of analysis, then it is impossible to break out "variables" as being causes or consequences of one another. However, one can often break down events and discern steps at which an agent – for example, a norm entrepreneur – is contesting social structures, and steps at which a structure prevents agents from acting upon or even conceiving of courses of action that are taboo. In fact, several prominent (conventional) constructivists have endorsed such a bracketing strategy (Wendt 1987; Finnemore 1996).

A third, radical or post-modern view maintains that language, arguably the most central of all social structures, is inherently ambiguous and open to many interpretations. The danger here is that all narratives are reduced to story-telling, a critique that has also been raised against process tracing (Norkus 2005). We should note, however, that even these radical forms of constructivism have increasingly developed standards of evidence. We now have clear "how to" guides for conducting systematic discourse and textual analysis (Hansen 2006; Neumann 2008; Hopf 2002: chapter 1). Moreover, genealogical methods – the historical reconstruction of discourses – bear a strong family resemblance to historical forms of process tracing (Price 1997). Finally, in recent years, there has been a strong move to "bring practice back in" to the study of discourse (Pouliot 2010), which provides an interpretive nod to the central importance of process.

In sum, while there are philosophical hurdles to surmount – or perhaps better said, to be bracketed – we see intriguing possibilities for developing a richer understanding of process tracing by drawing upon these various strands of interpretive social science (see also Guzzini 2012: chapter 11). This is precisely the challenge that Pouliot takes up in his contribution in Chapter 9 (this volume).

Bayesianism and process tracing

Bayesian logic provides a way to use evidence to update one's beliefs in the likelihood that alternative explanations are true. Bayesianism has become a popular general approach to theory choice in the philosophy of science (Earman 1992), and it is closely related to process tracing in ways that illuminate the latter's strengths and limits (Bennett 2008; Rohlfing 2012: 180–199; Beach and Pedersen 2013a: 83–88, 96–99). We provide an overview of Bayesianism and process tracing here, and an Appendix (Bennett, this volume) outlines the technical details.

Bayesianism and process tracing do not overlap entirely. Bayesianism, for example, does not encompass the inductive theory-generating side of process tracing. Nor is Bayesianism the only logic useful for clarifying process tracing; directed acyclic graphs (Waldner, this volume, Chapter 5) and set theory (Mahoney 2012) are also helpful in this regard.

Yet, Bayesianism is the most developed logic in the context of process tracing, and the two are in agreement in key respects. Both use evidence to affirm some explanations and cast doubt upon others (the latter process involves "eliminative induction," whereby rendering alternative explanations less likely makes those that remain more likely). They both put importance on the probative value of evidence relative to competing explanations, and on diverse or independent evidentiary tests, rather than on the number of pieces of evidence. Both also allow for the possibility that a few pieces or even one piece of evidence with high probative value can help observers, who approach a case with different theoretical priors, to converge in their views on the proper explanation of the case. Finally, they both warn against becoming 100 percent confident in any theory or explanation due to the limits on observational evidence and the possibility that undiscovered theories may yet prove superior to existing ones.

Central to Bayesianism and process tracing is the idea that some pieces of evidence provide higher inferential power than others. Stephen Van Evera has developed useful shorthand terms for the probative value of alternative evidentiary tests in process tracing. In Van Evera's view, the probative value of evidence depends on the degree to which a hypothesis uniquely predicts that evidence, and the degree to which it is certain in doing so (Van Evera

1997: 31–32; see also Bennett 2010; Collier 2011). From the four possible combinations of (non-)uniqueness and (un)certainty, Van Evera derives four tests. *Hoop tests* involve evidence that is certain, but not unique; failing a hoop test disqualifies an explanation, but passing it does not greatly increase confidence in that explanation. Hoop tests are thus most useful in excluding alternative hypotheses. Van Evera's example of a hoop test is: "Was the accused in the state on the day of the murder?" Failing this hoop test falsifies the hypothesis that the accused was the murderer. Whether passing a hoop test constitutes strong evidence in favor of a hypothesis depends on how frequently the pass condition occurs naturally (Mahoney 2012: 575–576). The higher the number of suspects that were in the state at the time of the murder, the less this hoop test increases the likelihood that any particular one of them is the murderer.

Smoking-gun tests are unique, but not certain. Passing a smoking-gun test strongly affirms an explanation, but passing such a test is not necessary to build confidence in an explanation. In Van Evera's example, a smoking gun in a suspect's hands right after a murder strongly implicates that suspect, but the absence of such a smoking gun does not exonerate this suspect because murderers have incentives to hide smoking-gun evidence. Again, the strength of a smoking-gun test depends on how often the condition in question occurs on its own (Mahoney 2012: 578).

Doubly decisive tests use evidence that is both unique and certain, or that is necessary and sufficient to provide great confidence in an explanation. Van Evera uses the example of a bank camera that catches the faces of bank robbers, thereby strongly implicating the guilty and exonerating the innocent. Conversely, *straw-in-the-wind tests* provide weak or circumstantial evidence that is neither unique nor certain. Any one such test is not very decisive, but a series of such tests can increase confidence in one explanation and decrease that in others if all or even most of the test results point in the same direction (Mahoney 2012: 584).[6]

Techniques and best practices of process tracing

Process tracing usually proceeds through a combination of induction and deduction. The particular mix in a research project depends on the prior state

---

[6] Such tests – and the Bayesian logic underlying them – can be further elaborated in important ways. See Bennett, this volume, Appendix; and Waldner, this volume, Chapter 5.

as all ~~good~~ the best research, no?

of knowledge and theorizing about the phenomenon and the case selected for study, and on whether the case is similar to a defined population of cases or is an outlier vis-à-vis this population. For phenomena on which there is little prior knowledge and for cases that are not well explained by extant theories, process tracing proceeds primarily through inductive study. This often involves analyzing events backward through time from the outcome of interest to potential antecedent causes, much as a homicide detective might start by trying to piece together the last few hours or days in the life of a victim.

In such situations, the researcher takes in a significant amount of information that may or may not later become part of the hypothesized explanation, a phase that some have colloquially called "soaking and poking." Here, one immerses oneself in the details of the case and tries out proto-hypotheses that may either quickly prove to be dead ends or become plausible and worthy of more rigorous testing. It is important that the investigator be open to all kinds of possible explanations and willing to follow the evidence wherever it leads. The more promising potential explanations uncovered in this way can then be rendered more formal and deductive and tested more rigorously against evidence in the case or in other cases that is independent of the evidence that gave rise to each hypothesis.

If theories that appear to offer potential explanations of a case already exist, or after such theories have been developed inductively, process tracing can proceed more deductively. A key step here is to develop case-specific observable implications of the theories in question (Bakke 2013, for an excellent example; see also the discussion in Jacobs, this volume, Chapter 2), as theories are seldom specified in such precise ways that they offer tight predictions on the observable implications that should be evident in particular cases.

It is also important to cast the net widely for alternative explanations, including theoretical explanations in the academic literature, the more context-specific arguments that historians or regional or functional experts have offered, the implicit theories of journalists or others following the case, and the understandings participants have about what they are doing and why they are doing it. As researchers develop observable implications of hypothesized mechanisms, they should be on the lookout for particularly valuable kinds of evidence that allow for hoop, smoking-gun, and doubly decisive tests.

When iterating between the inductive and deductive sides of process tracing, it is important that researchers seek to identify additional observable implications or what Imre Lakatos called "new facts" to test each modification to a hypothesis, so as to avoid confirmation bias. Particularly valuable are new testable implications that, if found, would fit only the modified theory and not the alternative explanations, or that had not already been observed and had not been used to construct the hypothesis (Lakatos 1970).

There is a related distinction between evidence that is unavailable and evidence that is contrary to the process tracing expectations of a hypothesis. Evidence that is unavailable at the time of the research, such as classified information, lowers the upper limit of the probability one can attach to the likely truth of an explanation. One useful technique here is to predict what the unavailable evidence will indicate once it becomes available; such predictions, if borne out, provide strong confirmatory evidence. This was precisely the strategy followed by one of us where process tracing was employed to test hypotheses on socialization mechanisms in small group settings within international organizations. On the basis of interviews and a reading of primary documentation, predictions were made about socialization dynamics; these were subsequently confirmed through the release of previously classified meeting minutes (Checkel 2003).

Evidence that is contrary to the process-tracing predictions of an explanation lowers the likelihood that the explanation is true. It may therefore need to be modified if it is to become convincing once again. This modification may be a trivial one involving a substitutable and logically equivalent step in the hypothesized process, or it could be a more fundamental change to the explanation. The bigger the modification, the more important it is to generate and test new observable implications to guard against "just so" stories that explain away anomalies one at a time.

Inferences from process tracing also depend in part on judgments of when "absence of evidence" constitutes "evidence of absence." If we expect evidence to be readily accessible and doubly decisive – as when we feel around for change in our pocket – failure to find something constitutes strong evidence it does not exist. When social actors have incentives and capabilities for hiding evidence, however, the absence of evidence might not greatly lower our expectation that an entity or relationship exists (see also Bennett, this volume, Appendix).

In addition, process tracing helps to address the limits of Mill's methods of comparison. Mill himself recognized that the possible presence of equifinality – that is, multiple paths to the same outcome – could threaten inferences based on comparisons of small numbers of cases. Process tracing can address this by affirming particular paths as viable explanations in individual cases, even if the paths differ from one case to another. Mill also noted that omitted variables can undermine case comparisons. For example, comparisons of "most similar cases," or cases that are similar in the values of all but one independent variable and different in the value of the dependent variable, are always potentially flawed because of residual differences between the two cases in variables that are outside of the theoretical framework. Process tracing on such omitted variables, and on the independent variable that differs between the two cases, can help determine if either or both help explain the differing outcomes in the two cases (George and Bennett 2005: 153–160, 254).

Process tracing can also be readily combined with quantitative techniques in a mixed-method design. Building upon Lieberman's (2005, 2009) idea of nested analysis, for example, it can be applied to a few cases selected from a statistical analysis to clarify whether the direction of causal influence is indeed from the independent variable to the dependent variable, and not the reverse, and to help assess whether any observed correlations might be spurious.[7] In these ways, process tracing on the mechanisms hypothesized in statistical models can greatly increase the confidence in the causal significance of the correlations identified in them (see also Lyall, this volume, Chapter 7).

In a variation on the above, (quasi-)quantitative techniques such as agent-based modeling can be used to check the plausibility of inferences about causal mechanisms derived from process tracing. Consider contemporary research on civil war, where a central finding is that such conflicts are anything but "civil": mechanisms of transnational diffusion play central roles. Scholars have now utilized process tracing to document a number of these mechanisms, including framing, resource mobilization, and social learning (Checkel 2013b).

Such findings can be strengthened through the careful application of agent-based modeling, where one assesses the plausibility of the mechanisms by using computer simulation. If the results of the simulations resemble the empirical patterns of conflict diffusion uncovered through process tracing, then the validity of the posited causal relation is strengthened (Nome and Weidmann 2013; see also Hoffmann 2008; and Hedström and Ylikoski 2010: 62–63).

Process tracing: best practices

With these definitional, philosophical, and operational preliminaries in hand, we now return to the challenge highlighted in the chapter's opening pages. How do we know a particular piece of process tracing research is good process tracing? More colloquially, how would we recognize good process tracing if it were to walk through the door?

---

[7] Nested analysis is just one of several mixed-method designs where process tracing can play a central role. See Dunning, this volume, Chapter 8.

We argue for a three-part standard for what counts as a good application of process tracing (see also Bennett and Elman 2007; Bennett 2010; Checkel 2008; Rohlfing 2012: 188; Beach and Pederson 2013a: 163–170; and Checkel 2013b: chapter 1). *Meta-theoretically,* it will be grounded in a philosophical base that is ontologically consistent with mechanism-based understandings of social reality and methodologically plural. While we favored scientific realism above, there is sufficient (and inevitable) uncertainty at this philosophical level to leave the door open for related approaches such as analytic eclecticism (Katzenstein and Sil 2010), pragmatism (Johnson 2006; Friedrichs and Kratochwil 2009: 719), as well as interpretivism (Pouliot, this volume, Chapter 9).[8] *Contextually,* it will utilize this pluralism both to reconstruct carefully hypothesized causal processes and keep sight of broader structural-discursive contexts. *Methodologically,* it will take equifinality seriously and consider the alternative causal pathways through which the outcome of interest might have occurred.

Building on these three broad signposts, we advance ten best practices for what constitutes a systematic, operational, and transparent application of process tracing – summarized in Table 1.1 below. We start with four general criteria that follow in part from standard injunctions and checks that are applicable to an array of qualitative methods. These include attention to

Table 1.1 Process tracing best practices

1. Cast the net widely for alternative explanations
2. Be equally tough on the alternative explanations
3. Consider the potential biases of evidentiary sources
4. Take into account whether the case is most or least likely for alternative explanations
5. Make a justifiable decision on when to start
6. Be relentless in gathering diverse and relevant evidence, but make a justifiable decision on when to stop
7. Combine process tracing with case comparisons when useful for the research goal and feasible
8. Be open to inductive insights
9. Use deduction to ask "if my explanation is true, what will be the specific process leading to the outcome?"
10. Remember that conclusive process tracing is good, but not all good process tracing is conclusive

---

[8] We are not arguing for an explicit discussion of meta-theory for each empirical application of process tracing. Rather, we urge recognition that traditional positivism is inadequate for dealing with concepts such as mechanisms and techniques like process tracing.

research design and potential biases in evidentiary sources, as well as caution in the application of triangulation among evidentiary sources. At the same time, the use of process tracing demands adherence to additional best practices (criteria 5 to 10) that address problems related to testing inductively generated insights in ways that reduce the risks of "curve-fitting."

For sure, these criteria are not immune to criticism. Some may prefer a greater emphasis on logical consistency (Mahoney 2012) or quantification (see also Bennett, this volume, Appendix). Others may have the opposite reaction, fearing they strip away the theoretical creativity and playfulness that characterize process tracing at its best (Pouliot, this volume, Chapter 9; Checkel, this volume, Chapter 3).

We have three reactions to such concerns. First, we stand by these ten criteria. They are not pulled from thin air, but emerge from recent advances in qualitative methodology, philosophy of science, and Bayesian analysis, as well as findings from cognitive psychology regarding confirmation bias and other biases that often befall researchers. They also reflect our own use of process tracing in a wide variety of contexts over the last several decades. They demonstrate that the technique is far more than a temporal sequencing of events or mere "detective work" based on hunches and intuition (Gerring 2007a: 178). Second, we view these ten practices as a starting point, and not the final word. Indeed, we invited our contributors to push back, modify, and argue against us as they felt necessary. Chapter 10 thus revisits the criteria in light of this "intervening process."

Finally, we appreciate that our list – especially for graduate students – looks daunting, perhaps leading them to give up before ever attempting any process tracing. This is not our intent! In fact, not all criteria may be relevant for any given study. However, they should serve as a starting point and checklist, thus maximizing the likelihood of conducting good process tracing. Moreover, the ten criteria are more or less relevant depending upon the stage of the research cycle. Some are clearly important during research design (criterion 1, broad search for alternative explanations), while others are key during data collection (5 and 6, determining and justifying start and stop points, and 9, using deduction to specify what one expects to see). Still others are most important during data analysis, for example criterion 3, on evidentiary biases, and 8, on the inductive discovery of new insights. The ten best practices can thus often be addressed sequentially, over time, and not all at once.[9]

---

[9] We thank an anonymous reviewer for Cambridge University Press for discussion on this point.

1. Cast the net widely for alternative explanations

Explanations are more convincing to the extent that the evidence is inconsistent with alternative explanations. Put differently, failing to consider a potentially viable explanation that readily occurs to the readers and critics of a case study can make the process tracing unconvincing. The consequences of leaving out a viable explanation are thus sufficiently serious that it is important to consider a wide range of alternatives despite the effort this entails.[10]

Specifically, and at a minimum, researchers should assess the process tracing evidence on the explanations that regional specialists and functional experts have offered for the specific case at hand and for the class(es) of cases or phenomena of which it is an instance. In addition, it is often useful to render in theoretical terms and undertake process tracing upon the understandings of actor behavior offered by participants and journalists. Often these will overlap with scholars' explanations of the case, but occasionally they point to viable explanations that have been overlooked.

An additional criterion for assessing the adequacy of potential explanations is to ask whether any major theoretical categories of social explanation have been omitted. These include explanations based on actors' material power, institutional constraints and opportunities, and social norms or legitimacy (Mahoney 2000). Another taxonomic dimension to check is whether both agent-based and structural explanations have been considered. Structural constraints can be material, institutional, or normative, for example, and agents can be motivated by rational calculations of material interests, cognitive biases, emotional drives, or normative concerns.

As process tracing often involves exploring what individuals knew when and how they behaved, there is a risk of overlooking normative or material structural contexts (see also Pouliot, this volume, Chapter 9). For example, in earlier work, one of us used process tracing to explore the social–psychological factors that might lead decision-makers to change their minds in light of persuasive appeals (Checkel 2003). Yet, as critics noted, the argument overlooked structural context, simply assuming that persuasive arguments were a function of individual-level dynamics alone. It was equally plausible, however, that the persuader's arguments were legitimated by the broader social discourse in which he or she was embedded. Checkel, in conducting his process tracing, had thus failed to address equifinality, or the possibility of multiple pathways leading to the same outcome.

---

[10] Schimmelfennig, this volume, Chapter 4, notes the trade-off here between comprehensiveness and efficiency, and – compared to the present discussion – he puts more emphasis on the latter.

2. Be equally tough on the alternative explanations

Being equally tough on alternative explanations does not require going into equal depth in process tracing on every one of them. Some explanations may be quickly undermined by the evidence, while others will require deeper investigation. Some explanations may be more counterintuitive or, put another way, have a lower prior expectation of being true, and may thus require more evidence to convince ourselves and others even if initial process tracing evidence suggests they may be true. Some explanations may be more novel than others, and there may be more value added in exploring these. There is also a tendency, and a justifiable one in the Bayesian view, to generate more detailed evidence on the explanations that appear to be increasingly likely to be true as the evidence cumulates (Bennett, this volume, Appendix).

Research in cognitive science, however, reminds us of a common tendency toward confirmation bias, and one goal of methodology should be to counter-act it. In this regard, fairness to alternative explanations requires that we fully consider evidence that fails to fit the explanations that interest us most, as well as evidence that fits explanations that initially interest or convince us the least. Some case studies accord an unduly privileged status to one explanation by granting it "first mover advantage" (Caporaso *et al.* 2003). That is, they per-form process tracing on this explanation and turn to evidence on the alter-native explanations only to address the anomalies that confront the privileged first mover. A far better procedure is to outline the process tracing predictions of a wide range of alternative explanations of a case in advance, and then consider the actual evidence for and against each explanation (Schimmelfennig 2003, for a superb example; see also Evangelista, this volume, Chapter 6; and Richards 2011).

3. Consider the potential biases of evidentiary sources

A pervasive problem in the social sciences is how to judge, or discount, evidence provided by agents who have instrumental motives to convince observers that some explanations are stronger than others – and Bayesianism offers a useful framework for addressing it. When those pro-viding evidence may have instrumental motives for putting forth particular explanations of their own or others' behavior, researchers should apply a two-step Bayesian analysis. First, they should attach Bayesian priors to the possible instrumental motives of those providing evidence and weigh the evidence they give in light of those priors. Then, in a second step, researchers should use the evidence provided by the sources to update prior expectations on their motives, and use these updated priors in assessing subsequent evidence.[11]

This sounds complex, but we in fact make such judgments every day. Given A's possible motives, how much should I trust what he or she says? Given what he or she has said, what are A's likely motives? Social psychologists have long noted that audiences find an individual more convincing when that person espouses a view that is seemingly contrary to his or her instrumental goals. When Warren Buffett argues that wealthy Americans should pay more taxes, this is more convincing than when a person of moderate income argues for raising taxes on the rich. Bayesian logic suggests that this is a sensible procedure for accrediting or discounting evidence from individuals with potential instrumental goals for providing, distorting, or hiding evidence (see also the excellent discussion in Jacobs, this volume, Chapter 2).

For similar reasons, researchers should follow established advice on considering issues of context and authorship in assessing evidence. Spontaneous statements have a different evidentiary status from prepared remarks. Public statements have a different evidentiary status from private ones or from those that will remain classified for a period of time. Statements in front of some audiences may reflect different instrumental purposes from those in front of other audiences. In addition to weighing such factors in judging what individuals say, write, or do, researchers should also consider the instrumental motivations that can lead to selection bias by participants in which statements, documents, and other sources they make accessible or available. Newly empowered actors in control of the archives are likely to make available only negative information about their opponents and positive information about themselves.

It is important to consider as well any potential selection biases in secondary sources. Historians are always at risk of selectively choosing the primary and secondary sources that confirm their arguments. For this reason, it is important to consider a wide range of secondary accounts representing contending historiographical schools and explanations, a point nicely demonstrated in Evangelista's systematic, process-tracing reconstruction of the Cold War endgame (Evangelista, this volume, Chapter 6; see also Lustick 1996).

4. Take into account whether the case is most or least likely for alternative explanations

Prior expectations on the strength and scope conditions of a theory require the most updating when it fails to explain a case in which it is most likely to apply,

---

[11] See the Appendix for more detail and further examples.

or succeeds in explaining a case in which it is least likely to apply. Process tracing can play an important role in insuring that such cases are not flukes, and that the scope conditions of prior theories need to be revised. If, for example, a theory's failure in a most-likely case is caused by a variable that occurs only rarely or even only once, the scope conditions of the prior theory may need revision for only one or a few cases. However, if process tracing demonstrates that the prior theory failed due to a variable or interaction that is common, its scope conditions will require more radical revision.

5. Make a justifiable decision on when to start

Process tracing requires a researcher to choose and justify a starting point for investigating evidence on alternative explanations. Do we begin process tracing on the Cuban Missile Crisis, for example, at the point when President Kennedy learned of the Soviet effort to deploy missiles in Cuba, with the Russian Revolution in 1917, or with the environmental context in which humans have evolved over the centuries? There is no universal answer to such questions, as a justifiable starting point depends on how a researcher defines the puzzle or question they are trying to explain: crisis decision-making, Great Power ideological rivalry, or the extent to which humans have genetic predispositions regarding conflictual and cooperative behavior.

Even within one well-defined research question, the proper starting point can be subject to debate. Just as any researcher's decision on how far down to go in gathering detailed evidence can be critiqued for going too far or not far enough, the selection of the point in time at which to start process tracing can be critiqued for being too far back or too proximate. Robert Putnam's account of political differences between northern and southern Italy at the end of the twentieth century, for example, has been criticized for starting the explanatory story in the eleventh century, skipping over long periods of history, and downplaying or ignoring more historically proximate events that may have had powerful effects on regional politics (Putnam 1993; Tarrow 1996: 393).

Yet, process tracing has to begin somewhere, and there are useful rules of thumb for deciding when to start. A reasonable place may be a critical juncture at which an institution or practice was contingent or open to alternative paths, and actors or exogenous events determined which path it would take. Path dependency theories suggest that institutions, once set on a particular path, often become locked in to that path by increasing returns, externalities, or other mechanisms (Pierson 2000). A common critique of critical junctures is that they are identifiable only in retrospect, but process tracers have the luxury of always looking at them in retrospect.

Still, in choosing a critical juncture as a starting point for process tracing, researchers have to consider whether earlier and later ones might also be relevant (hence Tarrow's critique of Putnam), and they should also consider whether it is necessary to do process tracing on other potential but unrealized critical junctures before or after their chosen starting point (see also Capoccia and Kelemen 2007). These are the times at which institutions could have changed, perhaps due to some exogenous shock, but did not. Such potential junctures are subject to more conceptual and interpretive debate than the junctures that in fact led to institutional change. In general, to the extent that a researcher locates the starting point for process tracing in the distant past, it is important to show how institutions or practices could have reproduced themselves for long periods of time, even if resources and word limits do not allow continuous process tracing on the long period between the starting point and the outcome.

Another kind of starting point is the time at which a key actor or agent enters the scene or gains some material, ideational or informational capacity. This can be effective when alternative explanations hinge upon or work through the motivations, knowledge, and capacities of individual agents, and when particular agents behave differently, or with different effects, from their predecessors.[12]

6. Be relentless in gathering diverse and relevant evidence, but make a justifiable decision on when to stop

When assessing alternative explanations of a case, process tracers should be relentless in tracking down primary sources or seeking interviews with participants. A single meeting or memo may prove to be the crucial piece of evidence that instantiates one explanation or undermines another. Yet, not all evidence is equal: the more probative we expect it to be, the more effort we should expend to obtain it. Here, process tracers should use the Bayesian-inspired criteria discussed above and in the Appendix – smoking-gun, doubly decisive, straw-in-the-wind, and hoop tests – to assess the potential probative value of data not yet obtained.

Furthermore, Bayesian logic indicates they should seek diverse and independent streams of evidence. If you want to know whether an animal is a duck, instead of just looking at how it walks, you should also consider how it flies, sounds, looks, and so on. This insight is consistent with arguments

---

[12] Evangelista, this volume, Chapter 6, offers an excellent, historically grounded application of our arguments here regarding starting points.

concerning triangulation among diverse data sources. With triangulation, a researcher cross-checks the causal inferences derived from his or her process tracing by drawing upon distinct data streams (interviews, media reports, documents, say).

Yet, triangulation is not a panacea, as its successful use requires that the error term in each stream of evidence, on average, points in such a way that it cancels those in others. If all the streams are subject to the same selection bias, however, then errors can accumulate, making researchers unaware of this problem ever-more confident in a false explanation (Symposium 2007: 10; Kuehn and Rohlfing 2009). Seemingly diverse sources of evidence could actually all originate from one or a few individuals with instrumental reasons to convince observers of a particular explanation.

As it can demand both diverse and deep evidence, and may require significant "straw-in-the-wind" evidence when the more definitive kind is not available, process tracing can be quite time consuming. Elisabeth Wood's excellent study of the Salvadoran civil war, for example, advances a rich, process-based argument that draws on an enormous amount of information. Yet, it was also fifteen years in the making (Wood 2003: xi–xv; see also Lyall, this volume, Chapter 7). Carefully executed process tracing thus requires that researchers think at an early point about their own financial limits and temporal constraints.

This point highlights the necessity of deciding when to stop gathering and analyzing evidence. There is no simple algorithm for deciding when to stop, and stopping at any point makes the researcher vulnerable to the possibility that just a little more research would have turned up evidence that would have greatly revised their estimate of the likely truth of alternative explanations. However, Bayesianism offers a sensible argument here: one stops when repetition occurs. That is, a researcher should stop pursuing any one stream of evidence when it becomes so repetitive that gathering more of that same kind of evidence has a low probability of revising their estimate of the likely accuracy of alternative explanations.[13]

For each test in determining whether an animal is a duck – walk, sounds, etc. – a small sample is sufficient. A thousand steps or quacks provide no more convincing evidence than a few. Yet in deciding when to stop, there is no escaping the de facto trade-off between the risk of stopping too soon and making poor inferences, and the risk of stopping too late and wasting time,

---

[13] While using different language, ethnographers advance a strikingly similar decision rule: Gusterson 2008.

effort, and resources on evidence that proves to have no effect on one's estimates on the verisimilitude of alternative explanations.

7. Combine process tracing with case comparisons when useful for the research goal and feasible

Although some have argued that single-case or no-variance designs are weak (King *et al.* 1994), process tracing within single cases can in fact lead to convincing explanations if appropriate evidence is accessible. Moreover, if the explanations of these cases disprove claims of necessity or sufficiency, or if the cases are most likely for a theory that fails to explain them or least likely for an explanation that succeeds, their explanation can have more general implications for the veracity and scope conditions of contending theories (see also Mahoney 2012). Yet for many inferential purposes, comparative case studies can be more powerful sources of inference than single-case designs.

In a most-similar case comparison, in which two cases differ on one independent variable and on the dependent variable, process tracing can help establish that the one independent variable that differs is related through a convincing hypothesized causal process to the difference in the cases' outcomes. As noted above, most-similar cases rarely control for all but one potentially causal factor, and process tracing can establish that other differences between the cases do not account for the difference in their outcomes. Similarly, it can help affirm that the one independent variable shared between two least-similar cases accounts for the similarity in their outcomes, and that similarities in other potential causal factors do not explain the common outcome.

An additional synergy between process tracing and case comparisons is that an explanation inductively derived from process tracing might lead the researcher to reconsider his or her case selection. If the close study of a case leads to the discovery of an omitted variable, adding this variable to the theoretical framework can change the definition of the relevant population of cases. This can also change which cases are most similar, least similar, or deviant, hence changing which are most useful to study for theory testing or theory development.

8. Be open to inductive insights

One of the great advantages of process tracing is that it puts researchers at risk of stumbling upon many potential causal factors, evident in the details and sequences of events within a case, which they had not anticipated on the basis of their prior alternative hypotheses. Encountering such surprises provides opportunities to rethink prior explanations of the case. It may be possible to revise these prior explanations in trivial ways to accommodate unexpected facts, or it may prove necessary to build new explanations or link surprising facts to extant theories that the researcher had not previously thought would apply to the case. In any event, it is important to pay attention to the feeling of surprise and to follow it up with efforts to explain surprising facts theoretically.

9. Use deduction to ask "if my explanation is true, what will be the specific process leading to the outcome?"

Prior to embarking on process tracing, researchers should clarify as much as possible the facts and sequences within a case that should be true if each of the alternative hypothesized explanations of the case is true. Which actors should have known, said, and did what, and when? Who should have interacted with, worried about, or allied with whom? We cannot stress enough that theories are usually stated in very general terms; they must therefore be operationalized and adapted to the specific processes predicted in particular cases (see also the discussion in Jacobs, this volume, Chapter 2).

For new explanations inductively derived from the evidence within a case, it is doubly important to forestall any confirmation bias by considering what other observable implications must be true if the new explanation is true. As noted above, these observable implications may be in other cases, but they could also be within the case from which the new theory was derived as long as they are independent from the evidence that gave rise to it. Either way, if additional observable implications can be derived from the new explanation and tested against new evidence, this can provide a check against confirmation bias.

10. Remember that conclusive process tracing is good, but not all good process tracing is conclusive

The more continuous a narrative explanation of a case, and the closer the evidence fits some explanations and not others, the more confidence we can have in explanatory inferences based on process tracing (but see also Schimmelfennig, this volume, Chapter 4). There may well be temporal or spatial gaps in the evidence bearing on hypothesized processes, however, such as documents that have been destroyed or remain classified, or participants who are unwilling or unable to submit to interviews. In addition, in some case studies the available evidence may be equally consistent with two or more hypotheses that offer incompatible explanations of the case. When the evidence does not allow high levels of confidence in supporting some hypotheses and discounting others, it is important to acknowledge the level of uncertainty that remains.

Some may worry that such transparency will undercut their argument. However, the opposite is in fact the case. The explanation – its veracity and the soundness of its causal inferences – will only be enhanced (see also Evangelista, this volume, Chapter 6; Checkel, this volume, Chapter 3). Indeed, the intellectual honesty and rigor of this approach is vastly better than the so-called "gladiator style of analysis, where one perspective goes forth and slays all others" (Friedrichs and Kratochwil 2009: 721).

Process tracing on general categories of theories

The kinds of process tracing evidence that are relevant and the veracity, accessibility, and biases of this evidence are often specific to the explanations a researcher is considering and the cases they have chosen to study. The extent to which alternative explanations are mutually exclusive or complementary also varies greatly depending on the explanations and cases studied. Nonetheless, useful general observations can be made about the kinds of process tracing opportunities and challenges that arise with different general modes of explanation common in political science. Here, we consider process tracing on rational choice, cognitive, material/structural, normative/structural, and institutional/functional-efficiency theories.

Rational choice theories argue that actors have complete and transitive preferences and that they choose courses of behavior that maximize the expected value of likely outcomes given the information available to them. Some early theorists made "as-if" assumptions, or assumptions that obviated the need for process tracing by arguing that it was unnecessary to show that actors actually made rational calculations so long as outcomes arose as if actors had done so. So-called thick rational choice approaches make further assumptions by presuming that actors have certain preferences, such as for gains in material resources or power. Rational choice theorists, however, have increasingly been willing to eschew as-if assumptions and engage in process tracing. That is, they accept the challenge of making only thin assumptions to the effect that actors decide through rational processes. They then seek to discover actors' preferences by observation, demonstrating empirically that actors actually do make calculations and choices through rational processes to maximize their preferences (Bates *et al.* 1998; Schimmelfennig 2003; see also Checkel, this volume, Chapter 3).

This raises several challenges for process tracing. For one, there is the revealed preference problem. How can we infer actors' real preferences, given that they are often engaged in strategic contexts that provide incentives to misrepresent them? In addition, how can we avoid circularity or tautology by inferring preferences separately from the behavioral choices that these preferences are supposed to explain? There is a danger that – no matter what the outcome – the researcher can change his or her measurement of the actors' preferences so that the chosen outcome was a value-maximizing one.

In view of these challenges, the only option is to infer preferences from an actor's earlier rhetoric and actions and use these to explain subsequent behavior, while also investigating the possibility that preferences may change over time through learning or other processes. In particular, if actors engage in costly signaling – rhetoric or actions that impose high political or material costs if preferences are not consistent with these statements or acts – this may be taken as a relatively reliable indicator of preferences. A good example is David Laitin's study of how Russian speakers in the non-Russian former Soviet Republics chose between teaching their children the titular language of the country in which they resided (such as Latvian) or their native Russian. Laitin convincingly uses statements from the individuals making these choices, as well as aggregate data, to show that they were conceived as involving a trade-off between passing along to children an exclusive focus on Russian language and heritage and maximizing their employment opportunities. Those who chose to have their children invest in the newly dominant local language revealed their preference for employability over linguistic heritage (Laitin 1998).

Even if preferences can be reliably inferred, however, rational choice arguments face a second hurdle in demonstrating that decision processes maximized actors' expected utilities given their preferences and the information at their disposal. This makes it very important to establish the information actors had and when they had it. This stage of rational choice explanations is often tested through process tracing against the alternative explanation that actors' decisions are influenced by cognitive errors and biases. David Lake, for example, uses process tracing to compare a rational choice approach, in this case a bargaining theory model, and an "error and bias" explanation of US decision-making on the 2003 intervention in Iraq. Lake concludes that Iraqi leaders failed to consider readily available costly signals of American resolve, and American leaders ignored ample evidence on the likely costs of war, so that "misrepresentation by the other side was far less of a problem than self-delusion" (Lake 2010: 45).

If rational choice explanations face a revealed preference problem, cognitive theories face the challenge of accurately inferring revealed beliefs. Actors may have instrumental reasons, such as an interest in winning political support from groups or individuals, for publicly espousing ideas that they do not actually believe. One option here is to compare actors' public statements with available private deliberations that they expected would not be revealed for some time. Yuen Foong Khong, for example, compares the analogies American leaders used in public to justify the Vietnam War with those they used in private policy discussions that were de-classified many years later, checking to see if actors chose the same analogies in both settings. He concludes that they did so, with the sole exception of the analogy to France's disastrous experience in Vietnam, which was used only in private (Khong 1992: 60–61).

Actors may also make statements authored by their staffs or pushed upon them by powerful individuals or groups, so it is important to establish the provenance and authorship of public statements, and to give spontaneous and unplanned statements more weight than planned ones as indicators of genuine beliefs. Also, stated beliefs that incur substantial audience costs are more likely to reflect genuine beliefs, and recollections of beliefs held in the past that are backed up by documentary evidence are more credible than those lacking such supporting evidence. In addition, research by social psychologists shows that the recall of past beliefs is likely to be more accurate the more intense was the social context surrounding their creation (Wood 2003: 33–34). Finally, we should expect evidence that an actor holds socially stigmatized beliefs to be harder to find than evidence that he or she shares widely accepted ones, so we should treat absence of evidence on the former differently from absence of evidence on the latter.[14]

Theories that emphasize material power and structure require that actors be aware of power differentials and that they circumscribe their behavior when faced with more powerful opponents. This raises several challenges for process tracing. First, actors engaged in strategic interaction may have incentives to either exaggerate their capabilities (to bluff) or to understate them (to preserve the option of surprising adversaries). The same applies to actors' publicly stated assessments of others' power capabilities.

Second, power is often strongest as an explanation when it has a taken-for-granted quality. It may successfully deter actors from publicly discussing or

---

[14] On all these points, see Jacobs, this volume, Chapter 2.

even contemplating possible courses of action.[15] This makes it difficult to distinguish whether an actor was deterred from doing something or never had an interest in doing it in the first place. It also means that exceptions to power explanations – cases in which actors thought their higher level of commitment would enable them to prevail over better-endowed adversaries – are more evident and easier to document because these situations become overt conflicts, such as wars, labor strikes, or attempted revolutions, rather than being non-events.

Nonetheless, it is possible to use process tracing to assess power explanations by paying careful attention to sequencing and to what information actors had and when they had it. For example, scholars have offered two competing explanations of the 1898 Fashoda crisis between Great Britain and France over control of the headwaters region of the Nile. Christopher Layne advances a straightforward power argument: France backed down because Britain had superior military power (Layne 1994: 28–33). Kenneth Schultz offers an explanation based not only on power differentials, but also on the ability of democracies to commit credibly to using military power when both ruling and opposition parties support this stance (Schultz 2001: 175–195). Schultz's process tracing makes his explanation more convincing because it explains the puzzle of why a weaker France challenged Britain in the first place, when Britain's resolve was unclear, and it demonstrates that France backed down precisely when Britain's democratic institutions made its threat to use force credible and France's democracy laid bare the political divisions that undermined its resolve.

Like material structure arguments, theories about norms – a form of social structure – need to show that norms prevented actors from doing things they otherwise would have done. A good example is Nina Tannenwald's research on the non-use of nuclear weapons since the bombings of Hiroshima and Nagasaki. To show that normative constraints explain this outcome, Tannenwald has to demonstrate that norms against the use of nuclear weapons – rather than their limited battlefield utility – explain their non-use. Accordingly, Tannenwald provides direct, process-tracing evidence that American presidents and their advisors chafed at the perceived normative constraint of the American public's revulsion at the idea of using nuclear weapons after the effects of nuclear fallout became more widely known. She also demonstrates that these same leaders often

---

[15] It is only a short step from this understanding to what interpretive theorists call productive power, or power that is constitutive of agent interests and identities: Barnett and Duvall 2005; see also Pouliot, this volume, Chapter 9.

avoided even officially considering the option of using nuclear weapons for fear that their deliberations would be leaked to the public (Tannenwald 2007; see also Bennett, this volume, Appendix).

Finally, institutional explanations that rely on functional efficiency and transaction costs must be able to demonstrate through process tracing how such costs affect compliance. A good example is Ron Mitchell's study of international environmental cooperation over the sea. In particular, he uses process tracing to demonstrate that the international regime to prevent the dumping of oil residue from tankers failed to reach high compliance levels due to high transaction costs. In contrast, the international regime to force oil tanker owners to install expensive anti-pollution equipment succeeded in motivating high compliance because it made non-compliance transparent and provided low-cost means of sanctioning owners who failed to comply (Mitchell 1994).

Conclusion and preview

This introduction and the chapters that follow seek to consolidate the turn to process and mechanisms in contemporary political science. We do this not by exploring new substantive empirical domains or developing novel theories; rather, we focus on the prior, operational, and methodological issue of how we come to know when studying process. As has been argued elsewhere, the central challenge here is to avoid "lazy mechanism-based storytelling" (Hedström and Ylikoski 2010: 58, 64).

Preview

The volume has three parts. Part I comprises this introductory essay. It historicizes the term "process tracing," grounds it philosophically, and advances specific best practices for distinguishing good process tracing from bad.

The six chapters in Part II are the manuscript's core, assessing the contributions of process tracing in particular research programs or bodies of theory, including ideational theory (Chapter 2 – Jacobs), work on international institutions (Chapter 3 – Checkel), the European Union (Chapter 4 – Schimmelfennig), the comparative politics subfield (Chapter 5 – Waldner), the end of the Cold War (Chapter 6 – Evangelista), and the literature on conflict processes (Chapter 7 – Lyall). These chapters are resolutely applied – connecting method to practice – with recognized experts assessing the strengths and weaknesses of process tracing as used in particular substantive domains. They include process tracing for deductive/theory-testing purposes (Chapter 4 – Schimmelfennig), micro-level process tracing on cognitive theories (Chapter 2 – Jacobs), process tracing and design-based inference (Chapter 7 – Lyall), macro-level process tracing on structural theories (Chapter 5 – Waldner), process tracing on the interplay of individuals and institutions (Chapter 3 – Checkel), and process tracing that focuses on explaining key historical cases (Chapter 6 – Evangelista).

Whatever the application and type of process tracing, all chapters address the best practices articulated in the present chapter and work from a common template of questions. We asked the contributors to analyze cutting-edge examples of process tracing in their subfields; to assess the evidentiary and interpretive matters relevant to the topics they research; to identify the process tracing issues specific to the kinds of theories on which they have focused; and to assess critically the good and bad in applications of process tracing. Collectively, the analyses highlight issues of data quality, the role of hypothesized causal mechanisms, time and resource constraints, research ethics, multi-method strategies where process tracing is one technique in play, and theory development.

In Part III, we step back and – in three separate chapters – explore the research frontier. In Chapter 8, Thad Dunning makes explicit a theme touched upon in several earlier contributions – the relation of process tracing to quantitative methods – and does so by highlighting the key role it can and should play in multi-method research. In particular, Dunning shows how process tracing can help to interrogate the assumptions behind quantitative inferences. For example, it can be used to assess whether assignment to treatment was in fact "as if random" in a setting that a researcher has identified as a possible natural experiment. Building upon a theme in this opening chapter, Dunning also argues that transparency regarding evidentiary claims and inferences is critical to process tracing because it fosters open contestation among scholars with empirical and theoretical expertise on the case or cases in question; in turn, this produces more considered and shared judgments on the evidence.

If Dunning's analysis bridges different methodological traditions, then Chapter 9, by Vincent Pouliot, goes a step further, examining the role of process tracing in interpretive social science. Pouliot explores the gap that separates positivist and post-positivist understandings of the technique, and argues that an engagement around the concept of practice can minimize the meta-theoretical challenges involved in bridging such a divide. In a subtle, fair-minded, and empirically grounded analysis, he simultaneously both engages with and pushes back against the best practices we articulate above.

In Chapter 10, the co-editors revisit the best practices of good process tracing, synthesize and critique the volume as a whole, and outline an agenda for future development of and research on process tracing. In particular, proponents of process tracing need to remember that method is not an end in itself; rather, it is a tool helping us to build and test theory. And the latter remains a central challenge for process tracers – how to combine the technique's use with the development of cumulable social science theory (see also Hedström and Ylikoski 2010: 61–62). Moreover, process tracing is only one way to capture process. Future work thus needs to integrate this volume's findings with insights gleaned from statistical approaches, agent-based modeling exercises, and applications of discourse analysis, among others.

Finally, in the Appendix, Andrew Bennett explores in more detail the relation of Bayesianism to process tracing. Arguing that the technique shares much in common with Bayesian approaches to the logic of explanation, he outlines the similarities and differences between it and Bayesian inference. To make the exposition accessible to all with a general interest in process tracing, Bennett grounds his conceptual and logical analysis in the illustrative example of Nina Tannenwald's study of the "nuclear taboo" (Tannenwald 2007).

Part II

Process tracing in action

2 Process tracing the effects of ideas

Alan M. Jacobs

This chapter examines the uses of process tracing for empirically testing ideational explanations and theories of political decision-making. Ideational mechanisms have characteristics that make them especially difficult to study, as compared to materially driven causal processes. Ideas are unusually difficult to measure and are often highly correlated with other plausible causes of political outcomes. Moreover, key mechanisms of ideational influence operate within a "black box" of unobservability from the perspective of the historical researcher. These challenges of ideational analysis motivate this chapter's arguments in two respects. On one level, the chapter seeks to demonstrate that process tracing represents an especially powerful empirical approach for distinguishing between ideational and material effects. At the same time, the chapter reckons with the considerable challenges that the study of ideational causation presents, even for careful process tracing.

The chapter offers ideational analysts a set of process tracing strategies as well as guidance in identifying the conditions under which each strategy can be fruitfully applied. Broadly, it emphasizes three hallmarks of effective tracing of ideational processes. The first of these is "expansive empirical scope." It is tempting for analysts testing ideational explanations to zero in on key moments of political decision, on the handful of elite actors who were "at the table," and on the reasons that they provided for their choices. However, for reasons outlined below, a narrow focus on critical choice points will rarely be sufficient for distinguishing ideational from alternative explanations. To detect ideational effects, our analytic field of view must be expansive in terms of both temporal range and level of analysis. A well-specified theory of ideas will imply predictions not just about individual elites' statements and behavior at key moments of choice, but also about continuity and change, sequences of events, flows of information, and movements of actors across institutional settings over time.

The author thanks Justin Shoemaker for invaluable research assistance and the volume's editors and participants at the Georgetown Authors' Workshop for helpful comments.

Second, in outlining, illustrating, and assessing a set of empirical strategies, the chapter emphasizes the importance of careful and explicit reasoning about *the processes that generated the data* under analysis. As in all inferential endeavors, analysts seeking to trace ideational processes must relentlessly confront their interpretations of the data with plausible alternatives. In ideational analysis, this means paying especially close attention to the ways in which the institutional and political contexts of choice generate *strategic incentives*. These incentives include pressures for actors to speak, behave, or keep records in ways that occlude, rather than reveal, the considerations motivating their decisions.

Finally, the chapter underlines the role of "theory-specification" in process tracing. Tightly specified theories with detailed mechanisms can substantially enhance the discriminating power of process tracing by generating relatively sharp and unique empirical predictions. In the realm of ideational analysis, analysts can often fruitfully draw more detailed causal logics from psychological theories of how individuals process information and form beliefs. At the same time, the chapter points to the risk that an *overly* narrow specification of mechanisms may lead analysts to miss ideational processes that are in fact present.

As the editors indicate in their introductory chapter, process tracing is a versatile analytic approach that can be put to different kinds of knowledge-generating purposes. The analysis below is primarily focused on the deductive testing of claims about ideational effects, rather than the inductive generation of hypotheses (see also Schimmelfennig, this volume, Chapter 4). The tools assessed here, however, may be equally applied to the testing of general theories as to the testing of explanations of specific cases. The causal processes of concern here, moreover, operate at multiple levels of analysis. Viewed narrowly, the effect of ideas on decision-making may play out on a very "micro" scale, at the level of individual-level cognition and short-run governmental processes. Yet, as I have foreshadowed, the chapter will argue that substantial empirical leverage can be gained from a more macroscopic approach: from the analysis of patterns of behavior and interaction among individuals and across organizations over extended stretches of time.

The remainder of this chapter proceeds in four sections. The first substantive section lays conceptual foundations by defining an ideational theory and distinguishing it from alternative logics of explanation. The second section then outlines three acute empirical challenges that afflict the testing of ideational claims. Next, taking into account these challenges, the third section outlines, illustrates, and assesses several types of process-tracing tests of ideational influence. These tests involve a variety of forms of data and logics of inference, including the analysis of communication; the examination of within-unit co-variation (both over time and cross-sectionally); the tracing of paths of ideational diffusion; and analysis of the substantive content of decision outcomes. The chapter closes with reflections on the core analytical investments scholars must make if they are to effectively trace ideational causation in politics.

Defining an ideational theory

As the volume editors point out in their introductory chapter, good process tracing involves, first, casting a wide net for plausible alternative accounts and, second, being as empirically "tough" on one's primary explanation as on the alternatives (see Chapter 1, pp. 23–24). Testing a theory against its competitors, however, first requires a clear conceptual distinction between alternative causal logics. In this section, I offer a definition of an ideational causal theory and logically distinguish ideational theories from non-ideational alternatives.

I conceptualize an ideational theory (or explanation of an outcome) as a causal theory (or explanation) in which the content of a cognitive structure influences actors' responses to a choice situation, and in which that cognitive structure is not wholly endogenous to objective, material features of the choice situation being explained.[1]

The first part of this definition is straightforward: an ideational theory posits a causal effect of the content of actors' cognitions on their choices. These cognitions may include normative commitments, causal or descriptive beliefs about the world, or mental models or analogies from which actors draw specific beliefs or policy prescriptions.

It is the second part of the definition, however, that distinguishes an ideational theory from most alternative lines of explanation. It is a common feature of most theories of political choice that actors' choices flow causally from their cognitions. In standard game-theoretic accounts, for instance, actors' choices of strategy result from (among other things) their beliefs and preferences. Nearly all theories of choice could, in this trivial sense, be considered "ideational."

How, then, can we conceptually distinguish ideational theories from non-ideational alternatives? In this chapter, I refer to non-ideational explanations

---

[1] Herein, I refer interchangeably to ideational theories and explanations; the arguments I make are intended to apply to both.

of choice, broadly, as *materialist* explanations. We can conceptualize one key difference between ideational and materialist explanations by thinking about how each accounts for *variation* in actors' choices. In a materialist logic of explanation, variation in choices is caused by variation in *the objective, material parameters of actors' choice situations*. Material causes may include differences across cases in the relative material pay-offs of the alternatives, arising from variation across those cases in the causal relations linking options to material outcomes. Material causes may also include differences in the menu of feasible alternatives (or strategies), arising from differing material capabilities or differing institutional or technical constraints. Rationalist institutional theories, theories grounded in class-based, sectoral, or geographic economic interests, and neo-realist theories of strategic interaction in international relations are among the more common forms of materialist explanation in political science.

In an ideational theory, by contrast, variation in choices across cases is explained by reference to variation in the *content of actors' cognitions*. This may include variation in the relative value placed by actors on different material outcomes (i.e. goals or normative commitments); differences in actors' mental maps of the causal relations linking alternatives to outcomes (i.e. causal beliefs); or differences in actors' descriptive beliefs about the state of the world. A requisite feature of an ideational account, moreover, is that this variation in cognitions must not be purely a function of material conditions. The ideas in question, that is, must have a source *exogenous* to material features of the present choice situation.[2] Such prior causes may include exposure to ideas held by other actors through policy networks or processes of political socialization. Alternatively, actors' beliefs may arise from the lessons they draw from a disproportionately formative historical experience. Whatever the idea's prior cause, however, a claim of ideational causation necessarily implies that decision-makers' beliefs or goals are not fully determined by the material parameters of the choice being explained.

Thus, an account in which actors in different cases hold different causal beliefs because the *true* causal relations objectively differ across those cases would not be an ideational explanation: the ultimate cause here would be the material conditions of choice. On the other hand, an account in which actors operating in environments governed by similar true causal relations act on different *beliefs* about those causal relations – beliefs which were shaped by

---

[2] One may be able to trace the origins of many ideas to some set of material conditions: e.g. the past economic or sociological circumstances of their original formulation and dissemination. The key requirement here is that the ideas cannot be endogenous to material features of the choice situation *which is presently being explained.*

something other than the objective causal relations themselves – would be an ideational explanation. As should be clear, ideational accounts are fully compatible with an instrumentalist logic of choice in which actors select the goal-maximizing option given their causal beliefs. The key distinguishing feature of an ideational theory is that those goals and beliefs can *vary* independently of objective material conditions, generating differing decisions.

This extended definition now allows us to delineate the empirical task of testing an ideational theory. In particular, the definition implies three elements that must be operationalized in order to establish ideational causation. Any test of an ideational explanation must seek evidence that: (1) decision-makers possessed particular cognitions (a measure of the independent variable); (2) those cognitions shaped their choices (evidence of a mechanism of influence); and (3) those cognitions were not simply reducible to material features of the circumstances of choice (evidence of exogeneity of the independent variable).

The challenges of testing ideational theories

Attempts to adduce evidence of these three elements – to empirically distinguish ideational from material influences – confront a distinct set of challenges. I identify here three hurdles to ideational analysis, which roughly parallel the three evidentiary tasks identified above: the unusual difficulty of observing the independent variable; the difficulty of observing key mechanisms of influence; and a frequently close alignment between actors' ideational commitments and their material incentives.

First, the independent variable in an ideational theory – the ideas to which political decision-makers subscribe – is particularly difficult to observe. Error in the measurement of ideas can arise from the fact that the most readily interpretable manifestation of actors' cognitive commitments – their own verbal expressions of their ideas – is often a systematically biased indicator. As the volume's editors point out in Chapter 1, evidence that is provided by political actors themselves is subject to bias whenever those actors have incentives to conceal their true motives (see pp. 24–25, 33). Politics generates strong pressures for actors to employ verbal communication to strategically misrepresent the reasoning underlying their choices (Shepsle 1985; Goldstein 1993). In particular, officeholders or interest-group leaders, seeking to broaden support coalitions and advance their careers, have strong incentives to occlude many of the material and self-interested motives that might underlie their policy positions. They likewise have incentives to exaggerate the importance of "good policy" motives and broad social benefits. They will in turn select "good policy" justifications that conform to widely embraced normative frameworks and causal models connecting chosen policies to valued goals.

The result will often be systematic measurement error and a tilt of the inferential scales in favor of ideational explanations – in particular, those centered around "pro-social" or widely accepted ideas – and against material explanations based on a logic of decision-maker self-interest.[3] Importantly, this problem is not limited to utterances made at the time of decision: in recounting decisions in later memoirs and interviews, actors may face similar incentives to forge reputations for disinterested, civic-minded leadership.

Second, even where ideas can be well measured, analysts will face difficulty in assembling evidence of the mechanisms through which those ideas influence choices. Consider the mechanisms through which other commonly studied independent variables – such as institutions or the organization of interests – shape political outcomes. Many of these mechanisms operate at the level of *social interaction*. Institutional models of policymaking – such as theories of veto points or veto players – posit efforts by opponents of policy change to exercise influence at points of institutional opportunity, and efforts by proponents to bargain their way to winning coalitions across institutional venues. While some of this activity may be (strategically) hidden from view, much of it will be at least in principle observable by virtue of the fact that it involves communication and behavioral interaction *among* individuals and organizations.

Far more of the causal action in an ideational theory, by contrast, is *intra*personal, taking place inside the minds of individual decision-makers, as their pre-existing conceptual frameworks lead them to prioritize particular goals, attend to particular pieces of information, or employ particular causal logics. The challenge here is one of connecting independent variable to outcome: even if the analyst can establish that actors *hold* certain beliefs or goals, the intrapersonal nature of much of the causal process makes it more difficult to establish that actors *applied* those ideas to the choice being explained.

Finally, ideational analysis will often confront a challenge of multicollinearity. Competitive theory-testing is much easier when the analyst can

---

[3] By the same logic, it may also generate bias against explanations centered around "anti-social" ideas (e.g. racist ideas).

observe suspected alternative causes varying independently of one another across cases. In politics, however, actors' ideas and their material circumstances are not independently "assigned." In fact, common patterns of political interaction will often select for ideas that push actors' choices in the same direction as their material incentives. One important selection process derives from the logic of delegation. Many influential actors in politics – from elected officials to agency directors to interest-group leaders – owe their positions of authority to an act of delegation by one or more principals (for example, voters or legislators). These agents often face, on the one hand, strong material incentives to make choices that satisfy their principals (for example, the threat of electoral punishment). Yet, whenever principals have a choice among agents, they will seek to reduce the risk of "agency loss" by *selecting* agents who share their goals (Bendor *et al.* 2001). Wherever an effective agent-selection mechanism is operating, the result will tend to be a high correlation between the principal's demands and the ideational world-view of the agent. The result is a causal confound: the agent's material incentives to satisfy the principal will tend to dictate similar choices to those implied by the agent's own ideas. So, for instance, members of the US Congress who take conservative stances on social issues are more likely than those taking liberal stances to: (a) sincerely hold conservative social attitudes; and (b) come from districts in which a large share of the voting public holds conservative social attitudes. While this may be good news for democratic representation, it is bad news for causal inference: if the former fact supports an ideational explanation of roll-call voting patterns, the latter will suggest an equally plausible office-seeking motive. In sum, in many political contexts, processes of agent-selection will deprive analysts of independent variation in ideational and material causal variables, making it harder to sort out potential causal confounds. In addition, a high correlation between actors' ideas and their material circumstances makes it harder for the analyst to establish that the former are exogenous to the latter.

To summarize, I have argued that testing an ideational theory requires looking for evidence that decision-makers' choices were influenced by the content of their cognitions and that those cognitions are not reducible to material parameters of the choice situation. I have now contended that cognitive content is difficult to observe without bias; that mechanisms of individual-level cognitive influence are unusually elusive; and that cognitions and the material conditions of choice will often be highly correlated. How, in light of these challenges, should the testing of ideational theories proceed?

Strategies for process tracing ideational effects

In the remainder of this chapter, I consider how scholars can use process tracing to discriminate between ideational explanations of political choice and plausible materialist alternatives. In some ways, process-tracing methods are ideally suited to addressing the challenges of studying ideational causation. For instance, the detailed, context-sensitive analysis of cases allows scholars to closely examine the strategic incentives generated by particular choice situations and to exploit variation at multiple levels of analysis and over time. At the same time, the nature of ideational causation creates unique challenges for process tracing. The difficulty of detecting the operation of individual-level cognitive mechanisms is particularly problematic for an analytic approach that is so dependent on mechanism-related evidence. In crafting research designs based around process tracing, we must therefore think carefully about the ways in which ideational mechanisms might leave behind observable clues at *higher* levels of aggregation: in interpersonal interactions and communication, in organizational dynamics, and in the substance of the outcomes chosen.

In this section, I outline a set of empirical tests centered on the core elements of the definition of ideational causation introduced earlier in the chapter. Each empirical test contributes to one or more of the three evidentiary tasks that we have derived from that definition:

1. *measuring the independent variable*: identifying decision-makers' sincere ideational commitments;
2. *establishing the exogeneity of the independent variable*: identifying an ideational source external to the choice situation being explained;
3. *finding evidence of a causal mechanism*: establishing that the relevant ideas were applied to the choice being explained.

In addition, certain tests discussed below complement the first three tasks by:

4. *reducing multicollinearity*: identifying and exploiting independent variation in possible material and ideational causes.

In discussing each test, I do four things. First, I elaborate the logic of inference underlying the test, specifying the observable implication (of an ideational theory) that it examines. Second, I identify the probative value of each test. The tests contribute differentially to the four evidentiary tasks identified above. Moreover, they vary in the degree to which they refer to unique evidence for an ideational theory (that is, in their *sufficiency*) and in the degree to which they test for a certain prediction of that theory (that is, in their *necessity*) (see also Van Evera 1997). I thus characterize each test according to its degree of necessity and sufficiency: the degree to which a test's failure impugns an ideational theory and to which its passage adds to the theory's credibility. Third, the probative value of each test depends on certain assumptions about the processes generating the data. For each test, I therefore outline key conditions that determine the strength or validity of the test. Fourth, I provide illustrations of each test drawn from prominent studies of the role of ideas in politics.

To structure the exposition, I group the empirical tests roughly according to the kinds of data on which they draw. In particular, I consider tests that draw on:

- the analysis of communication,
- the examination of within-unit covariation over time,
- the examination of within-case covariation cross-sectionally,
- patterns of ideational diffusion, and
- the substance of decision outputs.

Table 2.1 summarizes the tests, the evidentiary tasks to which they contribute, and the assumptions on which they hinge.

Throughout, the discussion emphasizes key themes foreshadowed in the chapter's introduction: the advantages of expanding the scope of inquiry both temporally and across levels of analysis; the importance of careful reasoning about processes of data-generation, including actors' strategic incentives; and the benefits of theoretical specificity.

Analyzing (mostly private) communication

The most legible manifestation of an idea will sometimes be its verbal expression. Often, the tracing of ideational causal processes relies heavily on an analysis of the things that decision-makers say and write. Indeed, among the most intuitive observable implications of most ideational theories of influence is the expectation that *we should observe communication, during the process of decision-making, that is congruent with the idea.* Under favorable conditions, testing for this implication can serve two evidentiary purposes: it can provide a measure of the independent variable – revealing what ideas actors hold – and provide evidence of the operation of an

Table 2.1 Strategies of process tracing ideational effects

Empirical test	Evidentiary task to which it contributes	Assumptions or limitations
Analyzing (mostly private) communication	– **Measurement of independent variable:** observing statements under reduced strategic pressure – **Establishing causal mechanism:** application of ideas to decision	– Requires relatively complete deliberative record – Must take into account internal (e.g. intra-governmental) strategic motives for persuasion – More decisive when specific psychological mechanisms theorized and evidence of those specific mechanisms sought
Examining covariation over time *Analyzing ideational stability and change*	– **Reducing multicollinearity:** examining whether materialist factors vary over time, while ideational measures and outcomes remain constant; or ideas and outcomes change as predicted by learning-based theory – **Establishing exogeneity of ideas** – **Measurement of independent variable:** stable beliefs more likely to be sincere than rapidly changing ones	– Requires establishing wide variation in material incentives; greater material change → greater sufficiency – Requires theoretical specificity about conditions under which ideas should persist or change – Learning-based theory will have less certain and unique predictions than theory of ideational persistence
Examining within-case sequences	– **Reducing multicollinearity:** temporally separates out potential influences	– Must rule out strong role of strategic anticipation of preferences of actors involved later in process
Examining within-case cross-sectional covariation	– **Reducing multicollinearity:** tests for within-case covariation between actors' issue positions and their exposure to ideas and material incentives	– Must rule out correlational confounds (omitted variables, etc.)

Tracing ideational diffusion *Identifying ideational origins*	– **Establishing exogeneity of ideas** – **Measurement of independent variable**: helps validate communication as an unbiased measure of sincere ideas	– A "hoop test" for ideational theory, but low in uniqueness – Must rule out strategic "cherry-picking" of ideas – Test more applicable to shared cognitions than individuals' idiosyncratic beliefs
Tracing paths of ideational transmission	– **Measurement of independent variable** – **Establishing exogeneity of ideas** – **Reducing multicollinearity**: variation in transmission over time tests for causal necessity of ideas	– Generally, a "hoop test": ideas must be available to actors hypothesized to have used them – May also be satisfied with evidence of "mobile carriers"
Identifying mobile "carriers"	– **Measurement of independent variable** – **Establishing exogeneity of ideas** – **Reducing multicollinearity**: can test for covariation between policy and mobile carriers' entry/exit	– Carriers' ideational commitments must be readily identifiable (e.g. based on professional affiliation) – Carriers must move into key loci of authority – Must rule out strategic *selection* of carriers by political principals at time of outcome to be explained
Unpacking the substance of decision outputs	– **Establishing causal mechanism**: costs and benefits of decision outputs, and their visibility, helps discriminate between strategic and ideational motives	– Must take into account collective nature of decision-making and potentially diverse motives

ideational mechanism, suggesting that actors *applied* a particular set of values, beliefs, analogies, etc. to the decision in question.

For reasons outlined above, verbal communication by strategic political actors can be misleading. As this volume's editors point out in Chapter 1, the analyst must interpret actors' statements with careful attention to the motives or incentives that the speaker may have had to say particular things (see pp. 24–25). Among the determinants of those incentives is the *context* in which utterances are made. I unpack here the implications of one specific element of context that Bennett and Checkel discuss: the speaker's audience. More particularly, I explore the implications of *privacy*: whether statements are made to a small circle of fellow elites or to the general public.

Analysts of ideational effects often privilege statements delivered in more private settings – for example, discussions within cabinet or correspondence between officials – over public statements. There is good reason to make this distinction. In more public settings, political elites will, in general, have stronger incentives to justify predetermined decisions in socially acceptable terms. In private settings, on the other hand, decision-makers can let down their guard. Especially where actors with similar goals are deliberating together, it is more likely that they will understand themselves to be engaged in the collective pursuit of optimal (from their shared perspective) choices. In such a setting, actors are more likely to candidly reveal their goals, their causal beliefs, and their lines of reasoning in order to maximize the effectiveness of deliberation. Where an assumption of "collective deliberation" is justified, privately communicated statements can be a rich source of data on actors' cognitive commitments and their sources.[4]

One of the most striking uses of private communication to test an ideational argument appears in Yuen Foong Khong's (1992) study of US decision-making during the Vietnam War. The ideas posited as influential in Khong's study are *analogies* between past historical events – particularly, the appeasement of Hitler at Munich, and the Korean War – and current choice situations. In testing his analogical theory, Khong relies heavily on quotations from correspondence, meeting minutes, and other primary documentation of closed-door deliberations over Vietnam among top US officials. These communications reveal actors repeatedly reasoning about the risks and potential benefits of military options in Vietnam by reference to events in Europe in the 1930s and the Korean peninsula in the 1950s. Khong shows

---

[4] Public statements may also be revealing for some evidentiary purposes: for instance, where the analyst is interested in the kinds of policy justifications that public audiences find legitimate.

actors engaging in this process of selective historical inference repeatedly, across numerous contexts, and often in great detail.

In some cases, records of private deliberations may also be revealing for their silences. The analysis of reasoning in which actors do *not* engage plays an important role in my own study of governments' long-term choices in the field of pension policy (Jacobs 2011). The study seeks to explain the choices that governments have made between two alternative methods of financing public retirement schemes: pay-as-you-go, or PAYGO, financing (the collection of enough tax revenue each year to match annual spending) and pre-funding (the accumulation of a fund to meet long-term pension commitments). Among the propositions tested is the claim that policymakers' choices were influenced by the "mental model" that they employed to conceptualize pension arrangements: in particular, by whether they understood a state retirement program as: (a) a form of insurance, analogous to private insurance; or (b) a social mechanism for the redistribution of resources. While the insurance model was expected to tilt actors' preferences toward pre-funding, a redistributive understanding was expected to yield preferences for PAYGO financing. Further, these ideational effects were theorized to arise through an *attentional* mechanism: a given mental model was expected to direct actors' attention disproportionately toward those particular lines of reasoning logically implied by the model, and away from logics extrinsic to it.

The case of the design of the world's first public pension scheme, in Germany in 1889, yields especially clear verbal evidence of this effect (Jacobs 2011: 84–90). On the one hand, archival records show actors in closed-door settings drawing repeatedly on an understanding of public pensions as a form of "insurance" and articulating actuarial lines of reasoning that flow from this private-sector analogy. Equally revealing, however, is the *absence* of any record that officials considered key lines of reasoning that were inconsistent with the model. For instance, in their tight focus on the actuarial logic of commercial insurance, Bismarckian officials never spoke about the *political* consequences of fund-accumulation: in particular, the possibility that a pension fund accumulated in state coffers might be misused or diverted by future governments. This silence is particularly revealing – as evidence of biased information-processing – by comparison to two further observations. First, actors in other cases analyzed – where the redistributive model was dominant – referred frequently to the political considerations ignored by German officials. Second, the political risks to fund-accumulation appear to have been objectively present in the German case: within thirty years of the program's enactment, its fund had been wiped out by political misappropriation.

What is the probative value, for an ideational theory, of a test for private communicative evidence? How necessary is the discovery of such evidence to the survival of the theory? And how sufficient is such evidence for concluding that ideas had an effect on the outcome? The answers to these questions depend on the assumptions that we can plausibly make about the process generating the data in a given case.[5]

We would seem to be on most solid ground in characterizing communicative evidence as *necessary* for the survival of an ideational explanation: it would seem hard to credit such an explanation if we had looked hard and failed to find significant verbal references to the ideational constructs hypothesized to have been influential. The wrinkle, though, is that an absence of evidence cannot always be interpreted as evidence of absence. For many political and policy decisions, a sufficiently complete and reliable set of records of actors' closed-door deliberations may not exist or be available to the researcher, especially where actors were intent on keeping their discussions secret. Moreover, some widely held beliefs may never be voiced by actors during deliberations precisely because they are understood to be common knowledge.

Following the Bayesian intuition that the editors outline in this volume's introduction as well as its Appendix, the degree to which communicative evidence can serve as a "hoop test" – high in necessity – depends on the likelihood that we *would* have found verbal evidence of a set of ideas if actors had in fact held and applied those ideas to the decision. When assessing an absence of evidence, we must ask several questions about the data-generating process, including: Do we have evidence of deliberations in the *venues* within which actors would have been likely to apply and give voice to the idea in question? How *complete* is the available record of the deliberations in those venues? Would actors have had an *incentive* to voice the idea during deliberations if they subscribed to it? In my study of German pensions, the absence of evidence of certain lines of reasoning is made more compelling because the data are drawn from: (a) relatively comprehensive transcripts; (b) across several deliberative venues; and (c) containing participants who, if they *had* thought of the unmentioned considerations, would have had clear incentives to draw on them because the arguments would have bolstered the case for their desired outcome.

What about the sufficiency of the test? When is verbal evidence sufficient to establish actors' ideational commitments or that actors applied those ideas in

---

[5] The following builds upon Bennett and Checkel, this volume, Chapter 1 (pp. 16–17); Bennett, this volume, Appendix; George and Bennett 2005; and Trachtenberg 2006.

reasoning about the choice? One threat to the sufficiency of communicative evidence is the fact that actors' statements in internal deliberations may – despite their private nature – be affected by strategic dynamics. Even in closed-door settings, political elites may frame arguments for the purpose of coalition-building, rather than open-minded deliberation, selecting lines of reasoning to maximize the persuasive effect on fellow decision-makers. Moreover, available records of deliberations may have been created or released strategically by participants in the decision-making process; records revealing less pro-social material motives may tend to be suppressed. As George and Bennett (2005) emphasize, assessing the probative value of archival evidence thus requires knowledge of the broader context within which deliberations unfolded: the role of a given discussion and deliberative venue within the larger decision-making process; the incentives and pressures faced by actors; and the procedures by which records were kept, stored, and declassified in the political context under analysis. The sufficiency of verbal evidence will be higher to the extent that we can, through empirical and logical argumentation, rule out strategic motives among both speakers and record-keepers.

The examples above also suggest that we can increase the sufficiency of the test – that is, the uniqueness of the empirical predictions – by increasing the specificity of the theory itself (see also Chapter 1, p. 30). Effective causal-theory-testing via process tracing always depends on a clear specification of the causal logic or mechanisms underlying a causal effect (see also Schimmelfennig, this volume, Chapter 4; Hall 2003; Collier *et al.* 2004; George and Bennett 2005). And the pay-offs to relatively high theoretical specificity are apparent in both Khong's and my own analyses of communicative evidence. Both studies set out to test ideational claims grounded in relatively detailed cognitive mechanisms, drawn from psychological models of mental representation and information-processing. These theories do not posit simply that a given set of ideas will influence decisions: they also supply a more specific set of predictions about the ways in which ideas should shape the *processes* through which actors arrive at those decisions, yielding a substantially more demanding test of ideational claims.

Drawing on schema theory, Khong, for instance, predicts not just that actors will make use of analogies, but that they will ignore or discount information inconsistent with the analogy and interpret ambiguous information in ways that support the analogy. In my study of German pension politics, the theory yields the "risky" prediction that actors on both sides of an issue will display the same allocation of attention across considerations: thus, even opponents of a policy option should fail to attend to some considerations (those outside the dominant schema) that would speak strongly against the option. Such observations would be hard to reconcile with a strategic account of deliberation. By generating predictions that are less likely to be observed under alternative theories, a better-specified theory increases the sufficiency of supporting evidence.

At the same time, the analyst should weigh an important risk of crisp specification of mechanisms: while rendering ideational accounts more falsifiable, positing a particular cognitive mechanism of causation raises the probability of *falsely rejecting* an ideational explanation. In my own study, it was possible that ideas influenced German policymakers' choices through a cognitive mechanism *other* than the attentional mechanism that I theorized (say, by shaping actors' underlying goals). Deductive process tracing based on my tightly specified attentional theory would then have led me to understate the importance of ideas in shaping the outcome. How should the analyst manage this trade-off between Type I and Type II errors? One way to guard against the danger of false negatives is by theorizing multiple cognitive mechanisms, although this tactic will reduce the sufficiency of the tests. A strong familiarity with the relevant findings in cognitive and social psychology can also help to rule out the least-plausible mechanisms. Moreover, the analyst should consider leavening deduction with induction. As Bennett and Checkel (this volume, Chapter 1, pp. 17–18) explain, a key advantage of process tracing is that in-depth engagement with cases provides opportunities for uncovering evidence of causes and mechanisms that had not been previously theorized. Thus, the researcher might begin with one tightly specified ideational mechanism. If no evidence for that mechanism is found, he or she inductively searches for clues of other ideational processes; and if another ideational logic is suggested, derives empirical predictions from that new logic and collects additional evidence to test them.

Examining covariation over time

For reasons outlined above, material pressures and actors' ideational commitments will often be systematically correlated. However, analysts can enhance their prospects of finding independent variation in suspected causes by studying decision-making over time. Suspected causes that push in the same direction at the level of a case may diverge (a) over stretches of time extending *beyond* the case or (b) across temporal stages *within* the case. The analyst can exploit such independent variation to test for the distinct over-time correlations predicted by alternative theories. Temporally structured evidence can, further, permit inferences about both the exogeneity and the sincerity of actors' apparent ideational commitments. I discuss here two types of tests drawing on over-time covariational evidence: one grounded in the analysis of ideational stability and change across decision-making episodes in a single unit; another based on the inspection of sequences within a single case of decision-making.

Covariation over time: analyzing ideational stability and change

Observation of the behavior of key decision-makers over substantial stretches of time can help distinguish ideational from material causes by uncovering independent variation in these two sets of factors. One strategy of longitudinal analysis exploits the fact that cognitive commitments are typically slow to change and that beliefs are robust to new information (see, for example, Nickerson 1998). By analyzing decision-making over an extended time horizon, the analyst can test the following observable implication of many ideational theories: *that, because cognitive constructs are relatively resistant to change, we should see evidence of relative stability over time in both actors' ideas and in the choices that are hypothesized to result from them, even as material conditions change.*

In effect, this test multiplies the number of cases available for analysis within a single unit (for example, a country) by taking in a stretch of time covering a series of decisions. This will often mean extending the temporal scope of analysis prior to or beyond the decision(s) initially of central interest to the investigator (see also Bennett and Checkel, this volume, Chapter 1, pp. 26–29). The analyst then applies a longitudinal form of Mill's (1868) Method of Agreement to rule out alternative causes. If actors' statements and choices remain consistent with a hypothesized ideational commitment at multiple points in time, even as material pressures shift, then those material factors become less plausible as an explanation of actors' decisions. Furthermore, the case for both the exogeneity and the sincerity of actors' stated ideational commitments is considerably strengthened if they do not change with material conditions. If suspected "ideas" shift with the material winds, they are more likely to be endogenous or insincere post hoc justifications of choices that are actually driven by those material forces.

Students of ideational effects have frequently engaged in long-term longitudinal analysis to exploit this logic. Judith Goldstein (1993), for instance, in her landmark study of US trade policy, examined decision-making over the course of more than a century. This time frame included two decades-long periods during which a single idea – protectionism in one period, free-trade liberalism in the other – was dominant. Examining decision-making across several episodes in each period, Goldstein demonstrates that commitments to protectionism and free trade, respectively, were little moved by changes in economic conditions to which, under a materialist explanation, they ought to have been highly sensitive. During the post-war era of liberal dominance, for instance, Congress and the President continued to reduce tariff barriers even as the country's trade position dramatically worsened and well-organized interests lobbied hard for protectionism (Goldstein 1993: 167–169).

Sheri Berman (1998), in her comparative study of social democratic parties, similarly leverages a longitudinal design to examine the presence and effects of specific ideas. She demonstrates the cognitive grip of Marxist doctrine on German social democrats by outlining party leaders' rigid adherence to it over time; most strikingly, during the Weimar period the party refused to broaden its appeal beyond the working class or embrace Keynesian responses to unemployment despite strong electoral incentives and pressures to do so.

To summarize, the longitudinal, within-unit Method of Agreement can lend support to an ideational theory to the extent that expressed ideas and observed choices remain constant as possible material incentives vary. Such an observed pattern lends support to the claims that: (1) actors truly hold the beliefs that they profess; (2) those beliefs are not merely a function of (changing) material circumstances; and (3) the material factors that vary are not the explanation. A variant of this logic is to examine whether actors' positions are consistent with their expressed ideas across *issue* areas. Observing an actor who supports a social welfare program from which he or she happens to benefit, but defends that program with egalitarian arguments, one can ask whether the actor also supports a redistributive program from which he or she derives no pecuniary or electoral advantage.

The *necessity* of a longitudinal Method-of-Agreement test is greater the less change there is in the matrix of material pay-offs in the period under analysis: if actors' verbal reasoning or choices shift frequently with relatively modest change in material conditions, then the ideational theory is seriously impugned. The *sufficiency* of the test is greater the more change there is in material pay-offs: the more material pressures change while actors' choices and statements remain the same, the more decisively those incentives are ruled out. Analyzing longer stretches of time can thus tend to increase sufficiency.

Even so, evidence of consistency over long periods of time will not always imply support for an ideational theory. For some ideational theories – particularly, those that allow for learning – evidence of *change* in ideas and outcomes under particular circumstances can provide crucial support. For instance, when existing ideas and their policy implications fail in spectacular fashion, a theory of learning might expect actors motivated by "good policy" reasoning to reconsider prior understandings and adjust course. Here again, a clear specification of an ideational theory's mechanisms becomes important. At a cognitive level, are actors understood to engage in such strongly confirmatory reasoning that we should expect consistency over time *regardless* of the outcome? Or are there conditions under which actors are expected to attend to discrepant information and revise their ideas – i.e. learn? Are there sociological processes through which old ideas and their adherents get replaced by new?

Often, ideational theories do not explicitly answer these questions, but some do. Berman (1998) and Hall (1993) usefully adopt relatively clear – and differing – positions on the conditions for ideational change and, as a result, look for distinctive kinds of longitudinal evidence. Berman emphasizes the biasing effect of ideas on how actors process information, arguing that "ideas play a crucial role in structuring actors' views of the world by providing a filter or channel through which information about the external environment must pass" (Berman 1998: 30). Given this model of cognitive self-reinforcement, Berman seeks evidence of over-time ideational and policy *rigidity*, even in the face of failure and seemingly clear objective indications that other options might be preferable.

Hall, in contrast, sees prior ideas as constraining only up to a certain point. Actors will tend to draw by default on existing paradigms, even in the face of considerable policy failure. But when failures sufficiently accumulate – and if they are inexplicable in the terms of the old paradigm – then social learning may occur.[6] In support of this argument, Hall demonstrates, on the one hand, rather remarkable consistency in British policymakers' adherence to Keynesian principles and prescriptions – despite their ineffectiveness – through the stagflation of the 1970s. At the same time, he shows that Keynesian doctrine lost credibility and was replaced following persistent

---

[6] The process of learning documented by Hall appears to be more sociological than cognitive, driven as much by shifts in the locus of authority as by individual-level information-processing.

failures that were incomprehensible from the standpoint of Keynesian theory. In Hall's argument, that is, it is precisely because British policy *does* change in response to a strong form of objective feedback that the case for a particular kind of ideational influence receives support.[7]

As these examples illustrate, the longitudinal pattern for which analysts should go looking depends strongly on their theoretical priors about the conditions under which ideas change. It is worth noting that not all claims about ideational change and persistence are equally falsifiable. A prediction of strict rigidity is relatively easy to test for: any evidence of significant ideational change undermines the theory. The predictions of a learning mechanism are much harder to specify and operationalize (see Levy 1994). If learning can occur in the wake of dramatic failure, what counts as "dramatic"? If repeated failure is necessary, how much repetition is required? When exactly does an unexpected failure become an anomaly that forces ideational revision? Moreover, different theories might make different predictions about *which* actors will be most likely to change their minds: for instance, those with a material stake in the policy outcome, or those most directly exposed to information about the failure? Without well-crystallized theoretical accounts of the mechanisms through which learning operates, empirical tests based on a logic of learning can only be relatively weak "straws in the wind" (Van Evera 1997).

Finally, important considerations flow from the reliance of this test on the inspection of covariation between independent and dependent variables. Much of the recent literature on qualitative methods has drawn a sharp contrast between the logics of causal inference underlying process tracing, on the one hand, and correlational analysis (whether small-n or large-n), on the other. This contrast, for instance, underlies Collier *et al.*'s (2004) distinction between a correlational "data-set observation" (DSO) and a "causal-process observation" (CPO). As scholars have pointed out, many canonical methodological principles (most prominently expressed, in King *et al.* 1994) are drawn from a logic of covariation and apply differently or not at all to the analysis of CPOs (see also Dunning, this volume, Chapter 8).

In practice, small-n case-study research partakes of both logics, blending causal-process analysis with correlational analysis. As in the test described here, case analysts often unpack cases into multiple sub-cases (temporally or cross-sectionally) and analyze the correlation of suspected causes and outcomes across those sub-cases. And whenever they are drawing leverage from the inspection of covariation – whatever the level of analysis – the standard

---

[7] For a related argument, see Culpepper 2008.

assumptions required for drawing unbiased causal inferences from correlations must be defensible. Crucially, familiar concerns about omitted variables and endogeneity apply in full force to these "within-case" covariational strategies.

The case-study researcher will be in an especially strong position to rule out endogeneity: indeed, a number of the tests explored here are specifically aimed at establishing the exogeneity of ideas. But scholars employing tests based on covariation – including other covariation-based tests described below – must think especially hard about the threat of omitted confounding factors. In particular, they must ask: are there other material conditions that remained constant alongside ideas (or that covaried with ideas) that might also have influenced the outcome? If there are, then the analyst will need to employ additional tests (which may themselves draw on CPOs) to rule out those variables' confounding influence on the outcome.

Covariation over time: examining the sequence of decision-making

As discussed above, process tracing over time may mean examining covariation across decisions within a given unit. Yet the analyst can also leverage useful variation across the sequence of steps *within* a single decision-making process. Sequential analysis can take advantage of the fact that different actors and different venues are likely to play an important role at different stages in processes of policymaking or institutional design. Sequential analysis begins by examining a decision-making trajectory to determine a stage in the process, S, at which a plausible alternative was removed from the menu of viable options. The analyst can then inspect most closely the motives of actors at and prior to S, relative to the motives of actors involved after that watershed moment had passed. This test relies on the following empirical prediction: if an option was removed from the menu of active alternatives for ideational (or material) reasons at stage S, then *we should be able to observe actors who plausibly held that idea (or who had that material interest) centrally engaged in the policymaking process at or before S*. This test contributes to causal inference by generating independent variation – over time within a decision-making episode – in material and ideational factors that are correlated at the level of the episode taken as a whole.

In my analysis of pension policymaking (Jacobs 2011), I seek to distinguish between electoral and ideational motives in governments' choices between PAYGO financing and pre-funding. In general, PAYGO financing tended to be the more appealing option in electoral terms because it imposed the lowest costs on constituents and delivered the largest pensions in the near term. At the same time, prominent ideas about the political economy in some of the cases analyzed also favored PAYGO financing, particularly the notion that elected governments cannot credibly commit themselves to saving large reserves for future use. Cases in which pro-PAYGO ideas were dominant are thus especially difficult to decipher because material pressures (electoral incentives) and ideas push in the same direction.

The study's analysis of British pension politics illustrates how sequential evidence can help to pry apart correlated potential causes. The outcome to be explained in this case was the decision by British ministers to place their pension system on a PAYGO basis in 1925 (Jacobs 2011: 104–107). As secondary histories and archival records make clear, Conservative ministers in Britain initially designed a scheme with full pre-funding. This blueprint was then sent to an influential interdepartmental committee of civil servants for vetting and, according to an internal report, was rejected by this committee on the grounds that elected officials could not be trusted to resist short-term political pressures to spend the fund – a view with a long pedigree within Whitehall. After this stage, there is no evidence in the historical or archival record of pre-funding having been considered further by elected or unelected officeholders. These temporally ordered data are revealing on two points: (a) those actors with the *strongest* electoral motivations (ministers) placed the less electorally appealing option on the agenda; and (b) that option no longer appeared on the menu after those actors with the *weakest* electoral motivations (career bureaucrats) – and a strong set of cognitive commitments running counter to the plan – had rejected it. In short, the observed sequence is far less consistent with an electoral than with an ideational explanation.

Tightly assembled sequential evidence can prove quite decisive against either ideational explanations or rival hypotheses by helping to eliminate, as potential causes, the beliefs or motives of downstream actors (whether ideationally or materially generated). At the same time, temporal orderings must be interpreted with caution. If political actors are even moderately strategic, they will frequently take positions and make choices *in anticipation* of other actors' reactions. Perhaps British civil servants simply discarded an option that they knew their political masters would, if presented with it, later reject. Or perhaps ministers sent the plan to committee precisely in the hope that senior bureaucrats would kill it.[8] In social causation, temporally prior

---

[8] What makes both possibilities unlikely in the present example is the prior step in the sequence: the initial design and proposal of the idea by ministers themselves.

events and political behavior can be endogenous to subsequent (expected) outcomes. Sequential analysis should thus be informed by evidence or reasoning about the incentives that actors involved early in the process might have had to pander to the preferences of those who would arrive on the scene later.

Examining within-case cross-sectional covariation

We have considered the use of over-time within-unit variation to cut against multicollinearity of ideational and material forces. A similar logic also applies to the disaggregation of cases *cross-sectionally* – across subunits within a case. Some ideational theories, for instance, may usefully imply predictions about the positions that *individual actors* should be observed to take on the issues up for decision.[9]

The logic of inference here closely follows the familiar logic of analyzing cross-case variation, but at a lower level of aggregation. Actors within a case (individuals or organizations) will display varying degrees of exposure to experiences, information, or argumentation that might shape their beliefs, goals, or conceptual toolkits. They will also vary in their material stakes in the choice. This information will be analytically useful whenever those two patterns diverge: when the cross-actor distribution of ideational exposure is only weakly correlated with the distribution of material stakes. If the relevant ideational and material influences and actor positions can be well measured, the resulting test approaches "double decisiveness." That is, it would seriously impugn *either* an ideational explanation or the materialist alternatives if well-measured variation in actors' stances on the issue did not correspond to variation in their exposure to ideational influences or to their material stakes in the issue, respectively.

Andrew Bennett's (1999) study of Soviet military interventionism in the 1970s and 1980s makes substantial use of this method. Bennett seeks to explain why the Soviet Union (and, later, Russia) sometimes chose to intervene in some places, but not others. His prime theory yields an ideational explanation in which Soviet and Russian leaders' beliefs about the effectiveness of military intervention derive from personal experiences: personal involvement in a successful intervention is expected to reinforce actors' beliefs

---

[9] Related strategies could involve unpacking a country-level case into subnational units or institutional settings across which suspected causal conditions and actor positions vary.

in the efficacy of the use of force, while involvement in a failed intervention is theorized to lead to learning and belief change.

At the level of the cases as a whole, the outcomes to be explained appear over-determined: we observe the presence of both material and ideational forces that could explain Soviet and Russian policy choices. Several of Bennett's most decisive tests thus leverage variation *within* the state in actors' exposure to formative experiences from which lessons could be drawn. This differential exposure derives, for instance, from generational differences and variation in whether or not actors were directly involved in the Soviet Union's disastrous intervention in Afghanistan. Crucially, moreover, Bennett attends closely to points of divergence between the distribution of material stakes and the distribution of learning opportunities. So, for instance, while the military as an organization had a material stake in an expansion of its turf and resources, not all members of the organization had personal experience of the Afghan war; veterans of that failed intervention were, in turn, among the fiercest uniformed opponents of the war in Chechnya. This within-case correlational pattern helps to carry the ideational explanation through a critical hoop, while simultaneously casting significant doubt on an important materialist alternative.

The probative value of this type of test depends on a number of conditions. First, the certainty of the prediction, for either an ideational or materialist theory, depends on how well actors' sincere positions on the issue can be measured. And, like measurement of ideas themselves, measurement of actor positions needs to take into account potential strategic dynamics: the possibility that actors may have had strategic reasons to take public positions that differed from their sincere preferences.

Second, theoretical clarity is once again crucial. In particular, the method relies on a clear specification of what kind of "exposure" is causally important: what kind of stimulus ought to generate or transmit a given set of ideational commitments? Bennett draws heavily on cognitive psychology to identify the ways in which particular kinds of experience and information ought to translate into actor beliefs. Only with this specification in hand can he determine which actors have been "exposed" and which have not. On the other hand, as discussed above, the choice of degree of specification presents a dilemma. The more precise the specification, the more closely this test approaches a smoking gun for an ideational explanation. Yet unwarranted precision also risks setting up an overly restrictive hoop test and a false negative finding. (And the same issues apply to postulating the sources of actors' material interests.)

Third, because it draws on the inspection of covariation, this test is vulnerable to familiar threats to correlation-based inference. To avoid omitted variable bias, for instance, the analyst must be careful to account for all plausible influences on actors' positions that are also correlated with their ideas.

Tracing ideational diffusion

While individual-level cognitive structures may be difficult for the political analyst to observe, discriminating evidence often lies in the observable pathways along which ideas travel through a political system. I turn now to three tests for ideational influence that center on paths of ideational diffusion. I discuss tests for: (1) the origins of ideas; (2) the transmission of ideas across actors; and (3) the movement of ideational "carriers" across institutional settings.

Identifying ideational origins

Establishing that ideas mattered in a decision-making process requires establishing that they are *exogenous* to the material circumstances of choice. If an ideational framework is indeed exogenous, then the following prediction should usually hold: *there should be evidence of a source for the idea that is both external and antecedent to the decision being explained.* Where the exogeneity assumption is valid, such evidence will usually be easy to find: typically, proponents of new issue understandings or ideological frameworks *want* to transmit them in order to influence the course of social events – and are thus likely to make and disseminate statements of their views. This strategy, in most cases, is thus a hoop test: without a demonstration of prior intellectual ancestry, the case for ideational influence should usually be considered weak.

Such demonstrations are, unsurprisingly, quite common in ideational accounts. Berman exhaustively documents how the Swedish Social Democrats' programmatic beliefs emerged from the thinking of early party leader Hjalmar Branting, while those of the German SPD emerged from the thinking and argumentation of theoreticians Friedrich Engels and Karl Kautsky (Berman 1998: 38–65, 66–95). Goldstein traces the free-trade ideas that dominated the post-war era back to work being done in economics departments at US universities decades earlier (Goldstein 1993: 88–91). And

Hall (1993) can readily establish that monetarist ideas had become well established within the US economics profession and had been, subsequently, taken up by British right-of-center think tanks and journalists prior to the policy shifts that he seeks to explain.

Demonstrations of antecedent origins do not, by themselves, establish exogeneity. One reason is that actors within the decision-making episode being explained could have "cherry-picked" – from among the pre-existing ideas available in their environment – those that were most compatible with their material interests. The ideas employed during the decision-making process would, in such a situation, be endogenous "hooks" for policies chosen on other grounds. Moreover, not just any intellectual antecedent will satisfy the hoop test. The source must have been sufficiently prominent and credible to have influenced the intellectual environment in which the case is situated.

But should we always consider the search for an ideational antecedent to be a hoop test? What if the causally important idea is the "brainchild" of the episode's key decision-maker, who never had occasion to express this belief prior to the choice being explained? In such a situation, there might be no observable intellectual antecedent, even if an ideational explanation is right. A crucial implication is that not all ideational claims are equally amenable to empirical analysis. The idiosyncratic beliefs of lone individuals will usually be harder to study, and claims about them harder to falsify, than arguments about the influence of socially shared cognitions with identifiable origins.

Tracing paths of ideational transmission

A prior source for an idea is itself insufficient to sustain an ideational account: the analyst should also be able to demonstrate that the idea was *available* to decision-makers prior to the decision being explained. In this subsection and the next, I suggest two types of evidence that may, independently, help satisfy this hoop test of ideational influence. First, the analyst could identify *a pathway – an organizational structure or a social interaction – through which information or argumentation was likely to have been transmitted to authoritative actors.*

Alastair Iain Johnston (1996), in his case study of Chinese security policy, examines an ideational explanation of China's apparent shift toward a more constructive engagement in arms control. One form of evidence for which Johnston looks is indications that Chinese officials were exposed to new, more dovish security ideas through transnational communities of experts. He uncovers evidence of several pathways of dissemination, finding that considerable numbers of Chinese officials spent time at Western security institutes and took part in bilateral meetings and training programs with US organizations committed to arms control – much of this prior to the policy shift being explained (Johnston 1996: 43–46). These data help to keep an ideational explanation in contention.

Erik Bleich (2003), in his study of race politics in Britain and France, similarly provides evidence of transnational contacts as a pathway of ideational dissemination. He shows that an influential group of British Labour Party politicians was exposed to new understandings of racism – as a problem of access and discrimination, best handled through civil penalties and administrative procedures – both through visits to North America and through the study of US and Canadian models of race relations (Bleich 2003: 53–56).

Identifying mobile "carriers"

As discussed above, one way to establish ideational availability is to find evidence that actors in positions of institutional authority came into contact with the relevant ideas. Alternatively, availability can be established with evidence of the *movement of individuals* – individuals reliably known to hold a given set of ideas – into decision-making institutions. In this second version of the test, *changes in outcomes should follow the entry of identifiable "carriers" of the relevant ideas into key loci of political authority* (see also the process-tracing account of the role of "policy entrepreneurs" in Checkel 1997).

The institutional analysis of mobile carriers is central to Margaret Weir's (1989) explanation of the differing fates of Keynesian policy prescriptions in the United States and Britain. Weir begins with the observation that Keynesian policies were introduced earlier in the United States, but proved less enduring there than in Britain. She accounts for this temporal pattern, in large part, by reference to differing patterns of recruitment and distributions of power in the two political systems (for a parallel argument in another context, see Risse-Kappen 1994). Staffed by a large number of political appointees, the US bureaucracy is a relatively porous environment characterized by rapid turnover in personnel and without a single, centralized locus of policymaking authority. With high turnover across a fragmented system, disciples of Keynesian thought gained relatively quick entry to federal economic councils and agencies in the 1930s. The dispersion of authority, however, limited their ability to enact the type of coordinated policy responses that Keynesian theory prescribed. Moreover, serving at the pleasure of the President, Keynesian advisors never achieved a stable and secure foothold within government. The result was the quick adoption of, but unsteady commitment to, countercyclical macroeconomic management.

Weir also documents, by contrast, the far more regimented environment of the UK Treasury: not only was the department dominated by career bureaucrats (making turnover slow), but recruitment procedures and lines of authority severely limited the entry or influence of carriers of new ideas. The Treasury's virtual monopoly of economic policymaking authority within the state further restricted access opportunities for ideational upstarts. It took the national emergency of World War II to pry the system open: Treasury authority was temporarily diluted, and Keynesian economists (including Keynes himself) were brought into government to help manage the wartime economy. Following the war, the same organizational rigidities and concentration of authority that had postponed the Keynesians' entry then secured their position within the state, leaving them ensconced in career positions at the Treasury. Keynesian principles came to dominate British fiscal and economic policy-making for the next thirty years (on a similar point, see Blyth 2002).

Analyses based on personnel movements across institutions hinge on a few important assumptions. First, we must be able to reliably identify the carriers' ideational commitments. Indeed, what makes a carrier analytically "useful" is that his or her cognitive commitments are more readily knowable than those of other actors involved in decision-making, especially elected officials. Carriers' belief systems can often be inferred by reference to their sociological context – such as their embeddedness within professional networks or the site of their training – or from past verbal communication. In this respect, the most "useful" carriers will have a prior track record of activity *outside* of politics – i.e. in an intellectual or professional setting in which the incentives for strategic misrepresentation of beliefs are limited. Second, for their ideas to have explanatory power, the carriers must not only take up residence within major loci of authority; they must have sufficient influence *within* a venue for their ideas to shape its outputs.

Finally, the analyst must dispense with an alternative explanation: that the carriers were *selected* by a set of political principals in order to provide intellectual cover for an option that was appealing to those principals for reasons of material interest. Where experts are hand-picked for political convenience, these carriers – and their ideas – are epiphenomenal. One response to this quandary is to employ the carriers as an explanation of *longer*-term rather than immediate choices: even if politicians choose carriers strategically, those carriers may exert long-term influence if they remain in place – like entrenched Whitehall bureaucrats – long after their political masters have departed the scene.

Where key assumptions can be met, analyses of ideational availability – based on either transmission paths or mobile carriers – can aid causal inference in a few ways. First, they can contribute to an unbiased measure of decision-makers' ideational commitments by helping to establish that actors had access to the relevant ideas or (in the case of mobile carriers) providing evidence of their views under reduced strategic pressures. Second, in doing so, these tests can lend support to claims of ideational exogeneity. Third, as Weir's study demonstrates, the analysis of ideational movement can exploit distinctive temporal variation in ideational availability: it can demonstrate that a given idea was "on the scene" when congruent policy change occurred, the absence of policy change prior to the idea's arrival, and the fragility of policy change after mobile carriers' exit. Such over-time patterns can significantly undermine the sufficiency of non-ideational alternatives, suggesting that the availability of the relevant idea was *necessary* for the outcome to occur. Of course, since this logic draws on patterns of covariation between potential causes and outcomes, the standard cautions about correlational inference – discussed above – apply here.[10]

Unpacking the substance of decision outputs

In large-n analyses, scholars are usually forced to code decision outputs relatively crudely – along a single dimension or using a very small number of categories. Small-n analysis, in contrast, affords the opportunity to attend much more closely to qualitative features of actors' decisions, and such scrutiny can sometimes produce evidence with substantial potential to discriminate among possible motives. The analyst can usefully ask the following question of a policy or institutional choice: is this precisely the way in which actors would have constructed the policy or institution if they had been motivated by a given normative commitment or causal belief? A detailed examination of the "fit" between the outcome and alternative lines of reasoning can contribute to a demonstration of the mechanisms at work: in the best case, it can help discriminate among the possible considerations or motives that actors might have applied when making the decision.

---

[10] The process-tracing strategies outlined here should also be highly relevant for the extensive international relations literature on so-called norm entrepreneurs; see Finnemore and Sikkink (1998).

Inspection of decision outputs can test an observable implication of the following form: if a choice was driven by policymakers' commitment to Goal X, then the output should be take a form that, given the state of knowledge at the time, was likely to effectively promote Goal X. A simple example will help illustrate: President George W. Bush's tax cuts of 2001 were partly sold to the public as a much-needed stimulus for a slowing economy. A detailed inspection of the package's provisions would cast doubt, however, on an explanation based on a commitment to quickly boosting the economy. For instance, a large majority of the revenue cuts were both substantially delayed in time and targeted to those (the wealthy) least likely to spend the additional disposable income (Hacker and Pierson 2005). On the other hand, these policy details are highly congruent with an electoral logic of redistribution toward wealthy supporters.[11]

In his study of Chinese security policies, Johnston (1996) undertakes a systematic unpacking of the dependent variable and tests for ideational fit. The starting point for his analysis is an apparent shift toward greater cooperation in Chinese arms control policy. The question is whether this shift is generated by a strategic interest in improving China's image or by a new set of more internationalist ideas about the sources of global security. By closely examining the specific international agreements to which China has been willing to accede, Johnston is able to derive considerable discriminatory leverage. In particular, he finds that Chinese leaders have largely cooperated with international arms control efforts when those efforts would exact a low cost to China's military capabilities, but walked away from efforts that would impose substantial, binding constraints (Johnston 1996: 49–57).

A test for the "fit" between outcome and motive may serve as a hoop test not only for an ideational explanation, but also for materialist alternatives. That is, one can ask: Is the outcome precisely what an actor with a hypothesized political or economic motive would have chosen? Were the material benefits of the policy, for instance, carefully directed toward those constituencies most critical to the government's re-election prospects, or more broadly diffused? Moreover, as the Johnston example illustrates, *costly* features of the output are often the most illuminating. The fact that a choice imposes costs on decision-makers or their constituents to more effectively advance Goal X is an especially informative signal about the importance of that goal to decision-makers.

---

[11] They might also be congruent with a goal of long-term growth combined with a supply-side belief about the beneficial effects of tax cuts on the rich.

The application of this test also confronts an important complication. Because political decisions are usually collective choices, they often involve compromise among actors with divergent beliefs or goals. Deviations from an ideational (or material) logic may, therefore, reflect not the absence of that logic's operation, but the comingling of that logic with other motivations. This complication is not intractable, however; indeed, it can be turned into a testable hypothesis. By closely examining the decision-making process alongside the details of the outcome, the analyst should be able to determine how well any departures from the prescriptive logic of an idea held by one set of actors "fit" the demands of other actors with veto power or strong bargaining leverage.

Conclusion

The process-tracing strategies explored here require, on the whole, three types of analytic investment. The first is an investment in *breadth of empirical scope*. In measuring politicians' and policymakers' ideational commitments, analysts might begin by examining actors' statements at or just prior to the critical moment of choice. But an ideational theory's observable implications can be readily multiplied, and their uniqueness enhanced, by expanding the inquiry both temporally and across levels of analysis. Establishing the exogeneity of actors' ideas almost always requires expanding the historical scope of inquiry to periods prior to the choice being explained. By examining extended stretches of time, analysts can also make discriminating observations about the degree of stability of, or the timing of change in, actors' statements and issue positions, relative to change in the material context of choice. Likewise, by shifting the focus from the individual level toward larger patterns of social interaction, scholars can track the movement of ideas and their adherents across organizational settings and institutions. Substantial leverage can also be gained by disaggregating episodes to inspect within-case correlations across both participants and sequenced steps in the decision-making process.

At the same time, the chapter has argued that none of this is straightforward. Each of these strategies can only be credibly employed when key assumptions can be made plausible. To put the point another way, the sufficiency of these empirical tests – for substantiating an ideational account – depends on the analyst's ability to rule out alternative interpretations of the evidence. Hence, the second analytic commitment required of good process tracing of ideational effects: close attention to the *assumptions* required for drawing valid inferences from evidence. In part, this means close attention to the incentives generated by the institutional, organizational, and societal context. Analyzing these incentives means deploying case-specific knowledge of formal and informal institutional structures, patterns of political competition, economic and social conditions, and details of the substantive issue at hand. For those tests that rely on assessing within-case covariation, the analyst must also attend carefully to the assumptions necessary for drawing causal inferences from correlations, including taking potential confounds into account.

Third, I have emphasized the value of *richly theorized mechanisms* for effective process-tracing. Ideational mechanisms can be fruitfully specified in terms of both individual-level cognitive processes and sociological processes through which ideational frameworks are disseminated, embedded within organizations, and replaced over time. Theoretical refinement can go a long way toward rendering ideational theories more falsifiable. Yet, as I have cautioned, tight specification of mechanisms also has risks: a deductive search for evidence of narrowly theorized mechanisms may render ideational effects more elusive, generating more false negatives. Thus, where more than one mechanism is plausible for a given effect, the analyst will often want to test multiple ideational logics, trading a measure of falsifiability for an increased chance of picking up ideational effects.

Although it has not been a focus of this chapter, a final word of caution is in order about the selection of cases. As noted in Chapter 1, any inferences drawn from process tracing must take into account whether the case examined is most or least likely for the theories being tested (pp. 25–26). Whether it makes sense to choose cases that are most or least likely loci of ideational influence depends on the analyst's goals. Most likely cases will be especially informative for the inductive *building* of ideational theories, as they are good places to observe ideational mechanisms unfold (see, for example, Parsons 2002). Inductive theory-generation may be aided by the selection of cases across which outcomes appear to align poorly with material conditions or in which actors faced high uncertainty about their material interests – and, thus, where there was greater room for the operation of ideational processes (see, for example, Berman 1998; Blyth 2002).

However, if the analyst seeks to test a *general* theory of political decision-making, a procedure that selects most likely cases from a domain of decisions will, on average, lead us to overstate the overall influence of ideas in that domain. A more balanced test would involve a selection rule uncorrelated with the likelihood of ideas mattering – for instance, choosing for wide variation in the outcomes to be explained. Alternatively, if the analyst wants to subject an ideational theory to an especially *hard* test, then he or she should seek out least likely cases, such as those in which actors' material stakes were high and pushed strongly in favor of the observed decision (George and Bennett 2005). Evidence that actors' decisions in such cases were nonetheless shaped by their particular cognitive commitments would offer especially strong support to a general claim of ideational influence.

3 Mechanisms, process, and the study of international institutions

Jeffrey T. Checkel

Introduction

In an agenda-setting essay first published in 2002, Lisa Martin and Beth Simmons argued that the study of international organizations (IOs) and institutions (IIs) had reached an important threshold, focusing less on why they exist and more on "whether and how they significantly impact governmental behavior and international outcomes" (Martin and Simmons 2002: 192). Put differently, the past decade has seen a sustained move by students of international institutions and organizations to viewing their subject matter as independent variables affecting state interests and policy. Conceptually, this has put a premium on identifying the mechanisms connecting institutions to states; methodologically, there has been a growing concern with measuring process.

In this chapter, I assess several studies that make claims about international institutions influencing state-level action through various processes and mechanisms. The move to process and to the method of process tracing has been salutary, I argue, producing rich and analytically rigorous studies that demonstrate the multiple roles – good and bad – played by institutions in global politics.

At the same time, challenges remain. In terms of design, scholars often fail to address the problem of equifinality – where multiple causal pathways may lead to the same outcome – and instead conduct process tracing only on their preferred argument. Theoretically, the power and generalizability of arguments about institutions seem to decrease as the focus shifts to process. Finally, the potential for process tracing to help scholars produce integrative

An early version of this chapter was presented at the workshop "Compliance and Beyond: Assessing and Explaining the Impact of Global Governance Arrangements," University of St. Gallen, Switzerland, May 2013. I thank the workshop participants, as well as Andy Bennett, Tim Buethe, Marty Finnemore, Andy Mack, and Frank Schimmelfennig for detailed and helpful comments.

frameworks about international institutions – combining insights from different social-theoretic toolkits – remains unfulfilled.

Work on IOs and IIs addresses a number of the criteria for good process tracing outlined in Chapter 1. The more general standards (alternative explanations, possible biases in evidentiary sources) are often explicitly invoked. However, those specifically relevant for process tracing – most important, addressing equifinality; and the a priori specification of observable implications – are too often left unaddressed. Certainly, discussing the latter will clutter the empirical narrative and story, but the trade-off will be more robust explanations (see also Jacobs, this volume, Chapter 2). Thus, an important challenge for future work is to be more explicit, both in the operationalization of process tracing and the evaluative standards behind its use.

The remainder of the chapter is structured as follows. I begin with a brief review of work on international institutions and organizations, focusing largely on research conducted by political scientists and international relations (IR) theorists; this provides the context for the current focus on mechanisms and process.[1] I then discuss four works that are empirical examinations of the processes and mechanisms through which IIs/IOs shape behavior and interests; two are rationalist in orientation (Wallander 1999; Schimmelfennig 2003), while two are broadly constructivist (Kelley 2004a; Autesserre 2010). My purpose is not to recount the stories they tell, but to provide a net assessment of their turn to mechanisms and use of process tracing. In a third, concluding section, I argue that students of IOs need to remember that method is no substitute for theory, and that they can strengthen their arguments by combining process tracing with other techniques, such as agent-based modeling.

The study of international institutions

By the mid- to late 1990s, IR research on institutions and IOs had reached a new level of sophistication. Some rationalists built upon Keohane's neo-liberal institutionalism (Keohane 1984; see also Mitchell 1994; Simmons 1994), but applied it to new issue areas (security – Wallander 1999) or new – domestic – levels of analysis (Martin 2000). A different set of rational choice scholars advanced a principal–agent perspective to think more specifically about the

---

[1] This neglects II/IO research in other disciplines. Process and a mechanism-based understanding of causality are not emphasized in some – economics, for example. In other cases – sociology, organizational studies – I reference relevant work where appropriate, while bearing in mind the volume's political science focus and audience.

relation between states and IOs (Pollack 2003; Hawkins *et al.* 2006). From a more sociological perspective, constructivists began to document a different, social role for IIs and IOs, where they created meaning and senses of community that subsequently shaped state interests (Finnemore 1996; Risse *et al.* 1999; Barnett and Finnemore 2004). Among all scholars, the focus was shifting away from asking why such institutions existed to a logical follow-on question: given their existence, how and in what ways did they influence politics within and between states (Martin and Simmons 1998)?

Finnemore's 1996 study exemplifies these achievements and shift in emphasis. In its first pages, she argues that political science has focused too much "attention on the problem of how states pursue their interests," rather than "figur[ing] out what those interests are" (Finnemore 1996: ix). She then goes on to develop an argument on IIs and IOs as the source for those state interests. And it is an argument not simply couched in terms of independent (an IO, in this case) and dependent variables (state policy and interests). Rather, Finnemore is concerned with the intervening process that connects the two.

Analytically, she was thus capturing the workings of what we now call causal mechanisms, or "the pathway or process by which an effect is produced or a purpose is accomplished" (Gerring 2007a: 178). In her study of state adoption of science policy bureaucracies, UNESCO is not simply some black hole magically diffusing policy; instead, Finnemore theorizes and empirically documents the teaching process behind such diffusion (Finnemore 1996: chapter 2).

At the same time, this turn to process and state properties raises new challenges. In particular, studying IO influence on states means that, to some extent, one must examine their domestic politics, which arguably requires some theory of the latter. However, at this point (the mid 1990s), IR scholars were devoting relatively little attention to politics at the state level (Schultz 2013: 478). Extending these arguments about international institutions to include the domestic level, I argue below, raises additional challenges for those employing process tracing, especially in the absence of any explicit theory of domestic politics.

Another feature of this work was to accord primacy to international-level factors. At first glance, this makes sense; after all, these were IR scholars studying the causal effects of IIs and IOs. Consider the case of international human rights. The assumption was that the real action was at the international level, with international human rights norms diffusing to the domestic arena to bring about change (Risse *et al.* 1999; Thomas 2001). More recently, however, some students of IIs and human rights have reversed the causal arrows, arguing for the primacy of domestic factors (Simmons 2009). At this domestic level and mirroring the thrust of system-level analyses, the emphasis was again on mechanisms and processes (Simmons 2009: chapters 6–7).

In summary, by the early years of the new millennium, arguments about international institutions were becoming more determinate and fine grained. They were also becoming more empirical, with richly detailed case studies and new data sets replacing the illustrative empirics of earlier work (Keohane 1984). The language might vary – middle-range approach, intervening variables, process, causal mechanisms – but the goal was the same: to theorize and empirically document the pathways through which IIs and IOs influenced states and state-level processes. More and more scholars, it would seem, were joining the process and mechanism bandwagon.

The process and mechanism turn

Perhaps the strongest evidence of a clear move among students of IIs and IOs to study process and mechanisms is a non-event: IR scholars currently have no grand theories in this area. Among rational-choice scholars, Keohane's neo-liberal institutionalism serves at best as a starting point for contemporary analyses (Simmons 2009, for example); and there certainly is no single, widely accepted constructivist theory of international institutions. Instead, we have a growing collection of partial, mid-range theories, which are largely the result of the analytic and methodological choice in favor of process and mechanisms.

My analysis in this section is structured around the four books noted earlier, taken in chronological order so as better to assess progress over time in process-based studies of institutions and IOs. They cover different issues (security, IO membership expansion, human rights, post-conflict intervention), different parts of the world (Eurasia, Europe, Africa), and a variety of IOs (NATO, OSCE, Council of Europe, UN system). While they likely are not a representative sample – there are many other books, articles and chapters produced in recent years that study institutions and IOs from a process perspective – they nicely capture the changes at work over time.

For each of the four books, I begin with a summary of its subject matter and core argument. However, the bulk of the analysis is a net assessment of a given author's turn to mechanisms and process. What was gained? And, equally important, what new challenges arose?

International institutions and the Great Powers

Celeste Wallander's 1999 book is quite explicit in its debt to Keohane's neo-liberal institutionalism (Wallander 1999: chapter 2). However, she moved beyond it in several important ways. First, addressing a criticism lodged against Keohane's early work, she applied his theory to the study of high politics security institutions, in contrast to the low-politics/economics emphasis of Keohane's own research (1984) and that of his early followers (Simmons 1994). Second, and as discussed in more detail below, Wallander added elements of process to what was largely a structural approach.

Wallander's topic is security relations between the two most powerful European powers in the Cold War's wake: unified Germany and post-Soviet Russia. The book's empirical core is a careful reconstruction of German–Russian security relations in the immediate post-Cold War period (1991 to 1996). In particular, she explores the role of international institutions in shaping relations between these two European powers in several areas.

Theoretically, the book develops an institutional argument that goes beyond saying institutions matter. Instead, Wallander theorizes (and then empirically documents) the specific ways and conditions under which international institutions influenced Russian–German relations. Her "stronger institutional theory of security relations" explores how variation in institutional form and function and the layering of international institutions affect the likelihood that states will choose cooperative security strategies (Wallander 1999: 27–40, at 28).

Writing in the late 1990s, and thus before the more recent revitalization of qualitative methodology, Wallander is – unsurprisingly – not explicit on her methods. However, the underlying approach is clear. Drawing upon an extensive set of interviews (over 100), she traces the process through which Russian and German interests – post-Cold War – were being formed through interaction with institutions such as NATO. This is process tracing in practice, if not in name.[2] That is, Wallander analyzes "evidence on processes, sequences, and conjunctures of events within a case for the purposes of either developing or testing hypotheses about causal mechanisms that might causally explain the case" (this volume, Chapter 1, p. 7; see also Checkel 2008). While she does not explicitly invoke the language of causal mechanisms, her

---

[2] Wallander wrote in the late 1990s and published her book in 1999. However, it was only in the early 2000s that the specific term "process tracing" began to receive considerable attention. Hall 2003; George and Bennett 2005: ch. 10.

analysis is very much in this spirit, seeking to fill the gap between the independent variable – European institutions – and the outcome (Russian–German security cooperation).

In contrast to earlier work on international institutions from a neo-liberal perspective, Wallander – by focusing more on process – provides a richly documented account of how institutions were shaping state behavior. Her extensive interview material gives the book a sense of "history in the making." More importantly, the analysis is not of the either/or type, where either power (realism) or institutions (institutionalism) carry all the causal weight. Instead, she offers a careful both/and argument, where power and interests are refracted through and, in some cases, shaped by institutions.

Wallander thus does not just conduct process tracing on her preferred – institutionalist – perspective. Rather, she takes seriously the possibility that there may be alternative causal pathways leading to the outcome she seeks to explain – so-called equifinality. This is a central requirement of good process tracing (this volume, Chapter 1, pp. 21–23).

Moreover, the evidence for her institutionalist argument is not presented as a loosely structured narrative. Rather, the book's case-study chapters carefully fit the evidence to the deductive logic of her theory, another criterion of well-executed process tracing (Chapter 1, p. 30). That is, through her interviews, readers see how Russian and German security officials are relying on key regional organizations to structure their relations and interests. Certainly, there is still an inferential gap here, as Wallander presents little "smoking-gun" evidence establishing a direct institution-interest tie (this volume, Chapter 1, p. 17). Yet, her careful theorization and attention to process has decisively shrunk that gap, especially when compared to earlier neo-liberal work.

In summary, Wallander's book marks an important advance in the study of international institutions. It is theoretically innovative, empirically rich and – central to my argument – begins to add an element of much-needed process to its subject matter. Institutions are not magically reducing abstract transaction costs – an analytic claim typically undocumented in earlier work; rather, they are reshaping state strategies in specific and empirically measurable ways.

At the same time, her turn to process is not without weaknesses and limitations. Most importantly, when Wallander uncovers evidence that does not fit within the neat causal arrows of the institutions → state strategy relation, it is either set aside or left under-utilized. Consider two examples. For one, the manuscript provides ample documentation that international institutions have not just influenced German strategies, but, at a much deeper level, helped to construct its very interests and preferences. Over and over,

Wallander's interviews with high-level German policymakers and analysts show them to be almost reflexively institutionalist. They find it exceedingly hard to conceive or define German interests outside the dense institutional network within which their country is embedded. Unfortunately, except for a brief mention in the concluding chapter, the author fails to exploit fully such findings. Put differently, her process tracing would have been stronger if she had been open to inductive insights "not anticipated on the basis of . . . prior alternative hypotheses," as argued in Chapter 1 (pp. 29–30).

In addition, Wallander portrays European and other international institutions as passive actors, as a resource to be exploited by self-interested states. They have no sense of agency in their own right. Throughout the book, though, institutions often play a very active and social role, serving as forums for political dialogue, as settings where learning and education occur, or where states are socialized into the ways of the international community.

As these examples suggest, Wallander has also uncovered evidence of the causal mechanisms behind what constructivist IR theory would call the constitutive power of institutions (Adler 2013). If she had systematically theorized and measured such dynamics, the pay-off would have been threefold. Substantively, her account of the role of institutions in shaping German–Russian relations would have been richer; conceptually, she would have expanded her understanding of process; and, theoretically, she would have contributed to the then nascent literature on theoretical bridge building between rational choice and constructivism (Adler 1997, for example).

International institutions and membership expansion

If Wallander (1999) is suggestive of a greater emphasis on process in the study of international institutions, then Schimmelfennig's study on the post-Cold War enlargement of European institutions is explicit on this score (Schimmelfennig 2003; see also Gheciu 2005; Checkel 2007). Indeed, his central theoretical innovation is to theorize – and then empirically document – the role of rhetorical action as "the mechanism" and "causal link" between rule-ignoring, egoistic individual state preferences and a rule-conforming, collective outcome: EU and NATO membership being offered to the formerly communist states of East and Central Europe (Schimmelfennig 2003: 6).

Schimmelfennig argues that explaining the enlargement of regional organizations is a neglected area of study, and that post-Cold War Europe offers an ideal laboratory to both theorize and document such processes. This is precisely the task he sets for himself in the book, which begins by conceptualizing

Europe as a community environment for state action. He then proceeds to specify the constraints under which states act in such an environment and describes how the rhetorical use of arguments can result in rule-compliant behavior (Schimmelfennig 2003: 6).

The concept of rhetorical action, or the strategic use of norms and arguments, serves several purposes for Schimmelfennig. First and theoretically, it moves his argument away from structure and decisively to the level of process, where agents strategically deploy arguments. Second, and again theoretically, it positions his argument to bridge rationalist and constructivist modes of social action. After all, arguing, at least before Schimmelfennig wrote, was thought to be a core constructivist concept (Risse 2000). It was part and parcel of following a so-called logic of appropriateness. For Schimmelfennig, however, arguments are strategically deployed by egoistic agents operating under a so-called logic of consequences.

Thus, the book promises a process-based, social-theoretically plural account of the role played by IOs. And it delivers, with Schimmelfennig operationalizing his argument and testing it against rich empirical material. At the time of writing, it was probably the best example of how one theorizes and measures process in the IO/state relation.

The book is especially strong at the level of methods. In particular, Schimmelfennig does not simply assert the central importance of rhetorical action as the causal mechanism linking IOs to outcomes; he directly addresses the challenge of measuring such mechanisms. Much more so than Wallander – and more explicitly – he carefully thinks through the challenges involved in observing mechanisms. Writing several years before George and Bennett (2005) would popularize the term, Schimmelfennig tells his readers how to conduct process tracing or what he calls "looking into the *causal process* that links independent and dependent variables . . . in which the researcher explains an event by detailing the sequence of happenings leading up to it" (Schimmelfennig 2003: 13 [emphasis in original], quoting in part Dessler 1999: 129).

In conducting the process tracing, Schimmelfennig follows several of the best practices advanced in Chapter 1 (pp. 20–31). For one, he increases readers' confidence in his findings by explicitly addressing equifinality, theorizing and empirically testing for mechanisms other than rhetorical action that might also explain the outcomes he observes. Thus, in an entire chapter on "Process Hypotheses" (Schimmelfennig 2003: chapter 7), Schimmelfennig theorizes four different processes for how the decision to expand NATO and the EU came about. However, the analysis is anything but abstract, for he then moves to specifying the observable implications of each mechanism. That is, he asks "if this mechanism were at work, then I would expect to see the following in my empirical data" (Schimmelfennig 2003: 160–162; see also Schimmelfennig 2005).

In addition, and as his invocation of the various mechanisms suggests, Schimmelfennig casts his net widely for alternative explanations, as counseled by Bennett and Checkel (this volume, Chapter 1, p. 23). In so doing, he grounds the discussion specifically in other accounts that seek to explain similar European/EU/NATO outcomes. Finally, throughout the book, Schimmelfennig takes care to present the different theories in detailed, operational form – a procedure advocated in Chapter 1 above (p. 30; see also Jacobs, this volume, Chapter 2). This level of detail enhances the reader's confidence in the validity of the inferences he draws from the process tracing.

The result of this theoretical innovation – the turn to and operational use of causal mechanisms – and methodological rigor – the systematic application of process tracing techniques – is a study that significantly advances our knowledge of IOs. For students of European institutions, Schimmelfennig's argument fills the gap left by general and hence highly underspecified theories of integration such as intergovernmentalism or supranationalism. For the more general study of institutions and IOs, Schimmelfennig – by focusing on mechanisms – demonstrates the value added in taking process seriously. Instead of abstract and general theories that at best hint at how institutions matter, Schimmelfennig's work details the exact causal pathway through which they influence state behavior.

At the same time, the book's overall argument and approach raise a troubling issue, one that would only become more apparent – in the broader II/IO literature – in the years following its publication. Simply put, what is the theoretical take-away? Yes, Schimmelfennig demonstrates the important role of rhetorical action. However, what more general theory of IOs emerges? It would seem that there is none. Instead, one gets a middle-range argument (George 1993), where a set of factors interact to produce an outcome, but that very complexity limits the generalizability of the argument. Today, ten years after the publication of Schimmelfennig's book, do we have a cumulative research program on rhetorical action and the study of international institutions? No, we do not. The time of the general "isms" in the study of IOs may have passed; what, though, has replaced them (see also Bennett 2013b)?

A second theoretical limitation is less troubling, but still worth highlighting. Despite Schimmelfennig's claim to be utilizing insights from rational choice and constructivism (Schimmelfennig 2003: 159, 281–287), the book essentially offers a clever rational-choice argument where central elements of constructivism – social structure, recursivity, interpretation, holism (Adler 2013) – are notable only by their absence. There is some recognition of the importance of theoretical pluralism in the book, but it is quite minimal in the end. To be fair to Schimmelfennig, however, such limited efforts at building theoretical bridges have become the norm (Checkel 2013a), despite the optimism of its early proponents (Adler 1997; Katzenstein *et al.* 1998; Fearon and Wendt 2002).[3]

International organizations and minority rights

Like those by Wallander and Schimmelfennig, Judith Kelley's (2004a) book seeks to theorize and empirically measure the mechanisms linking IOs to state behavior (see also Kelley 2004b). In at least two ways, however, her study advances the research frontier in work on international organizations. First, she explores possible IO influence in a policy area – the rights of ethnic minorities – with enormous implications for state sovereignty and identity. Second, and more important, she addresses a neglected point: IOs ultimately matter and shape state behavior only when they work through the domestic politics of particular countries.

The latter is perhaps Kelley's central contribution. For over two decades, there have been persistent calls for IR theorists to take domestic politics seriously. Kelley does this in a theoretically plural way that seeks to combine elements of rational choice and constructivism. Her 2004 book is essential reading not because she shows us that international institutions matter – others had by that time made and documented such claims. Instead, by thinking systematically about the mechanisms – cost/benefit calculations and incentives as well as normative pressure – that connect the international with domestic politics, Kelley shows us how this occurs. She can thus explain domestic implementation dynamics and ultimate policy outcomes ignored by virtually all other scholars studying IOs at that point in time.

The danger – or, better said, challenge – in modeling the interaction between IOs and domestic politics is that the enterprise can get messy. In social science terms, the result may be over-determined outcomes, where a host of causal factors are in play, but it is difficult to parse out which matter most. Kelley mostly avoids this problem by careful, upfront attention to design and methods.

---

[3] Indeed, the "efficient process tracing" advocated by Schimmelfennig in Chapter 4 below is not suited for theoretical bridge building (pp. 100–101).

Kelley's focus is post-Cold War East Europe and the efforts by regional organizations to influence state policy on ethnic minorities. Like the other books assessed here, her concern is to connect these institutions to states by conceptualizing and empirically measuring the causal mechanisms at work. Theoretically, her aim is to combine previously separate compliance schools – enforcement and management – to explain why and how states might abide by IO injunctions. To do this, Kelley focuses on two specific causal mechanisms: membership conditionality and normative pressure. With the former, rationalist mechanism, states respond to incentives and sanctions imposed by IOs. With normative pressure – the constructivist mechanism – IOs rely on the use of norms to persuade, shame, or praise states into changing their policies (Kelley 2004a: 7–8).

If Kelley were to stop here, her study would resemble others – specifying the mechanisms between independent (IO) and dependent (state policy) variables. She goes an important step further, however, introducing domestic politics into the analysis, basically as an intervening variable, with the degree of domestic opposition (high or low) affecting the likelihood of one or the other of the two mechanisms having effects on state policy (Kelley 2004a: 32, Figure 2.1). This analytic move is to be applauded, for it highlights the important point that international actors affect states by working through, shaping, and influencing their domestic politics.

The argument is tested through a combination of quantitative and qualitative methods, as well as carefully executed counterfactual analysis. On the qualitative techniques, process tracing is explicitly invoked as playing a key role (Kelley 2004a: 23–24, 67). While its use is not as systematic as in the case of Schimmelfennig (2003) – Kelley fails to address the challenge of equifinality – she nonetheless provides the reader with a clear and transparent discussion of how it will be applied. For example, she considers potential biases in her empirical material, which is especially important given that interviews are a major data source; combines process tracing with case comparisons to strengthen her inferences; and adapts and operationalizes the general argument about conditionality and socialization to her specific cases, clearly stating the observable implications of each (Kelley 2004a: chapter 3; 2004b: 435–437, 449–453) – which are all key criteria of good process tracing (this volume, Chapter 1, pp. 20–31).

Overall, then, the book makes an important contribution, both methodologically and theoretically. It illuminates the specific conditions and mechanisms that allow regional organizations to influence policy on highly sensitive issues (policy on ethnic minorities). For students of IOs, it offers a nuanced understanding of when conditionality is likely to work, which is a welcome contrast to broad-brush critiques asserting that it is rarely if ever effective (Kelley 2004a: 9). Moreover, and in a fashion similar to the other two books discussed, Kelley demonstrates that a focus on process and mechanisms is fully consistent with theoretical and methodological rigor. Finally, with a greater emphasis on policy, she demonstrates how a mechanisms/process approach can and should play a key role in designing policy interventions by the international community (Kelley 2004a: 189–191).

At the same time, Kelley's argument can be criticized on three grounds. First and at the risk of sounding like a broken record, what is the broader contribution to theory? Her nuanced, mechanism-based argument is not easily generalized; moreover, it may only work in post-Cold War Europe, where the EU had a particularly strong ability to insist on states adopting certain standards of behavior as a condition of membership (see also Kelley 2004a: 192–193).

Second, while Kelley's turn to the domestic level is an important and progressive theoretical move in the study of IOs, it can nonetheless be criticized for being rather simplistic. One gets no theory of domestic politics, be it one emphasizing institutions, interest groups, elites, or the like. Instead, we are told that high levels of domestic opposition make it harder for the international community to influence policy. This is surely no surprise, and does not get beyond, or even up to, the level of earlier theories on two-level games between international and domestic politics (Putnam 1988).

Third, and similar to Schimmelfennig, Kelley's theoretical bridge building is biased and thus ultimately weak. In particular – and in keeping with Kelley's strong positivist commitments – if she cannot carefully measure and operationalize a concept, it falls by the wayside. Thus, while she claims in the book to be speaking to constructivist social theory, she in fact does this in only a very minimal sense. For example, Kelley invokes the concept of socialization (Kelley 2004a: 7–8, 31, 34–35), the sociological core of which is all about processes of internalization. Yet, she shies away from measuring the latter and instead searches for (weak) proxies as observable implications of it.

While this is a trade-off the author explicitly acknowledges (Kelley 2004b: 428–429), it does limit the argument in important ways. For her, socialization thus boils down to measuring behavioral change; internalization and belief change are absent. Yet, the latter are crucially important for the longevity and durability of the domestic policy change to which Kelley gives pride of place.

For someone who argues that a central goal of her research is to promote conversation across theoretical traditions (Kelley 2004a: 9, 187–188), Kelley therefore comes up short, especially on constructivism. The only constructivism that works for her is that measurable in a way (pre-)determined by her positivist epistemological starting point.

International institutions and post-conflict interventions

In her recent study, Severine Autesserre uses a focus on mechanisms and process to demonstrate that IOs need not always be a force for good, helping states cooperate or promoting global governance (Autesserre 2010; see also Autesserre 2009). The three other books reviewed here all highlight the role of IOs in fostering interstate cooperation or in promoting normatively good outcomes as intended consequences (enlargement of European institutions; fair treatment of ethnic minorities). There is nothing wrong with such a focus, which has clear roots in Keohane's (1984) original formulation of neo-liberal institutionalism as well as the normative commitment by many of those studying IOs to improve world order.

At the same time, it is entirely plausible – once one grants IOs some degree of autonomy and agency – that they may perform suboptimally and even pathologically and produce unintended consequences. These latter outcomes need not be caused by member states, but may arise because of processes and mechanisms at work within the organizations themselves (Barnett and Finnemore 2004).

Picking up on this line of reasoning, Autesserre's book explores the role of international organizations in post-conflict interventions.[4] In the post-Cold War era, this has typically meant IO efforts to promote/preserve peace in states where a civil war has occurred. Her specific focus is sub-Saharan Africa and the international community's efforts to intervene in the long-running internal conflict in the Democratic Republic of Congo (DRC). These interventions, in Congo and elsewhere, typically do not succeed; in nearly 70 percent of the cases, they fail to build a durable, post-conflict peace (Autesserre 2010: 5). Why?

The answer, Autesserre argues, lies not in the national interests of states or specific organizational interests (Autesserre 2009: 272–275; 2010: 14–23), but in a powerful framing mechanism that shapes the understanding and actions of intervening organizations. This peace-building culture – as Autesserre calls it – establishes the parameters of acceptable action on the ground by UN peacekeepers; it "shaped the intervention in the Congo in a way that precluded

---

[4] Autesserre's focus is actually the broader set of international interveners, including diplomats, non-governmental organizations (NGOs), and IOs. Given my concerns in this chapter, I consider only the IO part of her argument.

action on local violence, ultimately dooming the international efforts" (Autesserre 2010: 10–11).

This is an argument about how process – framing dynamics first theorized by sociologists – shapes what IOs do and the effects they have. To make it, Autesserre conducts multi-sited ethnography, semi-structured interviews (over 330), and document analysis, spending a total of eighteen months in the field – mainly in Congo (Autesserre 2010: 31–37). While she never explicitly cites process tracing, this is in fact a central technique she employs. In the article version of the study, Autesserre makes clear her concern is less to capture the relation between independent and dependent variables, and more "to document a dispersed process, where social objects have multiple sources, and where ideas, actions and environmental constraints mutually constitute each other" (Autesserre 2009: 255, n. 21).

Despite its implicit application, the process tracing is carefully executed. For example, while she does not use the language of observable implications, Autesserre does just this throughout the study's empirical chapters, exploring what she ought to see if the dominant frame/peace-building-culture is at work (Autesserre 2010: chapters 2–5). In particular, she captures a process whereby a post-conflict frame is first established at the IO level and then, at later times, affects the attitudes and behaviors of numerous other actors. Autesserre measures these frame effects by carefully triangulating across multiple data streams. Thus, she examines UN documents, reports findings from field observations, and – more ethnographically – engages in participant observation, all with the purpose of documenting both the frame's existence and its effects (Autesserre 2009: 261–263). This triangulation exercise increases confidence in the validity of Autesserre's inferences – another of the process-tracing best practices discussed in Chapter 1 of this volume (pp. 27–28).

It should also be noted that her process tracing was being conducted in an unstable post-conflict situation. This raises additional challenges for the researcher, including enhanced incentives for interviewees to lie, personal safety concerns, and ethical issues. Concerning the former, Autesserre shows how careful attention to what has been called the "meta data" (gestures, silences, rumors) surrounding an interview context (see also Fujii 2010) allows one to minimize the likelihood of being misled by interviewees. The bottom line – as also argued by Lyall in his chapter on process tracing and civil war (Lyall, this volume, Chapter 7) – is that rigorous, systematic process tracing is feasible even in conflict settings (see also Wood 2003).

Bringing it all together – the innovative sociological theory, the carefully executed methods, the rich empirics – Autesserre develops a powerful, process-based argument that helps scholars better understand the role (good and bad) that IOs can play in rebuilding war-torn societies. At the same time, this study of IOs, mechanisms, and process will leave readers with lingering questions and concerns.

First, does the argument about frames and the failures of peace building travel? Does it explain anything but the – clearly very important – case of Congo? Are there certain scope conditions for the operation of the framing mechanism – that is, when it is likely to affect the behavior of different IOs seeking to intervene in other conflict situations? It would appear not.

As Autesserre makes clear from the beginning (Autesserre 2010: 14–16), her argument about framing supplements existing explanations based on material constraints, national interests, and the like. Such both/and theorizing is appealing as it captures the reality of a complex social world where it really is a "bit of this and a bit of that factor" that combine to explain an outcome. At the same time, it is difficult – in a more social science sense – to parse out the exact role played by framing in the Congolese case. If we cannot determine its precise influence here, how can we apply it elsewhere?

Despite this concern, in the book's concluding chapter Autesserre claims the "scope of this argument is not limited to the international intervention in the Congo. The approach ... is valuable to understanding peacebuilding success or failure in many unstable environments around the world" (Autesserre 2010: 247). The following pages provide a number of empirical examples broadly suggestive of the generalizability of her approach. However, it is difficult to see the analytic role – if any – played by framing and the peace-building culture in these illustrations.

Second, given her process tracing and mechanisms focus, Autesserre must address equifinality, which means considering the alternative causal pathways through which the outcome of interest might have occurred. However, it is not sufficient simply to consider alternative explanations for the observed outcome – failed interventions, in this case – which Autesserre nicely does (Autesserre 2010: 4–23). Rather, one needs to theorize the mechanisms suggested by alternative accounts, note their observable implications, and conduct process tracing on them (Bennett and Checkel, this volume, Chapter 1, pp. 23–24). In Autesserre's case, this would have involved taking the most plausible alternative, such as arguments based on national interests, and demonstrating that, at key points in the process, they generated observable implications different from what she found.

Third, Autesserre fails to offer a broader, integrative framework that combines different theoretical schools, which is a missed opportunity. After all, this is a book with a firm grounding in constructivist ontology (culture and frames creating meaning, making action possible), but one that simultaneously recognizes the importance of rationalist factors (material constraints, strategic action). That is, the building blocks for such a framework are there. Moreover, it is precisely a focus on mechanisms and process – as seen in Autesserre – that makes it easier to identify points of contact between different theories (Checkel 2013a).

Mechanisms and process tracing are not enough

For students of international organizations, the move to process and mechanisms and to the method of process tracing has been salutary. As the books reviewed attest, the result has been rich and analytically rigorous studies that demonstrate the multiple roles played by institutions in global politics. We now know much more about how these organizations really work and shape the behavior and interests of states. The embrace of a mechanism-based understanding of causality and application of process tracing have reduced reliance on "as if" assumptions and thus heightened theoretical-empirical concern with capturing better the complex social reality of IOs.

Yet, as my criticisms suggest, there is no such thing as a free lunch, even in the study of IOs. There are trade-offs, opportunity costs, and limitations to a mechanism-based/process-tracing understanding of the IO–state relation. And to be clear, my criticisms here are only possible thanks to the pioneering work of scholars like Wallander, Schimmelfennig, Kelley, and Autesserre. By taking mechanisms seriously and carefully operationalizing the process tracing, they have demonstrated the tremendous advantages of such an approach. These facts along with the transparency of their methods and designs make it easier to see what is working – and where challenges remain. On the latter, I see three issues of method and three regarding theory that deserve further attention.

Method

Given the subject matter of this volume and the centrality of causal mechanisms in the books reviewed, I focus here on a key method for measuring them – process tracing. All the authors do a good job at this level; this is all the more notable because they were mostly writing well before the recent literature seeking to systematize and establish good standards for it (Collier 2011; Beach and Pedersen 2013a, for example).

Nonetheless, future work on process tracing and measuring the causal mechanisms of the IO–state relation could improve on three counts. First, process tracers need carefully and fully to theorize their mechanisms. The more care at this stage, the clearer will be those mechanisms' observable implications. Put differently: "Theory must take primacy over method. Theory offers the perspective through which we can interpret empirical observation . . . [T]he interpretation of events in a process-tracing case study is shaped by theory" (Gates 2008: 27). As Jacobs argues elsewhere in this volume: "Tightly specified theories with detailed mechanisms can substantially enhance the discriminating power of process tracing by generating crisp and unique empirical predictions" (Jacobs, this volume, Chapter 2, p. 42; see also Checkel and Bennett, this volume, Chapter 10). Of the four books reviewed above, Schimmelfennig (2003) goes the furthest in this direction; it is no coincidence, then, that his process tracing is the most transparent and systematic in application.

This strategy of theoretical specification was also pursued by Checkel and collaborators in their work on European institutions and socialization. They took the mechanism of socialization, disaggregated it into three sub-mechanisms (strategic calculation, role playing, normative suasion), theorized scope conditions for each, and specified their differing observable implications (Checkel 2007: chapter 1). This allowed them not only to avoid "lazy mechanism-based storytelling" (Hedström and Ylikoski 2010: 64), but to advance the process-based research program on IOs and socialization.

Second, scholars studying IOs from a mechanism-based perspective must address fully the challenges raised by equifinality, where multiple causal pathways may lead to the same outcome. It is not sufficient to carry out process tracing on one's preferred mechanism, or to run through a list of alternative explanations. As argued in Chapter 1, a far better procedure is to outline the process-tracing predictions of a wide range of alternative explanations of a case in advance, and then to consider the actual evidence for and against each explanation (this volume, Chapter 1, pp. 23–24). Done properly, this takes time (and resources) and should thus be integrated into research designs at an early stage.

Moreover – and to link back to my first point – full, robust theorization of these various mechanisms will only facilitate this task. The point is not to eliminate equifinality; that is not possible given the complex social world we (and IOs) inhabit. Rather, by explicitly addressing it, the researcher increases readers' confidence in the validity of the mechanism-process story he or she relates.

Third, process tracing should not be viewed as the only way of capturing causal mechanisms. One promising strategy is to employ computer techniques known as agent-based modeling to explore the logic and hypothesized scope conditions of particular causal mechanisms. For example, in recent work on civil war, scholars have used such modeling to analyze the transnational diffusion of social identities as a key process underlying the spread of civil conflicts. They disaggregate – and thus better specify – diffusion as occurring through two possible causal mechanisms: social adaptation in a transnational context, and transnational norm entrepreneurship. The simulations – the computer modeling exercise – indicate that norm entrepreneurship is the more robust mechanism of diffusion, which is an important confirmation of a finding in the qualitative, process-tracing work (Nome and Weidman 2013).

Theory

Despite or because of the focus on mechanisms and process tracing over the past decade, one recent agenda-setting essay on IOs concluded that "more attention to the causal mechanisms advanced . . . would greatly enhance our ability to explain the world around us" (Martin and Simmons 2013: 344). Given the results achieved to date, such an endorsement makes sense – and is consistent with the move to mechanism-based theorizing in political science and other disciplines more generally (Johnson 2006; Gerring 2007a; Hedström and Ylikoski 2010).

Yet, in almost all cases – and this is my first theoretical concern – there is a trade-off. Mechanisms and process tracing provide nuance and fine-grained detail, filling in the all-important steps between independent and dependent variables, but do so at the expense of theoretical parsimony. More general theories of IOs have been replaced by a growing collection of partial, mid-range theories. This might not be a problem, especially if it was clear what was replacing the general theories (see also Checkel and Bennett, this volume, Chapter 10).

Unfortunately, it is not clear. Mind you, we have a name for the replacement – middle-range theory – which is repeated with mantra-like frequency by a growing number of graduate students and scholars. Missing, however, is an operational sense for how such theory is constructed and critical self-reflection on its limitations. For sure, the very name tells us something: middle-range theory is in between grand, parsimonious theories and complex, descriptive narratives.[5] Typically, it brings together several independent variables and

---

[5] So defined, it thus has a strong family resemblance to what sociologists call grounded theory (Glaser and Strauss 1967).

causal mechanisms to explain an outcome, leading some to term it "typological theory" (George and Bennett 2005). The ideal is that the resulting framework will have some degree of generalizability – in a particular region or during a particular period of time, say (George 1993; see also Checkel 2007). More recently, prominent scholars have endorsed such theorizing as the way forward for the IR subfield as a whole (Katzenstein and Sil 2010).

However, middle-range theory has three potential drawbacks about which students of IOs should be aware. For one, it will often be over-determined. That is, with several independent variables or mechanisms in play, it is not possible to isolate the causal impact of any single factor. One way to address and minimize this problem is by emphasizing research design at the early stages of a project, carefully choosing cases for process tracing that allow the isolation of particular theorized mechanisms. This may sound like Grad Seminar 101 advice, but it needs nonetheless to be stressed (Bennett, this volume, Appendix; see also Martin and Simmons 2013: 344; George and Bennett 2005; Seawright and Gerring 2008).

In addition, when large parts of a research program are characterized by mid-range approaches, the production of cumulative theoretical knowledge may be hindered. Specifically, for work on IOs and institutions, the various middle-range efforts – including those surveyed above – are not coalescing into a broader theoretical whole. Instead, we have proliferating lists of variables and causal mechanisms. Contrast this with neo-liberal institutionalism – a paradigm-based, non-plural body of theory on the same topic (Keohane 1984). Here, there has been theoretical advance and cumulation, as later efforts build upon earlier work – for example, by adding process and domestic politics variables while still keeping a rational-choice core (Mitchell 1994; Simmons 1994; Wallander 1999; Martin 2000, for example). Of course, some would argue that the neo-liberals' advances are mitigated and indeed perhaps made possible by empirics that are still too often illustrative or not systematically tested against alternative explanations.

Yet, this need not be a zero-sum game, where mechanisms and rich empirics automatically lead to less robust theory. Instead, students of IOs with a process focus need to more consistently place their explanations within families of theories on mechanisms – agent to structure, structure to agent, agent to agent, structure to structure mechanisms, for example. They should also explore whether their mechanisms relate to power, institutional efficiency, or legitimacy. Thinking along these lines, together with more careful attention to scope conditions and typological interactions among variables, can promote more cumulative theorizing (see also Bennett 2013a, 2013b).

Finally, there is a tendency with middle-range approaches to adopt a micro-focus, where one theorizes (interacting) causal mechanisms in some temporally or spatially delimited frame (Haas 2010: 11). The danger is then to miss the macro-level, where material power and social discourses – say – fundamentally shape and predetermine the mechanisms playing out at lower levels (see also Chapter 1, p. 23). This is precisely the trap into which Checkel and collaborators fell in their project developing theoretically plural, process-based, middle-range theories of European IOs and socialization. A global search of the resulting volume reveals virtually no hits for either power or discourse (Checkel 2007). More generally and as Nau has argued, middle-range theories "inevitably leave out 'big questions' posed from different or higher levels of analysis"; they may thus "not get rid of 'isms' [but] just hide them and make it harder to challenge prevailing ones" (Nau 2011: 489–490).

To be clear, the middle-range theory currently favored by many students of IOs is caused not by process tracing, but by the prior, analytic choice in favor of mechanisms. Yet, process tracing does play a supporting role, especially when it is used without sufficient prior attention to design, theory, and operationalization. And the latter is all the more likely given that many process tracers are problem-driven scholars who want – simply and admirably – "to get on with it," explaining better the world around us.[6]

One promising possibility for addressing these analytic problems is typological theory, or theories about how combinations of mechanisms interact in shaping outcomes for specified populations. Compared to middle-range approaches, this form of theorizing has several advantages. It provides a way to address interactions' effects and other forms of complexity; stimulates fruitful iteration between cases, the specification of populations, and theories; and creates a framework for cumulative progress. On the latter, subsequent researchers can add or change variables and re-code or add cases while still building on earlier attempts at typological theorizing on the phenomenon (George and Bennett 2005: chapter 11). For example, in a recent project on civil war (Checkel 2013b), it was demonstrated that typological theorizing is one way to promote cumulation, even in the hard case of mid-range, theoretically plural accounts (Bennett 2013a).

A second theoretical issue upon which IO scholars might reflect is their efforts at theoretical pluralism and bridge building. In principle, such efforts could be wide-ranging. After all, the philosophy of science literature reminds

---

[6] The ten best practice standards for process training outlined in Chapter 1 are designed precisely to combat this tendency.

us that accounts of IOs and institutions built on causal mechanisms should be "quite compatible with different social theories of action" (Mayntz 2004: 248) – rationalist or constructivist, say. Moreover, if process tracing is a central method for measuring mechanisms and if the technique captures fine-grained detail, then its use should facilitate the discovery of points of contact between alternative theoretical accounts. Yet, as argued above, attempts at pluralism have been limited.

An excellent example of a bridge-building effort in the area of international institutions and IOs – and the key role of process tracing in it – is work on human rights led by Thomas Risse, Stephen Ropp, and Kathryn Sikkink (1999, 2013).[7] However, it is the exception that proves the rule. Actually, it proves two rules: (1) that very few other students of IOs have shown this degree of theoretically plural ambition; and (2) even the bridge building of Risse *et al.* is quite limited.

Risse and collaborators sought to develop a model explaining the process through which international institutions and norms have effects at the national level; it was conceived from the beginning as a pluralist effort integrating causal mechanisms from both rational choice and social constructivism. To accomplish this integration, they employed a temporal-sequencing bridge-building strategy. That is, it was the combination of different theoretical approaches – first, rational choice; then, constructivism – working at different times, that explained the outcome.[8]

Using this theoretically plural frame, the two books employ process tracing to demonstrate that compliance with international prescriptions is not just about learning new appropriate behavior, as many constructivists might argue. Nor, however, is it all about calculating international or domestic costs. Rather, by combining these mechanisms, Risse and collaborators provide scholars with a richer picture of the multiple causal pathways through which norms matter. If earlier, the implicit assumption was that these various pathways were complementary and reinforcing, the authors now recognize they may also work at cross purposes, with some strengthening domestic norm implementation while others may hinder it (Risse *et al.* 2013: chapter 6).

All this said, it is important to note an important limitation in the authors' self-consciously plural theory. If we continue with the bridge-building

---

[7] The latter is a thoroughly revised version of the 1999 book. My concerns about bridge building apply equally to both volumes.

[8] In the more recent book, the authors maintain this commitment to theoretical pluralism and bridge building, while endorsing no one strategy, such as temporal sequencing (Risse *et al.* 2013: 12–13, chapter 6).

metaphor, then it is about a bridge not crossed – that of epistemology. Positivism or its close relation, scientific realism, is the philosophical starting point for both volumes – exactly as we saw for the Schimmelfennig (2003) and Kelley (2004a) books discussed above. It would thus appear that theoretically plural accounts of IIs and IOs built on mechanisms and process tracing can include the whole spectrum of rationalist scholarship, but only that part of constructivism with a foundation in positivism. This seems unduly limiting as constructivism is a rich theoretical tradition with equally strong roots in interpretive social science (Adler 2013).

One possibility is that interpretive constructivism is missing from these accounts because it is structural and holistic, while the IO work reviewed here is about mechanisms and processes. However, this is not correct. Over the past decade, interpretive constructivists have added a strong element of process to their accounts (Neumann 2002). They have done this through the concept of social practice, where "it is not only who we are that drives what we do; it is also what we do that determines who we are" (Pouliot 2010: 5–6). This has not been an abstract exercise, as the concept has been operationalized and rigor-ously applied – including to the study of IOs (ibid.). Moreover, and as Pouliot demonstrates elsewhere in this volume, scholars are now actively developing an interpretive variant of process tracing, thinking in concrete terms about how to do it well (see also Guzzini 2011; 2012: chapter 11).

So, the concepts and tools are there to allow for a bolder form of theoretical bridge building – one that crosses epistemological boundaries – when study-ing IOs. However, it has for the most part not happened. Perhaps combining (positivist) rationalism with (interpretive forms of) constructivism just cannot be done; it is an apples and oranges problem. The former is about cause, linearity, and fixed meanings, while the latter is about recursivity, fluidity, and the reconstruction of meaning. Yet, these black and white distinctions blur into "bridgeable" grays when the research is applied and empirical. Thus, in two important books, Hopf combines the interpretive recovery of meaning with causal, process-tracing case studies (Hopf 2002; 2012). These books are about Soviet/Russian foreign policy and the origins of the Cold War; however, the basic interpretive-positivist bridge-building design could just as easily be applied to the study of IOs (Holzscheiter 2010, for example).

My point here is straightforward. Research on IOs has gained considerably by focusing on mechanisms and process over the past fifteen years. It has also gained by integrating insights from both rational choice and constructivism. It may gain even more if it integrates practice and discourse – and interpretive forms of process tracing – into its accounts. And by gain, I simply mean it may acquire even more practical knowledge about why IOs do what they do in global politics (see also Checkel 2013a: 235–236).

A final theoretical issue concerns domestic politics. Kelley (2004a) shows the clear benefit of beginning to incorporate the domestic level into explanations of IO effects on states. More recently, Simmons (2009), while again having no theory of domestic politics, goes a step further – systematically linking the nature of domestic legal systems (common versus civil law) to state receptivity to IO norms and rules.

Beyond the theoretical rationale of offering more complete and thus determinate explanations, there is a real-world reason for bringing domestic process into our theories about IOs. Simply put, for many IOs, what they decide and do have become the subject of deep and intense domestic (and transnational) political contestation and mobilization. Consider the most powerful IO in the world – the European Union (EU). After decades when theorists of the EU ignored domestic process, national politics and politicization now occupy an increasingly central place in their arguments (Hooghe and Marks 2009; and, especially, Risse 2014).

If scholars of IOs make this move to the domestic realm, they could benefit by learning from those comparativists who have already thought about mechanisms and process tracing at the national level (Waldner, this volume, Chapter 5). Indeed, while the challenges of doing good process tracing are no different, the complexity of (most) domestic–political processes – compared to their system-level counterparts – enhances the importance of a clearly operationalized and transparent use of process tracing (Wood 2003, for a superb example).

At the same time, care should be exercised in not taking domestic politics and process too seriously, where system-level influences from IOs (and other actors) are ignored. This is precisely the (flawed) theoretical move taken by an increasingly influential branch of international political economy in the United States – open economy politics (Oatley 2011). It is possible that what some IOs do on some issues is driven entirely by the domestic politics of a particular member state. However, this should be a matter of empirical discovery and not theoretical diktat.

If we return to this chapter's title, "Mechanisms, process, and the study of international institutions," it is clear that the turn to causal mechanisms and process has delivered. We now have more complete, causally more robust understandings of how IOs and institutions contribute to – and detract from – governance at the global and regional levels, and of their relation to states.

This has helped to spur exciting new work on what one might call comparative regional organizations (Acharya and Johnston 2007).

However, this new knowledge has come with some unwanted baggage. The methodological challenges highlighted above are relatively easy fixes; basically, scholars need to do a bit better what they are already doing. The theoretical issues, though, are of another magnitude. Mechanism-based theorizing raises a number of challenges – most important, how to scale up from explanations grounded in mechanisms and process tracing to larger bodies of theory. We can and should do better than generating endless lists of case-specific causal mechanisms.

The days of paradigm wars and grand "isms" may be mostly past, which are surely good things. However, for students of IOs – and the broader discipline – their replacements are not clear. Terms and concepts such as mid-range theory, analytic eclecticism (Katzenstein and Sil 2010), and pragmatism (Johnson 2006) open up exciting, more plural theoretical (and epistemological) vistas, but are less clear in telling us how to get there in a way that maintains some degree of intellectual coherence.

4 Efficient process tracing
Analyzing the causal mechanisms of European integration

Frank Schimmelfennig

Introduction

Why a separate chapter on the European Union (EU) in a volume on process tracing? Is there anything distinct about the analysis of European politics that would merit a special treatment? In general, the answer is no. The methodological challenges of studying the EU are pretty much the same as in other areas of research (although, see Lyall, this volume, Chapter 7, on process tracing and civil war), and EU scholars have used the same toolboxes as those working on other polities. There is one major field of inquiry, however, in which process tracing has taken pride of place for both empirical and theoretical reasons: the study of European integration.

The study of European integration is about the development of the EU: the transfer of tasks from the state to the European level of governance, the growth of EU competences, and the expansion of membership. By contrast, the study of EU politics and policies deals with elections, legislation, compliance, and other topics that are well established in the analysis of other political systems. Standard methods of quantitative or comparative analysis are commonly used in these areas.

The study of European integration, however, starts from the premise that the EU is a rare or extreme phenomenon. According to a much criticized but also very durable assumption of EU research, the EU is a polity *sui generis*, "less" than a state but "more" than an international organization (Wallace 1983). Even if one treats the EU more generally as an instance of regional integration or multi-level governance, it is hard to avoid the conclusion that the combination of deep supranational centralization and

An earlier version was presented at the workshop on "Process Tracing in the Social Sciences," Georgetown University, March 2012. I thank the editors, Alan Jacobs, and the other the participants of the workshop, as well as Andrew Moravcsik and Craig Parsons for helpful comments.

broad functional scope – the EU covers all policy areas and some of them are exclusive competences of the Union – makes it an outlier in the population of international organizations. As a consequence, most students of European integration prefer focusing on within-case analysis rather than comparing the development of the EU to that of other organizations and polities.

In addition, European integration is generally studied as a series or sequence of individual big decisions: for instance, to establish the common market or monetary union, to expand to Eastern Europe and start accession negotiations with Turkey, to empower the European Parliament, or to conclude separate treaties on free travel (Schengen) and fiscal stability outside the Community framework. In the first decades of European integration, such big decisions were arguably too rare, too causally heterogeneous, or too dependent on each other, to qualify for comparative analysis.

Even though these obstacles do not necessarily hold any more, there are also theoretical reasons for process tracing. Many of the theoretical controversies in the study of European integration have to do with motivation and process. Take the traditional theoretical debate between intergovernmentalism and neofunctionalism (or supranationalism). Both schools of thought broadly agree that governments negotiate and decide on integration in order to cope with international interdependence. They disagree, however, regarding the sources of interdependence, the nature and sources of government preferences, the relevant actors in negotiations, and the ways in which decisions are reached.

Liberal intergovernmentalism (Moravcsik 1993; 1998) claims that interdependence is exogenous (to the integration process); government preferences are conditioned by the interests of powerful domestic interest groups; negotiations are intergovernmental; and outcomes are determined by the relative bargaining power of governments. By contrast, supranationalists (Pierson 1996; Stone Sweet and Sandholtz 1997) argue that interdependence is endogenous, i.e. generated by the "spill-over" of previous integration decisions; government preferences are reshaped and constrained by such spill-overs in addition to transnational interest groups and supranational institutions; and both negotiations and their outcomes are influenced by supranational actors such as the Commission. The more recent arrival of constructivism added more variation to this debate. According to constructivism, ideas matter for how governments deal with interdependence; government preferences are constituted by identities; and negotiations and their outcomes are constrained by European norms (Schimmelfennig 2012). Finally, on a more methodological note, studies of European integration are often outcome-centric and focus on examining cases of successful integration. In other words, they select cases on the dependent variable. This case selection procedure is useless for establishing sufficient conditions in comparative analysis (King *et al.* 1994; Geddes 2003).

Theory-testing analyses of European integration thus cannot rely on studying covariation between independent variables (for example, interdependence and convergence of government preferences) that do not vary sufficiently across theories and a dependent variable (integration) that does not vary sufficiently across cases. For theoretical reasons, such analyses would most probably run into problems of over-determination or equifinality. For methodological reasons, they would be unable to draw valid causal inferences. Rather, theory-testing requires examining how factors such as interdependence and government preferences are produced and in which causal order they affect the outcomes. In other words, theory-testing analyses of European integration require process tracing for both theoretical and methodological reasons.

It is therefore small wonder that many influential studies of European integration follow a process-tracing design – implicitly or explicitly. This methodological choice cuts across theoretical positions. Andrew Moravcsik's *Choice for Europe* "is a series of structured narratives" of the EU's grand bargains designed to test observable "process-level" implications of competing theories of preference formation, bargaining, and institutional choice (1998: 2, 79). The critics of liberal intergovernmentalism have objected to Moravcsik's selection of units of analysis and cases or his interpretation of data, but not the design as such. Paul Pierson illustrates his historical-institutionalist, process-level explanation of the "path to European integration" with a case study of European social policy (1996). Craig Parsons traces the process of how a specific set of ideas on the construction of European regional organization prevailed over its competitors in the French political elite and was subsequently institutionalized (2003). Adrienne Héritier (2007) examines institutional development in the EU on the basis of process implications of several theories of institutional change. This list could easily be extended.

In this chapter, I draw on several of these studies in addition to an example of my own work to illustrate how process tracing is done in the study of European integration. Before doing so, however, I make an argument in favor of "efficient" process tracing. The core point of efficient process tracing is that it maximizes analytical leverage in relation to the invested resources. It starts from a causal relationship provisionally established through correlation, comparative, or congruence analysis and from a causal mechanism that is specified ex ante; it selects cases that promise external validity in addition to the internal validity established by process tracing; and it confines itself to analyzing those process links that are crucial for an explanation and for discriminating between alternative explanations. As a result, efficient process tracing is designed to avoid three major problems of the method: the potential waste of resources, the temptation of storytelling, and the lack of generalizability. In elaborating on the concept of "efficient process-tracing," I focus on deductive, theory-testing process tracing in contrast to the inductive, theory-building type (this volume, Chapter 1, pp. 7–8; see also Beach and Pedersen 2013a); I also emphasize design issues over the actual conduct of process tracing, which is an important complement to the "best practices" articulated in Chapter 1.

I then assess key process-tracing studies of European integration. Andrew Moravcsik's *Choice for Europe* (1998) and Paul Pierson's "Path to European Integration" (1996) represent the intergovernmental-ist–supranationalist debate, while *A Certain Idea of Europe* by Craig Parsons (2003) and my analysis of enlargement in *The EU, NATO, and the Integration of Europe* (2003) are two ideational accounts. These are all examples of efficient process tracing, but the criteria established earlier in the chapter also provide grounds for partial criticism. In the concluding section, I summarize the insights gained from the comparison of these studies and discuss the prerequisites, trade-offs, and limitations of efficient process tracing.

Efficient process tracing

Challenges of process tracing

As a within-case method focusing on the causal mechanism linking factors or conditions to outcomes, process tracing occupies a unique position among observational research designs. Other single-case designs such as the "congruence method" (George and Bennett 2005: 181–204), which relies on the consistency between the theoretically expected and the observed outcome, are fraught with problems of causal interpretation such as omitted-variable bias or equifinality. Comparative or large-n analysis gives us more confidence in the relationship between "independent" and "dependent variables," but does not provide information on the causal mechanism linking the two. By analyzing process-level evidence on causal mechanisms, process tracing can claim, in principle, to increase the internal validity of causal inferences dramatically and thereby strengthen our causal interpretations of both single case studies and studies based on covariation (see also Lyall, Chapter 7; Dunning, Chapter 8 – both this volume). Yet these unique and useful features of process tracing also produce severe challenges. I will focus on four core problems: the resource problem; the measure-of-fit problem; the storytelling problem; and the problem of generalization.

Resource

It is generally agreed that process tracing can "require enormous amounts of information" (George and Bennett 2005: 223). To some extent, the process-tracing best practices proposed in Chapter 1 are general standards of good scientific practice: the search for alternative explanations, the consideration of potential bias in sources, and the gathering of diverse evidence. In addition, any research design needs to make a decision on how far "down" and "back" the researcher wants to go in the search for "the cause."

In process tracing, however, the per-unit (case) investment of time and resources is likely to be much higher than in comparative analyses. This has mainly to do with design: whereas comparative analysis may work with a few data-set observations per case measuring the independent variables and the dependent variable, the sequence of causal-process observations in process-tracing analysis can become very long. This is especially true if process taking is of the "soaking and poking" kind requiring immersion in the details of a case (Chapter 1, p. 18) or if researchers heed the warning by George and Bennett that process tracing "provides a strong basis for causal inference only if it can establish an uninterrupted causal path" (George and Bennett 2005: 222). Because we never really know whether we have soaked and poked enough, and any causal path can always be more fine-grained and extended into history, process tracers are at risk of ending up in an "infinite regress." Moreover, process tracing analyses cannot use the standardized, computer-based data-processing techniques on offer for comparative analysis.[1] Finally, process tracing analyses generally take up much more space – again on a per-case basis – for presenting findings than comparative analyses.

---

[1] A partial exception would be the application of agent-based modeling to process-tracing accounts, as discussed by Checkel, this volume, Chapter 3.

Measures of fit

How do we know that the process-tracing evidence is good enough to accept or discard a hypothesis? Statistical analyses work with levels of significance for individual factors or measures of fit for entire models. Qualitative comparative analysis (QCA) (Ragin 1987) tests for necessity and sufficiency of conditions, and uses consistency and coverage to assess the fit of causal configurations. Both designs benefit from analyzing a data set with clearly delineated and (ideally) independent units of analysis and a defined number of observations. Such formal measures of significance and fit do not seem to exist in process tracing. In part, this has to do with "the non-comparability of adjacent pieces of evidence" in process tracing (Gerring 2007a: 178; Beach and Pedersen 2013a: 72–76). The units of process tracing, the individual steps in a causal path or the elements of a causal sequence, are neither independent nor comparable. Moreover, Gerring claims that the elements of the causal process chosen by the researcher, and how many of them, can be arbitrary (Gerring 2007a: 179). It is also difficult to say what qualifies as an "uninterrupted" causal path in George and Bennett's criterion for causal inference. Finally, whereas Bayes's Theorem provides a general standard for evaluating process-level evidence, its application to process tracing remains informal and less quantifiable than the measures of fit for QCA with which process-tracing shares the non-frequentist mode of inference (Bennett 2008: 708–709; Bennett, this volume, Appendix).

Storytelling

Because the standards for selecting causal-process observations and making valid inferences are relatively open and malleable in process tracing, it is relatively easy to select, arrange, and present the material more or less consciously in a way that appears plausible to the reader (see also the discussion in Dunning, this volume, Chapter 8). We may extend Popper's classical critique of empiricism by saying that humans have an innate propensity not only for seeing patterns and regularities (Popper 1963: 62), but also for constructing and telling coherent stories.

Generalization

Whereas process tracing maximizes the internal validity of causal inferences, it does not generate any external validity per se. In all fairness, process tracing is not meant to produce external validity, and other methods suffer from the same trade-off between internal and external validity. However, in combination with the high costs of process tracing for producing a highly valid explanation of a single event of the past, the uncertainty about generalizability can be discouraging (see also Checkel and Bennett, this volume, Chapter 10).

The ten criteria of good process tracing proposed by Bennett and Checkel go a long way in acknowledging these challenges and devising ways to bound them (Chapter 1, pp. 20–22). "Efficient process tracing" builds on these criteria, in particular on the Bayesian intuition guiding process-tracing inferences, but seeks to increase the efficiency of theory-testing process-tracing designs.

Efficient solutions

I suggest that process tracing deals best with these challenges and is used most efficiently if it is complementary to the analysis of congruence or covariation; if it is used on cases that promise a maximum of external validity; if the causal mechanism is specified ex ante; and if the process links to be examined are carefully selected to provide for crucial, competitive theory tests.

Complementarity

First, process tracing is best used to complement analyses of congruence (for single cases) and comparative analyses (for two or more cases). The high investment in process tracing is most efficient if we have an "initial suspicion" that the causal mechanism has actually been at work *and* effective. For a single case, preliminary evidence is given if the values for the outcome and the explanatory factor(s) match the hypothetical expectation (congruence). Statistically significant and substantively relevant correlations serve as a useful starting point in quantitative studies. In QCA, conditional configurations with high consistency and substantial coverage are worth exploring further. Process tracing then serves the purpose of checking the causal mechanism that is supposed to link the factors or configurations with the outcome. Sometimes, it may also be interesting to find out why a condition that is present and that we assumed to be causally relevant did not produce the outcome – but even for process tracing of a deviant case, we need first to establish the relationship between cause and effect to know that it is deviant.

Case selection

If process tracing follows a single-case congruence analysis or explores a deviant case, case selection is not an issue. If it is designed to probe further into the causal validity of small-n or large-n correlations, however, the researcher needs to decide which case or cases to select for process tracing – assuming that it is so resource-intensive that it can only be conducted for one or two cases. This selection should again be based on considerations of efficiency: to maximize external validity while checking internal validity. Gerring and Seawright suggest selecting a typical case, which represents a cross-case relationship well, to explore causal mechanisms (Gerring 2007a: 93; Seawright and Gerring 2008: 299). If there is time for two process tracing analyses, the study of diverse cases that illuminate the full range of variation in the population is also advisable in order to see how the causal mechanism plays out for different starting conditions (Gerring 2007a: 97–99; Seawright and Gerring 2008: 300–301). Both typical and diverse case-study types maximize external validity on the basis of the assumption that the findings of process tracing in the selected case(s) are representative for the entire population.

Alternatively, the process tracing analysis of a crucial case also promises to be efficient. When dealing with positive outcomes, the best case is a hard or least-likely case. Based on theoretical expectations, the researchers choose a case in which the presumed cause is only weakly present, whereas presumed counteracting factors are strong. If process tracing shows that the causal process triggered by the presumed cause produces the positive outcome nevertheless, there is good reason to conclude that this is even more likely in cases in which the causal condition is more strongly present and counteracting factors are weaker.

Ex-ante specification of the causal mechanism

As a safeguard against storytelling, process tracing should be based on causal mechanisms that are derived ex ante from theories and follow a basic analytical template (see also Jacobs, this volume, Chapter 2). Such causal mechanisms tell us what to look for in a causal process rather than inducing us to make up a "just so" story of our own. "Coleman's bathtub" (Coleman 1986) or similar standards for a fully specified causal mechanism in the analytic social sciences (for example, Hedström and Swedberg 1998) provide a useful template.[2] They usually stipulate:

1. who the relevant actors are;
2. how their beliefs and preferences are formed (macro-micro link or situational mechanism);
3. how they choose their actions (micro-micro link or action formation mechanism); and
4. how the individual actions of multiple actors are aggregated to produce the collective outcome (micro-macro link or transformational mechanism).

In addition, Gerring claims that "process tracing is convincing insofar as the multiple links in a causal chain can be formalized, that is, diagrammed in an explicit way" (Gerring 2007a: 181; see also Waldner, this volume, Chapter 5). I concur with his advice that "the formal diagram is a useful heuristic, forcing the author to make a precise and explicit statement of her argument" (Gerring 2007a: 182).

Selection of theories and causal-process observations

Embedding a process-tracing analysis in competitive theory testing provides a further safeguard against the "infinite regress" and "storytelling" problems, and it helps to allocate research investments efficiently. Usually, there are a manageable number of theories or causal mechanisms that are relevant for the case at hand *and* compatible with the initial finding of congruence or correlation. In other words, process tracing can be limited to probing into and discriminating between alternative explanations that attribute the outcome to the condition (independent variable), but different causal mechanisms.

Once theories are selected, we can further focus on those links of the causal mechanism that are crucial for each theory and for discriminating between rival theories. This matches Gerring's advice to focus our attention "on those links in the causal chain that are (a) weakest (that is, most contested between theories) and (b) most crucial for the overall argument" (Gerring 2007a: 184), and it is in line with Bayesian reasoning (Bennett, this volume, Appendix). If two theories agree that only states are relevant actors, we can focus on states for the process-tracing analysis and do not need to probe into the potential role of other actors. If two theories agree that states are rational, we can skip examining evidence on

[2] "Coleman's bathtub" or "boat" refers to the way in which James Coleman's scheme of macro-micro-macro linkages is usually drawn.

their decision-making process and focus on the preferences or constraints on which the theories may differ. In other words, theory helps us target decisive – and, if possible, "doubly decisive" – tests right from the start rather than investing time and other resources in tests that will give us less information.

By the same token, competitive theory testing gives us a clearer idea of the data requirements. It focuses our attention on those episodes that offer the possibility to discriminate between competing theories and to collect the data that are needed for this purpose. It helps us distinguish between irrelevant data and relevant data. Rather than wasting resources and space on a full, uninterrupted narrative from cause to outcome, we can focus on a small number of crucial steps in the process that are worth exploring.

Which process links should we examine and which ones are dispensable? Process tracing starts from the assumption of a temporal and analytical sequence, in which later stages in the process are dependent on earlier stages. For this reason, we start with the first link in the causal process which is (a) a crucial or *the* crucial process element for at least one of the competing theories and (b) for which we have competing hypotheses and observable implications of the candidate theory and at least one alternative theory. In other words, there is no need to examine process links which are marginal or secondary for the theories involved or on which the competing theories agree. Under the same assumption of temporal and analytical sequence, any theory that is decisively disconfirmed in the empirical analysis of the first link is eliminated and does not need to be considered further at later stages. The process of selecting and testing additional links is reiterated until a single theory or explanation is left.

This means that if we have only two competing causal mechanisms and the first link provides for a doubly decisive test that confirms one theory and disconfirms the other, process tracing could stop in principle after the first iteration. There are, however, three considerations for pursuing process tracing further. First, subsequent stages in the causal process may be at least partly independent from earlier processes. Transformational mechanisms are, for instance, often independent of preference formation mechanisms. This is a core insight of the theory of collective action and other social theories explaining unintended consequences. Second, the crucial process element for a theory may only come after it would have been eliminated on a less important link. Unless the later link was strongly causally dependent on the earlier link, it would thus be "fair" to keep the theory in the race until its most important process implications have been tested. Finally, the evidence may not be sufficiently strong to discard one theory and confirm the other. In this case, further testing is also necessary.

Table 4.1 "Good/best-practice" and "efficient" process tracing compared

Good/best-practice process tracing	Efficient process tracing
1. Cast the net widely for alternative explanations	Yes, but focus on those that are compatible with findings from analysis of congruence or correlation
2. Be equally tough on the alternative explanations	Yes, but eliminate them if their core causal-process expectations are disconfirmed
4. Take into account whether the case is most or least likely for alternative explanations	Yes, but also select representative or crucial cases in order to maximize external validity
5. Make a justifiable decision on when to start	Yes, but let this decision be guided by the relevant theories and standard analytical templates
6. Be relentless in gathering diverse and relevant evidence	Yes, but limit yourself to the evidence that is needed to discriminate between competing theories
7. Combine process tracing with case comparisons	Yes, but start with comparison to establish correlation and select the best case for process tracing
8. Be open to inductive insights	Yes, if theoretically specified causal mechanisms fail to explain the case

Table 4.1 illustrates how "efficient process tracing" builds on and further develops most of the process-tracing "best practices" advanced in Chapter 1. Efficient process tracing strongly concurs with the advice to specify testable process-tracing expectations deductively (criterion 9), and it agrees with the caveats that process tracers need to consider biases in the evidentiary sources (criterion 3) and take into account that process tracing may be inconclusive in the end (criterion 10). For the other criteria, it puts the emphasis on efficiency-enhancing deduction, selection, and generalizability. Deduction helps us make a justifiable decision on when to start and how to specify causal mechanisms (criterion 5); it helps us design more decisive and focused tests (criteria 2 and 6); and it limits the relevance of inductive insights to instances of general theory failure (criterion 8). Selection of theories based on prior evidence derived from congruence or correlation limits the number of explanations to be considered (criteria 1 and 7); and selection of cases based on representativeness increases external validity and generalizability (criterion 4).

Process tracing in studies of European integration

In this main part of the chapter, I present and discuss examples from the literature on European integration. As already mentioned in the introduction, many if not most studies of integration use process tracing as their main method or as an important part of the analysis. I reconstruct how they *design* process tracing and how efficient the designs are in light of the above considerations. In contrast, I will not discuss how they actually *conduct* process tracing, that is, what data they use, how they analyze them, and how they draw substantive conclusions from them.

I start with two contributions to the debate of the 1990s between inter-governmentalism and supranationalism (or neofunctionalism): Andrew Moravcsik's *Choice for Europe* and Paul Pierson's "Path to European Integration." I then move on to the more recent debate between ideational (or constructivist) and rational–institutionalist approaches and present two studies that seek to demonstrate the relevance of ideas through process tracing: Craig Parsons's *Certain Idea of Europe* and my own book, *The EU, NATO, and the Integration of Europe.*

Andrew Moravcsik, *The Choice for Europe*

Andrew Moravcsik's *Choice for Europe* (1998) starts from the major theories that claim to explain the history-making decisions in European integration: neofunctionalism, federalism, realism, and his own liberal intergovernment-alism. He develops a parsimonious "rationalist framework" of the stages of negotiation in international cooperation. Moravcsik uses this framework to model the causal mechanisms proposed by the various theories in a commensurable way and to establish at which junctures in the causal process their propositions differ (see Table 4.2). In each case, these propositions

Table 4.2 Process-tracing framework of *The Choice for Europe*

Stages of negotiation	National preference formation	Interstate bargaining	Institutional choice
Alternative independent variables	Economic vs. geopolitical interests	Asymmetrical interdependence vs. supranational entrepreneurship?	Federalist ideology vs. centralized technocratic management vs. credible commitments
	↓	↓	↓
Observed outcomes	Underlying national preferences →	Agreements on substance →	Choice to delegate or pool decision-making in international institutions

Source: Simplified reproduction from Moravcsik 1998: 24.

are translated into different observable implications and confronted with historical evidence. Although Moravcsik does not use the term "process tracing," his methodological principles match the method well:

In each case, a consistent set of competing hypotheses is derived from general theories; the decision is disaggregated to generate sufficient observations to test those hypotheses; and, wherever possible, potentially controversial attributes of motive or strategy are backed by "hard" primary sources (direct evidence of decision-making) rather than "soft" or secondary sources.

Moravcsik is also aware of the advantages and disadvantages of process tracing: "Adherence to these three methodological principles has disadvantages – it accounts for the length of the book, as well as its continuous alternation between narrative and analysis – but the aim is to facilitate more reliable causal inference" (Moravcsik 1998: 10).

In more detail, the rationalist framework of the stages of negotiation in international cooperation and integration is an actor-centered framework providing the micro foundations for integration outcomes at the macro level (ibid.: 24). It is thus in line with the methodologically individualist recipes for constructing causal mechanisms in the social sciences. The first stage is about national preference formation (macro-micro) followed by interstate bargaining and institutional choice (micro-macro) with bounded rationality providing the (unobserved and untested) micro-micro link. At the stage of national preference formation, Moravcsik distinguishes between economic and geopolitical interests. At the stage of interstate bargaining, agreements could be explained either on the basis of asymmetrical interdependence or supranational entrepreneurship. Finally, institutional choice may be the result of federalist ideology, centralized technocratic management, or the need for credible commitment. Economic interests, asymmetrical interdependence, and the search for credible commitments constitute the main elements of the liberal-intergovernmentalist mechanism of integration.

Moravcsik disaggregates each of the three stages into further process-level indicators. For the preference formation stage, for instance, he checks whether variation in interests is across issues (evidence for liberal intergovernmentalism) or across countries (evidence for geopolitical ideas and interests); when shifts in preferences occurred; how consistent EC policy was with other policies; who the key actors and coalitions were; and which interests or concerns were prioritized in domestic deliberations. Some of the indicators are based on characteristic patterns of cross-case variation; others correspond more closely to the idea that causal factors (such as interests) leave "traces," for example, in the temporal sequence of events or discourses. But Moravcsik's selection is typical for the eclectic use of different kinds of "non-comparable" (Gerring) pieces of evidence in process tracing.

In general, Moravcsik's three-stage rationalist framework of the stages of negotiation is not a straightjacket for comparative theory testing and does not do injustice to the competitors of liberal intergovernmentalism. All theories under scrutiny are actor-centered and rationalist theories. All of them make assumptions about preferences and negotiations. In addition, the omission of the micro-micro link of "rational choice" from process tracing is perfectly justified. If all theories share this assumption, there is no analytical leverage to be gained from examining it empirically.

Liberal intergovernmentalism does not compete with each theory at each stage of the process. For instance, neofunctionalism also assumes economic interests; hard intergovernmental bargaining and asymmetrical interdependence are in line with realism. To overcome theoretical indeterminacy and to demonstrate that the liberal-intergovernmentalist explanation is better than the alternatives, it would therefore not have been sufficient to just focus on a single stage of the process. In other words, national preference formation and interstate bargaining each provide a "smoking-gun" test for liberal intergovernmentalism. Taken together, they qualify as a "doubly decisive test" because they not only demonstrate sufficiency, but also "shrink the hoop" until none of the competitors fits through it (Chapter 1; Bennett, this volume, Appendix; see also Mahoney 2012).

Does this mean that, from the point of view of efficient process tracing, the final stage – institutional choice – would have been dispensable? This depends on the two considerations explicated in the previous section. First, is institutional choice the crucial process element for any of the theories involved? Institutional choice as such is an important but secondary concern for liberal intergovernmentalism; the emphasis is clearly on preference formation and interstate bargaining. It is certainly not crucial for realism (which does not even feature as one of the alternative explanations here). As I will argue in a moment, it is also not the defining process feature for neofunctionalism. One may argue, however, that institutional choice is the key feature of federalism. In general, federalist theory (in European integration) is poorly specified. Yet, it has always put a clear emphasis on the "form" of integration. Whereas functionalism argued that "form follows function," federalism stipulated that "function follows form." In this perspective, examining the choice of institutional form is crucial for eliminating federalism as a competitor and should be part of an efficient process-tracing analysis.

Second, however, is institutional choice an independent stage of the causal process? In Moravcsik's process-tracing framework, the first stage is national preference formation. Since the analysis shows that national preferences are indeed predominantly economic and only to a minor extent motivated by geopolitical concerns or federalist ideology, realism and federalism are "out." If, as rationalist institutionalism assumes, institutional choice is functional and depends on the interests of the participating actors, it is hard to see how institutional choice should have been motivated by federalist or anti-federalist ideology or how it should have led to federal (state-like, democratic) European institutions as a result of economic preferences and intergovernmental bargaining. In this perspective, the study of institutional choice would indeed have been dispensable for efficiency reasons. If federalism is disconfirmed by an analysis of preference formation and if institutional choice is largely dependent on preferences, federalism could hardly have been supported by an analysis of institutional choice.

There is, however, one omission in the framework that stacks the deck unfairly in favor of liberal intergovernmentalism and to the disadvantage of neofunctionalism: the feedback link between integration outcomes and preferences. This is not just one additional part of the causal process on which liberal intergovernmentalism and neofunctionalism disagree. The feedback loop is central to a fully specified causal mechanism in the social sciences; and it is the essential element of the neofunctionalist causal mechanism of integration.

Neofunctionalism is a historical–institutionalist and dynamic theory. It does not dispute that the initial steps of integration match liberal intergovernmentalist assumptions about the centrality of exogenous state preferences and intergovernmental bargaining power. It stipulates, however, that once supranational organizations and rules are in place, integration produces unanticipated, unintended, and often undesired consequences and escapes the control of the states. For instance, integration may create additional transnational interactions that create demand for more integration. Supranational organizations use the regime rules and the competences they have been given by the states not only to stabilize cooperation, but also to further develop the rules and expand their own powers. The externalities of integration in one policy create demand for integration in functionally adjacent policy areas. As a result, the integration outcome modifies the material and institutional constraints under which the states operate and likely also affects societal and governmental interests. Moravcsik's framework, however, does not include the feedback process and thus does not allow us to study whether or not national preferences become endogenous.

Finally, Moravcsik achieves external validity not by carefully selecting typical, diverse, or hard cases of integration, but by doing a series of process-tracing analyses for all major treaty revisions in European integration up to the time of writing. The result is a book of 500 pages. This is hardly efficient, but is justifiable given the problems of heterogeneity, time dependence, and small-n for a comparative analysis of integration decisions from the 1950s to the early 1990s. It would also have been difficult to find an uncontroversial hard case for confirming liberal intergovernmentalism vis-à-vis all competing explanations. In summary, Moravcsik's *Choice for Europe* is an excellent example of efficient process tracing – with the exception of being "too efficient" regarding the omission of the feedback link from the causal process.

Paul Pierson, "The Path to European Integration"

Paul Pierson focuses precisely on the gap in Moravcsik's process-tracing framework. He criticizes the "snapshot" view of European integration that omits the consequences of integration decisions for member-state control. Whereas he concedes that "*at any given point in time*, the key propositions of intergovernmentalist theory are likely to hold" (Pierson 1996: 126 [emphasis in original]), the theory seriously underestimates "the lags between decisions and long-term consequences, as well as the constraints that emerge from societal adaptations and shifts in policy preferences that occur during the interim" (ibid.).

Based on historical–institutionalist assumptions that elaborate on and partly contradict those of Moravcsik's functional theory of institutions, Pierson develops a causal mechanism for the "missing link" in Moravcsik's framework. In a first step, he argues that member states are likely to lose control of the institutions they created owing to the partial autonomy of EC institutions, the restricted time horizons of political decision-makers, unanticipated consequences such as overload and spill-over resulting from high issue density, and unexpected shifts in government preferences. In a second step, he claims that member states are unable to reassert control because of supranational actors' resistance, institutional barriers to reform (such as veto powers or high voting thresholds), or sunk costs that raise the price of exit to the point that exit threats by member states lose credibility.

Pierson then combines these elements of the causal mechanism in an arrow diagram (see Figure 4.1) that illustrates the feedback link between "institutional and policy outcomes" at T_0 (as explained by liberal intergovernmentalism) and the member-state preferences, bargaining power, and power of other actors

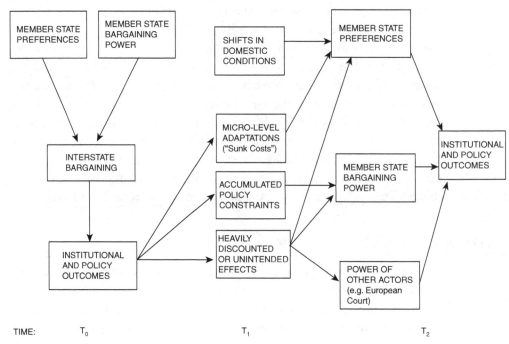

Figure 4.1   The causal mechanism in "The Path to European Integration"
Source: Reproduction from Pierson 1996: 149

that shape institutional and policy outcomes at T_2. At T_1 "micro-level adaptations ('sunk costs')," "accumulated policy constraints," "heavily discounted or unintended effects" as well as "shifts in domestic conditions" modify member-state preferences, constrain or rebalance member-state bargaining power, and/or increase the power of other actors, thereby producing outcomes that would not have occurred in the absence of the institutional effects that liberal intergovernmentalism does not include. In a final step, Pierson briefly analyzes three cases in the area of social policy to illustrate these institutional effects (for a more extensive analysis of EC social policy, see Leibfried and Pierson 1995).

Pierson's article is again an excellent example of an efficient process-tracing design. First, it demonstrates how theories can and need to be elaborated for the process tracing of causal mechanisms (Chapter 1, p. 30; Jacobs, this volume, Chapter 2). Pierson explicates process-level arguments that are merely implicit and underdeveloped in the original formulation of neofunctionalism. In addition, he provides micro foundations for the various spill-over effects theorized by neofunctionalism. Finally, he combines the elements of the causal mechanism in a process model that is represented as an arrow diagram.

Second, Pierson picks a hard case for neofunctionalism to build external validity for his analysis. According to Pierson: "Social policy is widely considered to be an area where member-state control remains unchallenged" (Pierson 1996: 148). He goes on to argue that the "need for action at the European level has not been self-evident" (ibid.), presumably because issue-specific international interdependence was low. In addition, "member states have been quite sensitive to intrusions on a core area of national sovereignty" (ibid.), and earlier attempts by the Commission to strengthen the social dimension of European integration have not been met with success. In a typical justification for a hard-case design, he concludes that "even in this area – where an intergovernmentalist account seems highly plausible – a historical institutionalist perspective casts the development of European policy in quite a different light" (Pierson 1996: 150). By extension, we can infer that if the mechanism proposed by historical institutionalism works effectively under these unfavorable circumstances, it is likely to be even more powerful in "easier" policy fields.

This is not to say that the process-tracing design could not be improved. Although it is clear that the process-tracing case study is placed in a competitive setting between historical institutionalism and intergovernmentalism, the alternative expectations of liberal intergovernmentalism for the feedback link are not explicitly formulated. For one, it is sometimes not sufficiently clear how compatible and incompatible elements of the historical–institutionalist mechanism are with liberal intergovernmentalism. For instance, shifts in domestic conditions, one element in Pierson's account, would fit a liberal-intergovernmentalist account as well and thus do not help to discriminate between the two theories. The question is rather whether such shifts could have been anticipated at the time of the negotiations, but were discarded in favor of short-term gains and at the price of long-term losses. This is, indeed, Pierson's argument in the case of British Prime Minister Major's refusal to sign a Social Protocol at Maastricht (Pierson 1996: 155).

In addition, the crucial element in the feedback mechanism for the theory competition is not that institutions develop in ways that governments did not fully foresee at the time of their making – remember that Moravcsik starts from the assumption of bounded rationality, and elaborating incomplete contracts and dealing with uncertainty are the major reasons for creating supranational organizations. The core issue is whether governments are able to correct institutional developments that run counter to their own preferences. Efficient process tracing would thus focus less on the link between T_0 and T_1 and more on the link between T_1 and T_2. It would need to show that member-state preferences at T_2 were based not on exogenous domestic or international situations (such as changes in the domestic power of interest groups or changes in international interdependence), but on endogenous institutional effects of European integration. In case member-state preferences did not differ from T_0, the analysis would have to show that even powerful governments tried in vain to rein in supranational organizations or change European rules because of resistance, institutional barriers, or weak credibility of exit threats.

The case studies in Pierson's article either do not engage in such focused process-level competitive tests (as in the case of workplace health and safety) or provide less than conclusive results (as in the case of gender policy). Finally, the Social Protocol was still too recent at the time of writing to observe longer-term institutional effects. However, Pierson correctly predicted that the next Labour Government would sign the protocol and thus constrain British social policy more than if Major had negotiated and signed a watered-down version in Maastricht.

In all fairness, it also needs to be mentioned that Pierson's 1996 article was mainly meant to set the agenda for and design a competitive process-tracing analysis rather than conducting it at the necessary level of detail (Pierson 1996: 158). He admits to "daunting" challenges "for those wishing to advance a historical institutionalist account" (ibid.: 157), such as "to trace the motivations of political actors in order to separate the intended from the unintended" or "determining the impact of sunk costs on current decision-making" (ibid.: 158). Pierson is also keenly aware of the fundamental trade-off involved in process tracing: "The evidentiary requirements encourage a focus on detailed analyses of particular cases, rendering investigations vulnerable to the critique that the cases examined are unrepresentative" (ibid.). This statement again points to the need to design process-tracing analyses efficiently in terms of both internal and external validity. By choosing hard cases from the area of social policy, Pierson did much to strengthen the potential generalizability of his results. In contrast, the specification of competitive observable implications for the crucial process elements was still underdeveloped in the 1996 article.

Craig Parsons, *A Certain Idea of Europe*

Craig Parsons shares the interest of all integration theories in explaining the EU as "the major exception in the thinly institutionalized world of international politics" (Parsons 2003: 1). In contrast to liberal intergovernmentalism, however, he claims that a "set of ideas" rather than structural economic incentives was responsible for this development; and while he agrees with historical institutionalists about the centrality of path-dependent institutionalization, he puts the emphasis on the "institutionalization of ideas," "effectively defining the interests even of actors who long advocated other ideas" (ibid.: 2), rather than on institutional constraints on governments' material interests and cost–benefit calculations.

Parsons's book is a study of French policy-making on European integration from 1947 to 1997. He subdivides this period into five steps of integration from the European Coal and Steel Community (ECSC) to Maastricht, but also analyzes two instances of failure: the European Defence Community of the early 1950s and the "empty chair crisis" of 1965 and 1966. The temporal scope of the book is thus similar to Moravcsik's *Choice of Europe*, except that he focuses on France (rather than France, Germany, and the UK, as Moravcsik does).

According to Parsons, the selection of France is justified because France was the pivotal country for supranational integration in Europe: "The victory of the community project was not determined solely in France, but the key battle of European ideas occurred here." In addition, he classifies France as a hard case for his ideational account and an easy case for its competitors. Parsons claims to tell "the story of how the state that invented the state, famous for its jealous defense of autonomy, with a deep bias toward dirigiste economic policies, delegated unprecedented amounts of sovereignty to a neoliberal and monetarist framework" (Parsons 2003: 33). From the point of view of efficient process tracing, France is thus a good choice.

More than Moravcsik or Pierson, Parsons refers directly to process tracing – probably because the term had become more familiar to integration scholars in the meantime. For instance, he laments that other work has claimed the causal impact of ideas "without tracing the process by which certain ideas become embedded as constitutive norms or identities" and vows "to focus on this link" (Parsons 2003: 6).

Parsons does not develop the same kind of semi-formalized and graphically illustrated process model as Moravcsik and Pierson, but a causal mechanism starting with preferences, moving on to collective interaction, and ending with feedback can easily be reconstructed from the theoretical chapter of his book. In addition, the ideational argument is contrasted with and tested against structural alternatives (realism, liberalism, and functional institutionalism) and institutionalism (neofunctionalism).

The first stage is preferences. Parsons argues that initial preferences on integration are ideational rather than structural. Conflict takes place between traditionalists, confederalists, and advocates of supranational community rather than between parties, bureaucracies, or economic groups. Correspondingly, the first step of process tracing is to determine whether or not preferences on integration are cross-cutting groups based on structural interests and positions. In addition, Parsons looks for persisting debate along ideational lines. "As long as current patterns of mobilization do not trace to current objective conditions (and do trace to differences in rhetoric), we have evidence that ideational factors are currently influencing action" (Parsons 2003: 14).

The second, transformational stage analyzes how individual preferences of policymakers are transformed into French governmental policy. After all, "variation in individuals' ideas does not mean ideas matter in government strategies" (Parsons 2003: 14). Parsons's argument in this part of the causal process is not "inherently ideational." Rather, leaders that have been (s)elected on the basis of other cleavages use the discretionary space they have on the integration issue to pursue their supranational ideas. It is therefore historically contingent and not part of an ideational, structural, or institutional mechanism whether leaders with supranational ideas or leaders with traditionalist or confederal ideas come to power. Parsons makes an interesting and non-trivial point which completes the narrative sequence from individual preferences to government policy. Yet, the function of analyzing this stage of the process is unclear: because it does not directly test ideational effects against its alternatives, efficient process tracing could have done without the analysis of this stage.

Moreover, a second part of the transformational mechanism is missing in Parsons's argument: the micro-macro link from individual state preferences to European integration outcomes, which features prominently in Moravcsik's account of intergovernmental bargaining, is dealt with only in passing. Parsons claims that "without the community ideas of French leaders, today's Europe would look much like the rest of modern international politics" (Parsons 2003: 27). Whereas all other governments would have been willing to settle for less ambitious institutional solutions, "French insistence on the community model repeatedly decided the outcome" (ibid.: 2). Yet, this is not a mechanism-based argument. It is not clear how France has been able to impose its community ideas on its partners. Was it bargaining power, as structuralists would claim, or was it persuasion or social influence as an ideational account would have to show? If institutional feedback is the missing link in liberal intergovernmentalism, intergovernmental negotiations are the missing link in Parsons's "certain idea of Europe."

In contrast, Parsons returns to the competitive testing of causal mechanisms at the final stage: the institutional feedback. From an efficiency point of view, we can ask again whether the analysis of this link is necessary. First, is this link the crucial one for any of the competing theories? Second, is it conceivable that structuralism or institutionalism explains the feedback stage if the study shows that the French debate on European integration does not follow structural lines (and that government leaders pursue European policy independent of structural cleavages)? Both questions can be answered in the affirmative. First, as I have argued in my criticism of Moravcsik, the institutional feedback is central for neofunctionalism. Second, Parsons argues that even if structural factors were indeterminate at the beginning, structural signals may "have clarified over time" and shape preferences at subsequent stages of the integration process (Parsons 2003: 15).

Were it correct, we would expect that the earlier dissidents' adjustments traced to identifiable structural shifts (economic, geopolitical, or electoral); that French groups or parties displayed greater internal agreement before deciding on later institutional steps (the imperatives forward now being clear); and that dissidents pointed to exogenous pressures to justify their alignment. (Parsons 2003: 16)

This is a clear process-tracing agenda. Against structuralism, Parsons claims that:

broader elite agreement on European strategies arose in discrete steps that followed institutional initiatives by pro-community leaders, not clear structural shifts. Only after advocates of that agenda successfully asserted it in a new European deal did proponents of other views reluctantly adjust their strategies to a revised institutional status quo. In so doing, they consistently referred to pressures from the new institutions themselves. In a short period of time after each deal, they changed their strategies and rhetoric to present the institutional steps they had opposed as "in French interests." (Parsons 2003: 16)

At the theoretical level, Parsons also distinguishes ideational and rational–institutionalist mechanisms of institutional feedback in terms of conversion versus constraint logics. In the end, however, he does not really engage in competitive process tracing for the reason that both logics would be hard to distinguish empirically (ibid.: 18). That means, however, that Parsons's criticism of neofunctionalism ultimately rests on the rejection of interest-based integration preferences rather than on the core claim of Pierson and others that integrated institutions affect policymakers' preferences and behavior through rational adaptation and constraints.

As a final consideration, could Parsons have worked with fewer cases to make his point? First, the argument about the institutional construction of interests requires a longitudinal analysis. Second, it is most effective if it includes a period in which anti-supranationalist leaders made French policy. Thus, an analysis spanning the time period from the 1950s via the "Gaullist" 1960s to the relaunch of supranationalism in the internal market program was necessary. Only the analysis of monetary policy in addition to single-market policies may have been redundant.

In summary, Craig Parsons's study is highly efficiently designed to demonstrate the ideational formation of integration preferences against materialist, structuralist accounts of "objective" preferences. By contrast, the transformation and feedback stages contribute less to confirming an ideational explanation of integration and defending it against alternative explanations. For these stages of the process, the process-tracing design would have benefited from an additional process link to be studied (transformation of French preferences to European outcomes) and from the specification of observable implications discriminating between conversion and constraints as institutional feedback mechanisms.

Frank Schimmelfennig, *The EU, NATO, and the Integration of Europe*

My book on "rules and rhetoric" in the enlargement of the EU and NATO (Schimmelfennig 2003) deals with an aspect of integration that had long been neglected by the literature. Whereas integration theory has almost exclusively been concerned with "vertical integration," the transfer of powers from the nation-state to an international organization, integration also has a "horizontal" dimension, the expansion of integrated rules and institutions to additional states and territories. Concerning this horizontal dimension, integration theory asks why and under which conditions non-member countries seek to join an international organization and member countries agree to admit a new member state.

In terms of theory, the book is similar to that of Parsons (2003) in that it puts forward an ideational explanation of integration. In particular, it claims that rationalist institutionalism can only partly explain the Eastern enlargement of the EU (and NATO). The book starts with a congruence analysis of Eastern enlargement, which shows that rationalist institutionalism accounts for the interest of Central and Eastern European countries (CEECs) to join the EU, but not for the interest of the member states to admit them. The CEECs were highly dependent on trade with and investments from the EU and were poorer than the member states. They therefore stood to gain from full access to the internal market, subsidies from the EU budget, and decision-making power in the integrated institutions. The member states, however, had few incentives to admit the CEECs. First, the CEECs' economic and trade relevance for most member states was low. Second, the prospect of their accession raised concerns about trade and budget competition. Third, massive enlargement dilutes the old members' voting power. Finally, the CEECs depended much more on the EU than the other way around and did not have the bargaining power to put pressure on the EU to admit them.

In contrast, a second congruence analysis based on sociological or constructivist institutionalism shows a strong fit of explanatory conditions and outcome. Starting from the assumption that the EU is a community of liberal European states, the sociological or constructivist hypothesis posits that all liberal European states are entitled to membership in the EU if they so desire. This holds even if their admission produces net costs for the organization or individual old member states. In cases of conflict between material (economic) interests and liberal community norms, the norm of liberal membership overrides the economic interests and the superior bargaining power of member states. The analysis shows that the EU invited those ex-communist countries to accession negotiations that had consolidated liberal democracy; in addition, those that had become consolidated democracies earlier were in general also invited to membership talks earlier. In a next step, the book reports a large-n event-history analysis of enlargement decisions in three major Western European international organizations: the EU, NATO, and the Council of Europe. This analysis confirms democracy in European non-member countries as the most relevant factor of enlargement. In summary, the study establishes a robust correlation between liberal democracy and EU enlargement, which serves as a starting point for the exploration of the causal mechanism linking community norms with enlargement decisions.

The need for process tracing arises from the fact that various modes of action are theoretically compatible with the covariation between community norms and enlargement decisions: habitual, normative, communicative, and rhetorical action. I suggest that the causal mechanism of social action can be conceived as a sequence of four stages or links (Schimmelfennig 2003: 157–159). The first is *cognitions*, that is, the set of beliefs or ideas actors hold about the world and the actors' ways of thinking and making decisions. The second level is the *goals* actors set for themselves and seek to attain through their actions. The third is the individual *behavior* actors choose in light of their goals and cognitions. Finally, two or more individual behaviors form an *interaction* that brings about a collective outcome. Social norms can become influential at each of these stages or levels. The earlier in the process they do, the deeper the institutional impact on social action. Each of the four modes of action is based on the assumption

Table 4.3 Modes of action in *The EU, NATO, and the Integration of Europe*

	Norm impact on			
Logic of action	Cognitions	Goals	Behavior	Outcome
Habitual	X	X	X	X
Normative		X	X	X
Communicative			X	X
Rhetorical				X
Rational				

Source: Slightly modified reproduction from Schimmelfennig 2003: 158.

that rules have an impact on decision-making at different stages in the process of social action (Table 4.3).

The stages of rule impact match the major links in the "bathtub" template of analytic social science. The habitual mode of action is the most structuralist one and leaves the least room for individual agency. According to this mode, rules have the deepest possible impact because they already shape social action at the level of cognitions. Normative action leaves more room for agency. It conceives the goals of the actors as norm-based. But they are a result of reflective and purposive choice, not of habit. Communicative action does not postulate norm-based goals and preferences, but norm-based behavior. It assumes that actors with conflicting preferences enter into a discourse about legitimate political ends and means in which they argue according to normative standards of true reasoning and rational argument. Unlike communicative action, rhetorical action starts from the assumption that both the preferences and the behavior of the actors are determined by individual and instrumental choices. According to this mode of action, social norms will, however, affect the process of interaction and, as a consequence, the collective outcome. Rational action is the null hypothesis. It excludes the impact of norms at any stage of the causal mechanism. It was already disconfirmed by the congruence analysis and therefore did not need to be included in the process tracing. Note that whereas Moravcsik's process-tracing analysis does not deal with the modes of action because all theories in his set of competitors are rationalist theories, the micro-micro link is of key interest here.

While it is difficult to test the dispositional features and cognitive mechanisms assumed by the modes of action directly, they leave characteristic traces in verbal and non-verbal behaviors. To facilitate comparison and competitive evaluation, the observable implications that I specify for each process hypothesis refer to a common set of phenomena: (1) the CEECs' enlargement preferences; (2) the member states' enlargement preferences; (3) the initial reaction of the organizations to the CEECs' bid for membership; (4) the decision-making process within the organizations; and (5) the effects of enlargement on later enlargement rounds. I further refer to several features of efficient process tracing:

Finally, note that, even though process analysis results in a more narrative form of presentation than the correlational outcome analysis of NATO and EU enlargement, I do not provide a full chronological account of the enlargement decision-making processes that one would expect in a historiographical perspective. Rather, I present "analytical episodes" focused on examining the empirical implications of the process hypotheses under scrutiny. These episodes sometimes violate the chronological order and regularly neglect those aspects of the enlargement process that are not relevant for hypothesis-testing. (Schimmelfennig 2003: 159)

I then formulate five expectations (relating to the five types of observable implications) for each mode of action. The empirical analysis starts with the candidates' and the member states' enlargement preferences and the initial decision-making process. Because the observations do not meet the expectations based on the habitual and normative modes of action, these modes are excluded from further analysis. In contrast, the egoistic state preferences and the strategic initial reaction of the member states were compatible with the communicative and rhetorical modes of action. In the next step, I therefore focus on the further negotiating and decision-making process of the EU and NATO as well as on subsequent enlargement rounds in order to discriminate between the two remaining modes. In the end, the observational implications of "rhetorical action" are shown to be more consistent with the actual process than those of "communicative action." Rhetorical action thus demonstrates how egoistic preferences and strategic action can still result in norm-conforming outcomes.

Does this design meet the criteria of efficiency set up above? First, the process tracing is clearly complementary to a set of congruence and comparative analyses that put into question rationalist–institutionalist theories such as liberal intergovernmentalism and establish a correlation between community norms and enlargement decisions. It is used to resolve a problem of equifinality: multiple mechanisms through which norms may bring about norm-conforming behavior (Chapter 1, pp. 19, 21). Second, I contrasted several causal mechanisms and their observational consequences resulting from different assumptions about the actors' modes of action.

But was it necessary to study all five links in order to determine the causal mechanism linking community norms and enlargement decisions? In hindsight, two of them appear redundant. First, since what really matters is the decision-making of the international organization, the preferences of the applicants do not seem to be relevant. The four modes of social action under study could have been causally effective regardless of the motivations and goals of the CEECs. (And, indeed, the analysis of their preferences proved inconclusive.) Second, the brief analysis of subsequent enlargement rounds was not necessary either. Even though this analysis provides further evidence for the rhetorical action hypothesis, the effect of the first round of Eastern enlargement in the EU or NATO was not crucial for any of the competing hypotheses nor needed to discriminate between any of them. From the point of view of efficiency, it would have been enough to study the member states' enlargement preferences and initial reactions as well as the subsequent negotiating behavior resulting in the decision to admit the democratically consolidated CEECs.

Finally, I do not explicitly discuss the generalizability of the findings of the process-tracing analysis. I chose the case of Eastern enlargement out of interest in the issue and based on the perception that Eastern enlargement was a highly relevant event in the history of European integration. Whereas it is plausible to assume that Eastern enlargement constitutes a hard case for rationalist institutionalism, it may well constitute an easy case for sociological institutionalism. The external validity of my 2003 findings is thus uncertain (see also Checkel, this volume, Chapter 3).

Conclusions

In this chapter, I have made the case for "efficient" process tracing, which builds on the best practices advanced by Bennett and Checkel in the introductory chapter. However, I further elaborate on these practices to cope with four core challenges that hamper the effectiveness and efficiency of process tracing as an inferential method: the large amount of resources needed; the absence of formal, quantifiable measures of fit; the temptation of storytelling; and the limits to generalization.

As a partial remedy to these problems, I proposed making process tracing complementary to analyses of congruence and correlation; selecting representative or crucial cases; specifying causal mechanisms and their observable implications ex ante and according to basic templates of analytic social science; and designing process tracing as competitive theory testing with a focus on the crucial process links on which the theories differ. Following these recommendations, I suggest, helps us design harder tests, impedes storytelling, reduces the required time and resources for conducting process tracing, and improves generalizability. It thus makes process tracing both more rigorous and more efficient.

There are several prerequisites of efficient process tracing. It requires studies establishing congruence or correlation in our area of interest; theories with a well-specified causal mechanism; and clear and observable implications of this causal mechanism. These prerequisites for engaging in efficient process tracing may not be fulfilled. This does not mean, however, that the researcher should delve inductively into the case. Often, time and resources are better spent by doing a comparative analysis that helps us pick a suitable case for process tracing and by elaborating and operationalizing the causal mechanism. In principle, social scientists have a big toolbox full of the "nuts and bolts" or "cogs and wheels" (Elster 1989) to construct theoretically plausible and consistent causal mechanisms deductively.

Efficient process tracing will also be undermined if either the implications of the theories or the available evidence do not lend themselves to rigorous tests that allow the researcher to accept and reject theories "beyond reasonable doubt." But this applies to research in general. Importantly, because of its deductive design, efficient process tracing is more likely to alert us to problems of indeterminacy than the inductive search for causal processes.

At the same time, efficient process tracing does come at a price in that it passes over several features that researchers may particularly value. First, it replaces the full narrative from cause to outcome with a few process snapshots. Second, we may rashly accept an explanation if one theory quickly outperforms alternative explanations at an early stage of process-tracing analysis. It may well be that this explanation would not have performed well at later stages of the causal process or with regard to process links that were not tested because they were uncontroversial. Third, by privileging hypothesis testing over hypothesis generation or the open exploration of explanations, efficient process tracing discourages or even prevents researchers from discovering new causal mechanisms or process features. Fourth, efficient process tracing is mainly designed to bring about scientific development. It is certainly not the best approach to make process tracing relevant for policy.

As a final thought, we need to bear in mind that efficiency is about *designing* process-tracing studies, rather than actually conducting the analysis. In the end, the quality of the data, their analysis, and their interpretation are decisive for the conclusions we draw on the basis of efficient process tracing.

5 What makes process tracing good?
Causal mechanisms, causal inference, and the completeness standard in comparative politics

David Waldner

Introduction

Why did some European democracies survive the interwar period while others were replaced by fascist dictatorships? Why do some instances of civil war culminate in democratic transitions? What are the causes of the emergence of sovereign nation-states in early modern Europe? Scholars addressing these foundational questions of comparative politics have been among the pioneers of process tracing. A close examination of a small number of such important studies should be illuminating for our efforts to articulate "best practices" for causal inference via within-case analysis, or process tracing. On the one hand, these studies give us an opportunity to observe closely the procedures and standards that have emerged over the past decade – practices that are summarized concisely in the editors' introduction to this volume. On the other, they give us the raw material for thinking about a refined and expanded set of best practices and evaluative standards.

I develop these arguments by closely examining a small number of exemplars of process tracing. Before conducting that assessment, however, it is helpful to highlight where these studies overlap with our extant understanding of process tracing, but also where they direct us toward some new methodological directions.

First, the studies assessed here completely comport with the claim that process tracing works by "using evidence to affirm some explanations and cast doubt upon others," an approach that "emphasizes that the probative value of evidence relative to competing explanations is more important than the

For comments on earlier versions, I thank the volume's editors, as well as Gerard Alexander, Robert Mickey, and Elisabeth Wood.

number of pieces of evidence" (Bennett and Checkel, this volume, Chapter 1, p. 16). Second, the logic of hypothesis testing can be readily and fruitfully reconstructed according to Van Evera's framework, in which hypotheses have varying degrees of certitude and uniqueness and therefore can be used to affirm or disconfirm explanations (1997: 31–32).[1] Hoop tests, for example, are tests of hypotheses that have certitude, but not uniqueness. Failing these tests eliminates a hypothesis, but passing them does not confirm it; in other words, passing a hoop test is necessary but not sufficient for confirming a hypothesis. Smoking-gun tests, on the other hand, have uniqueness, but not certitude: passing them is thus sufficient but not necessary for confirming a hypothesis. As Bennett (this volume, Appendix; 2008) argues, we can fruitfully interpret passage or failure of these tests within a Bayesian framework.

Third, the works reviewed below are consistent with many of the ten standards enumerated in the editors' introduction. They systematically consider alternative explanations; they are aware of and take measures to safeguard against confirmation bias; they amass considerable amounts of evidence from varied sources, including archival research and interviews; and they combine process tracing with cross-case comparisons to good effect (Chapter 1, pp. 21–31). It is reassuring to know that some standards of good process tracing have general applicability.

Yet, there are ways in which these studies either depart from the conventional wisdom or embody standards and practices that have not yet been explicitly discussed. First, while all research no doubt reflects a balance between inductive and deductive reasoning, those explored below had their origins in long-standing theoretical disputes, not in the type of "soaking and poking" discussed in the editors' introduction (Chapter 1, p. 18). Indeed, the majority of the works covered here begin with models of decision-making that link macro-structures to micro-level action. Consequently, it is clear that each author was able to construct a relatively lengthy and dense causal chain prior to beginning his or her research, even if that chain was not presented in the format I recommend below. Second, these studies invite us to pay close attention to the issue of *exogeneity*, a topic which is not sufficiently discussed in the literature on process tracing. In statistical parlance, exogeneity – or conditional assignment of treatment and outcomes – is the assumption that assignment to treatment is independent of outcome variables conditional on a set of pre-treatment covariates. The concept of a critical juncture is a metaphor for

---

[1] For further discussion of Van Evera's framework, see Chapter 1, pp. 16–17, as well as Bennett 2008; 2010; Mahoney 2010; and Collier 2011.

conditions that might satisfy exogeneity. However, as the studies here demonstrate, we need more refined analytic tools to better justify assumptions about it.

Finally, and most importantly, these works direct us toward an important standard for assessing causal inference based on process tracing, which I formulate in the following way.

Process tracing yields causal and explanatory adequacy insofar as: (1) it is based on a causal graph whose individual nodes are connected in such a way that they are jointly sufficient for the outcome; (2) it is also based on an *event-history map* that establishes valid correspondence between the events in each particular case study and the nodes in the causal graph; (3) theoretical statements about causal mechanisms link the nodes in the causal graph to their descendants and the empirics of the case studies allow us to infer that the events were in actuality generated by the relevant mechanisms; and (4) rival explanations have been credibly eliminated, by direct hypothesis testing or by demonstrating that they cannot satisfy the first three criteria listed above.

Let us call this the *completeness standard*, for it requires a complete causal graph, a complete set of descriptive inferences from particular historical settings to the graph, and a complete set of inferences about the causal mechanisms that generate realizations of the causal graph.

I argue that the completeness standard makes three significant contributions to our collective understanding of how we make valid causal judgments using process tracing. For one, it clarifies the concept of a process. We all know that a process is the set of intermediary links between a cause and its effect. Beyond this minimal understanding, we have not developed any standards for appraising the validity of a claim to have correctly articulated these connections. In their pioneering volume on case studies, George and Bennett state what I call the "continuity criterion":

> [*All*] the intervening steps in a case must be predicted by a hypothesis, or else that hypothesis must be amended – perhaps trivially or perhaps fundamentally – to explain that case. It is not sufficient that a hypothesis be consistent with a statistically significant number of intervening steps. (George and Bennett 2005: 207)

This is an immensely important, albeit underdeveloped, statement of a key criterion of good process tracing. Surprisingly, to the best of my knowledge, the continuity criterion has been largely ignored in all subsequent discussions of the technique. Qualitative methodologists have devoted their attention to Van Evera's framework of hypothesis testing and its connection to the concept of causal-process observations, as defined by Collier *et al.* (2010: 184–191). Along the way, the continuity criterion appears to have gotten lost. My proposal is that we use the instrument of a causal graph as the best measure of what constitutes continuity; that is, the nodes in a causal graph constitute "all the intervening steps" of a hypothesis.

A second contribution of the completeness standard is that it adds needed content to the procedure of *tracing* a causal process. Subjecting a hypothesis to a set of hoop or smoking-gun tests cannot be unproblematically equated with tracing a causal process. Many hypotheses are not causal, and many causal hypotheses do not specify a causal mechanism. The instrument of the causal graph serves the function of specifying a delimited set of causal hypotheses, each based on the identification of a set of causal mechanisms, and which collectively stand in a particular relationship to the outcome. We trace this process not by passing an arbitrary number of tests, but rather by showing that in the case or cases under study, events constitute each node of the causal graph and that a set of events is sufficient to generate the subsequent set of events by way of the relevant mechanism. We affirm this tracing of the causal process with reference to the usual criteria: construct validity, measurement validity, and measurement reliability.

A third contribution of the standard introduced here is that it supplies a much-needed *stopping rule* (see also Chapter 1, p. 21). To see why this is important, consider two scenarios. In the first scenario, hypothesis h^* competes against three rival hypotheses that exhaust the set of available alternative explanations. Each of the three rivals fails a hoop test on its independent variable; h^* passes a hoop test on its independent variable. By the logic of eliminative induction, h^* is fully vindicated by these relatively simple congruence tests; it literally has no rivals.[2] Yet, the analyst has not conducted process tracing on the intervening links between the independent variable and the outcome. To ask about a stopping rule is to ask how much additional work is required to claim that h^* is confirmed: is further process tracing necessary and, if so, how much?

In a second scenario, h^* passes a smoking-gun test. Given that passage of a smoking-gun test is sufficient to accept a hypothesis, we again ask how much additional process tracing is required to claim that h^* is confirmed. My reading of the existing literature is that there are no unambiguous answers to these questions. Therefore, we need a stopping rule, a standard that once met is sufficient to justify the belief that a claim about a cause–effect relationship "has weathered sufficient scrutiny relative to its rivals and to the current state of theory and data gathering that belief in its approximate truth is more

---

[2] This is the basis of the "modus operandi" method advanced by Scriven 1976.

reasonable than disbelief but is also subject to revision in the face of future data gathering or theorizing" (Waldner 2007: 145).

In summary, the completeness standard adds important content to the concepts of both process and tracing. It outlines a standard for determining when a process has been sufficiently traced to be descriptively valid; and it demarcates a standard for determining when process tracing yields valid causal and explanatory adequacy. My claim is not that the hypothesis testing framework adduced by Van Evera (1997) or the Bayesian analysis proposed by Bennett (this volume, Appendix) are dispensable elements of process tracing; both are central to the enterprise and consistent with the standard I propose. The value added of the completeness standard is to impose relatively heavy obligations on process tracing scholarship that wishes to claim causal and explanatory adequacy, obligations that are not explicitly addressed by existing standards. In other words, the standard is critical to closing the gap that separates the generic claim that process tracing is good from the particular claim that this or that scholarship represents good process tracing – a point explicitly recognized in this volume's opening pages (Chapter 1, p. 4). While my terminology and approach differ, I thus join with Schimmelfennig (this volume, Chapter 4) in arguing that good process tracing builds on, but goes beyond, the ten best practices advanced by the editors.

A cautionary note before proceeding – the scholarship reviewed below does not make explicit use of the completeness standard, and I cannot attest that the authors would endorse my application of it to their work. My intention is to show that some of this scholarship can be readily evaluated in light of this standard, and, perhaps more important, some does not meet it. This is key because any justifiable method must be able to distinguish competent executions from applications that, for all their worthwhile qualities, fall short of that standard (see also Checkel and Bennett, this volume, Chapter 10). My focus remains on best practices, as developed here and in Chapter 1. Beyond a few necessary preliminaries discussed in the next section, I do not provide any lengthy discussion and justification of the completeness standard, as this is done elsewhere (Waldner 2012; 2014).

Conceptual preliminaries

The foundational element of the completeness standard is the causal graph. A causal graph, depicted in Figure 5.1, is a representation or model of a chain of cause-and-effect relations, beginning with an independent variable, X,

$$X \longrightarrow M_1 \longrightarrow M_2 \longrightarrow Y$$

Figure 5.1   A causal graph

running through intervening variables or mediators, M_1, M_2, and concluding with its terminal node, Y, representing the outcome variable.

Nodes or vertices of the graph represent random variables; for simplicity, we can treat these random variables as binary variables that are either true or false. Directed edges, or arrows, refer to relations of conditional dependence. Arrows therefore represent causal mechanisms. Mechanisms should not be confused with intervening variables or mediators; M_1 and M_2 are random variables that are contingently located in non-initial and non-terminal nodes; they are not mechanisms.

Causal graphs are composed of random variables, not events. They are designed to be estimated using statistical techniques, not process tracing. Their function in the completeness standard is to represent, as fully as possible, *the set of causal relationships that constitute the process being traced by within-case evidence*. This function, in turn, aids evaluation in two ways. First, it allows us to consider the qualities of the causal process itself, in particular whether the nodes of the causal graph are collectively sufficient to generate the outcome. As we shall see below, establishing causal sufficiency for the graph is not an easy task. Second, the causal graph highlights the location of the relevant causal mechanisms that must be identified and confirmed. Both of these foci of evaluation can take place prior to considering the within-case evidence that will constitute the tracing of the process.

These two functions of the causal graph refer to causal adequacy and explanatory adequacy, respectively. By causal adequacy, I mean our assessment of the logical coherence and sufficiency of a causal graph. Our considerations should include the following: Does each node in the causal graph imply its successor? Are there missing nodes? Is the set of non-terminal nodes sufficient to reach the outcome node? Insofar as we answer these questions affirmatively, we can have greater confidence that the empirical confirmation of the graph supports the valid causal inference that X causes Y. Explanatory adequacy, on the other hand, refers to our knowledge of the relevant causal mechanisms linking each node in the causal graph. It is perfectly possible and permissible to have confidence in a causal relationship that supports intervention without knowing the underlying causal mechanisms; causal inference, in other words, is distinct from causal explanation and so we can have causal adequacy without explanatory adequacy. Humans have known for millennia that willow bark has therapeutic value; only recently have we discovered the mechanisms by which synthetic forms of willow bark – aspirin – reduce pain, fever, and swelling. Only in the past few decades have researchers gained insight into the underlying causal mechanisms and thus become able to *explain why* aspirin has therapeutic properties.[3]

Finally, let us consider how to trace the process represented by the causal graph. For each realization of the causal graph in a particular case study, process tracing requires the specification of a set of events that correspond to each node in the causal graph. Call the complete set of such correspondences an *event-history map*. Process tracing first and foremost requires this descriptive inference from event-history map to causal graph. Note, therefore, that process tracing begins by establishing some degree of analytic equivalence between a set of events and a random variable. In effect, one claims that the set of events are equivalent to a random variable realizing a particular value. This correspondence requires satisfaction of the standard desiderata: construct validity, measurement validity, and measurement reliability. Note as well that event history maps can only be formally represented by works that also provide a causal graph; because this is not yet considered a best practice, I consider only informal correspondences in the works considered below. Furthermore, process tracing involves providing warrant for the claim that each subset of events generates the next subset of events by virtue of the causal mechanisms contained in the causal graph.

Process tracing democratic transitions

Two important studies of democratic transitions, Moore (1966) and Rueschemeyer *et al.* (1992), helped to establish the value and the feasibility of using historical evidence to support causal claims. Despite their enduring theoretical and methodological influence, neither work meets some minimal standards for review here. Moore gave priority to his event-rich historical narratives over a clear statement of his theory; it is thus difficult to extract a causal graph from his immensely significant work. The completeness standard, to be clear, is by no means the exclusive measure of scholarly value.

Rueschemeyer *et al.* (1992: 29) further developed Moore's ideas about class conflict and democracy, while also providing one of the first explicit statements of how historical case studies can confirm causal claims. Specifically,

---

[3] On the distinction between causal adequacy and explanatory adequacy, see also Shadish *et al.* 2002.

one uses them to uncover the "causal forces that stand behind the relationship between development and democracy," causal forces that remain, in quantitative studies, a "black box." For two reasons, however, I omit discussion of this seminal work. First, the theoretical arguments consist of three distinct "clusters" of structural conditions that are relevant to democracy: the balance of class power, the power and autonomy of the state and its articulation with civil society, and transnational structures of power (1992: 75). It is not clear how one might combine these clusters of structural conditions into a causal graph. Second, the historical case studies are relatively abbreviated, do not cover all of this material in sufficient detail, and – in the end – the study relies heavily on exploiting cross-national variation. Therefore, while acknowledging the book's enduring significance for the study of democracy, it is not an appropriate starting point for exploring best practices and the completeness standard in process tracing.

Regime change in interwar europe

I therefore begin with Gerard Alexander's (2002) account of the sources of democratic consolidation in twentieth-century Europe. Alexander focuses on the political preferences of rightist political actors, showing in great detail how pro-authoritarian preferences in interwar Europe were gradually replaced by the acceptance of democracy in post-war Europe. His main case study is Spain, which suffered civil war in the 1930s, a long period of authoritarian rule, and then a successful transition to democracy in 1978. Alexander exerts considerable effort at falsifying rival hypotheses. Of particular interest is his claim that Rueschemeyer *et al.* are not vindicated by his case studies, for transitions to democracy were emphatically not preceded by observable shifts in the balance of class power in a way that favored workers and their pro-democratic preferences. Still, the book's claims to causal and explanatory adequacy rely heavily on the completeness standard, so I concentrate on the procedures followed by Alexander to establish rightist political preferences and then to connect those preferences to regime outcomes.

Alexander posits that rightist calculations are based on two basic interests: material well-being, such as protection of property or generating higher incomes, and physical well-being. The two interests can conflict with one another if, for example, an authoritarian regime might more reliably protect property, but less reliably protect property owners from arbitrary state violence. Given these basic interests, actors derive political preferences over regimes. These preferences are formed in specific contexts: it is not the case,

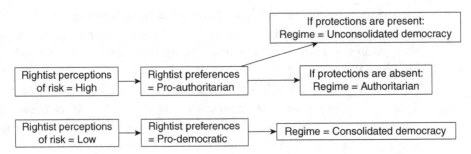

Figure 5.2   Comparative statics in *The Sources of Democratic Consolidation* (Alexander 2000)

Alexander avers, that rightists always prefer authoritarianism. The key condition is the behavior of the specific people who will be influential in either type of regime. Thus, actors' generic basic preferences merge with their highly contextualized beliefs about likely outcomes under different regimes to produce preferences for democracy or authoritarianism. When the right considers the left an unreliable partner that poses high risks to its basic interests, rightists might tolerate democracy if there are contingent protections present, such as political pacts or protective institutions (including links to paramilitaries); when these contingent protections are absent, rightists commit to authoritarianism. Democracy is consolidated only when rightists believe that the left is reliably low risk, that leftist moderation is a genuine commitment, not a tactical gesture.

I reconstruct this argument as the causal graph depicted in Figure 5.2, where the upper graph corresponds to the interwar breakdown of Spanish democracy, and the lower one to the post-war transition to democracy.

We might ask three questions about the sufficiency of this causal graph: (1) are rightist perceptions of risk exogenous variables or is there a prior variable that both determines perceptions of risk and directly influences the type of regime? (2) Are protections for rightists under democracy exogenous variables? and (3) What is the causal connection between rightist preferences and the survival or failure of democracy? That we ask such questions generates some concern that the causal graphs are not complete and sufficient for the outcome.

Turn next to the procedure by which Alexander makes descriptive inferences from the case studies to the causal graphs. Alexander devotes lengthy chapters to the breakdown of Spanish democracy in the 1930s and the transition to democracy in the 1970s. In the first half of the 1930s, the main leftist party, the Spanish Socialist Workers' Party (Partido Socialista Obrero Español or PSOE), enjoyed substantial political support. But despite the party's relatively moderate electoral platform, the Spanish right perceived a substantial threat of radicalization, from both the large social base of urban and rural (landless) workers and from the revolutionary groups to the right of the PSOE. As Alexander summarizes:

Despite the presence of several favorable conditions, the right did not commit to democracy, and the Republic never consolidated, because rightists detected high risks in democracy. These high risks were the result of the perceived susceptibility of millions of landless laborers and industrial and mining workers to revolutionary appeals threatening the right's safety, property, income, control of the workplace, and church. (Alexander 2002: 103)

Alexander provides three types of evidence in this chapter. First, he details rightist perceptions of a potentially radicalized left, showing not only that major rightist actors and groups perceived this risk, but that even leaders of the PSOE worried that the rank-and-file membership, together with millions of landless laborers, were moving to the left of the party's position. This claim is based on extensive research using local newspapers, party archives, and other contemporaneous commentaries, together with references to a large secondary literature.

Second, he compiles evidence about rightist political preferences in light of this perceived risk of leftist radicalization and violent confrontation. Most strikingly, he documents a shift from rightist acquiescence to democracy as late as 1935 to rightist defection from democracy in 1936. Again, Alexander is able to quote directly from leading rightists to demonstrate that, as long as its own electoral performance was adequate, Spanish rightists had no need to resort to an authoritarian solution. Alexander then turns to changes in 1936, when rightist preferences for an authoritarian solution, while hard to measure, were communicated to coup plotters who were assured of widespread civilian support. This "demand" for a coup was, apparently, crucial to its supply; having witnessed the failure of "socially isolated coups" in the early years of the decade, coup leaders, including Franco, took sustained measures to align their actions with civilian rightist opinion.

Finally, Alexander provides the links between rightist preferences and political outcomes. Unlike Italy, Weimar Germany, or even France, rightists did not need to cultivate paramilitary forces, for the Spanish army was large, politicized, and sympathetic to the right. As concerns about leftist radicalization intensified, Spain's rightists assiduously worked to "protect the strength of the state security apparatus and cultivate as conservative an orientation within it as possible" (Alexander 2002: 122). Thus, although this final link is not depicted in the causal graph, we can reconstruct the logic of the argument from the case-study details.

Spanish rightists' preferences for authoritarianism were historically contingent. By the late 1970s, rightists' regime preferences shifted once again, this time favoring democracy. In analogous chapter-length detail, Alexander documents changing perceptions of risk from leftist radicalism, changing political preferences among rightists, and a transition to democracy. After 1977, the PSOE continued its moderate electoral position, and the right no longer perceived a revolutionary threat stemming either from the party's working-class base or from political groups to the left of the PSOE. Importantly, Alexander provides abundant evidence that Spanish rightists came to believe that the likelihood of class conflict had been attenuated by several decades of economic growth. Consequently, the attempted military coup of 1981 did not, as many argued, reveal the fragility of Spanish democracy. While pro-coup plotters had access to coercive resources, the coup's failure draws our attention to "the heavily pro-democratic distribution of regime preferences, including among the overwhelming majority of conservatives surveyed. This distribution helped ensure the coup's failure and suggested authoritarianism's inherent implausibility" (Alexander 2002: 180–181).

Alexander's work exemplifies the careful collection of qualitative evidence to buttress claims about preferences and their consequences. Every step of the argument, from basic preferences to perceptions of risk to the availability of protective institutions and other hedging devices to ultimate regime outcomes is carefully documented for both historical periods. Particularly for the latter period, he is able to show that political actors were able to forecast, with high confidence, what the likely consequences would be of a transition to democracy. It appears that in both Spanish cases, the values of the random variable in each node are properly coded. This is an exemplary execution of descriptive inference from event-history map to causal graph. It is historical process tracing (see also Evangelista, this volume, Chapter 6) that conforms to many of the best practices – consideration of alternative explanations, the careful use of multiple data sources, and the like – discussed in Chapter 1 (pp. 20–31).

Missing from the work, however, is theoretical and empirical analysis of the determinants of leftist moderation. While vigorously arguing against a modernization theory that would claim that growing wealth bred political moderation, Alexander states that he is "agnostic as to the causes of left moderation vs. potential radicalism" (Alexander 2002: 8). Given this explicit agnosticism, we cannot say for sure that the causal graphs initiate with exogenous variables and we remain agnostic about the possibility of subsuming this work into a more extensive causal graph. In addition, as a consequence of his agnosticism about the origins of risk perceptions, the two causal graphs in Figure 5.2 are disconnected: we do not know why Spanish rightists switched from perceptions of high risk to perceptions of low risk. Finally, as we have noted, the links between rightist political preferences and regime outcomes are not adequately handled in the causal graphs. It appears correct that when rightist political preferences are predominantly pro-authoritarian, the outcome is a dictatorship, but when rightist political preferences are pro-democratic, the outcome is a democratic transition and subsequent democratic consolidation. But these final linkages await further theoretical explication and the construction of a more extensive causal graph.

Civil wars and democratic transitions in El Salvador and South Africa

Elisabeth Wood's (2000) explanation for democratic transitions in El Salvador and South Africa demonstrates that it is possible to endogenize shifts in regime preferences and hence explain more adequately the transition from democracy to dictatorship using a single unified causal graph. The core argument in *Forging Democracy from Below* is that economic and political elites calculate the costs and benefits of political exclusion and derive their regime preferences from those calculations. The key feature of oligarchic states is the reliance of elite incomes on repressive labor institutions; the need to control the political system to discipline labor induces authoritarian elite preferences. Political exclusion, however, motivates insurgent collective action. By itself, insurgent collective action will face almost insuperable challenges to overthrowing the oligarchic state.

The critical innovation introduced by Wood is that insurgent collective action transforms the nature of the economic system. In El Salvador, one of the book's two major case studies (South Africa is the other), the civil war triggered the decline of the export agriculture sector and a parallel boom in the urban commercial sector. Economic transformation directly altered elite interests, making it more likely that elites would favor compromise over stubborn commitment to political exclusion. As Wood summarizes:

> Insurgency dampens the usual returns for the elite – assets are destroyed, costly strikes occur, security costs rise, investment is suspended, and taxes increase. If sustained long enough, expected returns under democracy look attractive in comparison – if the distributional terms of the transition do not greatly threaten the status quo distribution of property rights. (Wood 2000: 15)

The process being traced in El Salvador is represented in Figure 5.3. The initial state is a labor-repressive economic system that induces elite preferences for an exclusionary regime. The comparative statics are generated by the intervention of an insurgency that in turn triggers a shift in the sectoral

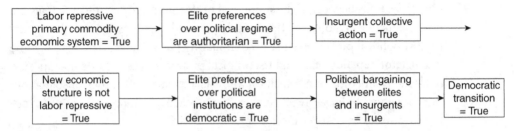

Figure 5.3   Wood's causal graph of post-insurgency democratic transition in El Salvador and South Africa

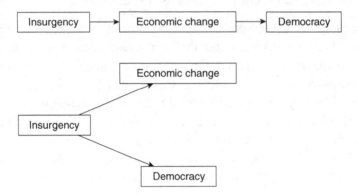

Figure 5.4   Two causal models

composition of the economy. New economic interests in turn transform political preferences, resulting in the final outcome of a democratic transition. It bears emphasis, however, that the change in key parameters is fully endogenous in the model: the oligarchic state causes an insurgency which in turn causes economic transformation. Wood contends that it was not the insurgency itself that pushed El Salvador along a democratic path; an insurgency that did not catalyze economic change would not have produced democracy. It is thus critical that Wood use process tracing to distinguish two potential causal models. In the top panel of Figure 5.4, economic change is a mediator between insurgency and democracy; because there is no edge between insurgency and democracy, insurgency acts as an exogenous instrument, allowing Wood to validate a claim that economic changes caused the democratic transition. But in the bottom panel of Figure 5.4, economic change and democracy are common effects of insurgency. Only careful process tracing can, potentially, distinguish these two causal models.

Returning to Figure 5.3, the causal model as I have reconstructed it consists of seven nodes and six edges. Wood devotes three full chapters to tracing this causal chain: the first chapter covers the first three nodes, from the labor-repressive agro-export system to the exclusionary political regime to civil war; the second chapter looks at the next two nodes in which a transformed economy induces new regime preferences – what Wood calls the "Structural Foundation" of a democratic pact; and the last chapter looks at the final two nodes, the political bargaining that culminated in the democratic transition. Let us stipulate that these chapters convincingly demonstrate that in El Salvador, each node took on the value assigned to it by the causal model. We can therefore focus on the critical question of *connectedness*: does process tracing demonstrate that the parent node determines the value of its descendant node?

The process tracing begins with the political economy of the agro-export sector: land, labor, and the state. Wood does not document, however, the regime preferences of economic elites. She is able to show that economic elites allied with hardliner military offers to undermine reformist military officers who sought to modernize politics and economics and thus were more tolerant of agrarian reform and liberalized politics. This fine discussion provides indirect evidence of the link between the first two nodes. Wood next turns her attention to the political stalemate of the late 1970s: she argues that rightist violence against both reformist political elites and non-elite political mobilization catalyzed the formation of a broad insurgent front, the Farabundo Martí National Liberation Front (Frente Farabundo Martí para la Liberación Nacional, or FMLN). The evidence is not abundant, but Wood's research largely confirms that many people joined the previously inconsequential insurgency following "outrage at the actions of the security forces against family members or neighbors . . . [or] in response to the killing of priests, particularly the assassination of Archbishop Oscar Romero in 1980" (Wood 2000: 47).

The next chapter examines in lavish detail how the insurgency transformed elite economic interests and the organs of elite political representation. This chapter provides abundant macro-level data on sectoral transformation along with a significant quantity of micro-level data – primarily interview data – about how Salvadoran elites relinquished their interests in export agriculture that required labor repression and tight control over the state and moved into new areas that permitted market disciplining of labor. A key transition point occurred when economic elites realized that the military were no longer crucial guarantors of their economic position and sought new forms of political representation, culminating in the establishment of ARENA, a political party capable of electoral dominance. While this chapter is persuasive that elite economic interests underwent massive changes, it is less attentive to elite political preferences and their turn to political liberalization. It is clear that ARENA's ideology shifted from rigid anti-communism to neo-liberal policies; and it is highly striking that this shift began with the ascendancy of Alfredo Cristiani, "a wealthy coffee grower and processor with a wide range of economic interests; an exemplar of the agrarian-financial-industrial group, he commuted by helicopter from his pharmaceutical company in San Salvador to his San Vicente coffee estate" (Wood 2000: 71). But Cristiani must stand as a proxy for the entire economic elite; and we do not observe his political preferences changing on the heels of his economic interests.

The third and final chapter traces the last steps in the causal chain, from political negotiations to democracy. There are two key points to be demonstrated here: first, that ARENA felt secure that elite economic interests would be safeguarded under democracy; and, second, the willingness of the FMLN to renounce violence and compete electorally. This second condition required that the FMLN first embrace democracy and second build a political organization and an economic base to induce its combatants to accept peace and to support the party at the ballot box. It is worth noting that the model does not explicitly theorize the determinants of the FMLN's embrace of democracy. Rather, Wood posits:

The politically exclusive nature of oligarchic societies makes the fundamental political bargain in capitalist democracies acceptable to insurgents despite their past rhetoric of socialist transformation. Insurgents value the realization of political democracy: leaders in part because they anticipate post-transition roles of power and status and their constituents because they value democratic participation per se. (Wood 2000: 15)

Wood provides parallel analysis of the South African transition from apartheid. For the most part, the South African case is fully consistent with the primary causal graph depicted above, and it embodies the same logic of endogenous preference change. Whereas in El Salvador insurgency triggered the transformation of the economic structure from agro-export to commercial interests, in South Africa, insurgency generated new elite preferences by depressing returns to investment in the existing economic structure and leading to a shift toward more capital-intensive production. Wood develops a formal model of returns on investment to create a causal connection between the critical middle three nodes. The economic logic of apartheid, according to the model, is that "the political control of labor keeps wages lower than they would be under liberal conditions whereby wages necessary for workers not to shirk increase with the employment rate." Once workers began sustained mobilization, on the other hand, the advantages of apartheid were sharply attenuated: "mobilization alters investment priorities and choice of technology, leading to increasing capital intensiveness of the economy as employers attempt to minimize their reliance on the restive factor ... the advantage of liberal over apartheid institutions decreases, so employers would have less reason to oppose political reform" (Wood 2000: 147–148). Wood verifies this claim through very careful consideration of macroeconomic trends. In contrast to the case study of El Salvador, which relied heavily on ethnographic evidence, here Wood bases her claims on a formal model that is consistent with a wide range of statistical data.

Like Alexander, Wood does not shy away from building confidence in her claims by rejecting alternative explanations. For example, to sustain her claim that it was labor insurgency that triggered new economic behavior by the business elite, she carefully considers an alternative liberal model that roots new economic conditions of rising capital intensity in labor-market dynamics. In particular, apartheid became non-viable in the late 1960s because of a shortage of skilled (i.e. white) labor that limited growth and prompted "inappropriately capital-intensive development" (Wood 2000: 159). Wood expends considerable energy showing that this model is not consistent with the data, that it was political mobilization that undermined the economic logic of apartheid. In other words, Wood and Alexander both use hoop tests to discredit alternative hypotheses and, more generally, follow many of the process-tracing best practices advanced in Chapter 1.

For both Wood and Alexander, however, the majority of their claim is based on the careful articulation and defense of causal graphs, a procedure that builds on but goes beyond those best practices. It is the relative completeness of their causal graphs, the high degree of confidence we have in their descriptive inferences from events to variables, and the efforts to identify causal mechanisms that lends credence to their claims of causal and explanatory adequacy. Neither work is without defect, but both demonstrate that it is possible for ambitious work to strive to meet very high standards and to approximate those standards in many respects.[4]

European state building

It is no exaggeration to state that Charles Tilly's (1990) magisterial work, *Coercion, Capital, and European States, AD 990–1992*, is the single most

---

[4] Wood's later work examining specifically the Salvadoran civil war is also exemplary in its systematic application of process tracing. See the discussion in Lyall, this volume, Chapter 7.

influential study of state building of the past half-century, with the same profound theoretical and methodological impact on the field as Barrington Moore's work has had on studies of democracy. Tilly's pithy summation, "war made the state and the state made war," has the same iconic status as Moore's "no bourgeoisie, no democracy." As the title suggests, the book covers 1,000 years of history over a vast geographic span. Its engagement with history is deep and wide. Yet, Tilly advertised his lack of interest in process-tracing methods of causal inference, identifying his work with "a rock skipping water, spinning quickly from high point to high point without settling for more than an instant at a time" (Tilly 1990: 35). Tilly was also frank about the casual nature by which he established causal linkages, settling for an implicit model populated by rulers, ruling elites, clients, opponents, and the population under a state's jurisdiction. Without explicit if not formal statements of the model, it is quite difficult to discern what is driving the sequence of events. In what I would consider the book's most insightful statement of mechanisms, Tilly suggests that alternative forms of taxation, ranging from tribute to income, both reflect different combinations of capital and coercion that are the argument's antecedent conditions, and also impose on rulers different forms of supervision and hence oblige revenue-hungry rulers to embark on different projects of institutional formation (Tilly 1990: 87–89). The argument, unfortunately, is unabashedly functionalist; Tilly never argues that rulers recognized these institutional obligations and that state-building trajectories follow from them.

The book's core arguments are thus composed of an under-theorized model of ruler-elite-mass bargaining coupled to a second under-theorized model of institutional selection; the latter has virtually no empirical support. In short, it is difficult if not impossible to reconstruct a detailed causal graph; and it is concomitantly difficult to claim that process tracing plays a major role in the empirical confirmation of Tilly's claims. This is not to say that Tilly's argument is wrong; it is to say that the argument's credibility rests on something other than the careful tracing of causal sequences that identifies their generating mechanisms within a given unit of analysis. The strength of the book, rather, stems from Tilly's imaginative construction of typologies, such as capital versus coercive-intensive regions; an attempt to demonstrate covariation between these antecedent conditions and elements of the state-building process; and the embedding within the historical narrative of processes such as changing forms of military recruitment. These virtues, however, do not yield causal and explanatory adequacy.

Rise of the sovereign state

We can find exemplars of process tracing in works that pursue rival claims, however. An excellent example is Hendryk Spruyt's (1994) *The Sovereign State and Its Competitors*, which tells a two-part story about the emergence and spread of the sovereign state in Europe. In the first stage, the sovereign state emerges out of the decline of feudalism. But other logics of organization also displace feudalism: city-states and city leagues. The second part of the argument is a selection model that accounts for the hegemony of the sovereign state and the disappearance of rival logics of authority. To focus attention on the process tracing of the model's core arguments – about the emergence of the sovereign state – I restrict discussion to its first half.

The initial outcome state consists of three types of non-territorial political organizations: feudalism, the Church, and the Holy Roman Empire. The key change that catalyzes political change is the emergence of a post-feudal economy in the late Middle Ages. Spruyt does not explicitly argue that this economic transformation was exogenous to political change; he simply side-steps an issue he considers irrelevant. Exogeneity should not be treated so informally, however; there are plausible arguments attributing economic revival to changing political conditions, and so Spruyt misses an opportunity to either reject these claims or to show how potential endogeneity does not threaten the validity of his causal claims.

Spruyt constructs a clear causal argument. The recovery of European commerce triggers both changing preferences over institutions of key actors (monarchs, nobilities, and townsmen) and a changing balance of power among these actors.[5] The result is the construction of new coalitions based on material and ideational interests. Coalition members, to complete the argument, select institutions that are compatible with their interests: either sovereign states in France, the Hanseatic League of commercial German cities, or city-states on the Italian peninsula. Clearly, getting the preferences right is a critical step in the argument. Spruyt warns against the functionalist fallacy of deducing preferences over institution from institutional outcomes. He theorizes how economic structures shape preferences over institutions, but his empirical challenge is to "inductively ascertain what preferences individuals actually had and what choices they made. I further examine

---

[5] Note the similarity to the core arguments in the literature on democratic transitions. There is an opportunity to recover a deeper causal model that underlies accounts of both democratic transitions and state building.

how preferences were aggregated and played out in political bargaining" (Spruyt 1994: 27).

Spruyt thus has two methodological challenges. First, he must reject rival theories of the rise of the sovereign state. The main rivals to Spruyt's theory are a family of neo-Marxist economic theories as well as the claim that warfare and the military revolution produced modern nation-states. Spruyt dispatches the neo-Marxist accounts on logical grounds: all of these accounts are "unilinear evolutionary accounts" that ignore the substantial variation in forms of political organization that followed the commercial expansion of the late Middle Ages. Consequently, these accounts conflate two issues that must be kept separate: the emergence of rival logics of organization and the selection of the sovereign state as the hegemonic political organization. Note that the rejection of these arguments is not based on process tracing; he rejects them because – due to their functionalist reasoning – they cannot generate a causal graph. Spruyt acknowledges that Tilly's war-making account does not commit the same logical fallacy of the neo-Marxist economic theories. He makes an argument about timing: the slow development of the nation-state *preceded* the military revolution and so the military revolution cannot be the cause of the modern sovereign state. Instead, it is the institutional outcomes of different coalitions that explain relative military efficiency, a claim that receives some evidentiary support in the chapter on French history.

In addition to casting doubt on rival accounts, Spruyt must use process tracing to demonstrate how interests formed and how they aggregated into institutional selection, including the problem of collective action inherent in institutional formation. We thus expect Spruyt to carefully trace the intervening steps in the process he has demarcated, as represented in Figure 5.5. Note that this generic causal graph is consistent with all three outcomes, depending on the specific local character of the economic revival and the subsequent content of preferences over institutions.

Does process tracing fulfill this promise? In a chapter on the European commercial expansion following AD 1000, Spruyt proposes a model that correlates the character and level of trade with expected preferences over institutions. Townsmen have conflicting interests: for independence, on the one hand, and for relatively efficient provision of public goods such as

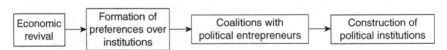

Figure 5.5　Spruyt's generic theory of institutional emergence

security, standardization of weights and measures, and reduction of transaction costs, on the other. How they balance these two conflicting preferences depends on three factors: the level of trade, the character of trade, and the degree of urbanization. Given low-volume trade in low value-added goods, French towns prefer centralized states to provide necessary collective goods. German towns traffic in high volumes of low value-added goods, and so also prefer a central actor to provide necessary collective goods. That central actor can be a state or a league of city-states that pools the resources of its members. Finally, Italian towns trade in a moderate volume of high value goods, and with a high level of urbanization; large towns do not need a central state to provide goods. Instead of collaborating to provide goods centrally, Italian towns create their own collective goods and compete with each other.

Given the important role this model plays in constructing the causal chain that will be traced by the historical case studies, we need to consider its internal logic, which is very promising, but also problematic. Each of the model's three dimensions – level of trade, character of trade, and degree of urbanization – is either dichotomous or trichotomous, and so the number of cells is quite large. Given eighteen possible cells and only three observed outcomes, Spruyt comes dangerously close to the type of fallacious rational-choice reasoning he has previously criticized.[6]

Furthermore, while recognizing that townsmen form coalitions and build institutions in concert with rulers, Spruyt does not theorize ruler preferences over institutions. In France, the preferences of the king for centralized rule are simply asserted. Although this assertion appears relatively non-controversial, the German monarchy (Holy Roman Emperor) holds contrary preferences and hence pursues an imperial strategy in Italy, ceding control over German towns to feudal lords. Thus, kings do not have uniform preferences over institutions and the failure to theorize these preferences undermines the validity of the causal argument, as we will see below.

It is a great strength of the book that the case studies directly amass evidence for these claims about merchant preference formation. Spruyt does not pretend to gain direct access to preferences. He takes some pains, however, to show that French towns were too small and revenue-starved to act independently; and that given low profit margins, townsmen would be keen to find cost-reducing forms of organization. Spruyt thus advances reasons

---

[6] The level of trade and the degree of urbanization can be low, moderate, or high; and the character of trade can be low or high value added. This creates eighteen possible cells.

why townsmen would prefer the regularized extractions of the crown to the irregular extractions of the nobility and hence why towns would help tip the balance of power away from lords and toward the throne. Spruyt is less attentive to the preferences of the crown, asserting but not demonstrating that "kings deliberately pursued the alliance with the towns as part of their overall strategy to centralize the kingdom" (Spruyt 1994: 93). Again, this claim of a centralizing strategy would not be problematic were it not for the absence of such a strategy in the German case; it cannot be the case that rulers have a strong tendency to ally with townsmen.

It must also be said that when Spruyt turns his attention to the construction of a centralized state, the French bourgeoisie basically drops out of the picture. Although Spruyt attributes the institutional outcome to a royal–bourgeois alliance, the discussion of state building is a remarkably royal affair. Indeed, given Spruyt's claim that the French monarchy was antagonistic to feudalism as a political mode of rule, it is not entirely clear that he can support the counterfactual that if French towns had not preferred a centralized state, the institutional outcome would have been very different. Thus, Spruyt theorizes the preferences of a class actor whose causal influence over institutional formation appears to be secondary to the non-theorized preferences of the monarchy.

Can Spruyt next explain why the German king (Holy Roman Emperor) allied with lords against towns, forcing the latter to form the Hanseatic League? The preferences of German towns did not diverge much from those of French towns: of intermediate size and wealth, they needed some form of authority to pool resources and provide collective goods. The German story thus hinges on the strategy of the monarchy. It appears that the balance of power between crown and nobility in Germany favored lords more heavily than in France: "Because of the continued strength of the German lords, the emperor opted for concessions to them" (Spruyt 1994: 115). In place of a strategy of building a territorial and sovereign state at home, German kings opted for the imperial strategy of conquering northern Italy. Spruyt offers plausible reasons why this strategy made sense, not least of which was that the imperial strategy promised access to large pots of revenue. But the main cause appears to be the superior strength of German lords, such that they were able to sabotage a crown–town alliance. Bereft of allies, German towns embarked on the city-league strategy as a substitute.

The case-study evidence appears to be uncovering under-theorized portions of the causal argument. In effect, Spruyt provides a "demand-side" argument explaining why townsmen might support the construction of a sovereign territorial state. But state building also requires a "supply side," and Spruyt's account does less well explaining royal strategies. In France, kings opt for a crown–town alliance, while in Germany, kings leave towns vulnerable to aristocratic dominance. There is some evidence that the key omitted variable is the balance of power between crown and nobility. To explain the rise of the territorial sovereign state, the preferences of the crown and balance of power between crown and nobility appear to be central in ways that are omitted in the causal graph. Put differently, the preferences of German townsmen were important to explaining why a league rather than independent city-states, but irrelevant to explaining why no territorial sovereign state emerged in Germany.

Let me be clear about the nature of the critique here. First and foremost, the critique does not support any rival arguments. Second, it retains Spruyt's emphasis on economic transformation and its capacity to induce new institutional preferences. Third, the critique does not cast doubt on the character of Spruyt's descriptive inferences. Rather, it focuses on the properties of the causal graph. My claim is that this graph omits at least one and perhaps two critical nodes, one accounting for royal preferences over institutions, and a second measuring the balance of power between crown and nobility. Therefore, despite the genuine accomplishments of this book, both theoretical and empirical, it is not clear that one can trace a continuous causal process from initial to terminal node. Spruyt's careful analysis, on the other hand, generates high expectations that a more highly elaborated causal graph could be fully vindicated by careful process tracing.

Disciplinary revolution and state building

Let us consider one final example of process tracing and European state building: Philip Gorski's (2003) account of Calvinism and state building. According to Gorski, Calvinism gave rise to a new infrastructure of religious governance and social control that subsequently generated new mechanisms for social and political order. Gorski's argument has three major links: confessionalization, social discipline, and state power. Confessionalization begins as the hardening of inter-confessional boundaries, followed by the imposition of intra-confessional uniformity by ecclesiastical authorities. The creation of territorially based churches directly boosted state power. Confessionalization also indirectly boosted state power by motivating new forms of social discipline. Social discipline is the internalization of externally imposed authority,

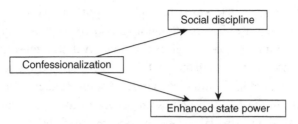

Figure 5.6   Gorski's causal model of Calvinism and state power

as members of confessions adapted to rigid frameworks of moral rectitude and behavior. Social discipline in turn generates state power by producing more honest and efficient administrators operating in a social environment populated by obedient, hard-working subjects and strong mechanisms of social control. These arguments are depicted in Figure 5.6.

Gorski does not pause to consider the potential endogeneity of confessionalization. Instead, he moves directly into the case-study evidence, which appears in two chapters: the first on the "disciplinary revolution from below" in the Low Countries; and the second on the "disciplinary revolution from above" in Prussia. The former begins with an interesting puzzle: how was the Dutch state, which was neither centralized nor bureaucratized, able to extract revenues and build a huge army while maintaining social order? The chapter begins with confessionalization, which took the form of the Dutch revolt against Spain. The next step is the system of church discipline. Gorski charts the link between social provision and social discipline with a highly detailed study of charity and morality in the Netherlands. The network of social provision was dense, but equally impressive were efforts to distinguish the deserving from the undeserving poor. Provision was accompanied by seemingly exhaustive efforts to combat moral degeneracy.

How did social discipline affect military and political discipline of soldiers and bureaucrats? Gorski has trouble making this crucial connection. He distinguishes political efficiency from administrative efficiency, and argues that the impact of the Calvinist disciplinary revolution on the former was slight. He goes on to posit that the impact of Calvinism on the latter

may have been somewhat more significant, not because it promoted administrative rationalization but rather because it hindered the sort of administrative irrationalization that occurred in other parts of the Spanish empire, where venality and corruption struck deep and lasting roots. Calvinism may also have had a positive impact on administrative efficiency insofar as it promoted ascetic values, such as diligence and self-denial, and created an institutional and political context that sanctioned their non-observance. That said, the impact of Calvinism on Dutch political institutions was certainly not as deep as its impact on Dutch social life. (Gorski 2003: 71–72)

To put it bluntly, Gorski is unable to establish any plausible connection between confessionalization and social discipline, on the one hand, and enhanced state efficiency, on the other hand. The problem here is not one of descriptive inference; the evidence supports the coding of each node of the causal graph. The problem is the failure to establish reasons to order the nodes as relations of causal dependence. It may be true that individuals disciplined by social institutions make better state administrators; but Gorski makes his case very elliptically, positing only that: "Other things being equal, we would expect that a state with obedient hard-working subjects and strong, effective mechanisms of social control will be stronger than one that does not" (Gorski 2003: 36). This is a surprisingly weak statement of the causal mechanism, and so we should not be surprised that the within-case evidence fails to corroborate the theory.

The same conclusion must be applied to Gorski's efforts to derive military efficiency from Calvinism. Recognizing that military reforms had sources other than Calvinism, he speculates as follows:

This is not to say that their military reforms were directly inspired by Calvinism; in this regard, Parma was surely a greater inspiration than Calvin! Still, one wonders whether there might not have been a psychological connection – an elective affinity – between their religious ethos and their military reforms because both placed so much stress on discipline, both as a value and as a practice. (Gorski 2003: 75)

This is perhaps an interesting speculation about an elective affinity, but it most certainly is not an adequately identified causal mechanism linking two nodes in a causal graph.

If process tracing the Dutch case uncovers a large gap between social disciplining and a strong state, process tracing the Prussian case shows the absence of ecclesiastical social disciplining. Strict inter-confessional boundaries were not created in Prussia; instead, a Calvinist court ruled over a predominately Lutheran population. Confessional conflict between the court and the Lutheran estates motivated the building of an autonomous state (although it cannot be claimed that the desire of a court to dominate nobles requires confessional conflict). Prussian puritanism, according to Gorski, was rooted in the personal beliefs and ethos of Frederick William I.

Gorski describes in lavish detail how Frederick William embarked on military reforms, inculcating discipline while rationalizing administration and finances. But he provides no evidence that these reforms had religious inspiration or that the success of the Prussian state was predicated on the broader social environment that had been disciplined by religious bodies. Indeed, Gorski explicitly states that he finds no evidence that the Pietist movement of social discipline "injected a new ethos into the Prussian state" (Gorski 2003: 112). The Prussian chapter, I conclude, provides evidence of a confessional conflict, but provides virtually no evidence that confessional conflict sparked a religious movement of social discipline that directly strengthened the state via the hypothesized mechanisms. Indeed, Gorski has a startlingly refreshing tendency to admit that he cannot make the critical causal connections.

In short, the causal graph corresponds reasonably well to the description of events in Holland, but Gorski fails to make the critical causal connections. In Prussia, on the other hand, there is very limited correspondence between the event-history maps and the causal graphs. Both case studies, then, fail to achieve causal or explanatory adequacy.

Summary and conclusions

This chapter has advanced a standard for the evaluation of the causal and explanatory adequacy of process-tracing methods. The completeness standard begins with the construction of a causal graph that embodies the causal process being traced. The standard next requires that scholars construct event-history maps, in which events of a particular case study correspond to nodes in the causal graph. A central function of process tracing is to establish a correspondence of descriptive inference between the event-history map(s) and the causal graph, showing that the events in a particular case constitute the theorized value of a random variable as expressed in the causal graph.

The causal graph and the event-history maps work in tandem: the causal graph supports the proposition that *if* the random variables take on their hypothesized values, then the graph is sufficient to produce the outcome. The event-history maps establish that the random variables took on the hypothesized values in the particular cases. If the causal graph is complete and hence sufficient to generate the outcome variable, and if descriptive inferences establish correspondence between the event-history map and the causal graph, the study has achieved causal adequacy. That is, the combination of causal graph and event-history mappings license us to make a valid causal claim about the causes of the outcome. Furthermore, if the causal graph includes a complete inventory of the causal mechanisms that connect nodes in the graph, and if the empirical evidence corroborates those mechanisms, the study has also achieved explanatory adequacy. We can say not only that X causes Y, but that X causes Y because the set of mechanisms connect X and Y in the relevant manner.

Note that the construction of a causal graph, the primary requirement of the completeness standard, is not always straightforward. As we saw, it is nearly impossible to reconstruct such graphs for major works by Moore and Tilly. Yet, working with them provides opportunities to think rigorously about process tracing and its relation to causal and explanatory adequacy. Consider our discussion of Spruyt's account of state building. As I have argued, his causal graph embodies a demand-side logic whereby townsmen derived institutional preferences based on their position within trade networks. But in the case studies, it is the crown that directly supplies new institutions; therefore, the causal graph requires one or more nodes that theorize royal preferences and reconcile royal with bourgeois preferences. This is not to claim that Spruyt's argument has been falsified, but rather to claim that it remains incomplete.

A second example of an insufficiently determinate causal graph is Alexander's account of regime change. The connection between perceptions of risk and rightist political preferences appears adequately stated and empirically corroborated; the problem is moving from these imputed preferences to observed outcomes. It is not sufficient to claim that relevant actors had incentives to produce an outcome; we must show that these relevant actors produced that outcome for the hypothesized reasons and by the hypothesized means. The causal graphs of both Spruyt and Alexander are indeterminate because they demonstrate incentive, but not capacity. We can make those judgments about the potential for causal adequacy *prior* to considering their empirical evidence.

At the same time, it is clear that additional work is needed on the completeness standard; this chapter is only a first step that moves us closer to a full statement of its relevant components. Indeed, a statement of standards is not equivalent to their operationalization.[7] Without the latter, we cannot determine when a causal graph fully meets the sufficiency

---

[7] This same "slippage" – between standards and their operationalization – explains why several other contributors to this book also modify Bennett and Checkel's ten process-tracing best practices in significant ways (Schimmelfennig, this volume, Chapter 4; Pouliot, this volume, Chapter 9).

criterion. In addition, more needs to be said about how to organize event-history maps and how to determine their correspondence with causal graphs. Our standard repertoire of hoop and smoking-gun tests will play an important role, but that framework does not yet exhaust the requirements of fair appraisal of causal claims.

Explaining the Cold War's end
Process tracing all the way down?

Matthew Evangelista

The fall of the Berlin Wall. The Soviet defeat in Afghanistan. The introduction of *glasnost* and competitive elections in the USSR. The withdrawal of Soviet armed forces from Central Europe. Such events have come to represent the end of the Cold War. Historians might not agree on precisely when the military–political–economic rivalry between the United States and the Soviet Union and their respective allies – and the attendant risk of global nuclear war – ended. They are left, instead, to explain the *events* that culminated in the undisputed demise of that rivalry. Political scientists' explanations for the end of the Cold War – a shift in the balance of power, the impact of economic globalization and relative Soviet decline, the normative appeal of democracy and capitalism – are, however, not well suited to explain events. Process tracing provides a way to evaluate explanations for the end of the Cold War by linking broad theories to specific events. The method depends on identifying evidence on the mechanisms behind the decisions of political leaders – something that the available archival record in many cases allows.

As the volume's editors point out in Chapter 1, this chapter differs from the others in that it does not seek to demonstrate the usefulness of process tracing for a particular domain of political science or how process tracing in one case can help evaluate the merits of a given theory more broadly. Scholars have used the case of the Cold War's end in this way – for example, to illustrate the impact of economic globalization on security (Brooks 2005), the factors influencing states' grand strategies (Evangelista 1993), and the conditions under which states pursue conflictual or cooperative security policies (Evangelista 1991). Indeed, process tracing has proved an effective method for evaluating competing theories of international relations applied to particular developments during the Cold War – from military intervention to arms control to the basic ideas underpinning foreign policy (for example, Bennett 1999; Checkel 1997; English 2000; Evangelista 1999; Mendelson 1998).[1]

This chapter's purpose is different. It focuses entirely on the Cold War's end, but it ranges broadly over the various explanations put forward by scholars. The goal is to link the main theoretical accounts to specific political, social, and psychological mechanisms that must come into play for these accounts to serve as explanations for the key events that constitute the end of the Cold War. The chapter offers a tentative assessment of the explanations on the basis of existing evidence. Its main intent, however, is to show how one would evaluate the mechanisms that each theoretical approach implies through examination of a single event – yet one intricately connected to many of the other most significant ones: Mikhail Gorbachev's December 1988 proclamation of "freedom of choice" for Eastern Europe and the unilateral defensive restructuring and reduction in the Soviet Army of half a million troops. Gorbachev's speech at the United Nations marked the most public articulation of the Soviet renunciation of the "Brezhnev Doctrine" (which had previously justified Soviet interventions) and helped to set in train the rejection of communist regimes throughout Eastern Europe and the peaceful reunification of Germany.

The justification for choosing the end of the Cold War for this exercise is twofold: (i) there is a remarkably rich array of contending theories whose underlying mechanisms are worth elucidating for potential application to other questions; and (ii) for many students of international relations, the end of the Cold War called into question some of the leading paradigms in the field, and thus enlivened the debate between the critics and defenders of those paradigms and offered the possibility of theoretical innovation and progress.

The chapter proceeds as follows. First, I review the range of possible events that could constitute the end of the Cold War and make my case for why Gorbachev's December 1988 initiative provides the most useful basis for this exercise. Throughout, I seek to fulfill the main criteria offered by the editors for "best practices" of process tracing, calling attention to the ones most relevant to my case. In the spirit of criterion 1, I "cast the net widely for alternative explanations," summarizing the main theoretical approaches to the end of the Cold War and the explanatory mechanisms associated with

---

[1] The theoretical and empirical work on the end of the Cold War is enormous and still growing. This chapter draws on important recent contributions to this literature in a special issue of the British journal *International Politics*; the special issue represents the main schools of thought on the topic and is based on papers presented at a March 2010 conference at Princeton University marking the twentieth anniversary of the end of the Cold War (Deudney and Ikenberry 2011a).

them. Then I examine a comparative case – Nikita Khrushchev's major reduction of conventional forces starting in the mid-1950s – of the sort that Bennett and Checkel recommend combining with process tracing to yield theoretical leverage and insight (criterion 7). The sections following take up competing explanations in the context of Stephen Van Evera's "hoop" and "smoking-gun" tests (Bennett and Checkel, this volume, Chapter 1; and Bennett, this volume, Appendix). I then pursue the question of whether "absence of evidence" constitutes "evidence of absence," and I suggest ways of uncovering observable evidence drawn from deductive hypotheses.

Next, I turn to a basic process-tracing exercise – what I dub "process-tracing lite" – to ponder the question, also raised by the editors, of "how far 'down' to go in gathering detailed evidence." My answer is: "the further the better." Thus, I agree with Alan Jacobs, who, in his chapter on ideational theories, advocates an expansive "analytic field," both in terms of *temporal range* and *level of analysis* (Jacobs, this volume, Chapter 2). By tracing a process further back in history (expanding temporal range), I argue, we can bring to light explanatory factors (at different levels of analysis) that were missing in the more delimited process-tracing exercise. More history saves us from creating "just so" stories and neglecting policy windows that were opened before the time of the specific event we sought to explain through process tracing. The same is so for going further into the future.

The exercise compels us to call into question the plausibility of a unitary-actor assumption founded on the apparent lack of resistance to Gorbachev's initiatives (in this case the December 1988 speech) at the time he made them. Resistance emerged later, in the implementation phase, and went to the extreme of inducing the resignation of Gorbachev's foreign minister and an attempted coup against Gorbachev himself. Finally, going further into the future – as Gorbachev became increasingly preoccupied with the situation in Eastern Europe – helps to uncover the "revealed preferences" motivating his policies there. Employing a counterfactual thought experiment – would Gorbachev have responded with force to political changes in Eastern Europe if the Soviet economy were not in crisis? – highlights the conflict between materialist explanations and ones favoring ideas, learning, and personality traits.

The end of the Cold War as a series of events

If the "dependent variable" to be explained in this exercise is an event or series of events representing the end of the Cold War, then we need to start by asking when that happened. Most accounts of the Cold War's end focus on events that include: the fall of the Berlin Wall (November 9, 1989); the Malta summit meeting between George H. W. Bush and Mikhail Gorbachev (December 2 to 3, 1989); Gorbachev's inauguration as the first president (albeit not popularly elected) of the Soviet Union (March 15, 1990), based on a new system that eliminated the political monopoly of the Communist Party (formally renounced at its 28th Congress on July 13, 1990); the successful military effort to reverse Iraq's invasion of Kuwait, which entailed unprecedented cooperation between the United States and the Soviet Union under the auspices of the UN Security Council (August 1990 to February 1991); negotiation and official reunification of Germany (September to October 1990); the signing of the Paris Charter for a New Europe and the Treaty on Conventional Armed Forces in Europe, which led to major reductions in the armed stand-off in Central Europe and promised a new European security order (November 19 to 21, 1990); the election of Solidarity leader Lech Wałęsa as president of Poland (December 22, 1990) signaling the end of Soviet-style communism in Eastern Europe; the dissolution of the Warsaw Treaty Organization (July 1, 1991); and the failed coup d'état against Gorbachev (August 19 to 21, 1991), which provoked a series of further events leading ultimately to the formal dissolution of the Soviet Union at the end of 1991.

What this long, yet still selective, list excludes is any event that happened *earlier*, which some observers might consider to have marked – or at least foreshadowed – the end of the Cold War: the start of Ronald Reagan's first term as president of the United States (January 20, 1981); Mikhail Gorbachev's accession to the top leadership of the Soviet Union (March 11, 1985); Ronald Reagan's visit to Moscow, where he characterized his statement calling the Soviet Union an "evil empire" as referring to "another time, another era" (May 31, 1988); or – my preferred choice for the purposes of this chapter – Gorbachev's speech at the United Nations where he declared that the countries of Eastern Europe should have "freedom of choice" about their political systems and announced a unilateral reduction of some 500,000 troops and withdrawal of offensively oriented military equipment from Europe (December 7, 1988).

Ronald Reagan and his Secretary of State George Shultz left office in January 1989 believing that they had overseen the end of the Cold War. But their successors George H. W. Bush and James Baker thought otherwise. They undertook a "strategic review" of US–Soviet relations that delayed for nearly a year the improvement of relations that had followed such initiatives as the Treaty on Intermediate-Range Nuclear Forces (INF Treaty – 1987), eliminating an entire class of nuclear weapons for the first time ever, and Gorbachev's UN speech and subsequent unilateral Soviet reductions of conventional armed forces.

Indeed, rather than welcome the INF Treaty, Bush and Baker seemed more concerned that it not prevent modernization of shorter-range US nuclear weapons, left uncovered by the treaty, and their deployment to West Germany (comments of Brent Scowcroft and James Baker in Wohlforth 2003: 31–32). George Bush was not convinced that the Cold War had ended until he developed a personal relationship with Mikhail Gorbachev at a summit meeting in Malta in December 1989, and Gorbachev revealed to him that "we don't consider you an enemy anymore" (Wohlforth 2003: 15). Some members of Bush's administration identified a later end – only with the reunification of Germany or Soviet cooperation in the war against Iraq were they convinced that the Cold War was history. At a retrospective conference of former US and Soviet officials, one of the Soviet participants responded that "unless the Cold War had ended at Malta, how could we have achieved the kind of German unification that was accomplished, [and cooperation in] the war in the Persian Gulf?" (Anatolii Cherniaev in Wohlforth 2003: 46). Another claimed that the Malta summit itself "proved that the Cold War had ended somewhat earlier" (Aleksandr Bessmertnykh in Wohlforth 2003: 22).

In trying to date the end of the Cold War, we might note that many people thought that it had already ended several times before the late 1980s. These include "The Thaw" period of the mid-1950s, when the successors of Josef Stalin drastically reduced Soviet ground forces and made efforts to improve relations with the United States, the "Spirit of Geneva" and the withdrawal of foreign troops from Austria in 1955, and the 1963 "Moscow Treaty" banning nuclear tests in the atmosphere, in outer space, and underwater. Moreover, the fact that observers could speak of a "Second Cold War" or a "New Cold War" breaking out in late 1979 – with the Soviet invasion of Afghanistan and plans for US deployment of new missiles in Europe – implies that the first Cold War had ended with the onset of the détente policies of the 1970s (Halliday 1983; Cox 1990). It is only because events of the 1980s and early 1990s went so much further than anyone anticipated that we do not feel obliged to explain those earlier "ends" of the Cold War (but see Evangelista 1991 for an attempt). Finally, a vocal minority, particularly in Russia, claims that the Cold War never really ended: one of its earliest institutions, the North Atlantic Treaty Alliance, is still going strong; it has expanded territorially to include parts of the former Soviet Union, along with contingency plans to defend them; and it has extended its military missions worldwide.[2]

A thicket of theories (and mechanisms)

The literature on the end of the Cold War is blessed (or cursed?) with what James Kurth (1971) in another context called a "thicket of theories" – many plausible contenders and no easy way to adjudicate among them. The theories I bring to bear can be grouped into four broad categories.

(1) *Realist approaches* emphasize a combination of the relative East–West balance of military and economic power. Scholars such as Stephen Brooks and William Wohlforth (2003) and Kenneth Oye (1995) explain the end of the Cold War in part as a response by the USSR to its relative decline vis-à-vis the United States. To the extent that mechanisms below the level of the international system (distribution of power) come into play, they entail rational adaptation to new information or so-called Bayesian updating (Bennett, this volume, Appendix) on the part of leaders who were slower than Gorbachev in grasping the implications of the long-term Soviet economic crisis.

(2) *Ideational approaches* represent the impact of new ways of understanding the Soviet security predicament and the relationship between foreign policy and the goals of domestic political reform. The main advocates of this approach do not neglect the impact of economic conditions and the East–West military rivalry, but consider these factors as indeterminate. Scholars such as Jeffrey Checkel (1997), Robert English (2000), and Sarah Mendelson (1998) tend to see economic and military conditions as factors that can be manipulated by *norm entrepreneurs* who favor "new thinking" in foreign policy and reform at home. Thus, their explanations often overlap with those that highlight institutions, coalition politics, and individual cognitive change.

(3) *Coalition-politics approaches* stress the interests of particular sectors of Soviet society and the concomitant foreign policies that would best serve them. The main locus of competition, as developed in the work of Jack Snyder (1987) most notably, pits Communist Party ideologues and stalwarts of the military-industrial sector against party reformers, the *intelligentsia*, and representatives of light and consumer industry and economic interests that would benefit from integration into the global economy. The principal mechanisms for this theoretical approach include political strategies such as log-rolling and agenda-setting.

---

[2] Oleg Baklanov *et al.*, letter to Thomas Biersteker, April 28, 1998.

(4) *Cognitive psychological and personality-based approaches*, applied to the end of the Cold War, seek to explain changes in Soviet security policy from confrontation to cooperation. They can work at both the group and individual level. Andrew Bennett (1999), for example, has studied the views and policy prescriptions of Soviet military officers regarding armed intervention based on their experience in previous conflicts (particularly the war in Afghanistan). His explanation employs mechanisms that stress the learning of lessons on a number of dimensions at the individual and group levels (cohorts of officers with similar histories of deployment). Janice Stein (1994) has also used a learning mechanism to explain the views of one particular individual – Mikhail Gorbachev – whose personality type ("uncommitted thinker and motivated learner") she finds particularly suitable to learning.

As these descriptions already reveal, there is considerable overlap among all of the explanations. Few observers would deny that economic decline played a role in Soviet policy changes of the 1980s. Ideas also play a role in many theories – either as long-standing views associated with particular individuals and groups; as products of individual, group, or organizational cognitive change ("learning"); or instrumentally to justify the self-interested policies of political coalitions. Thus, many of the difficulties identified by Jacobs (this volume, Chapter 2) for students of ideational theories, and the strategies he proposed for overcoming them, apply here.

This chapter will resolve neither when the Cold War ended nor which theories best explain that end. Presumably, some theories are better than others for explaining different dimensions of what we might consider the end of the Cold War – especially if we consider a range of topics from military intervention to arms control to democratization to economic reform and liberalization. The point is that different end points implicate different theories and perhaps entail different methods for resolving theoretical disputes. My claim, though, is that process tracing is probably the most powerful method for doing so, regardless of when precisely one dates the "dependent variable." My goal here is to illustrate the method not by a systematic evaluation of all of the rival theories – that exercise has already consumed volumes (for example, Brooks and Wohlforth 2000; 2002; English 2002; Kramer 2001; Lebow and Risse-Kappen 1995; Wohlforth 2003) – but by focusing on one plausible candidate event and considering the theories most associated with it. I use this event to suggest how process tracing sheds light on the strengths and weaknesses of the relevant contending theories and their attendant mechanisms.

In what follows, I seek to identify at what points in tracing the process that produced Gorbachev's UN speech we are able to adjudicate between particular explanations. While this bears some resemblance to Schimmelfennig's "efficient process tracing" (this volume, Chapter 4) as it analyzes those process links that are crucial for an explanation and for discriminating between alternative explanations, the exercise is primarily grounded in the concepts and "best practices" advanced by Bennett and Checkel (this volume, Chapter 1). Before proceeding, however, I justify my focus on this particular event.

Gorbachev's December 1988 speech as a key event

My choice is inspired by US journalist Walter Lippmann's series of articles, later published as *The Cold War*, which responded to George Kennan's famous 1947 article, penned under the pseudonym X. According to Lippmann, "until a settlement which results in withdrawal is reached, the Red Army at the center of Europe will control eastern Europe and will threaten western Europe" (quoted in Wagner 1993: 80).[3] Harrison Wagner (ibid.) cites Lippmann's identification of the key cause of the Cold War to give his definition of when it ended: "when Soviet control over Eastern Europe collapsed and the Soviet military threat to Western Europe ceased to be such a pressing concern." William Wohlforth (2011: 445) elaborates on the point and extends the end date a little: "The negotiated settlement of the German Question and the framework agreement on withdrawal of the Red Army from forward positions in Central Europe in 1990 constitute the end of the Cold War." Later, he reiterates the point: "the Cold War did not end at Reykjavik, it did not end with the INF agreement, it did not end because Ronald Reagan or George Bush conceded some fundamental position that had underlay the superpower rivalry. It ended when the Soviet Union credibly agreed to relinquish its military position in the center of Europe" (Wohlforth 2011: 450).

In my view, the December 1988 UN speech marked that end, but for Wohlforth it was the agreement on a unified Germany within NATO (see also Drozdiak 1990). Since Wohlforth and his critics have extensively plowed the theoretical ground concerning the reunification of Germany and the end of communism in Eastern Europe, I focus on the earlier and closely related event that helped pave the way for the ultimate settlement (Wohlforth 2003; Savranskaya *et al.* 2010).

The event I examine actually constitutes a longer-term process. Well before his December 1988 speech, Gorbachev made his intentions explicit when he

---

[3] My attention was drawn to Lippmann's article by Wohlforth (2011: 445), who in turn credits Wagner.

told his Politburo colleagues in July 1986: "The methods that were used in Czechoslovakia and Hungary now are no good, they will not work!" At a November 1986 meeting in Moscow with East European leaders, Gorbachev warned them that they could no longer rely on Soviet military intervention to maintain power (Savranskaya 2010: 39). The Berlin Wall fell exactly a year to the day after Gorbachev had ordered his Defense Ministry to draw up plans for the withdrawal of Soviet forces from Eastern Europe in anticipation of his UN speech. Gorbachev knew that the speech would be taken as a renunciation of the "Brezhnev Doctrine" that had arrogated to the Soviet Union the right to intervene militarily to prevent any threats to its understanding of "socialism" on the territory of its Warsaw Pact allies. Half a year before the speech, Gorbachev explained his intentions to Polish leader Wojciech Jaruzelski, whom he later encouraged to hold "roundtable" discussions with the Solidarity movement's Lech Wałęsa and to allow him to come to power when free elections gave his party 99 out of 100 of the seats in a new Polish parliament (Sejm). Svetlana Savranskaya reports that at a dinner with Jaruzelski in July 1988 and in a speech to the (unreformed) Sejm that same month "Gorbachev was already speaking explicitly about freedom of choice and non-interference, and how these fit into his grand design for the common European home – almost as if he were rehearsing his forthcoming UN speech" (Savranskaya 2010: 41–42).

Indeed, Gorbachev intended his December 1988 speech to mark the end of the Cold War. As Thomas Blanton (2010: 58) explains, he "sought to create a bookend for the Cold War that had been declared by Winston Churchill in Fulton, Missouri with his 'Iron Curtain' speech" of 1946. He told his advisors he wanted the UN speech to be "an anti-Fulton, Fulton in reverse." Many observers got the message. General Andrew Goodpaster, a former NATO supreme commander and military aide to President Dwight Eisenhower, called the announced reductions "the most significant step since NATO was founded" (Oberdorfer 1992: 319).

"Freedom of choice" and defensive restructuring

There was a precedent for the Soviet unilateral reduction of half a million troops, and it was the military reform carried out by Nikita Khrushchev in the second half of the 1950s. Soviet proponents of the December 1988 reductions had cited the Khrushchev example as inspiration for the Gorbachev initiative. In that respect, tracing the process leading to the 1988 event benefits from

using the earlier events in a cross-case comparison, as Bennett and Checkel
advocate in their criterion 7 (this volume, Chapter 1).

A plausible cross-case comparison

Khrushchev's initiative was driven in part by economic concerns, particularly a
slowdown in the growth of the workforce and in labor productivity that could
be addressed by an influx of demobilized soldiers into the economy (Tiedtke
1985; Tsentral'noe statisticheskoe upravlenie SSSR 1968). By analogy, one could
imagine Gorbachev's initiative as stimulated by similar economic concerns –
but a process-tracing effort would require evidence of the extent to which the
concern to cope with economic decline, rather than specific foreign-policy
goals, led to the troop-reduction proposal (something not clearly established
for the Khrushchev initiatives either). In any event, the Khrushchev–Gorbachev
comparison approximates Mill's most-similar design.

A key difference emerges from the comparison. Khrushchev combined his
conventional-force reductions with development of the Soviet nuclear and
missile arsenals (much as the Eisenhower administration was doing with its
"New Look" and nuclearization of NATO) and a policy of bluster and threat
intended to deter Western military action and achieve Soviet foreign-policy
goals (regarding Berlin, for example). Gorbachev, by contrast, sought to
reduce the level of nuclear threat overall and saw the conventional reductions
as complementary and contributing to that end. Gorbachev's decision to focus
on reducing the most offensively oriented components of his forward-
deployed troops (tanks and self-propelled artillery) was deliberately designed
to lessen the chances that an outbreak of war would trigger a nuclear response
from NATO. It marked a reversal of the Soviet military strategy that stressed a
quick offensive to suppress NATO's nuclear forces before they could be
launched (Lebow 1985). If a careful study of this comparative case found
enough similarities among the "independent variables" – for example, economic conditions, relative military balance, East–West political climate – then
one might use Mill's method of difference to account for their different
outcomes. The "dependent variable" would be the contribution of troop
reductions to ending the Cold War – in this interpretation explained by the
different attitudes and policies of the two leaders toward nuclear weapons.[4]

---

[4] For a more detailed process-tracing exercise comparing these cases, see Evangelista 1999.

I'm suprised isn't essay on this week's list

Economic decline and the "hoop test"

Given that the main realist accounts stress economic constraints as prompting Soviet military retrenchment, and that ideational and coalition-politics approaches also acknowledge the role of economic concerns, we might say that economic decline easily passes the "hoop test." If there were no evidence that Soviet leaders were concerned about economic conditions, we would exclude that factor from our explanations for the end of the Cold War. But, of course, there is plenty of evidence. The problem is quite the opposite. Dissatisfaction with the state of the Soviet economy and the system of central planning is evident throughout the history of the Soviet Union, reflected in the frequent attempts to reform economic management associated with names such as Evsei Liberman and Nikolai Kosygin during the Khrushchev and Brezhnev years. In that regard, to invoke the individual level of analysis, we might say that the person most responsible for the end of the Cold War was Stalin – the one who created the economic system that gave priority to military production through "extensive" mobilization of raw materials and labor, while sowing the seeds of agriculture's ruin through collectivization and allowing light industry and consumer welfare to languish (Kennan 1947: 577–578). Over time, as Jack Snyder's analysis explains, the policies of Stalin's coalition of heavy industrialists, party ideologues, and the military sector gave rise to the counter-coalition that backed Gorbachev, and before him, Georgii Malenkov, Khrushchev, and Kosygin (Snyder 1987).

Without further specificity, the economic explanation takes itself out of the competition for being the best account of the Cold War's end because it passes the hoop test so easily. To adjudicate between economic factors and other explanations, we need to "disaggregate" the economic explanation, by identifying more specific variants that we can evaluate against the existing evidence. William Wohlforth and his co-authors, for example, have stressed the influence of economic "burdens of empire," particularly energy subsidies to the East European allies and the opportunity costs to the USSR of selling its vast supply at below world-market prices. This analysis leads them to conclude that "the Soviet Union's economic crisis was to a significant degree endogenous to the international environment" (Brooks and Wohlforth 2003: 296).[5] Other analysts – by disaggregating the variable of economic burden – disagree

[5] The cost of oil hit a historic low during the Gorbachev years, so the opportunity costs were not as great as they were during the period 1973 to 1985. Thanks to Andrew Bennett for this point.

with Wohlforth's emphasis. Andrew Bennett (2003: 184), for example, argues that "the greatest drag on the Soviet economy was the inefficiency of central planning, the defense burden (even at 20 percent or more of GNP) was a distant second, and the costs of subsidies to the empire were a distant third."

"Breathing spaces" and "smoking guns"

One disaggregated variant of the economic-decline argument, quite popular in the late 1980s, related directly to the motivations for Gorbachev's December 1988 initiative. It suggested that Soviet political and military leaders were united in seeking to improve the Soviet military posture by short-term restraint in the interest of a longer-term competitive advantage. This explanation typically went by the name "breathing space" or "breathing spell." As late as October 1988, Robert Gates, then deputy director of Central Intelligence, was publicly and privately articulating this view (although not using it to explain the end of the Cold War, which he still considered an impossibility). Referring to the Soviet Union, which he had never visited, Gates offered his professional assessment: "The dictatorship of the Communist party remains untouched and untouchable."[6] He claimed that Gorbachev's goal was to use the improved international climate to obtain Western technology for the benefit of Soviet military modernization (Beschloss and Talbott 1993: 48). As he wrote in an intelligence assessment a year earlier, "a major purpose of economic modernization – as in Russia in those days of Peter the Great – remains the further increase in Soviet military power and political influence," but for now it needs "a prolonged breathing space" (Gates 2010).

Some studies do suggest that an unfavorable shift in the East–West military–technological balance underlay Gorbachev's reformist policies (Brooks 2005: 102–105). The implication is either that: Gorbachev lost control of the situation after opening his country to the West in the interest of narrow, instrumental military goals; or that he continued seeking Western integration for the sake of Soviet military objectives even at the expense of allowing a reunited Germany to remain in the US-led military alliance.

One could imagine a "smoking-gun" test to demonstrate Soviet military support for short-term retrenchment, including quantitative reductions and

---

[6] In fact, that summer, the 19th Party Conference had agreed to competitive elections with non-party candidates for the new Congress of People's Deputies (Savranskaya 2010: 61). For an ambitious effort to get Gates to visit Moscow, see Stone 1999, ch. 22.

budget cuts in the interest of longer-term qualitative advances to compete better with Western forces. The support would consist of public statements or internal documents where Soviet military officials would make their case to the civilian leadership. This would be an example of what Bennett and Checkel describe in their ninth criterion as a deductive "observable implication" of a claim that Soviet military officers were seeking a breathing space. We would expect to find some combination of cognitive and political causal mechanisms at work – persuasion and lobbying, for instance.

During the 1980s, a number of Western analysts thought this was precisely what was going on. They attributed a position in favor of near-term restraint in the interest of long-term competition to Marshal Nikolai Ogarkov, chief of the Soviet General Staff (Herspring 1990). As some critics recognized at the time, however, this view was based on a serious misreading of Ogarkov's writings (Parrott 1985; 1988; Phillips and Sands 1988; Snyder 1991; Ogarkov 1985). It was decisively refuted with the appearance of the memoir literature and internal documents recounting how Ogarkov lost his job. He was demoted for clashing with the civilian defense minister Dmitrii Ustinov and insisting on immediate increases in spending for research, development, and production of advanced conventional weapons in the service of a highly offensive strategy for war in Europe (Vorotnikov 1995: 45–48; Taylor 2003: 194–195). No one has yet found a smoking gun of advocacy by Soviet military officials for drastically reducing the military budget, much less thoroughgoing, market-oriented reforms and an opening to international trade and investment for the sake of rebuilding a high-tech Soviet military machine.

It is not so surprising that evidence of Soviet military support for retrenchment is so scarce. Before Gorbachev began undertaking his reforms, few in the West believed that retrenchment was on the agenda. The argument was widespread that the United States was in decline and that the Soviet Union had caught up and surpassed US military programs in both quantitative and qualitative terms. In 1983, President Reagan argued:

For 20 years the Soviet Union has been accumulating enormous military might. They didn't stop when their forces exceeded all requirements of a legitimate defensive capability. And they haven't stopped now . . . There was a time when we were able to offset superior Soviet numbers with higher quality, but today they are building weapons as sophisticated and modern as our own . . . With their present margin of superiority, why should they agree to arms reductions knowing that we were prohibited from catching up? (Reagan 1983)

Two prominent contributors to debates on the end of the Cold War have argued that the fact that people "were not aware of how close the Soviet-type economies were to utter collapse is not evidence that the collapse was not of central importance." They draw an analogy to predicting asteroids. "If, owing to limits on our powers of observation, we fail to foresee an asteroid impact on Earth, this predictive failure would indicate neither that the asteroid did not have an important impact, nor that our theories of astrophysics are flawed" (Brooks and Wohlforth 2003: 281). Thus, they seem to disagree with the editors of this volume who suggest that "theories that emphasize material power and structure require that actors be aware of power differentials and that they circumscribe their behavior when faced with more powerful opponents." In their view, "it is possible to use process tracing to assess power explanations by paying careful attention to sequencing and to what information actors had and when they had it" (Bennett and Checkel, this volume, Chapter 1, pp. 33, 34).

As it turns out, some analysts do argue that the Soviet military saw the asteroid coming and tried to do something about it. Following Bennett and Checkel, we can evaluate their explanations using process tracing. Proponents of the argument that military motives underlay Gorbachev's reforms claim to have found relevant evidence, but it does not come close to passing any reasonable process-tracing standard. William Odom, for example, argues that in the early 1980s: "Party officials throughout the country knew that the economy was in serious trouble, that social problems were acute, and that dramatic action, *particularly reductions in military spending*, was imperative to deal with the impending crises. The officer corps shared this view with party conservatives and reformers alike" (Odom 1998: 91 [emphasis added]).

Such an account, if true, would seriously undermine an explanation for the Gorbachev reforms that saw them stemming from "the natural constituency for reform, the well-educated urban middle class," intent on "breaking the fetters of the old mode of production," and seeking "to justify a shift in domestic arrangements away from the military industrial complex, central planning and obsessive secrecy," yet facing "resistance from the old-school military-industrial and ideological elites" (Snyder 2011: 563–564). In Odom's account, there is no such struggle between competing coalitions. Everyone is on the same page, in favor of retrenchment and reductions in military spending. And here is Odom's evidence: "Nine former Soviet officers, ranging from Marshal Yevgenii Shaposhnikov to a dissident lieutenant colonel, Aleksandr Rodin, said in retrospect that they believed at the time that the economy was in serious trouble and something had to be done about it, including significant cuts in military spending" (Odom 1998: 91, citing interviews from June and July 1995).

Absence of evidence as evidence of absence

From evidence of this quality, Odom (1998: 392) draws the conclusion that the military competition and pressure from the United States "contributed enormously to the economic and political climate that allowed Gorbachev to follow the new course he did." The mechanism associated with this explanation appears to mix cognitive and political elements. US policies put pressure on the Soviet economy. Military officers recognized that the struggling economy would provide a poor basis for defense, and therefore advocated reform and reductions in the military budget. They prevailed upon the party and government leaders to undertake the reforms. For such an argument, Odom's claim that the "officer corps shared this view with party conservatives and reformers alike" seems important. One wonders, though, whether the "absence of evidence" beyond nine retrospective interviews constitutes "evidence of absence" of genuine military support for the liberalizing reforms that entailed reducing the priority accorded to the military sector in the Soviet economy. If so, the economic-decline/breathing-space argument would be weakened vis-à-vis, for example, the political-coalition explanation for the end of the Cold War. The latter explanation makes a deductive assumption that the liberal supporters of Gorbachev's "new thinking" reforms would face opposition from old-thinking hardliners who populated the military-industrial sector and the party apparatus. That explanation would benefit from evidence of such opposition to reform – but it would also benefit from evidence of *absence* of support from the presumed opponents of reform.

I also interviewed Marshal Shaposhnikov (and others) in the mid-1990s, some months before Odom did. Shaposhnikov had served as head of the Soviet Air Forces and then Minister of Defense in 1991. I explicitly asked him whether US military-technological advances had induced the Soviet military to support *perestroika* and Gorbachev in the interest of a breathing space. He replied with a joke: "What do militarists and generals' wives have in common? A common enemy: disarmament and détente."[7] In other words, Soviet military officers were more concerned about the negative effects of Gorbachev's

---

[7] I posed the question in the context of an informal, small-group discussion at Harvard's Kennedy School of Government, October 18, 1994.

policies on their own careers and families – lower military budgets leading to the loss of their jobs – than to any long-term benefits to Soviet military technology some time in the distant future.

At this point on the evidentiary level, we would seem to be left with dueling interviews that fail to resolve a matter of equifinality, or the possibility that alternative causal pathways may lead to the same outcome (Bennett and Checkel, this volume, Chapter 1, pp. 19, 21). Both the claim that the reformers and the officer corps saw eye to eye on the need for retrenchment and the counterclaim that the reformers carried out retrenchment in the face of stiff opposition yield the same "dependent variable" – retrenchment. As our editors remind us, the absence of evidence does not necessarily mean the evidence of absence. Yet, with the advent to power of Mikhail Gorbachev, surely reform-oriented military officers would have had an incentive to make their views known – especially if those views constituted the most sensible response to external pressures. As Jacobs argues elsewhere in this volume, processes of political competition tend to select for actors who hold ideas that dovetail with the other exogenous, material influences on choice (Jacobs, this volume, Chapter 2, pp. 45–46). In May 1987, after an amateur West German pilot managed to fly unhindered all the way to Red Square, Gorbachev reached down into the ranks to choose Dmitrii Iazov to replace Sergei Sokolov as his defense minister. We now know that Gorbachev misjudged Iazov's reformist sympathies, given the latter's subsequent opposition to Soviet disarmament initiatives.[8] The absence of evidence of other high-level military officers ready to cut the military budget to win Gorbachev's favor or provide a breathing space strongly suggests that there were none. Otherwise, the processes of political competition – even in an authoritarian polity – should have revealed them.

Observable implications of deductive hypotheses

Stephen Brooks and William Wohlforth (2003: 298) have suggested that identifying disagreements on policy of the sort associated with domestic-coalition theories is beside the point. Highlighting a "lack of consensus," they write, "reflects a preoccupation with a different explanatory problem" from trying to account for the end of the Cold War – "namely, accounting for the specific

---

[8] A contemporaneous assessment of Soviet civilian and military views found military leaders publicly endorsing Gorbachev's call for reductions, but only in a multilateral, negotiated framework – whereas civilians were open to unilateral cuts. Most military officials – including Iazov – opposed a predominantly defense-oriented force structure; Phillips and Sands 1988.

details of individual decisions." "We do not claim," they write, "to account for each microanalytical decision or bargaining position adopted during the Cold War endgame." Moreover, they claim there are no "theoretical reasons to expect a consensus over the reorientation of Soviet foreign policy" (ibid.: 297).

For our purposes, however, seeking to explain "microanalytical" decisions is precisely how process tracing examines the deductive observable implications of hypothesized mechanisms (Bennett and Checkel, this volume, Chapter 1, p. 30). And there are indeed "theoretical reasons to expect a consensus" in the making of foreign policy – or, at least, that would seem an implication flowing from the deductive assumption of one particular school of thought: realism. One of realism's core assumptions is that states can be modeled as unitary, rational actors (Grieco 1997: 164–166). Even authors who identify disagreements between two particular forms of realism – "neo-realism" and "post-classical realism" – find little disagreement on this score: "both have a systemic focus; both are state-centric; both view international politics as inherently competitive; both emphasize material factors, rather than nonmaterial factors, such as ideas and institutions; and both assume states are egoistic actors that pursue self-help" (Brooks 1997: 446). On matters of national security, most realists posit that there are no meaningful differences at the domestic political level, arguing, with Stephen Krasner, that "it could be assumed that all groups in society would support the preservation of territorial and political integrity." In the "strategic arena," the state's "preferences are not likely to diverge from those of individual societal groups" (Krasner 1978: 70, 329).

So it does serve our explanatory purpose – especially adjudicating between realist and domestic-coalition accounts – to inquire into the relative degrees of support for Gorbachev's initiatives, and to ask which institutional actors favored which policy alternatives, as the competing theories make different predictions on these issues. An important distinction between the military reforms and the reductions announced in December 1988 and the earlier Khrushchev case is Gorbachev's focus on *defensive restructuring* of the Soviet armed forces to reduce their offensive capability. This was the military manifestation of the political decision to allow "freedom of choice" for the Eastern bloc countries. This political dimension was not always apparent to observers at the time, leading to explanations that favored material factors associated with realism. Some analysts maintained, for example, that the specifics of the force reductions and restructuring announced by Gorbachev at the United Nations were dictated by military needs and a heightened appreciation of defensive operations over offense. As one specialist put it, "few Westerners realize that new military technologies – first nuclear and then conventional – compelled Soviet force planners to reevaluate the role of the defense long before the arrival of Gorbachev" (FitzGerald 1989: 15; Sapir and Malleret 1990). If this is so, we would expect the domestic-coalition explanation to suffer: it does not deductively anticipate "Soviet force planners" to be members of the reformist coalition.

Evidence supporting such an interpretation of army-inspired reform would include Soviet military analyses – predating the December 1988 speech – that criticized overemphasis on offense and proposed the sorts of restructuring announced by Gorbachev. "Smoking-gun" evidence would include an actual plan from the Ministry of Defense upon which the UN speech was based.

When there is enough data: process-tracing lite

There is no such plan and no smoking gun affirming the Soviet military's role in initiating this reform. On the contrary, enough of the paper trail is available to show that the initiative came from the civilian side of Gorbachev's administration (and outside of it) and the military was tasked only with implementation of the reforms. This particular issue is well suited for addressing the questions raised in the introduction by Bennett and Checkel on how far down to go in gathering detailed evidence (this volume, Chapter 1, pp. 27–28). We know, for example, from his own admission, that Sergei Akhromeev, Ogarkov's deputy and then successor as chief of the General Staff, defended the marshal's views on warfare in Europe to Gorbachev, including their offensive orientation (Akhromeev and Kornienko 1992: 65–67). In April 1988, the Soviet Foreign Ministry commissioned an academic institution, the Institute of the World Economy and International Relations (known by its Russian acronym, IMEMO), to formulate a proposal for conventional-force reductions. The IMEMO team invited the Defense Ministry to send representatives, but it declined.[9]

In July 1988, Gorbachev instructed the General Staff to draw up a plan for a major cut in conventional forces. The study examined the possibility of reductions in the range of 300,000 to 700,000 troops in the context of multilateral negotiations, whereas the civilians favored unilateral cuts on the order of a million troops and a thoroughgoing defensive restructuring (Oberdorfer 1992: 319; Akhromeev and Kornienko 1992: 212).[10] On November 9, 1988,

---

[9] Author's interview with Gennadii Koloskov, IMEMO staff member, Ann Arbor, Michigan, October 19, 1990. IMEMO is a major focus of Checkel 1997.

[10] Aleksei Arbatov, interview with author, Washington, DC, June 10, 1991.

the Soviet defense council, chaired by Gorbachev, ordered the Defense Ministry to prepare a plan for the withdrawal of Soviet troops from Eastern Europe.[11] Armed with the IMEMO/Foreign Ministry proposal for unilateral reductions and defensive restructuring and the General Staff's implementation plan, Gorbachev presented the initiative to his colleagues in the leadership, pretty much at the last minute according to long-time Soviet ambassador to the United States and then Central Committee secretary for international affairs Anatolii Dobrynin (1995: 626).

For our purposes, two components of Gorbachev's resulting December 7 UN speech demand the most attention. The political component announced a rejection of class struggle as the basis of international relations in favor of an appreciation for diversity of political forms captured in the term "freedom of choice" – applied explicitly to the socialist bloc as "a universal principle to which there should be no exceptions." The military component announced the unilateral reduction of half a million troops and a restructuring of the remaining forces to remove the elements most suited to a rapid offensive invasion (Gorbachev 1988b). The combination of the two components implied that the countries of Eastern Europe could pursue their own political destiny without fear of Soviet invasion.

As presented here, the process-tracing exercise leading to Gorbachev's speech followed a simple chronological approach, one attentive to which actors – identified as theoretically relevant – were doing what and when. The civilian reformers took the initiative to put forward proposals. The top leader accepted the proposals and issued orders to the military to implement them. He then secured a pro forma approval from his fellow leaders at the last minute and made the public announcement of his initiative.

Maybe that would be enough "data" to satisfy political-science requirements of process tracing. The exercise seems to demonstrate that the military were not behind the initiative, even though "objectively" there was no need for so many troops in Europe, given the prospect that nuclear deterrence could maintain Soviet security, and a breathing space could provide the possibility of stronger, more technically advanced Soviet forces in the future. That "new thinkers" in the Foreign Ministry and civilian academics (representatives of the intelligentsia) promoted the initiative, and Gorbachev kept it secret from his more conservative Politburo colleagues (representatives of the KGB, the military-industrial sector, and other traditional constituencies), lends support to an explanation focused on divergent political coalitions.

---

[11] Politburo meeting, minutes, December 27, 1988, published in *Istochnik* 1993.

Process tracing further back: avoiding "just so" stories

Expanding the investigation temporally – and remaining "open to inductive insights," as our editors recommend in their eighth criterion – allow for the accumulation of more evidence that might help to evaluate these explanations further, together with others that have received less attention so far (see also Jacobs, this volume, Chapter 2). For example, examining the intellectual provenance of "freedom of choice" has taken Robert English (2000) back to the 1950s and 1960s, when many of the people who became Gorbachev's advisors were influenced by their interactions with socialists from Eastern Europe and elsewhere and the intellectual currents associated with concepts such as interdependence and globalization. English's book-length process-tracing exercise brings to the fore ideational factors that tend to line up with the more instrumental use of ideas in Snyder's political-coalition approach. Criticizing realists for their economic determinism, English downplays what he calls "arguments from hindsight – reading a near-desperate 'necessity' back into 1985 from the disintegration that came in 1991." On the contrary, "the anti-isolationist, globalist, social democratic-leaning intellectual current that provided the crucial soil for particular reformist policies was fertilized in the optimistic late 1950s and 1960s, not the crisis-ridden late 1970s" (English 2003: 245, 269).

Realists might find such an intellectual excursion superfluous. For them, key concepts, such as the "security dilemma" – developed by Robert Jervis – could have predicted the Soviet behavior announced on December 7, 1988 (Wohlforth 2011: 445). In fact, Gorbachev and his advisors read quite a lot and listened to people who espoused concepts similar to the insights provided by Jervis. But the provenance was different. Tracing the military component of the December 1988 announcement back in time reveals roots in a transnational community of US arms control activists and European peace researchers who introduced the concept of defensive restructuring into the Soviet debate. They made common cause with Soviet civilian analysts and a few retired military officers – mainly working at academic institutions – interested in uncovering a Soviet military tradition of defense and inspired by Khrushchev's example of unilateral reductions.[12] Important

---

[12] For the pre-Gorbachev period, see three articles by Shenfield (1984a; 1984b; 1985). For the reconstruction of a Soviet defensive tradition, see Kokoshin (1988), Kokoshin and Larionov (1987), and Kokoshin and Lobov (1990).

foreign influences included Anders Boserup, the Danish physicist and theo-retician of "non-offensive defense," and a number of German specialists work-ing on detailed technical proposals for what they called *strukturelle Nichtangriffsfähigkeit* – structural inability to attack (Ströber-Fassbender 1988). Particularly influential were ideas promoted mainly in social-democratic circles in West Germany and Scandinavia and reflected in the Independent Commission on Disarmament and Security Issues, directed by former Swedish Prime Minister Olof Palme. The Palme Commission, on which a couple of reform-oriented Soviet academic and retired military figures served, produced a report called "Common Security," which helped to introduce that concept into the Soviet political discourse (Risse-Kappen 1994; Risse 2011).

Calling attention to the role of the Palme Commission helps to address another popular explanation for the Soviet peaceful withdrawal from Eastern Europe, foreshadowed by Gorbachev's 1988 speech. Scholars representing many otherwise conflicting theoretical orientations typically agree that *nuclear weapons* played an important role. Once the Soviet Union achieved nuclear parity with the United States, the argument goes, the importance of Eastern Europe as a buffer zone lost its significance. Soviet security was assured by the threat of nuclear retaliation against any attack (Oye 1995; Deudney and Ikenberry 2011b). Process tracing the December 1988 initiative renders this explanation problematic. Multiple sources confirm that what Gorbachev found attractive about defensive restructuring was the prospect that it would *diminish* the nuclear threat for both sides ("common security") and enhance the prospects for nuclear *disarmament*. His allergy to nuclear weapons is one of his best-known characteristics – one that, significantly, he shared with Ronald Reagan. The Palme Commission and like-minded US and European researchers stressed the need to reduce conventional forces – and particularly to make disproportionate cuts in the offensively oriented Soviet army – as a prerequisite for the nuclear initiatives they favored, including a nuclear-free zone in Central Europe (Independent Commission on Disarmament and Security Issues 1982; Forsberg 1985).

Soviet researchers picked up on these ideas, developed them in their own studies, and arranged for their Western colleagues to travel to Moscow and meet high-level reformers, including Gorbachev himself, to promote specific initiatives (Institut mirovoi ekonomiki i mezhdunarodnykh otnoshenii 1987: 190–191, 202–206, 218–224; Forsberg 1981a; 1981b; 1987; 1989; Gorbachev 1988a). If Gorbachev had been reading Jervis rather than listening to the peace researchers, he would have been more sympathetic to the importance of a secure, "second-strike" retaliatory posture as Jervis's preferred way of dealing with the implications of nuclear weapons for the security dilemma. Instead, Gorbachev favored disarmament.

Gorbachev had already set himself the goal of nuclear disarmament long before the December 1988 speech. His first major foreign-policy initiative upon becoming Soviet leader in March 1985 was to impose a unilateral moratorium on Soviet nuclear testing, one that he extended multiple times during more than a year and a half, even as the United States refused to join it. In January 1986, Gorbachev launched a plan to eliminate all nuclear weapons by the year 2000. Few took it seriously at the time, but, as Robert English (2003: 256) points out, Gorbachev's plan "pointed the way toward precisely the agreements later reached" – including the complete elimination of intermediate-range nuclear missiles, a 50 percent reduction in strategic forces, and major cuts in conventional forces.[13]

Gorbachev was not a big believer in nuclear deterrence. At least he did not value it enough to prefer it over nuclear disarmament. That is why the Reykjavik summit meeting with Ronald Reagan made such an impression on him. A story from Reagan's Secretary of State George Shultz makes the point:

I recall meeting with Gorbachev after we both had left office. He came to my house on the Stanford campus and we sat in the backyard talking over what had taken place and where the world was going. I said to him, "When you and I entered office, the cold war was about as cold as it could get, and when we left, it was basically over. What do you think was the turning point?" He did not hesitate. "Reykjavik," he said. (Shultz 2007: xxiii–xxiv)

The Reykjavik summit of October 1986 was the occasion when both Gorbachev and Reagan publicly expressed support for a nuclear-free world and came close to negotiating the complete elimination of nuclear-armed missiles. Reagan recognized the effect that their mutual antipathy toward nuclear weapons had on Gorbachev. "I might have helped him see that the Soviet Union had less to fear from the West than he thought, and that the Soviet empire in Eastern Europe wasn't needed for the security of the Soviet Union" (Reagan 1992: 708). Anatolii Cherniaev, Gorbachev's main foreign policy aide, took Reagan's profession of the West's goodwill to heart more than anyone. In May 1990, he reassured Gorbachev that it would be safe to withdraw Soviet forces from Europe, for "no one will attack us even if we disarm totally."[14]

---

[13] For an analysis that did recognize the seriousness of Gorbachev's proposal, see Evangelista (1986).
[14] Anatolii Cherniaev, memorandum to Gorbachev, May 4, 1990, quoted in Savranskaya 2010: 17.

Process tracing further back still: policy windows remain open

Thus, process tracing back several years before the December 1988 speech and the later decisions to withdraw Soviet armed forces from Eastern Europe highlights other variables – such as the level of trust between the leaders and the importance of their shared commitment to nuclear disarmament – that might otherwise be missed.[15] Much of Gorbachev's foreign-policy orientation – including his nuclear allergy and his commitment to *glasnost* and transparency – comes into clearer focus if we consider the catastrophic nuclear explosion and fire at the Chernobyl plant in April 1986 in Ukraine, which "cost thousands of lives and billions of rubles," thus contributing to Soviet economic woes that only worsened over time. Yet, as Robert English (2003: 260) suggests, "its cognitive impact was still greater. Chernobyl absolutely consumed the Politburo for three months."

For the purposes of a process-tracing exercise, Chernobyl provided a "policy window" of the sort that explanations blending ideas and political coalitions would recognize (Checkel 1997). Gorbachev and his supporters used the tragedy to prolong the unilateral Soviet moratorium on nuclear testing against plainly evident domestic opposition in August 1986, for example, and to push through an agreement in September at the Stockholm Conference on Confidence- and Security-Building Measures and Disarmament in Europe to allow on-site "challenge" inspections – an unprecedented concession in the history of East–West arms control (Evangelista 1999).

Chernobyl also sheds light on the relevance of theories that link cognitive change to new ideas. Marshal Sergei Akhromeev, somewhat of a skeptic on Gorbachev's ambitious anti-nuclear initiatives, recalled the impact the nuclear explosion had on him personally – "imprinted in my memory like the start of the war with fascist Germany on 22 June 1941." He considered the event a turning point: "After Chernobyl . . . people began to regard all problems connected with nuclear weapons much differently" (Akhromeev and Kornienko 1992: 98–99). Responding to Akhromeev's remark, Robert English points out that "unlike Hitler's sudden and devastating strike of 1941, whose enduring lesson was to build up forces and heighten vigilance, Chernobyl's message was the opposite; traditional military principles such as surprise, superiority, and

---

[15] On the issue of trust, see Bennett (2003), whose attention to process tracing and competing explanations could merit the chapter a place in this volume.

even parity lost meaning when even a small reactor accident could wreak such havoc" (English 2000: 216).

As late as May 1988 – over two years after the accident – US Secretary of State George Shultz reported that he was "struck by how deeply affected Gorbachev appeared to be by the Chernobyl accident," when he and Reagan and their spouses spent an evening at the Gorbachev's dacha at the conclusion of a summit meeting in Moscow: "It was obvious from that evening that Chernobyl has left a strong anti-nuclear streak in Gorbachev's thinking" (quoted in Reagan 1992: 710–711). This was precisely the time when Gorbachev was drawing on the Foreign Ministry's proposal for unilateral conventional cuts, justifying it in part as a means to reduce the nuclear danger.

Process tracing forward: unitary actors exit the stage

Going back some years before the event one seeks to explain through process tracing reveals evident benefits in identifying important explanatory factors that might otherwise be missed. The same goes for looking into the future beyond the immediate event. Explanations founded on a unitary-actor assumption of state behavior would not expect problems of implementation of a decision once it is made. Explanations that describe the dependent variable as "why the Cold War ended peacefully on largely Western terms" (Brooks and Wohlforth 2003: 298) neglect Soviet initiatives that differed from or were orthogonal to what the United States and its NATO allies preferred. Yet, the period after December 1988 witnessed both developments, and they shed light on explanations for the end of the Cold War.

Opposition to Gorbachev's initiative emerged immediately in the wake of the UN speech. A senior aide to Foreign Minister Eduard Shevardnadze complained that "the unilateral cutbacks were the most difficult issue the diplomats had ever faced with the military, even more touchy than the problems of nuclear arms reductions" (Oberdorfer 1992: 319). On December 27, Gorbachev convened the Politburo to get its formal endorsement of his disarmament plan. Shevardnadze took the occasion to accuse Dmitrii Iazov, the defense minister, of conspiring to thwart Gorbachev's objectives. The military's position, he argued, "directly contradicts what was said from the tribune" by Gorbachev at the United Nations. "I have in mind the formulation of the defense ministry that the troops remaining on the territory of the socialist countries after the reductions will be given a 'large' – and, I stress – 'large' defensive 'orientation' [napravelenie]. These are only words, but they have principled significance. Comrade Gorbachev spoke of giving these forces a different, exclusively [*odnoznachno*] defensive structure."

The difference between the two formulations, argued Shevardnadze, was "large and important," especially given that the West would be following every subsequent move taken by the Soviets. Now the Defense Ministry was "proposing to speak not about structure but about some abstract orientation." Shevardnadze insisted that the reductions be carried out exactly in the spirit intended by Gorbachev, with maximum openness and publicity (*glasnost*), both toward the West and toward the new Soviet Congress of People's Deputies that was intended for the first time to submit the Soviet military budget to democratic scrutiny.[16]

Shevardnadze had good reason to be concerned. In his response to the foreign minister's accusations, Defense Minister Iazov explained that the army planned to bring about the "defensive orientation" simply by withdrawing tanks, as Gorbachev announced at the United Nations. Tank regiments would be removed from the larger tank divisions deployed with the Group of Soviet Forces in Germany, but within those divisions the motorized rifle regiments – with considerable offensive potential themselves – would remain. This was an augur of worse to come.

Gorbachev charged ahead with his attempt to create the "common European home" that he envisioned, demilitarized and denuclearized, and working toward what his foreign minister hoped would become "a unified economic, legal, humanitarian, cultural, and ecological space" (Savranskaya 2010: 45). His initiatives in this respect reveal the normative, ideational, and personal factors that a calculating instrumental approach hides. That approach holds that systemic constraints obliged Gorbachev to "acquiesce to western terms for the post-war settlement" (Wohlforth 2011: 445) in order to reduce the burden of supporting allies, to obtain financial credits, and to reap the supposed benefits of integration with the international economy (which in the event led post-Soviet Russia to suffer a 50 percent decline in its gross national product).

If acquiescing to Western terms was key to achieving Gorbachev's goals, why did he insist on doing such things as announcing the unilateral withdrawal of 500 tactical nuclear weapons from Eastern Europe at his first meeting with US Secretary of State James Baker in May 1989? President Bush and his national security advisor Brent Scowcroft "saw the event almost purely in terms of upstaging Baker and blindsiding him" (Blanton 2010: 69).

---

[16] Politburo meeting, minutes, December 27, 1988 (note 9), 137–138.

But Gorbachev was fixated on his normative goal of a nuclear-free world. This is a case that seems to fit Bennett and Checkel's requirement that "theories about norms – a form of social structure – need to show that norms prevented actors from doing things they otherwise would have done" (this volume, Chapter 1, pp. 34–35). A materialist theory would have Gorbachev do the minimum necessary to cash in on his surrender to the West. Gorbachev's normative concerns outweighed a more practical approach.

The cautious Bush administration would have been pleased had Gorbachev acquiesced to business as usual in European security – allowing the United States to upgrade its Lance missiles in West Germany, agreeing on token reductions under the auspices of the negotiations on Mutual and Balanced Force Reductions. But the Soviet leader had grander ambitions. He proposed a new forum that would entail serious reductions in military forces on both sides. Shevardnadze, at the opening session of the talks on Conventional Forces in Europe (CFE), claimed that the progress in disarmament had already "shaken the iron curtain, weakened its rusting foundations, pierced new openings, accelerated its corrosion." He proposed the withdrawal of all tactical nuclear weapons from Europe – something the United States eventually did on a unilateral basis in 1991, leaving only a couple of hundred out of what had amounted to some 7,000 at their peak (Blanton 2010: 63).

The opponents of Shevardnadze and Gorbachev were unenthusiastic about the CFE treaty for the same reason the foreign minister and his boss liked it (Baklanov 1991a; 1991b). In early 1990, a journalist close to the communist old guard and military hardliners wrote that "the sentimental theory of 'our common European home' has brought about the collapse of Eastern Europe's communist parties, a change in the state structures, and imminent reunification of the two Germanys" (Prokhanov 1990). The growing democratization of Soviet society and the open debates in the Congress of People's Deputies sharpened the division between liberal anti-militarists and the stalwarts of the traditional military-industrial sector highlighted in Jack Snyder's (2011) analysis. The situation became increasingly polarized, with military officers explicitly challenging the interference and competence of civilian reformers (Volkov 1989; Kirilenko 1990; Liubimov 1989; Moiseev 1989). The military diatribes in turn provoked Georgii Arbatov (1990), a usually cautious senior foreign policy analyst, to launch a direct attack against the military's priorities in a popular-magazine article he entitled "The Army for the Country, or the Country for the Army?" Evidence of the extent to which the political coalitions Snyder had identified were clearly aligned against each other was apparent in another widely circulated article; it expressed concern that too-rapid attempts to impose civilian control on the erstwhile privileged military sector of Soviet society might provoke a dangerous backlash (Snyder and Kortunov 1989).[17]

Military officials' unhappiness with Gorbachev's arms control agreements resulted in an attempt to undermine the CFE Treaty or at least reinterpret it in their favor. First, in the weeks prior to the signing of the Treaty in November 1990, the Soviet military moved enormous stocks of weapons and equipment out of the "Atlantic-to-the-Urals" area covered by the Treaty, thereby reducing the amount liable for reduction. Second, Soviet negotiators, relying on data supplied by their military representatives, provided figures for the amount of equipment subject to reduction that were much lower than Western assessments. Third, and most serious, the Soviet military reassigned three ground-forces divisions from the army to the navy in order to escape treaty limitations and claimed that four "naval infantry" or marine regiments were also exempt (*Sovetskaia Rossiia*, January 9, 1991, cited in Gelman 1992: 39). As one analyst has described, these actions threatened to open "a massive loophole in the treaty's numerical limits: the Soviets claimed, in essence, that a unit could be exempted from CFE limitation simply by giving the navy titular authority over it" (Falkenrath 1995: 132).

It seems certain that these initiatives were taken by the Soviet military without the knowledge of the civilian authorities. Soviet negotiators apparently learned for the first time of the magnitude of the withdrawal of equipment from Europe from their Western counterparts in September 1990. Shevardnadze (1991) described his position in an interview: "The transfer of huge quantities of equipment to areas beyond the Urals created an awkward situation in our relations with partners . . . I as Foreign Minister was presented with a fait accompli." As one observer has pointed out, "there is some reason to believe that this embarrassing revelation – or, more precisely, his indignation at having been lied to by his own military – contributed to Shevardnadze's decision to resign two weeks later" (Falkenrath 1995: 130).

On the other side of the barricades, Marshal Akhromeev was going through similar turmoil. Contrary to the breathing-space or unitary-actor approaches, Akhromeev was not a key figure in promoting Soviet disarmament initiatives. Much of the time, he was frozen out of discussions related to military reform. "Not once in my memory," wrote Akhromeev in his memoirs, "did M. S. Gorbachev thoroughly discuss with the military leadership the military-political situation in Europe and perspectives on its development

---

[17] This evidence might be slightly contaminated by Snyder's co-authorship, however.

during 1986–1988." Only "in relation to concrete decisions already taken did the military introduce proposals concerning the armed forces" (Akhromeev and Kornienko 1992: 70–72). In his own memoirs, Gorbachev (1995b: 13) flatly states that the Ministry of Defense never once proposed reductions in forces or the production of weapons. Akhromeev reports that Gorbachev repeatedly insisted that the military give up its monopoly on analysis of security affairs: "We value your opinion as professionals, as theoreticians and practitioners of military affairs," argued Gorbachev, "But you, as the interested parties, try to arrange things so that the problem gets resolved the way you propose. Let's listen to the opinions of others, including politicians and scholars." Akhromeev agreed "in principle," but he sincerely believed that the military "as the people responsible for the country's defense, were the most competent in these matters" (Akhromeev and Kornienko 1992: 70–72).

Akhromeev suggests that Gorbachev knew what kind of reaction he would receive from the military if he forthrightly revealed his proposals for reductions, retrenchment, and restructuring. Gorbachev's policy would have been recognized as a radical break with "the entire understanding by the military leadership of the essence of the country's defense capability in Europe." Withdrawal from Eastern Europe meant giving up "that which had been won at a cost of enormous amounts of blood and millions of lives" (Akhromeev and Kornienko 1992: 72). In an interview conducted four years after the marshal's death, his wife Tamara Vasil'evna summarized the sources of her husband's resistance to Gorbachev's reforms: "Sergei Fedorovich [Akhromeev] understood that Gorbachev's policy would lead to the breakup of the Warsaw Pact, the whole system of security in Europe. He considered his participation in the creation [of that system] his life's work . . . Having left the General Staff, he couldn't work as Gorbachev's adviser for very long. He wrote several letters of resignation" (Akhromeeva 1995: 16–17).

Akhromeev carried out the ultimate act of insubordination when he involved himself with other key national security figures – including Defense Minister Dmitrii Iazov and KGB chief Vladimir Kriuchkov – in the unsuccessful coup against Gorbachev in August 1991. When it failed in the face of resistance from Russian President Boris Yeltsin and thousands of mobilized citizens, the other plotters went to jail. Akhromeev committed suicide.

Realist accounts insist that there was simply no alternative to the policies pursued by Gorbachev. If his opponents were unhappy enough to kill themselves, that only reinforced the fact that there was no way out. But, as Savranskaya (2010: 45) reminds us, "during the second half of the 1980s the USSR still had the capability to dominate its allies militarily; even in 1990 several hundred thousand troops remained in Eastern Europe." Robert Zoellick, a top State Department aide to James Baker, explained at the time that "the presence of 380,000 Soviet troops in the GDR was means enough for obstruction" (quoted in Sarotte 2009: 125). The would-be putschists were certainly obstruction-minded when it came to Gorbachev's policy on Germany. If they had been able to convince Gorbachev to implement their own preferences – say, simply by leaving Soviet troops in East Germany – they would have undermined Gorbachev's hopes for integrating the Soviet economy into the global market system and reaping whatever benefits it had to offer. But a successful coup would have yielded the same result even quicker. Clearly, the opponents of *perestroika* and "new thinking" had different priorities from its supporters – a conclusion that supports both the "ideas" approach associated with English (2000) and Checkel (1997) and the domestic-coalition approach favored by Snyder (2011).

Process tracing further forward: uncovering revealed preferences

Brooks and Wohlforth (2003: 299) acknowledge reluctance among some of the more conservative members of the Politburo, such as Yegor Ligachev, to weaken Soviet military might in the interest of retrenchment, but they deem such preferences quixotic under the circumstances. The way in which they make their point is revealing: "Ligachev wanted to slash defense outlays without reducing military capabilities. Doubtless Gorbachev would have loved to have been able to do this. What leader wouldn't?" This assumption about Gorbachev's own preferences points up the limits of the realist approach. Every serious account of Gorbachev's personality and background stresses that he was not an enthusiast of Soviet military power. From his 1969 visit to Czechoslovakia in the wake of the Soviet invasion, if not earlier (given how his family and hometown suffered during World War II), Gorbachev harbored clear anti-militarist tendencies that he managed to hide just long enough to get elected General Secretary (Bennett 2003; Brown 1996; 2007; English 2000; Zubok 2003). They provided a key impetus to his foreign policy and explain many initiatives that are hard to understand from the standpoint of a rational cost–benefit calculus (such as nuclear test moratoria or unilateral withdrawals of missiles that put Soviet "partners" in a difficult position, but saved little money).

A useful counterfactual experiment would be to wonder what Gorbachev would have done had the Soviet Union during his tenure as leader benefited from the high oil prices that Vladimir Putin's Russia subsequently enjoyed, or (less plausibly) if his domestic reforms had brought economic growth and prosperity. He probably would have been in less of a hurry to "off-load" the burden of the East European subsidies, but would he have been satisfied with a status quo that kept the likes of Erich Honecker and Gustáv Husák in power and maintained history's highest concentration of conventional and nuclear weaponry on the Soviet doorstep in Central Europe? If the East Europeans had sought to leave the Warsaw Pact, would a Gorbachev-led USSR, rich in oil money and/or with a vigorous reformed economy, have used military force to prevent them? The economic costs that the realists cite for Soviet non-use of force in 1989 to 1990 – Western refusal to allow Soviet integration into the global market in the wake of an invasion – would not have served as a deterrent. Still, it would be hard to imagine Gorbachev wielding the military instrument under such circumstances. A counterfactual thought experiment of this type highlights the elements of an explanation that stress Gorbachev's ideational commitments and personality.

Another element of Gorbachev's personality which is hard for realists to understand is how much he was concerned for the well-being of ordinary Soviet citizens. His preoccupation about the relative economic performance of the Soviet Union and the West was not founded primarily on worries about the security implications, as the "breathing space" arguments hold. Gorbachev traveled widely in Western Europe, not only in his professional capacity, but also on vacations with his wife, Raisa Maksimovna. He admired the reform communists of Italy and the social democrats of West Germany, Scandinavia, and the Low Countries, and was impressed by their societies' ability to provide a high level of material welfare. "Why do we live worse than other developed countries?" he asked himself during his foreign trips (Gorbachev 1995a: 165; Lévesque 1997; Rubbi 1990).

Many observers still believe that Gorbachev was mainly motivated by an interest in maintaining the Soviet Union's international status as a super-power under the terms established by the Cold War. Retrenchment was the necessary approach in order for the Soviet Union to re-emerge as the worthy rival of the United States in a bipolar world. Retrenchment dictated "freedom of choice" in Eastern Europe and the withdrawal of Soviet armed forces. Missing from this interpretation is Gorbachev's antipathy to things military and his concern for popular welfare as motives for his reforms. Our editors make good suggestions for how to uncover "revealed preferences" – by comparing public statements to private ones and giving "spontaneous and unplanned statements more weight than planned statements as indicators of genuine beliefs" (Bennett and Checkel, this volume, Chapter 1, p. 33; see also Jacobs, this volume, Chapter 2). This technique works rather well in surfacing Gorbachev's concerns in the face of the deteriorating economic situation in Eastern Europe. In March 1989, for example, Gorbachev met with the Soviet ambassadors to the Eastern European allies, nearly all in an advanced state of turmoil. This group of officials "traditionally consisted of party functionaries picked for their ideological correctness rather than their diplomatic skills," and many were outspoken critics of Gorbachev's conciliatory approach.

This would have been an audience potentially receptive to a case for retrenchment in the interest of long-term Soviet military power. Yet, in evidently impromptu remarks, Gorbachev did not mention this factor at all. Certainly, he complained about the burden of the subsidies to the ungrateful allies – but mainly out of a sense of injustice and resentment: "There is 100 kilograms of meat per capita in the GDR. And they continue to demand raw materials for special prices. This is solidarity! They could not care less about our problems and difficulties ... They resell the specially priced resources they get from us to the West for hard currency. Such is their reciprocity!" The ambassadors might also have welcomed some indication of Soviet willingness to use force to intimidate the proponents of democratic change. Yet, Gorbachev insisted: "We are excluding the possibility of bloody methods." His bottom line was the importance of *perestroika* at home. "We, the Soviet Union need *perestroika*. We must find a new kind of society with it. We can no longer tolerate the situation our people find themselves in now. *Perestroika* is vitally important to us ... We need *perestroika*. The people deserve it."[18]

Conclusion: process tracing all the way down

The extensive range of theories brought to bear to explain the end of the Cold War, and the fact that the topic has continued to engage scholars for more than twenty years, belie early claims that the event constitutes "a mere data point" that could not serve to test or develop theories of international politics.[19] The first claim made by this chapter is that the "event" of the Cold War

---

[18] Notes of Mikhail Gorbachev's meeting with Soviet ambassadors to socialist countries, March 3, 1989, in Savranskaya *et al.* 2010: 414–417. The characterization of the ambassadors is Savranskaya's.
[19] Robert Keohane, quoted anonymously in Lebow 1994.

is made up of many events, and therefore many possible data points. The second claim is that process tracing is a useful method for evaluating the competing theoretical explanations. The third claim, consistent with the volume editors' expectations, is that evaluating explanations entails identifying their underlying mechanisms and their observable implications. This effort reveals, again as the editors expected, that several mechanisms can account for the same events – the problem of equifinality.

A close examination of one particular key event in the end of the Cold War – Mikhail Gorbachev's 1988 declaration of "freedom of choice" for the states of Eastern Europe and the substantial unilateral reduction and restructuring of Soviet armed forces that made the declaration credible – yields no definitive victor in the "paradigm wars" that have often consumed the field of international relations. Instead, I argued that moving forward or backward in history from a limited process-tracing exercise not only sheds more light on the event in question, but also serves to identify other types of explanations and mechanisms that a narrow focus on the event itself kept hidden.

William Wohlforth concludes what by his count was roughly his twenty-fifth publication relating to the end of the Cold War with a wise comment about the relationship between the broad theoretical approaches favored by scholars and the events that make up the phenomena they seek to explain. He and his co-authors had endeavored over a period of some twenty years to account for the end of the Cold War by appealing to some of the fundamental tenets of realist theory. He was relatively satisfied with the results, whereas his critics typically continued to favor their own alternative approaches.[20] Wohlforth's concession to those approaches is that they may be necessary to account for the fact that even if realism tells us how states *should* behave in a given international environment, particular leaders might not follow its prescriptions.

Gorbachev, in Wohlforth's view, followed the dictates of realism only to a point because he failed to steer the Soviet ship of state to safer harbors, wrecking it on the shoals of nationalism and economic chaos instead. "In this case as in all cases," Wohlforth argued, "the confrontation between general theories and unique events yields puzzles. To answer the puzzle of why Gorbachev did not adopt a more realist grand strategy, one clearly must consider personality, ideas, domestic politics, contingency, and, in a word, history" (Wohlforth 2011: 456). Process tracing is the method of choice for

---

[20] This point is amply evident in the special issue of *International Politics* that I have frequently cited here.

explaining rich historical events such as the end of the Cold War, but unlike the Cold War itself – at least as realists understand it – we should not expect that process tracing will lead to any definitive victory of one side over the other. As Bennett and Checkel wisely counsel, analysts need to "remember that conclusive process tracing is good, but not all good process tracing is conclusive" (this volume, Chapter 1, pp. 30–31).

7 Process tracing, causal inference, and civil war

Jason Lyall

Introduction

Process tracing is an invaluable tool in the civil war scholar's toolkit. Or, rather, it *should* be, for it provides the ability to move beyond statistical association toward causal inference about why (and how) outcomes are produced in civil war settings. Yet, scholars have too often neglected its use. Instead, great pains have been taken to construct research designs that (at best) are able to identify suggestive correlations between variables, but lack the ability to test the mechanism(s) at work. Qualitative research is not immune to this criticism, either, for process tracing, when properly conducted, establishes a standard for rigor that often goes unmet even in detailed historical cases (see also Evangelista, this volume, Chapter 6). This is an unfortunate state of affairs; without understanding the causal processes that underpin associations, we foreclose opportunities to advance our theories of civil war and contribute to debates about the efficacy of different policies in violent settings.[1]

This chapter emphasizes the practicalities of marrying design-based inference with the strengths of process tracing to improve our ability to build and (especially) test theories about civil war onset and dynamics. Bennett and Checkel's ten best practices for process tracing (this volume, pp. 20–31) provide a springboard for a discussion of how to identify and conduct rigorous process tracing in settings marked by poor (or no) data, security concerns, and fluid events. The chapter also introduces ideas from the now-burgeoning literature on causal inference to help guide decisions about case

I thank Jeff Checkel and Andrew Bennett for helpful comments on an earlier draft, and Helinna Ayalew, Nicole Pflug, Andrey Semenov, and Boloroo Uuganbayar for excellent research assistance. Support from the Air Force Office of Scientific Research (Grant FA#9550-09-1-0314) is gratefully acknowledged. All errors are mine.

[1] Civil war is defined here as an armed confrontation resulting in at least 1,000 battle deaths between two or more combatants that were subject to the same political and legal system prior to the war.

selection and evidentiary standards. In particular, the approach advocated here draws on a potential outcomes framework that hinges on the use of counterfactual observations, "elaborate" theory, and qualitative evidence on treatment assignment to facilitate drawing causal inferences about why wars break out and how they are fought (see also Dunning, this volume, Chapter 8, on using process tracing to assess assignment to treatment).

I proceed as follows. The first section details the near absence of process tracing as a methodological approach in journal articles published since 1994 on civil war onset and dynamics. The second section draws on Elisabeth Wood's *Insurgent Collective Action and Civil War in El Salvador* (2003) as an illustration of Bennett and Checkel's ten "best practices" of process tracing. The third section discusses four additional "best practices" that arise from the causal inference literature and that are especially likely to be useful in civil war settings. Next, I detail potential research designs and the utility of process tracing for two literatures: the cross-national study of why civil wars break out, and the micro-level (for example, subnational) study of civilian victimization and its effects on subsequent participation in an insurgency. A fifth section briefly details the ethical and practical challenges faced by researchers in these environments. I conclude with thoughts about the use of process tracing to further our theoretical and practical understandings of civil war.

Process tracing and civil war

The meteoric rise of research on civil war has largely centered around two questions. One research agenda, heavily dominated by cross-national statistical analyses of the post-1945 era, has sought to explain civil war onset. These studies seek to draw an association between structural factors – state capacity, lootable resources, and ethnic exclusion from political power, to name three – and the outbreak of civil war. A second research program has drawn on a "micro-level" framework that explores the dynamics of violence – including its location, nature, and timing, especially toward civilians – at the subnational level. Unlike cross-national studies, these micro-level studies typically pay close attention to identifying the causal relationship between independent variables and outcomes using disaggregated time-series data and a host of sophisticated approaches, including quasi- and natural experiments, matching, and instrumental variable regression.

What role has process tracing played in these two research programs? Very little, it turns out. Figure 7.1 plots the sharp increase in the number of articles

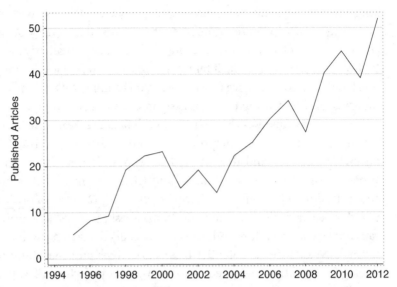

Figure 7.1 Number of articles published on civil war onset or dynamics in fifteen political science journals, 1995–2012

Note: The sample consists of 448 articles. Review articles and those in related fields (for example, genocide studies) were not included.

published annually in fifteen political science journals on the topic of civil war from 1995 to 2012.[2] Of these 448 articles, only 12 explicitly claim to be employing process tracing (all since 2004). While other work may be drawing implicitly on process-tracing insights (Checkel 2013b: 6), these articles reflect a more general trend away from the use of case studies, process tracing's natural habitat. Indeed, the share of articles with evidence from at least one case study has fallen from 80 percent in 1995 to about 50 percent in 2012. Over the past five years, an average of 44 percent of articles have had some form of case study, generously defined as a systematic discussion of a particular historical case at least four paragraphs in length.

The curious under-utilization of process tracing in civil war studies to date likely has several causes. Detailed process tracing can be difficult to execute within journal word limits. Perhaps relatedly, both cross-national and micro-level studies have increasingly adopted research designs built to measure the

[2] The journals surveyed include: *American Political Science Review, American Journal of Political Science, Perspectives on Politics, Journal of Conflict Resolution, International Organization, International Security, Journal of Peace Research, Security Studies, Journal of Politics, World Politics, Comparative Politics, Comparative Political Studies, Civil Wars, Terrorism and Political Violence,* and *International Studies Quarterly.*

direction and magnitude of the relationship between independent variables and outcomes rather than the mechanisms that underpin this relationship. This is a pragmatic move for research programs in their early stages. It can be difficult enough simply to identify the existence of a relationship given the multiple threats to inference, poor or absent data, and noisy proxy measures that often characterize research in conflict settings. Moreover, research designs that are tasked with establishing associations between variables may not be suitable for testing mechanisms. Yet, without moving beyond correlation, we are left blind about the processes and dynamics that drive these relationships, impoverishing both our theories and our ability to contribute to policy debates.

Process tracing in action: an example

The apparent neglect of process tracing in journal articles notwithstanding, there are still exemplars of the craft within political science and civil war studies. I use Elisabeth Wood's (2003) book, *Insurgent Collective Action and Civil War in El Salvador*, as an illustration of the ten "best practices" of process tracing outlined by Bennett and Checkel (this volume, pp. 20–31).[3] *Insurgent Collective Action* tackles the twin questions of why peasants supported (and joined) an armed insurrection against El Salvador's government during the 1970s and 1980s and how that participation evolved over time. Wood's argument, developed inductively and deductively in equal measure, is a nuanced one. Individuals supported the armed opposition, she argues, through a series of emotional mechanisms, including a belief in the moral purpose of acting, defiance in the face of state repression, and "pleasure in changing unjust social structures through intentional action" (Wood 2003: 235). More simply, pride in the "authorship" of their wartime actions (ibid.: 231) led some individuals to eschew the relative safety of fence-sitting in favor of risky acts that carried no credible promise of immediate (or future) material pay-off.

This interpretation of high-risk collective action is pitted against alternative explanations that emphasize the need for material incentives (Olson 1965; Popkin 1979), protection from state violence (Mason and Krane 1989; Goodwin 2001), or strong horizontal networks among peasants (Moore 1978; Scott 1976) to induce participation. In the language of this volume's best practices, Wood clearly "casts her net widely" for alternative explanations

---

[3] Waldner, this volume, Chapter 5, assesses Wood's use of process tracing in a different book – and comes to similar conclusions on its quality.

(criterion 1). She is also equally tough on these alternative explanations (criterion 2), marshaling an impressive array of ethnographic evidence from prolonged fieldwork to build her case.

To test these claims about the connection between emotions and participation, Wood initially engaged in eighteen months of fieldwork in four different sites in Usulután, a wealthy but conflicted department of El Salvador, and one site in Tenancingo in the northern department of Cuscatán.[4] Interviews with 200 *campesinos*, all but 24 of whom participated in the insurgency in some fashion, and mid-level Farabundo Martí National Liberation Front (Frente Farabundo Martí para la Liberación Nacional, or FMLN) commanders comprise the bulk of her evidence. In a particularly innovative (and non-intrusive) practice, twelve *campesino* teams engaged in collective map-making during three workshops in 1992 to provide a window into how peasant culture, especially pride in collective achievements, manifested itself. Wood is alert to the potential biases of her sources (criterion 3), particularly the problems associated with memory and (selective) recall of wartime activities. She also notes that her interviewees were not randomly selected, but instead chosen through *campesino* organizations, skewing her sample toward individuals who participated in the insurgency.

These materials, and the process of gathering them, enable Wood to generate inductively a wealth of insights (criterion 8). Yet, Wood's empirical claims do not rest solely on induction, for she also outlined the argument a priori using a formal model of individual decision-making (Wood 2003: 267–274). The micro-level motives for individual actions are also supported by insights from laboratory experiments developed by social psychologists. As a result, the book's argument draws on both inductive and deductive approaches to discipline its data gathering and to identify the specific processes that lead to *campesino* participation (criterion 9).

Wood selected her five field sites according to a fourfold criterion: their accessibility to an outside researcher; the presence of both supporters and non-supporters (for example, the regions had to be "contested"); variation in agrarian economies (to examine multiple pathways that peasants could take into the insurgency); and the presence of only one or two guerrilla factions (Wood 2003: 52–54). Taken together, it appears that these regions do offer representative examples of broader patterns of participation and violence in El Salvador's contested areas. What remains unclear, however, is whether these cases represent a "most likely" or "least likely" test for alternative explanations (criterion 4).

---

[4] The book draws on additional research and visits over the following twelve years (Wood 2003: xiii).

By truncating variation on the degree of state control or rebel presence, we may be working outside scope conditions where material incentives or desire for protection from state violence are most operative, for example.

Moreover, while Wood's "starting rule" (criterion 5) is clearly justified – sometimes researchers must simply take advantage of opportunities to start work that are created exogenously by lulls in fighting – her "stopping rule" is less clear (criterion 6). It appears that repetition in the *campesino*'s own stories for why they participated was the decision rule for ceasing data collection; once the researcher has heard the same stories repeated across different respondents, data collection stops.

In this instance, however, the process tracing is not necessarily conclusive (criterion 10). The decision to over-sample participants, for example, even though two-thirds of the population did not participate meaningfully in the insurgency (Wood 2003: 242), could overestimate the importance of emotive mechanisms. Wood herself notes how past patterns of state violence and proximity to insurgent forces (ibid.: 237–238) conditioned whether these emotions could be acted upon. Sorting out the relative causal weight between emotions and mechanisms of control or prior exposure to violence would require additional interviews among non-participants both within and out-side of these five areas. Not all process tracing is definitive – indeed, the best examples typically raise more questions that could be tackled by adjusting the research design or sample frame to provide additional empirical leverage on the original process under study.

Avoiding "just-so" stories: additional best practices

In the spirit of this volume's emphasis on practicality, I offer four additional process-tracing best practices that can help researchers avoid "just-so" stories when exploring civil war dynamics. These include: (1) identifying counter-factual ("control") observations to help isolate causal processes and effects; (2) creating "elaborate" theories where congruence across multiple primary indicators and auxiliary measures ("clues") is used to assess the relative performance of competing explanations; (3) using process tracing to under-stand the nature of treatment assignment and possible threats to causal inference; and (4) out-of-sample testing. The emphasis here is on situations where researchers wish to test empirical claims, but cannot randomize the "treatment" (for example, state violence, rough terrain, etc.) due to practical limitations or ethical concerns.

First – and taking the Rubin Causal Model (RCM) as a point of departure – I emphasize the need for counterfactual reasoning to measure causal effects (Rubin 2006; Rosenbaum 2010; see also Evangelista, this volume, Chapter 6). The intuition here is a simple one: every unit – be it a village, province, or state – has a different potential outcome depending on its assignment to a particular treatment. Since we cannot by definition observe all outcomes in the same unit, we must engage in counterfactual reasoning to supply the "match" (or "control") for the unit where an outcome was unobserved. The more similar the control and treated observations along the values of their independent variables, the greater the confidence we have in our estimates of the treatment's causal effects.

The comparative nature of the RCM framework strengthens inferences from process tracing in several ways. By matching treated and control observations, the number of possible alternative explanations is reduced, simplifying the task of process tracing since some (ideally all but one, but hopefully many or even most) mechanisms are being held constant by a research design pairing cases that have similar values on independent variables. Process tracing can then be used to assess whether the treatment variable and the variables that could not be properly controlled for might account for observed outcomes. More generally, without the counterfactual, we cannot rule out the possibility that the same causal process is present in both the treated and control cases. To be confident about one's inferences, within-case process tracing should thus be paired with cross-case process tracing in a control observation where the presumed relationship between treatment and outcomes is not present.

The RCM framework also provides a natural bridge to emerging Bayesian approaches to process tracing (Bennett, this volume, Appendix; see also Beach and Pedersen 2013a: 83–88).[5] At its core, the Bayesian principle of "updating" one's prior beliefs in light of new evidence hinges on counterfactual reasoning. Bayesian updating is guided by the prior probability of a theory's validity and the likelihood ratio between "true positives" (instances where the evidence suggests a theory is true and the theory is in fact true) and "false positives" (instances where the evidence is consistent with a theory, but the theory itself is in fact false). The likelihood ratio itself relies, often implicitly, on control observations to provide both affirmative evidence for the preferred theory and eliminative induction that rules out alternative explanations and the possibility that a theory's claims are false. As Bayesian reasoning underscores, ruling

---

[5] See also Humphreys and Jacobs 2013: 20–22.

out alternative explanations can sometimes generate greater discriminatory power for a test between hypotheses than discovering evidence that (further) confirms a preferred theory's validity.

Second, scholars should craft elaborate theories (Rosenbaum 2010: 329) that articulate multiple measures for the mechanism(s) at work (see also Jacobs, this volume, Chapter 2; Schimmelfennig, this volume, Chapter 4). If multiple mechanisms are thought to be present, then the sequence by which a process or effect is created should also be mapped out.[6] These hypotheses and measures should be specified before moving to empirical testing. Backward induction from a known outcome to the mechanisms that produced the outcome should be avoided, especially if counterfactuals are not used to eliminate the possibility that these mechanisms are also present in control cases.

Specifying multiple measures a priori enables the researcher to test for the congruence between these observations, helping to differentiate competing explanations that might rely on the same mechanism to explain an outcome. Put differently, the comparative strength of a particular argument may be decided not on the strength of evidence linking a variable to a mechanism, but instead on its ability to account for auxiliary observations as well as the sequence producing the outcome itself. From a Bayesian perspective, these auxiliary observations are "clues" that can shift beliefs about a theory's validity since their presence denotes that a specified process – and only that process – is responsible for the observed outcome.[7]

Third, treating potential outcomes explicitly also focuses one's attention on the key question of treatment assignment. The non-random nature of most "treatments" that interest civil war scholars means dealing with a host of methodological issues that can frustrate causal inference. Process tracing can help here, too. Qualitative data can be used to trace how the treatment was assigned to treated and control units, for example, a procedure Thad Dunning in Chapter 8 refers to as a treatment-assignment causal-process observation (see also Dunning 2012: 209). Understanding how the treatment was assigned, and whether it was truly assigned "as-if" random across units, is pivotal for micro-level studies that rely on natural or quasi-experiments to find starting points in the dynamics of civil war violence. Tracing the logic of assignment is especially important when evidence for these conditioning variables is private information among combatants, making it difficult to match across cases.

---

[6] In Chapter 5, Waldner formalizes this insight through the use of "causal graphs."

[7] It is worth emphasizing that the probative value of these clues hinges on whether they are uncovered in a treated, but not a control, case.

More broadly, process tracing can be used to explore whether the proposed causal pathway between an independent variable (or treatment) and the suggested mechanism is even plausible. This task is especially relevant for cross-national studies, where the language of mechanisms is often invoked in fairly coarse terms – "state capture," for example, or "opportunity costs" – which obscures rather than reveals the causal processes unfolding at different subnational levels (Sambanis 2004; see also Checkel 2013b: chapter 1).[8] Similarly, cross-national studies that rely on exogenous events such as price commodity shocks to explore changes in conflict incidence across different states could be strengthened by using process tracing to clarify the channel(s) through which a shock affects state capacity or rebel recruitment at the subnational level. In this setting, since numerous mechanisms are plausible, process tracing the link between the shock and the mechanism would also be an important step in reducing the problem of equifinality that plagues cross-national studies.

Fourth, the distinction between process tracing for theory building versus theory testing is an important one (Bennett and Checkel, this volume, Chapter 1, pp. 7–8; see also Beach and Pedersen 2013a). While comparative observations (say, villages) within a particular case (say, a region within a country) are useful for theory building, out-of-sample tests are generally preferred for empirical testing to avoid "fitting" one's argument to the cases used to develop it. Lubkemann (2008) provides a neat illustration of this principle at work. Seeking to explain forced migration as a function of war, he began his empirical investigation in the Machaze district of Mozambique, which witnessed a high degree of violence and refugee outflow. He then followed the trail of internally displaced persons to new field sites, treating "dispersion as a field site" (ibid.: 25), including dispersion to the capital of the neighboring district and to the area across the border in South Africa. While his fieldwork in Machaze was formative in establishing propositions about refugee flows, it is the testing of these insights in locations not originally envisaged by the research design – process tracing out-of-sample, as it were – that provides greater confidence in his claims about the nature of wartime forced migration.

Working examples

I draw on two empirical examples to demonstrate the importance of process tracing to civil war studies. I first concentrate on the (mostly) cross-national

---

[8]   See also Bazzi and Blattman 2011; and Berman and Couttenier 2013.

debate about the determinants of civil war onset. I then turn to emerging micro-level debates about the effects of civilian victimization on subsequent insurgent violence. In each case, I suggest possible research designs that use process tracing within a potential outcomes framework to adjudicate between proposed mechanisms linking independent variables to outcomes.

Working example 1: civil war onset

Why do civil wars break out? To date, scholars have sought answers to this question by predominantly utilizing cross-national regressions that link national level characteristics to the probability of civil war onset. In one notable example, James Fearon and David Laitin draw on data from 127 conflicts in the 1945 to 1999 era to argue that war is driven by opportunities for rebellion, not percolating grievances within the population. Instead, weak state capacity, as proxied by per capita income, and mountainous terrain are key drivers of insurgency; the weaker and more mountainous the state, the more likely we are to witness war (Fearon and Laitin 2003).

A recent spate of work has taken exception to this state capacity claim, however, and has instead argued that the exclusion of ethnic groups from executive political office better captures the origins of civil war onset. The larger the size of the excluded ethnic group, the greater the likelihood of civil war, especially if the now-excluded group once held the reins of political power (Cederman and Girardin 2007; Buhaug *et al.* 2008; Cederman *et al.* 2010).

This is an important and productive debate, but one subject to diminishing returns if the underlying processes that produce these outcomes continue to be left unexamined or measured with crude national-level proxy indicators. Absent new cross-national data, the greatest returns to investment appear to lie in the testing of proposed mechanisms at the subnational level.[9]

Take the argument by Cederman *et al.* (2010). These authors identify 124 ethnic civil wars (1946 to 2005) and employ a new data set (Ethnic Political Relations, or EPR) that measures the annual level of political exclusion from executive power for relevant ethnic groups within a given state. Using multivariate regression and several measures of political exclusion, they conclude that "we are able to establish an unequivocal relationship between the degree of access to state power and the likelihood of armed rebellion" (Cederman *et al.* 2010: 114).

---

[9] For examples of the use of qualitative case studies to refine cross-national models, see Sambanis 2004; Collier and Sambanis 2005.

Table 7.1 Mechanisms and measures as proposed by Cederman *et al.* (2010)

Proposed mechanisms	Possible measures
Status reversal	Fear of domination; desire for revenge
Mobilization capacity	% of population (collective action)
Prior exposure to violence	Nationalist histories; violence as "thinkable"
State capacity	Force structure; deployment; bureaucracy; police
Spoils	Center-seeking behavior; spoil-seeking

Note: Below the dotted line are alternative mechanisms and proposed measures.

The authors cite five possible mechanisms that could undergird the relationship between rising ethnic exclusion and a greater likelihood of ethnic civil war. First, political exclusion can generate a fear of domination and resentment among excluded individuals, leading to a desire for (armed) revenge. Such motives are especially likely if the ethnic group was only recently excluded from political office. Second, the larger the excluded group, the greater its mobilizational capacity, and the greater its likelihood of leading an armed challenge against the state. Third, a history of prior conflict between ethnic groups can heighten the risk of war via three channels: (1) ethnonationalist activists glorify their group's history through one-sided narratives that stress their own victories and attribute blame for military losses to traitors, weak-spirited leaders, or a ruthless enemy; (2) past experiences of violence may become part of oral tradition or official narratives, nourishing calls for revenge; and (3) prior exposure to combat means that violence is no longer unthinkable, but constitutes part of the accepted repertoire of action.

These hypothesized mechanisms are summarized in Table 7.1. Mechanisms suggested by other theories are also listed, although these are illustrative rather than comprehensive. While the mechanisms offered by Cederman *et al.* (2010) are plausible, the evidence marshaled to support their presence is thin, consisting typically of a few short sentences (see, for example, ibid.: 110–111).

How could we go beyond statistical associations to examine the causal processes at work? One possible approach uses a potential outcomes framework to identify a series of comparative cases that isolate the mechanisms and their role in producing war onset. Political exclusion would be recast as a "treatment," while countries without ethnic group-based discrimination would represent the pool of available control observations. Matching could then be used to identify pairs of cases that have similar values across a range of theoretically important independent variables (or "covariates"), including level of state capacity, ruggedness of terrain, and size of standing army. Assuming the statistical relationship identified in the full data set survives the matching procedure, we could then identify matched pairs of cases that are dissimilar only in their treatment status and the outcome (war onset/no war onset). Since the proposed argument rests on at least five mechanisms, no one matched pair will be able to test all possible mechanisms and their relationship to war onset. Instead, the matching procedure creates a pool of available paired comparisons that could be used to isolate individual mechanisms through a series of cascading comparisons.

For example, Comparison A could involve process tracing within and across a pair of similar cases where civil war onset was observed in the treated case (for example, the politically exclusionary state), but not in the control case. Each state could also have been subjected to an external shock – ideally, the same shock, such as a sharp decrease in commodity prices – that impacts each in a similarly negative fashion. This type of design would allow for separation of the effects of political exclusion from those of state capacity, as the price shock should affect each state in equal measure, yet civil war is only observed in the politically exclusionary state. Similarly, matching on additional (new) measures of state capacity such as bureaucratic penetration or the nature of infrastructure would enable the sifting out of the effects of status reversal or mobilizational capacity from the potentially confounding effects of (weak) state capacity (Comparison B).

Disaggregating an ethnic group's experience with political exclusion can provide additional causal leverage. Comparison C could involve two states that have similar characteristics, including presence of political exclusion, but where one group has experienced a sudden and recent reversal, while the other excluded group has not. A related set-up could examine a matched pair where the size of the excluded group varies (one large group, one small group) to test the link between mobilizational capacity and war onset (Comparison D). Another matched pair could examine two similar states with equivalent levels of political exclusion, but where one marginalized ethnic group has experienced prior violence at the hands of the state, while the "control" group has not suffered prior victimization (Comparison E). More ambitious designs could use matched pairs that control for several mechanisms across cases – say, status reversal and mobilizational capacity – and vary a third mechanism such as prior exposure to state violence (Comparison F).

Once the relevant comparisons have been established via matching, the actual process tracing can begin. To establish the credibility of ties between ethnic exclusion and war onset, we might consider qualitative evidence from the recruitment drives of insurgent organizations. What types of appeals do they use to mobilize individuals? Are insurgents organized along ethnic lines? We should also observe that proportionately larger ethnic groups more readily overcome collective action problems when attempting to mobilize recruits. Ideally, evidence from both public and private claims about the nature of (ethnic) grievances would be uncovered and would dominate more tactical considerations such as perceptions of state weakness ("now is the time to strike because the state is weak") or a desire for spoils.

Process tracing is also essential for articulating the sequence of events leading up to the war. Cederman *et al.* (2010) suggest that rebels, not the state, should initiate the conflict. Did fear of ethnic domination precede the conflict, or were such concerns actually a product of the fighting? Were nationalist histories and memories of prior violence widespread, or did such myths emerge as a post-hoc rationalization for the war? And, perhaps most importantly, are these myths only actionable in political systems that exclude along ethnic lines, or can would-be rebels craft such narratives even in the absence of prior ethnic exclusion?

Finally, process tracing can play a crucial role in sifting out the indirect effects that state capacity might have on the mechanisms proposed by the ethnic exclusion argument. Although these arguments are typically pitted against one another, it is possible, indeed likely, that state actions can condition the effects of ethnic exclusion (and vice versa). Political exclusion may be a response to state weakness, for example, as an embattled elite seeks to "harden" its regime against potentially disloyal populations (Roessler 2011). More subtly, fear of ethnic domination may be a reflection of the military's ethnic composition, while opportunities for group mobilization may be conditioned by the size and deployment patterns of a state's armed forces. Cederman *et al.* (2010: 95, 106) also note that rapid and sudden ethnic reversal is especially likely in weak states, suggesting a more complicated relationship between state power (and violence) and grievance-based mechanisms (see also Wood 2003).

In short, adopting a potential outcomes framework involves the use of multiple comparisons ("cascades") to screen out competing theories and their mechanisms. It also enables a closer examination of the sequence by which ethnic exclusion translates into a heightened risk of conflict onset, helping to guard against reverse causation. Articulating an elaborate theory with numerous measures for each mechanism also strengthens our inferences about these processes by permitting congruence tests across multiple indicators, increasing our confidence that we have correctly identified the process(es) at work.

Working example 2: civilian casualties and insurgent violence

Civilian victimization and its effects on subsequent insurgent violence represents one of the fastest growing research areas in the study of civil war dynamics. Despite divergent methods, it has become a near article of faith that indiscriminate victimization of civilians facilitates the recruitment of newly abused individuals by insurgents, contributing to bloody spirals of escalatory violence between counterinsurgent and rebel forces (for example, Kalyvas 2006; US Army 2007; Jaeger and Paserman 2008; Kocher *et al.* 2011; Condra and Shapiro 2012; Schneider and Bussmann 2013). While this view is not uncontested (Lyall 2009), much of the debate now centers around the causal processes linking victimization to subsequent patterns of insurgent violence. To date, however, our research designs have not kept pace with the profusion of mechanisms cited by scholars as facilitating insurgent recruitment or producing escalatory spirals.

Setting aside for the moment the inherent difficulties in process tracing such a sensitive issue, the abundance of possible mechanisms, operating singularly or jointly, can frustrate efforts to establish defensible causal claims. Consider the following example from a January 2013 drone strike in Yemen, which killed at least one, and possibly five, innocent civilians:

As the five men stood arguing by a cluster of palm trees, a volley of remotely operated American missiles shot down from the night sky and incinerated them all, along with a camel that was tied up nearby.

In the days afterward, the people of the village vented their fury at the Americans with protests and briefly blocked a road. It is difficult to know what the long-term effects of the deaths will be, though some in the town – as in other areas where drones have killed civilians – say there was an upwelling of support for Al Qaeda, because such a move is seen as the only way to retaliate against the United States.

Innocents aside, even members of Al Qaeda invariably belong to a tribe, and when they are killed in drone strikes, their relatives – whatever their feelings about Al Qaeda – often swear to exact revenge on America.

"Al Qaeda always gives money to the family," said Hussein Ahmed Othman al Arwali, a tribal sheik from an area south of the capital called Mudhia, where Qaeda militants fought pitched battles with Yemeni soldiers last year. "Al Qaeda's leaders may be killed by drones, but the group still has its money, and people are still joining. For young men who are poor, the incentives are very strong: they offer you marriage, or money, and the ideological part works for some people."[10]

---

[10] "Drone Strikes Risks to Get Rare Moment in the Public Eye," *New York Times*, February 6, 2013, A1.

This brief example usefully highlights at least five of the mechanisms that scholars typically invoke to explain the process from victimization to participation in an insurgency. A desire for revenge, tribal (group) ties, selective incentives in the form of money and marriage, and ideology all intermingle as plausible mechanisms in just this one instance. We might also add property damage, which leads to economic hardship and shifting reservation values for joining an insurgency (Abadie 2006),[11] and the belief that greater risk is associated with non-participation in an insurgency (Kalyvas and Kocher 2007), as two additional mechanisms not captured by this example.

The example also illustrates a second, less appreciated, issue: without prior baseline levels for these mechanisms, and without a similar control village that was not struck, we cannot assess the relative importance of these mechanisms or the causal effects of the air strike on subsequent behavior. Once again, a potential outcomes framework that emphasizes counterfactual observations provides insights not possible with a singular focus on within-case observations. Without a control observation, for example, we cannot establish either the direction or the magnitude of the air strike's effect on support for Al Qaeda. Similarly, without a before-and-after comparison of civilian attitudes and behavior across cases, we cannot determine whether the air strike increased, decreased, or had no effect on subsequent insurgent recruitment and violence.

Given the number of plausible mechanisms and the possibility that they might interact, how could process tracing be used to explore the links between victimization, recruitment, and subsequent participation in an insurgency? Table 7.2 outlines one possible research design.[12]

The basic idea is again one of maximizing comparisons by exploiting variation in the nature of the victimization and how it was administered. More specifically, we can create additional comparisons by decomposing the "treatment" – here, experiencing a drone strike – into different types of victimization, while including individuals in the sample who were present (i.e. in the same village) at the time of the strike, but who were not hurt, as counterfactual observations.

Variation in civilian victimization, for example, can be used to create comparisons that enable process tracing to link state violence to insurgent behavior. To separate the "revenge" mechanism from an economic hardship

---

[11] See also Lyall 2013.
[12] This design draws on the author's experiences with USAID's Afghan Civilian Assistance Program II, administered by International Relief and Development (IRD) in Afghanistan during 2012 to 2013.

Table 7.2 Sample research design for assessing effects of civilian victimization using process tracing

Context (violence)	Assignment	
	Random ("as-if")	Targeted (selective)
Low	A, B, C	A, B, C
Medium	A, B, C	A, B, C
High	A, B, C	A, B, C

Note: A represents personal victimization; B represents property damage; C is a control individual in the selected location, but who was not victimized. A, B, and C are in the same village in this design. Violence is used as an important example of context. Assignment refers to the manner in which individual(s) were targeted, i.e. plausible claim to "as-if" random or selected according to some criteria. Context is by village.

one, we could compare individuals who are victimized but do not experience property damage (Type A) with those who only have property damage (Type B). We could then compare individuals A and B to individual C, who was present but unharmed by the drone strike. These individuals could be chosen via random selection (for example, from a list of victimized individuals and locations). A screening question could be used to insure that these individuals share similar socioeconomic characteristics. This procedure creates a two-control group comparison (Rosenbaum 2010) between individuals A and B, and between A and C, permitting in-depth process tracing to sort out the role played by different mechanisms in shaping an individual's attitudes.

We can also draw on process tracing inductively to explore the nature of the sample and the context in which the civilian victimization occurred. In particular, we should stratify our sample by levels of key covariates to account for victimization's conditional effects. In Table 7.2, I use the example of prior violence in a village by the counterinsurgent as one key conditioning factor with varying levels (here, high/medium/low). We might imagine that different mechanisms operate under different circumstances; a one-time event may have a different meaning from repeated violence, and so revenge motives or nationalism may have more purchase when heavy oppression is used rather than a one-time, possibly accidental, event. Stratifying our sample along these important covariates before process tracing also aids in illustrating gaps in our coverage. It may be impossible, for example, to access high violence areas, placing an important limit on the generalizability of our findings.

The credibility of our estimates about the effects of violence is also enhanced if we can demonstrate that this victimization occurred "as if" randomly. For most micro-level studies, the problem of selection bias looms large. That is, the individuals victimized differ in some important fashion from non-victims, since they were selected by the state for victimization. Some studies (for example, Condra and Shapiro 2012), however, contend that we can assume casualties are inflicted more or less randomly – unlucky individuals are in the "wrong place and time" – and so we can treat these casualties as unconnected ("plausibly exogenous") to broader patterns of war. The benefit, of course, is clear. If civilian casualties are not intimately tied to broader patterns of violence, then we are able to estimate cleanly the effects of these casualties on subsequent violence, without worrying about selection effects that might confound our study.

Whether this claim is plausible given the possibility of substantial heterogeneity in how civilians are victimized, variation in the meaning of victimization depending on the perpetrator's identity, and the prospect that civilians are often targeted strategically, is a central question for inductive process tracing. Determining whether (and when) the "as-if" random assumption holds also helps determine to which populations we can generalize when making claims about the effects of violence.

What form does the process tracing actually take? Given the observational equivalence of these mechanisms, it makes sense to shift the debate to examine how victimization affects attitudes, not behavior. Once again, we witness the virtues of elaborate theories, which force us (in this case) to create attitudinal measures for each mechanism that enable us to distinguish among causal pathways to insurgency. Table 7.3 offers an initial cut at measures for five

Table 7.3 Possible mechanisms linking civilian victimization to insurgent recruitment and violence

Proposed mechanisms	Possible measures
Revenge	View of government/counterinsurgent, sense of loss
Economic hardship	Changes in livelihood, beliefs about (future) well-being
Group identity	Perception of status; magnitude of co-ethnic bias
Risk	Willingness to consider risky actions
Selective incentives	Receipt and views of rebel provision of goods/services

Note: Proposed measures (not exhaustive) are designed to be consistent with multiple methodologies, including survey and behavioral experiments, focus groups, interviews, and ethnographic approaches that remain open to post-positivist notions of causation. Measured relative to control observations (individuals with no or different exposure to civilian victimization).

mechanisms that link victimization to increased participaion in an insurgency via changes in attitudes.

Creating multiple measures for each mechanism also creates more space to adopt different methodologies when process tracing (see also Checkel and Bennett, this volume, Chapter 10). Interviews with rebels, for example, have become a standard tool in the civil war scholar's methodological toolkit (Wood 2003; Weinstein 2007; Ladbury 2009), although care should be taken to insure that non-rebels are also interviewed. Survey experiments could also tap into these concepts using indirect measurement techniques that mitigate incentives for interview subjects to dissemble due to social desirability bias or concerns about reprisals (Humphreys and Weinstein 2008).[13] Focus groups provide an opportunity to explore not just individual level dynamics, but also the construction of narratives about civilian victimization and, in particular, how blame for these events is assigned. Behavioral "lab-in-the-field" experiments provide an additional means of measuring how violence affects attitudes, including preferences over risk, time horizons, and decision-making (Voors et al. 2012). Finally, ethnography may offer a window into how these dynamics shift over time. These processes are difficult to capture with surveys or one-off interviews, especially if the process between victimization and subsequent behavior has more of a "slow burn" than a "quick fuse" logic.

Each of these methods has its own particular strengths and weaknesses. Moreover, the environment after a civilian casualty event is among the most sensitive a researcher can experience. These factors combine to make "smoking-gun" evidence elusive in such settings; it is unlikely that evidence will be found to support one mechanism while trumping all others. Good process tracing may still not yield wholly conclusive evidence, as emphasized by Bennett and Checkel (this volume, Chapter 1). Instead, it may be more productive to explore the scope conditions that make certain pathways more or less likely to lead to insurgency. A potential outcomes framework that stresses the role of counterfactuals (i.e. non-victims), the need for multiple measures for each mechanism (i.e. "elaborate theory"), and a clear understanding of the selection mechanisms (was victimization deliberate or by chance?) offers one means for harnessing process tracing to the task of producing generalizable claims.[14]

---

[13] See also Lyall et al. 2013.

[14] The relation of process tracing to theory type (mid-range, typological, general) remains a key challenge for future work. See also Checkel (this volume, Chapter 3); and Checkel and Bennett (this volume, Chapter 10).

Practicalities

My arguments thus far have tacitly assumed that fieldwork is necessary to gather most, if not all, of the data required for process tracing. Indeed, many of the methodologies best suited for process tracing – including lab-in-the-field and survey experiments, in-depth interviews, and ethnography – mandate an often-substantial investment in field research.

Yet, fieldwork in (post-)conflict settings presents a host of methodological, logistical, and ethical challenges (Wood 2006). A short list of such issues includes: the threat of physical harm to the researcher, his or her team, and local respondents; variable (and unpredictable) access to field sites due to changing battlefield conditions; the twin dangers of social desirability bias and faulty memories that may creep into interview and survey responses, especially in areas contested between combatants; the often-poor quality of data for key measures; the changing nature of causal relationships, where effects of a particular intervention may be large in the initial conflict period, but diminish over time as the conflict churns on; and reliance on outside actors and organizations for access and logistics that might shape perceptions of the researcher's work among potential respondents.

Context typically trumps generalization in these environments, so solutions to these problems are necessarily local in nature. That said, there are three issues that all researchers are likely to face when gathering data for process tracing in conflict zones.

First, researchers must obtain the voluntary consent of would-be interviewees and respondents. Though this is a common injunction for Institutional Review Board (IRB) approval at American universities, the requirement takes on a special cast in conflict settings, where individuals may run risks for simply meeting with (foreign) researchers or survey teams. Informed consent in these settings requires that participants understand the nature of the study (at least broadly), its funding source, and plans for dissemination, so that they can properly judge the risk associated with participating. It also requires that individuals recognize that they will receive no material benefits – for example, new disbursements of economic assistance – from participation.

Moreover, in many settings, such as Afghanistan, obtaining consent is a two-step process: first, with the stakeholders who control access to a given village and, second, with the prospective participant(s). Obtaining consent from these gatekeepers, whether government officials, local authorities, or rebel commanders, can mean the difference between accessing or being excluded from certain locations. In addition, obtaining permission from local authorities can lower individuals' concerns about participating, potentially also reducing the bias in their responses to interview or survey questions. Consent from local authorities and individuals becomes especially important if one's process tracing hinges on gathering longitudinal data.

Second, maintaining the anonymity of interviewees and survey respondents is essential in wartime settings. Researchers must work to secure data and to insure that if compromised, it does not allow third parties to identify their sources. The simplest expedient is not to record an individual's name and instead use a randomized identification number. The advent of computers, cell phones, and portable data storage devices in the field has changed the calculus, however, making it possible to reconstruct an individual's identify even if his or her name was not recorded. Survey firms routinely use respondents' telephone numbers to call back for quality control purposes, while enumerators use GPS devices and maps to track their "random walks" in selected villages when creating samples.

Confidentiality and guarantees of anonymity must extend to these personal data, not simply an individual's identity, especially given the prospects for rapid dissemination if these electronic storage devices are compromised. In areas with good cell phone coverage – an increasing share of once remote locations – data from interviews, surveys, or maps should be stored remotely (for example, on a "cloud" storage site) and local copies deleted to mitigate the risks of unwanted data capture. Researchers should also maintain robust networks for returning surveys, interview notes, or other sensitive materials to a central safe location if electronic means are not available. In Afghanistan, for example, trucks carrying market wares to Kabul can be enlisted to deliver sealed packages of completed surveys back to Kabul, where they are then scanned and destroyed. This system avoids having dozens of enumerators risk exposure while carrying materials through potentially hundreds of checkpoints between their field sites and Kabul. Similarly, quality control call-backs can be completed by a manager at the field site; the phone's log is then deleted, thereby avoiding transporting these data across checkpoints.

Third, researchers must work to safeguard both themselves and members of their team. Surprisingly, existing IRB guidelines do not address the issue of researcher safety nor that of the enumerators, translators, fixers, and others who might work under the researcher's direction and who also assume risks by participating in the research. Establishing a baseline of risk before conducting research – How violent? Which actors are present? What types of movement restrictions exist? – can be useful in detecting sudden changes that suggest increased risk for one's team. This baseline is also useful in selecting potential field sites as well as replacements, often via matching, which enables researchers to switch sites quickly without compromising their research design. Locals, who often have a far better sense of security risks than outsiders, should also be consulted when establishing notions of baseline risk. Finally, it is useful to construct a "kill-switch" protocol that can be activated if team members have been threatened (or worse). Activating the "kill-switch" (often via SMS) would signal to team members to wipe their data and withdraw to central points to avoid a credible threat, such as specific targeting of the team by rebel or government forces.

Conclusion

The explosion of research on the origins and dynamics of civil wars has not (yet) been accompanied by a turn to process tracing to identify and test the causal mechanisms that underpin our theories. This state of affairs is unfortunate, not least because political scientists have developed an increasingly sophisticated and eclectic methodological toolkit that could be applied toward process tracing in violent settings. Certainly, feasibility and safety concerns are paramount in these environments. Yet, as this chapter has sought to demonstrate, there are research designs and strategies that can be adopted to heighten our ability to make casual inferences despite these challenges.

The advantages of incorporating process tracing into conflict research also spill over to the policy realm. Process tracing offers an excellent means of uncovering the contextual "support factors" (Cartwright and Hardie 2012: 50–53) that help produce a causal effect. Without exploring these contextual factors, as well as the nature of the link between treatment and its mechanisms, we are left on shaky ground when trying to determine whether a particular effect or process generalizes to other settings. Moreover, process tracing is ideally suited to investigating possible interactions between multiple mechanisms. Policymakers, not to mention scholars conducting impact evaluations, are likely operating in settings marked by multiple mechanisms that interact in complex ways to produce a given effect. Pre-specifying the possible causal pathways and identifying several measures for these mechanisms, as called for by elaborate theorizing, will also help to avoid fishing for the "correct" mechanism via backward induction. The result of these efforts is likely to be a better understanding of how these processes unfold, thus contributing to our theories of civil wars as well.

Process tracing does have its limits, however. Without explicitly incorporating counterfactuals to facilitate cross- and within-case comparisons, theory-testing process tracing can lead to mistaken causal inferences about the robustness of a presumed relationship between an independent variable and outcomes. Moreover, crafting research designs that are capable of both identifying a statistical association and then competitively testing the mechanisms responsible for it may be a bridge too far. What may be required is a shift toward designs that take a particular relationship as a given and instead explicitly engage in process tracing to detail why this pattern is present. Danger lies in this type of strategy, though: the more micro-level the process tracing, the more contextual factors trump abstraction. The result may be a wonderfully nuanced account of a specific process that doesn't generalize to other settings even within the same case. Finally, a too-specific focus on mechanisms and process tracing might lead to neglecting the importance of structural factors that might condition which mechanisms are present and the magnitude of their effects (Checkel 2013b: 19).

Of course, process tracing is not unique in having drawbacks; no methodological approach is without its shortcomings. And the pay-offs, measured in terms of theoretical progress and policy insights, are considerable. By seeking to move beyond statistical associations to understanding why these relationships are present, scholars can open new avenues for exciting research into substantively important questions about the onset and battlefield dynamics of civil wars.

Part III

Extensions, controversies, and conclusions

Improving process tracing
The case of multi-method research

Thad Dunning

Introduction

Social scientists increasingly champion multi-method research – in particular, the use of both quantitative and qualitative tools for causal inference.[1] Yet, what role does process tracing play in such research? I turn in this chapter to natural experiments, where process tracing can make especially useful and well-defined contributions. As I discuss, however, several lessons are relevant to other kinds of multi-method research.

With natural experiments, quantitative tools are often critical for assessing causation.[2] Random or "as-if" random assignment to comparison groups – the definitional criterion for a natural experiment – can obviate standard concerns about confounding variables, because only the putative cause varies across the groups. Other factors are balanced by randomization, up to chance error. Simple comparisons, such as differences of means or percentages, may then validly estimate the average effect of the cause, that is, the average difference due to its presence or absence. Controlling for confounding variables is not required, and can even be harmful.[3]

However, much more than data analysis is needed to make such research compelling. In the first place, researchers must ask the right research questions and formulate the right hypotheses; and they must create or discover research designs and gather data to test those hypotheses. Successful quantitative analysis also depends on the validity of causal models, in terms of which hypotheses are defined. The formulation of questions, discovery of strong designs, and

---

[1] See, inter alia, Brady and Collier 2010; Bennett 2007; Dunning 2008b; 2010; 2012.

[2] Natural experiments are observational studies – those lacking an experimental manipulation – in which causal variables are assigned at random or *as-if* at random. See Freedman 1999; 2009; Dunning 2008a; 2012; or Angrist and Pischke 2008.

[3] Freedman 2008a; 2008b; 2009; also Dunning 2012; Sekhon 2009; or Gerber and Green 2012.

validation of models require auxiliary information, which typically does not come from analysis of large data sets (Freedman 2010). This depends instead on disparate, qualitative fragments of evidence about context, process, or mechanism. What has come to be called process tracing – that is, the analysis of evidence on processes, sequences, and conjunctures of events within a case for the purposes of either developing or testing hypotheses about causal mechanisms that might causally explain the case (Bennett and Checkel, this volume, Chapter 1, p. 7) – is the major means of uncovering such pieces of diagnostic evidence, which Collier *et al.* (2010) describe as "causal-process observations" (CPOs).

For instance, researchers using natural experiments face the challenge of validating the definitional claim of as-if random. To do so, they require evidence on the *information, incentives,* and *capacities* of key actors with control over *processes* of treatment assignment (Dunning 2012: chapter 7). This helps them to assess whether actors had the desire and ability to undercut random assignment.[4] To appraise central assumptions of standard causal and statistical models (for example, "no interference"), researchers may use qualitative information on the mode and possible effects of interactions between units in the treatment and control groups. Finally, deep engagement with research contexts – even "soaking and poking" (Bennett and Checkel, this volume, Chapter 1, p. 18) – can generate the substantive knowledge required to discover the opportunity for a natural experiment, as well as to interpret effects. Qualitative evidence may thus be a requisite part of successful quantitative analysis, and it can also make vital contributions to causal inference on its own (Brady and Collier 2010).

Despite these virtues, scholars have encountered challenges in developing process tracing tools for multi-method research. In the first place, recognition of the general utility of evidence on context or process does not provide researchers with a ready guide to practice. It is one thing to say that causal-process observations play a critical role in causal inference; it is quite another to say which *particular* CPOs are most persuasive or credible (Bennett and Checkel, this volume, Chapter 1, pp. 20–31; see also Jacobs, this volume, Chapter 2; Waldner, this volume, Chapter 5). Indeed, qualitative evidence can also lead researchers astray, as useful examples from the biological sciences surveyed in this chapter's third section suggest. Reflecting such concerns, methodologists have focused more centrally on the challenge of distinguishing more and less valid CPOs. The elaboration of standards to evaluate process tracing

---

[4] When "as-if random" fails, treatment assignment is not independent of potential outcomes – that is, the hypothetical outcomes each unit *would* experience if exposed to treatment or control.

is an important part of improving research practice – in terms of this volume's title, of turning process tracing from metaphor to analytic tool (see also Collier 2011).

There are several difficulties with implementing such standards, however. Bennett and Checkel's recommendation that process tracers "cast the net widely for alternative explanations" seems critical, as is their suggestion to "be equally tough on the alternative[s]" (Bennett and Checkel, this volume, Chapter 1, p. 23). Yet, it is not easy to demonstrate adherence to such advice. One challenge is that absence of evidence does not constitute evidence of absence (Bennett and Checkel, this volume, Chapter 1, p. 19). With natural experiments, failure to find information that disproves, say, the assumption of as-if random does not constitute positive proof of its validity. Thus, and to invoke Van Evera's (1997) framework, "hoop" or "straw-in-the-wind" tests of the assumption of as-if random assignment appear common: passing such tests increases the plausibility of as-if random, and may be necessary for as-if random to hold, but it is not alone sufficient.

In contrast, "smoking-gun" or "doubly decisive" evidence in favor of as-if random is rare – although smoking-gun evidence that assignment was not random may be sufficient to cast serious *doubt* on the assertion of as-if random assignment.[5] In other words, it is much easier to *disprove* the hypothesis of "as-if random" than it is to provide sufficient evidence in *favor* of this hypothesis. Thus, researchers may triangulate between quantitative tests – for example, evaluating whether assignment to categories of a treatment variable is *consistent* with a coin flip[6] – and qualitative information on the assignment process. Yet, without true randomization, there is always the possibility of lurking qualitative or quantitative information that would undermine the plausibility of random assignment, if it were only uncovered. Casting the net widely for alternative evidence on the process that assigns units to treatment or control groups is crucial; yet it can be difficult for researchers to know when they have cast the net widely enough.

Implementing standards for process tracing raises other epistemological and practical obstacles, related in part to the esoteric information that is often

---

[5] Recall that pieces of evidence are judged to have passed a "straw-in-the-wind test" if they merely increase the plausibility that a hypothesis is true; a "hoop test" if passing does not confirm the hypothesis but failing to pass disconfirms it; a "smoking-gun test" if passing confirms the hypothesis (but not passing does not disconfirm it); and a "doubly decisive test" if passing confirms, and not passing disconfirms, the hypothesis. See Bennett and Checkel (this volume, Chapter 1, pp. 16–17) and Bennett in the Appendix (this volume).

[6] E.g. they may demonstrate that the treatment and control groups are *balanced* on measured, pre-treatment covariates, just as they would be (in expectation) in a randomized experiment.

required. As with the discovery of natural experiments, process tracing typically requires deep substantive engagement with disparate research contexts; it involves sifting through both confirmatory and potentially falsifying pieces of evidence. Our expectations about the accessibility of evidence on the information, incentives, or capacities of key actors may also affect our assessment of the probative value of any qualitative fact (Bennett and Checkel, this volume, Chapter 1, p. 16; see also Jacobs, this volume, Chapter 2). Yet, precisely in consequence of the deep engagement and specialized knowledge required, the number of scholars who possess the requisite knowledge to evaluate the quality of process tracing may be small.[7]

This creates challenges relating to the ways in which observations on causal process are reported and evaluated by communities of scholars. Contrary evidence that would invalidate a given research design or causal model may indeed exist in the historical record or at a given field site. Unless it is elicited and offered by scholars, however, readers cannot use it to evaluate the persuasiveness of the process tracing. How are we in the community of scholars to know whether individual researchers have indeed sufficiently canvassed the available evidence – both supportive and potentially disconfirming? And how can researchers successfully demonstrate that they have done so, thereby bolstering the transparency and credibility of their findings (see also Waldner, this volume, Chapter 5)?

In this chapter, I discuss these challenges further, focusing on both the promise and the pitfalls of process tracing in multi-method research. I begin by describing two ways in which process tracing may help to validate design and modeling assumptions in natural experiments: through the discovery of what I have called treatment-assignment CPOs and the testing of model-validation CPOs (Dunning 2012: chapter 7).[8] While my illustrative examples show how qualitative evidence has been used productively in studying natural experiments, the discussion is also aspirational. In many studies, observations on causal process could be used more effectively to assess design and modeling assumptions.

I then turn to the challenge of appraising the quality of process tracing, describing in more detail the epistemological and practical difficulties mentioned above. I argue that while the formulation of *best practices* for what constitutes good process tracing is appealing – and the criteria suggested by

---

[7] The number of scholars who possess the interest or expertise to evaluate critically both the quantitative and qualitative analysis may be even smaller.

[8] As I make clear below, qualitative evidence has many important roles to play besides bolstering the validity of quantitative analysis; however, this plays an especially critical role in multi-method research.

Bennett and Checkel in Chapter 1 are excellent – they may also be quite difficult to apply and enforce. In other words, it may be challenging to develop general criteria with which to evaluate the persuasiveness and evidentiary standing of given pieces of qualitative evidence, or specific instances of process tracing. For individual researchers, it may also be difficult to demonstrate that they have adhered to those criteria – although specific attention in published work to Bennett and Checkel's best practices would undoubtedly help.

Instead, I argue that it may be productive to focus on research *procedures* that can bolster the credibility of process tracing in multi-method research. A central question is whether and to what extent such procedures can facilitate open scholarly contestation about the probative value of qualitative evidence. Thus, transparent procedures – including the cataloguing of interview transcripts or archival documents – should assist scholars with relevant subject-matter expertise in debating the evidentiary weight to accord to specific observations on causal process (Moravcsik 2010).

The idea that scholarly contestation can improve the quality of process tracing has some parallels in the theory of "legal adversarialism," in which competing advocates offer evidence in support of different theories. While this seems unlikely to produce perfect validation of qualitative evidence – for reasons that reflect not just basic epistemological difficulties, but also the sociological organization of scholarly production – I pinpoint a few major challenges and suggest some modest proposals for improving process-tracing practice. These research procedures can complement the process-tracing best practices outlined by Bennett and Checkel and bolster our confidence that researchers have indeed adhered to several of those criteria.

Process tracing in multi-method research

How does process tracing contribute to causal inference in multi-method research? I use process tracing, as do Bennett and Checkel (this volume, Chapter 1, pp. 7–8), to denote a procedure for developing knowledge of context, sequence, or process – essentially, for generating causal-process observations (CPOs). Collier *et al.* describe a causal-process observation as "an insight or piece of data that provides information about context, process, or mechanism" (2010: 184).[9] At times, CPOs function like clues in detective stories (Collier 2011),

---

[9] These are contrasted with quantitative "data-set observations" (DSOs), i.e. the collection of values on the dependent and independent variables for a single case, i.e. a row of a "rectangular data set."

playing the role of "smoking guns" (Collier *et al.* 2010: 185); at other times, they are simply pieces of contextual information upon which researchers can draw to evaluate particular assumptions or hypotheses. My usage of process tracing also follows Mahoney (2010: 124), who notes "process tracing contributes to causal inference primarily through the discovery of CPOs."

In multi-method as in other forms of research, process tracing can in principle help confront two key challenges in making causal inferences:

1. the challenge of understanding the selection process that assigns units to categories of causal/treatment variables (i.e. levels of an independent variable);
2. the challenge of model validation, for instance, validation of assumptions about causal process that are embedded in quantitative models.

On the former, in observational studies, where treatment assignment is not under the control of an experimental researcher, confounding variables associated with both a putative cause and effect may play an important role. Control of confounding variables thus requires a close understanding of selection processes and, ideally, the discovery of research settings in which assignment to the causal variable is independent of other variables that may influence outcomes – as in strong natural experiments.

Regarding point 2 above, in experiments and observational studies alike, quantitative analysis proceeds according to maintained hypotheses about causal process. Yet, if these hypotheses are wrong, the results cannot be trusted (Freedman 2009). Finding ways to probe the credibility of modeling assumptions is thus a critical part of successful quantitative inference.

For both of these challenges, qualitative evidence can and should play a crucial role. Here, I would emphasize both *can* and *should*; in practice, qualitative evidence is not always (or even usually) explicitly deployed in this fashion, and some qualitative evidence may not always contribute decisively or productively to causal inference. Thus, a major theme for consideration is how qualitative evidence could be deployed more effectively in such settings to bolster causal inference (see also Schimmelfennig, this volume, Chapter 4).

To develop these ideas further, it is useful to introduce two running examples: Snow's famous study of cholera (Freedman 1999; 2009; see also Dunning 2008a; 2012) and the Argentina land-titling study of Galiani and Schargrodsky (2004; 2010). Snow used a natural experiment to study the causes of cholera transmission, and to test hypotheses engendered by a series of causal-process observations. His study was occasioned by the move of the intake pipe of the Lambeth Water Company to a purer water source, higher up-river on the Thames, prior to a cholera outbreak in 1853 to 1854; a competitor, Southwark & Vauxhall, left its own pipe in place, lower on the Thames and downstream from more sewage outlets. According to Snow, the move of the Lambeth Company's water pipe meant that more than 300,000 people were:

divided into two groups without their choice, and, in most cases, without their knowledge; one group being supplied with water containing the sewage of London, and, amongst it, whatever might have come from the cholera patients, the other group having water quite free from such impurity. (Snow 1855: 75)

The contrast in death rates from cholera was dramatic: the household death rate among Lambeth customers was 37 per 10,000, compared to 315 per 10,000 among customers of Southwark & Vauxhall (Freedman 2009). Why this study design provided a compelling natural experiment is discussed in the next subsection, but Snow touted it thus: "It is obvious that no experiment could have been devised which would more thoroughly test the effect of water supply on the progress of cholera than this" (Snow 1855: 74–75).

The Argentina land-titling study provides another example, with a design quite similar to Snow's. In 1981, squatters organized by the Catholic Church occupied an urban wasteland on the outskirts of metropolitan Buenos Aires, dividing the land into similar-sized parcels that were allocated to individual families. After the return to democracy in 1983, a 1984 law expropriated this land, with the intention of transferring title to the squatters. However, some of the original owners challenged the expropriation in a series of court cases, leading to delays of many years in the transfer of titles to the plots owned by those owners. Other titles were transferred to squatters immediately. The legal action therefore created a "treatment" group – squatters to whom titles were ceded immediately – and a "control" group – squatters to whom titles were not ceded. As in Snow's study, nearby households found themselves exposed in an apparently haphazard way to different treatment conditions. Galiani and Schargrodsky (2004; 2010) find significant differences across the groups in subsequent housing investment, household structure, and educational attainment of children, although not in access to credit markets (thus contradicting De Soto's (2000) theory that the poor will use de jure property rights to collateralize debt).

In both of these studies, qualitative information about context and process plays a number of critical roles. In the first place, such information is crucial for recognizing the existence of natural experiments. Indeed, substantive knowledge and "shoe leather" work is typically a *sine qua non* for discovering the opportunity for such research designs (Freedman 2010). Yet, process tracing and causal-process observations can also play an especially important role with respect to challenges 1 and 2 noted above, as I now describe.

Treatment-assignment CPOs

Regarding challenge 1, understanding the process of selection into categories of an independent variable is vital for evaluating threats to valid causal inference from confounding variables. Here, treatment-assignment CPOs (Dunning 2012) – pieces or nuggets of information about the *process* by which units were assigned to treatment and control conditions – are critical.

For example, qualitative evidence on the process of treatment assignment plays a central role in Snow's study. Information on the move of Lambeth's water pipe and, especially, on the nature of water markets helped to substantiate the claim that assignment of households to source of water supply was *as-if* random – the definitional criterion for a natural experiment. The decision of Lambeth Waterworks to move its intake pipe upstream on the Thames was taken before the cholera outbreak of 1853 to 1854, and contemporary scientific knowledge did not clearly link water source to cholera risk.[10]

Yet, there were some important subtleties. The Metropolis Water Act of 1852, which was enacted in order to "make provision for securing the supply to the Metropolis of pure and wholesome water," made it unlawful for any water company to supply houses with water from the tidal reaches of the Thames after August 31, 1855. While Lambeth's move was completed in 1852, Southwark & Vauxhall did not move its pipe until 1855.[11] In other words, Lambeth chose to move its pipe upstream earlier than it was legally required to do, while Southwark & Vauxhall opted to keep its pipe in place; for the companies, assignment to water supply source was self-selected. In principle, then, there could have been confounding variables associated with choice of water supply – for instance, if healthier, more adept customers noticed Lambeth's move of its intake pipe and switched water companies.

Here, qualitative knowledge on the nature of water markets becomes crucial. Snow emphasizes that many residents in the areas of London that he analyzed were renters; also, absentee landlords had often taken decisions

---

[10] The directors of the Lambeth Company had apparently decided to move the intake for their reservoirs in 1847, but facilities at Seething Wells were only completed in 1852. See *Lambeth Waterwork History*, UCLA Department of Epidemiology. Available at www.ph.ucla.edu/epi/snow/1859map/lambeth_waterworks_a2.html.

[11] To comply with the legislation, the Southwark & Vauxhall Company built new waterworks in Hampton above Molesey Lock in 1855. Ibid.

about water supply source years prior to the move of the Lambeth intake pipe. Moreover, the way in which the water supply reached households – with heavy interlocking fixed pipes making their way through the city and serving customers in side-by-side houses – also implied a limited potential for customer mobility, since landlords had signed up for either one company or the other (presumably when the pipes were being constructed). As Snow put it:

A few houses are supplied by one Company and a few by the other, *according to the decision of the owner or occupier at that time when the Water Companies were in active competition.* (Snow 1855: 74–75 [emphasis added])

This qualitative information thus suggests that residents did not largely self-select into their source of water supply – and especially not in ways that would be plausibly related to death risk from cholera. Even if the *companies* chose whether or not to move their intake pipes upstream, as Snow emphasizes, *households* were assigned sources of water supply without their choice, and often without their knowledge. Thus, qualitative knowledge on water markets is critical to buttressing the claim that assignment to water supply source was as good as random for households – in particular, that it was not linked to confounding variables that might explain the dramatic difference in death rates across households served by either company.

In the Argentina land-titling study, qualitative evidence on the process by which squatting took place, and plots and titles were obtained, also plays a central role. Recall that squatters organized by Catholic Church activists invaded the land in 1981, prior to the return to democracy in 1983. According to Galiani and Schargrodsky (2004), both Church organizers and the squatters themselves believed that the abandoned land was owned by the state, not by private owners; and neither squatters nor Catholic Church organizers could have successfully predicted which *particular* parcels would eventually have their titles transferred in 1984 and which would not. Thus, industrious or determined squatters who were particularly eager to receive titles would not have had reason to occupy one plot over another – which helps to rule out alternative explanations for the findings whereby, for instance, organizers allocated parcels to certain squatters, anticipating that these squatters would one day receive title to their property. Nor did the quality of the plots or attributes of the squatters explain the decisions of some owners and not others to challenge expropriation in court. On the basis of their interviews and other qualitative fieldwork, the authors argue that idiosyncratic factors explain these decisions. In summary, evidence on the *process* of treatment assignment suggests that potentially confounding characteristics of squatters that might

otherwise explain differences in housing investment or household structure –
such as family background, motivation, or determination – should not be
associated with whether they received title to their plots.[12]

For both the cholera and land-titling studies, such evidence does *not* come
in the form of systematic values of variables for each squatter – that is, as data-
set observations (DSOs). Instead, it comes in the form of disparate contextual
information that helps validate the claim that the treatment assignment is as
good as random – in other words, causal-process observations (CPOs).
Certainly, Galiani and Schargrodsky (2004) also use quantitative tests of
their design assumptions, for instance, assessing whether balance on pre-
treatment covariates across the treatment and control groups is consistent
with a coin flip.[13]

Yet, qualitative evidence on the process of treatment assignment is just as
critical: fine-grained knowledge about context and process is crucial for bolstering the case for as-if random assignment. In Snow's study, causal-process
observations are also central to supporting the claim of as-good-as-random
assignment – and causal-process observations would likely be needed to challenge Snow's account as well.[14] In many other natural experiments, qualitative
evidence is also critical for validating the assertion of as-if random.[15]

It is useful to note here that understanding the process of assignment to
treatment and control conditions is also critical in other kinds of research –
including conventional observational studies (i.e. those that lack plausible
random assignment). For instance, researchers may use multivariate regression
(or analogues such as matching) to compare units with similar values of
covariates (age, sex, and so on), but different exposure to treatment conditions.
There, analysts typically assume that within groups defined by the covariates,
treatment assignment is as good as random (i.e. that "conditional independence" holds). Yet, why would this be? Along with a priori arguments, qualitative evidence on the process of treatment assignment – that is, process
tracing – is critical for making this assertion credible, and thus for heightening
the plausibility of causal inferences drawn from the analysis. Explicitly addressing this process element may not be typical, but it is no less important in
conventional observational studies than in natural experiments – even if, in

---

[12] Thus, potential outcomes – the outcomes each squatter *would* experience under assignment to a title or
assignment to the control group – should be independent of actual assignment.

[13] For instance, characteristics of both squatters and parcels are similar across the treatment and control
groups; see Galiani and Schargrodsky (2004; 2010).

[14] For instance, evidence that customers did switch companies after Lambeth's move of its pipe might
undercut the claim of *as-if* random. This evidence might come in the form of DSOs or CPOs.

[15] Dunning (2012: chapter 7) provides further examples.

many cases, as-if random assignment is unlikely to hold even within matched groups.

Model-validation CPOs

Just as important in multi-method research as understanding selection into treatment is the specification of the causal model – that is, the *response schedule* that says how units respond to hypothetical manipulations of a treatment variable (Freedman 2009). Before a causal hypothesis is formulated and tested quantitatively, a causal model must be defined, and the link from observable variables to the parameters of that model must be posited. Thus, the credibility and validity of the underlying causal model is always at issue.

Hence stems the importance of (2) Model-Validation CPOs, that is, nuggets of information about causal process that support or invalidate core assumptions of causal models. As one example, both the Neyman causal model (also known as the Neyman-Rubin-Holland or potential outcomes model) and standard regression models posit that potential outcomes for each unit are invariant to the treatment assignment of other units (this is the so-called "no-interference" assumption).[16] Yet, how plausible is this assumption? Close examination of patterns of interaction between units – for instance, the information they possess about the treatment-assignment status of others – can heighten or mitigate concerns about such modeling assumptions.

Consider, for example, the Argentina land-titling study. A key hypothesis tested in this study is that land titling influenced household structure – in particular, fertility decisions by teenagers. The study indeed provides some evidence that titled households had fewer teenage pregnancies. Yet, does the difference between titled and untitled households provide a good estimator for the causal effect of interest – namely, the difference between average pregnancy rates if all households were assigned titles and average pregnancy rates if no households were assigned titles? It does not, if fertility decisions of people in untitled households are influenced by the assignment of titles to their neighbors in the treatment group. Indeed, if titling also influences neighbors in the control group to have fewer children, then comparing pregnancy rates in titled and untitled households does not provide a reliable guide to the causal effect of interest.

---

[16] Following Rubin (1978), this is sometimes called the Stable Unit Treatment Value Assumption (SUTVA).

The key point is that the plausibility of the assumption that no such "interference" between treatment and control groups exists could in principle be investigated using a range of methods – including process tracing. For example, detailed knowledge of interactions between neighbors – insights into how fertility decisions of households are linked to those of other squatters – may be quite helpful for assessing the extent to which interference poses obstacles for successful inferences about average causal effects.[17] In Snow's study, too, non-interference would be important to establish: are cholera death rates in households served by Southwark & Vauxhall plausibly influenced by the assignment of neighbors to water from Lambeth? Information on causal process can also help researchers appraise other modeling assumptions, such as whether or not there is clustered assignment to treatment conditions.[18]

In summary, process tracing can contribute to buttressing or undermining the validity of such modeling assumptions – and can therefore play a critical role in experiments and natural experiments, as in conventional observational studies. Of course, modeling assumptions are just that – assumptions – and they are therefore only partially subject to verification. Researchers would do well to heed Bennett and Checkel's advice to be "tough on alternative explanations" and "consider the potential biases of evidentiary sources" (this volume, Chapter 1, pp. 24–25). This will include imagining the ways in which their modeling assumptions might go off the rails in a given substantive context – say, by considering how interference between treatment and control groups could arise. This is not easy to do. Yet, the examples in this section illustrate the important contribution that qualitative evidence obtained via process tracing can make to quantitative analysis – thus suggesting how multi-method work may, in principle, lead to more valid causal inferences.

The challenges of validation

Despite the merits of process tracing, the examples in the previous section also suggest important difficulties that confront the use of causal-process observations. Process tracing can certainly "generate a line of scientific inquiry, or markedly

[17] Of course, quantitative measures of interactions between neighbors (DSOs) – for instance, survey self-reports in which respondents are asked systematically about interactions with their neighbors – may be useful as well, a point further developed by Checkel and Bennett in their concluding chapter (this volume, Chapter 10).

[18] For further examples of treatment-assignment and model-validation CPOs, see Dunning 2012, especially chs. 7–9.

shift the direction of the inquiry by overturning prior hypotheses, or provide striking evidence to confirm hypotheses" (Freedman 2010: 338). Yet, it can also lead researchers down the wrong path. The medical sciences provide useful illustrations. Snow, for instance, did not stop with cholera. In fact, he also believed:

> by analogy with cholera [that] plague, yellow fever, dysentery, typhoid fever, and malaria . . . were infectious waterborne diseases. His supporting arguments were thin. As it turns out, these diseases are infectious; however, only dysentery and typhoid fever are waterborne. (Freedman 2010: 353)

Another example comes from James Lind, who carried out an experiment of sorts in 1747 to show that the absence of citrus fruits is a cause of scurvy. Lind assigned twelve sailors suffering from scurvy to ingest different nutritional supplements, with two sailors assigned to each of six treatment regimes: (1) a daily quart of cider; (2) twenty-five gutts of elixir vitriol, three times a day; (3) two spoonfuls of vinegar, three times a day; (4) a course of sea water; (5) nutmeg, three times a day; or (6) two oranges and one lemon each day. At the end of a fortnight, "the most sudden and visible good effects were perceived from the use of the oranges and lemons" (Lind, cited in De Vreese 2008: 16).[19]

According to De Vreese (2008), Lind rejected the evidence from his own experiment because he could not imagine mechanisms linking nutritional deficiencies to scurvy. Rather, his explanatory framework, inherited from the eighteenth-century theory of disease, focused on how moisture blocked perspiration, thought to be vital for inhibiting disease. Lind thought that lemons and oranges counteracted this property of moisture. Instead, he focused on humidity as the ultimate cause of scurvy, due to a series of observations apparently consistent with his theory (moisture constricting skin pores, leading to corrupted fluids in the body). Lind's focus on a wrongly identified mechanism – apparently supported by causal-process observations – thus led him astray.

Such discouraging examples raise important questions, not only about how to validate hypotheses generated by causal-process observations, but also how to distinguish useful from misleading process tracing.[20] As Freedman puts it: "If guesses cannot be verified, progress may be illusory" (2010: 353). Success

---

[19] Note that treatment assignment was not randomized; and with only twelve sailors, chance variation would have been pronounced. I am grateful to David Waldner for suggesting the De Vreese reference.

[20] Waldner (this volume, Chapter 5) also explicitly addresses this issue, in his case, by advocating a "completeness standard" for process tracing. Also, Bennett, in the Appendix (this volume) notes that in some circumstances evidence consistent with a hypothesis can actually lower the likelihood that the hypothesis is true.

stories demonstrate the importance of qualitative evidence. Yet, few recent writings on qualitative or mixed-method research describe misleading quali- tative observations that lead scholars in the wrong direction.[21]

There seem to be two major challenges. First, how can we appraise the value of any discrete piece of evidence offered in support of a design assumption or a substantive conclusion – without knowledge of other relevant diagnostic pieces of evidence, or additional confirmatory testing? In fact, as I argue below, the probative value of a causal-process observation often depends on the existence or non-existence of certain *other* pieces of evidence, as well as analysis of data sets from strong designs. Yet, this leads to a second issue, because the full set of potential diagnostic evidence may or may not be elicited and reported by individual researchers. We thus face important challenges in terms of how we as individual researchers – and as a research community – can best operationalize Bennett and Checkel's injunction to "cast the net widely for alternative explanations" (this volume, Chapter 1, p. 23).

Consider, first, the probative value of particular causal-process observa- tions, taking Snow's compelling examples as illustrations. In one cholera epidemic, Snow found that the second person known to die from cholera had taken a room in a boarding house previously occupied by a deceased boarder, who was the epidemic's first recorded case – plausibly suggesting that cholera might have spread from the first to the second boarder through infected waste. In his famous study of the Broad Street pump, Snow probed several anomalous cases. Households located near the pump where no one died from cholera turned out to take water from another source, while some households that experienced cholera deaths but lived further away turned out, for disparate reasons, to have taken water from the Broad Street pump. This heightened the plausibility of Snow's inference that infected water from the pump was spreading the disease.

Finally, Snow noted that sailors who docked at cholera-affected ports did not contract the disease until they disembarked, striking a blow to the prevailing theory that cholera travels via miasma (bad air). According to this theory, sailors should have contracted cholera by breathing bad air before coming ashore. As a whole, these fragments of evidence are convincing. Combined with Snow's natural experiment, they lead strongly to the inference that cholera spreads through infected waste or water (even if this conclusion was not fully accepted by epidemiologists for another fifty years).

---

[21] Freedman's (2010) account could be accused of a mild form of this selection bias: it mainly narrates success stories, in which qualitative insights led to important medical discoveries.

The persuasiveness and probative value of each single causal-process observation is nonetheless debatable. For example, other evidence appeared consistent with the miasma theory (for example, territorial patterns of the disease's spread); and Snow's evidence from sailors does not suggest that cholera is borne by infected waste or water. The taxonomy of process-tracing tests proposed by Van Evera (1997) and discussed and further elaborated both in Chapter 1 and the Appendix (both this volume) provides a helpful way of organizing our thinking about the strength of Snow's evidence. Some of his CPOs appear to provide "straw-in-the-wind" tests; others might be "hoop" tests.[22] However, such taxonomies do not provide a ready guide for assessing whether any *particular* CPO provides strong evidence in favor of his hypothesis (see also Waldner, this volume, Chapter 5). Researchers would be left to argue that a particular piece of evidence is indeed a "smoking gun" or is "doubly decisive"; and their readers may lack firm criteria for deciding when these claims are true.

Moreover, there is a potential circularity involved in assessing the probative value of particular CPOs in light of subsequent testing. Snow's series of causal-process observations led him to develop his natural experiment, in an approach very much in the spirit of multi-method research: both qualitative and quantitative evidence are leveraged in complementary ways at different stages of a research program. However, validation of a hypothesis through a subsequent confirmatory natural experiment does not necessarily validate a hypothesis-generating causal-process observation *qua* causal-process observation. Even with Snow, there may be a tendency for "post hoc, ergo propter hoc" thinking. That is, we may tend to see the process tracing in Snow's (1855) cholera study as powerful – and his supporting arguments for yellow fever as thin – because subsequent studies showed that he was right about cholera and wrong about yellow fever. Yet, it does not follow that Snow's causal-process observations in the case of cholera were necessarily more powerful than in the case of yellow fever.

Of course, Snow's natural experiment (and subsequent studies, including later work by microbiologists) did ultimately confirm his conjecture that cholera is waterborne; other research helped to pin down the distinctive causes of transmission of plague, yellow fever, and malaria.[23] The quality of the evidence that led to Snow's initial conjecture about cholera, and to his

---

[22] E.g. the miasma theory may have failed a "hoop test," due to Snow's observation that sailors did not contract cholera until disembarking; yet, this is at best a "straw-in-the-wind test" for his theory that cholera is a waste- and waterborne disease.

[23] See, e.g. Freedman (2010) for references and a review of this research.

misleading hypotheses about yellow fever, may not appear to matter much in retrospect. This conclusion would be short sighted, however. In many settings, perhaps especially in the social sciences, things are not so clear-cut: the conclusions drawn from subsequent testing may not be so sharp. It is, therefore, important to try to validate particular CPOs – i.e. not only to establish the truth of some general hypothesis generated through process tracing, but also to confirm the evidentiary value of a causal-process observation itself.

However, Snow's study also suggests that it may be quite tricky to evaluate the independent persuasiveness of a given CPO *without* subsequent or complementary confirmatory evidence. Indeed, as the previous section showed, knowledge of context or process often plays a critical role in validating or invalidating research designs – including the very designs expected to provide critical tests of hypotheses. In Snow's natural experiment, qualitative knowledge of the nature of water markets in nineteenth-century London played a critical role in making plausible the "as-if" random assignment of households to sources of water supply. If such claims about water markets are mistaken, then the case for the natural experiment itself is substantially weakened. Thus, even in Snow's study, the quality of CPOs matters for interpreting the credibility of confirmatory tests: those pieces of evidence are used to validate the natural experiment – even as the results of the natural experiment seem to validate other CPOs.

In summary, the evidentiary value of a given causal-process observation may depend on the existence or non-existence of certain *other* pieces of evidence, as well as analysis of data sets from strong designs. As Collier (2011: 824–825) puts it: "Identifying evidence that can be interpreted as diagnostic depends centrally on prior knowledge . . . The decision to treat a given piece of evidence as the basis [for a process-tracing test] can depend on the researcher's prior knowledge, the assumptions that underlie the study, and the specific formulation of the hypothesis."[24] In particular, the quality of any piece of evidentiary support must be evaluated in the context of existing background knowledge and theory, and especially, in light of other diagnostic pieces of evidence. Thus, the evidentiary weight of a given CPO clearly depends not only on its own veracity, but also on the non-existence of other CPOs that might provide countervailing inferences. Situating pieces of diagnostic evidence within a broader field of other causal-process observations is therefore critical for buttressing the claim that process tracing has

---

[24] Zaks (2011), for instance, assesses the relationship of process tracing evidence to alternative theories and discusses how to use process tracing to adjudicate between them.

produced genuinely dispositive evidence in favor of a particular assumption or hypothesis.

This point raises a second major challenge, however, regarding how to elicit potentially disconfirming as well as confirmatory evidence – an important challenge in natural experiments, where much hinges on detailed information about the process of treatment assignment. In the Argentina land-titling study, for example, we are told that Catholic Church organizers did not know that the state would expropriate land and allocate titles to squatters; and even if they had, they could not have predicted which particular parcels would have been subject to court challenges. Thus, evidence that Church organizers *did* have reason to suspect that land would be expropriated from the original owners – or that they had a basis for predicting which absent landowners would challenge expropriation in court and which would not – could undermine the plausibility that land titles are assigned as-if at random. In Snow's natural experiment, evidence that residents did in fact self-select into source of water supply – for example, by changing suppliers after the move of Lambeth's pipe – could similarly invalidate the claim of as-if random.

I do not have reason to believe that such countervailing evidence exists in these particular examples. On the other hand, I do not have strong reason *not* to believe countervailing evidence exists: in the main, I know only what I am told by the authors of the studies. This again brings into focus an Achilles heel of natural experiments with as-if random assignment, relative to studies in which treatment assignment is truly randomized (Dunning 2008a). "Absence of evidence" is not "evidence of absence," a point emphasized in both this book's introduction (Bennett and Checkel, this volume, p. 19) and Appendix. To assess the evidentiary value of qualitative evidence offered by researchers in defense of a particular claim, the research community would benefit from access to a range of *other* potential causal-process observations that might have been offered, but perhaps were not.

How can individual researchers, and the research community, best meet this second challenge of validation? In the first place, it seems to be a responsibility of the original researchers not only to look for evidence that supports an assumption such as "as-if" random, but also evidence that would *undercut* it – again, similar to the admonition in Chapter 1 that scholars should "cast the net widely," yet "be equally tough on alternative explanations" (Bennett and Checkel, this volume, Chapter 1, pp. 23–24). Moreover – and especially if researchers fail to find such evidence – they should report how and where they looked. In other words, and as emphasized in both Bennett and Checkel's opening (this volume, pp. 30–31) and concluding chapters (this volume, Chapter 10, pp. 264–274), transparency in research procedures is all important. In our two running examples, for instance, researchers could report the types and number of people they interviewed and the other sources they consulted, and then state that they found no evidence that people could or did switch water companies on the basis of water quality (Snow 1855) or chose plots in anticipation of which landowners would challenge expropriation in the courts (Argentina land-titling study).[25]

Yet, researchers may still face challenges in communicating in a credible and transparent way that they have adhered to Bennett and Checkel's best practices. With many natural experiments, the requirements in terms of substantive knowledge and mastery of the details of the process of treatment assignment are demanding; such research designs often involve intensive fieldwork. Indeed, this is a major virtue of the approach, because it brings researchers into close engagement with the research context, thereby "extract-ing ideas at close range" (Collier 1999). At the same time, this very level of substantive knowledge implies that many other scholars may not have first-hand knowledge – for instance, of the incentives, information, and capacities of key actors involved in assigning a given treatment – that is required for evaluating the plausibility of as-if random. Moreover, researchers themselves can only be held accountable for the evidence they do uncover; but again, absence of evidence does not always constitute evidence of absence. In sum-mary, it is not easy to rule out completely the possibility that qualitative evidence not uncovered or offered by researchers might undermine their case for the research design.

Thus, it may often be quite tricky to assess whether Bennett and Checkel's criteria for good process tracing have been applied. The development of general best practices is surely a helpful step forward. Yet, it is just as critical for researchers to be able to communicate credibly that they have adhered to these standards – for instance, that they have "cast the net widely for alternative explanations" or have been "equally tough on the alternative explanations." At its core, the challenge is to verify that researchers have indeed successfully sought both confirming and potentially disconfirming causal-process observations – so that disconfirming evidence will appear, if it exists.

---

[25] Snow implicitly does something similar when he notes that water pipes were laid down in the years when companies "were in active competition" (1855: 75). Galiani and Schargrodsky point to such interviews, although do not always specifically report to whom they spoke. For more detailed descriptions, see Snow 1855; Freedman 1999; 2009; 2010; or Dunning 2008a; 2012.

The utility of adversarialism?

One potential solution to this challenge of validation might be found in specific research *procedures*. Thus, researchers could catalogue disparate pieces of qualitative evidence, so that communities of scholars working in particular substantive areas might more readily examine them. Scholars can then subject more easily to critical scrutiny the truth of crucial claims, such as assertions of as-if random that rest on somewhat esoteric details about treatment-assignment processes. One might therefore appeal to the utility of competition between scholars with different vested interests in upholding or subverting the veracity of a given claim. Such "organized skepticism" (Merton 1973; see MacCoun 1998) may provide the most feasible way of confronting the problem that absence of evidence is not evidence of absence. Indeed, competition between scholars may boost the chance that potentially disconfirming bits of qualitative evidence are fruitfully brought to light. Much as in a court of law (at least in the non-inquisitorial tradition), where competing advocates adduce evidence in favor of or against a particular interpretation or causal claim, scholars with different theoretical commitments might seek to uncover evidence that supports or undermines a particular hypothesis.[26]

This image of seeking truth through scholarly rivalry is familiar. In the case of multi-method, design-based research, however, the specific focus is novel. For instance, scholars claiming to use a natural experiment might point to the aspects of an assignment process that support as-if random. Other scholars might seek to bring forward evidence that makes this assertion less plausible.

Certainly, the analogy to courts of law is only partially appropriate for scholarly research. Legal adversarialism pre-commits dueling attorneys to providing whatever evidence is most consistent with the position they have been assigned to attack or defend, which one would hope (!) does not characterize scholars even with the very strongest theoretical commitments. And unlike, say, some civil courts – in which an ostensibly disinterested judge adjudicates between competing truth claims – in the academic realm there is no neutral third-party arbiter of justice. (The analogy to criminal trial by a jury of one's peers might be somewhat more apt.) Still, the more-than-passing resemblance of legal adversarialism to what some scholars do at least some of the time suggests that this analogy might be fruitfully explored.

---

[26] MacCoun (1998) contrasts the adversarial and inquisitorial traditions.

Thus, one might ask: how successfully has organized skepticism interrogated the validity of research designs or modeling assumptions in multi-method research – or put the validity of supporting causal-process observations themselves under dispute? At the most general level, one can find plentiful contemporary examples of disputes about the quality of evidence. Many of these seem to focus on questions of conceptualization and especially measurement. Examples include Albouy's (2012) critique of the settler mortality data used by Acemoglu *et al.* (2001); Kreuzer's (2010) criticism of Cusack *et al.* (2007); or Rothstein's (2007) appraisal of Hoxby's (2000) coding decisions. Such assessments of data quality can certainly require qualitative knowledge of context and process. They may even sometimes involve causal-process observations – perhaps of the type Mahoney (2010) calls "independent-variable CPOs," where the main issue involves verifying the presence or absence of a cause. However, they do not typically involve the research design and causal modeling assumptions on which I have focused in this chapter.

In contrast, critiques of modeling assumptions do abound in the literature on natural experiments; yet, these often take the form of assessing observable *quantitative* implications of these modeling assumptions. For example, the assertion of as-if random implies that variables not affected by the notional treatment should be about equally distributed across treatment and control groups – just as they would be, in expectation, if treatment were assigned through a coin flip.[27] Thus, Caughey and Sekhon (2011), critiquing Lee (2008), show that winners of close elections in the US House of Representatives are *not* like losers of those elections on various pre-treatment covariates, especially partisanship (Democratic incumbents tend to win the close races more than Republican challengers).

Sovey and Green (2011) critique the claim of as-if random in Miguel *et al.*'s (2004) study of the effect of economic growth on the probability of civil conflict in Africa. Here, rainfall growth is used as an instrumental variable for economic growth, implying an assumption that rainfall growth is assigned as-if at random; yet, using Miguel *et al.*'s replication data, Sovey and Green suggest that "factors such as population, mountainous terrain, and lagged GDP significantly predict rainfall growth or lagged rainfall growth, although these relationships are not particularly strong and the predictors as a group tend to fall short of joint significance" (2011: 197). Thus, here we see examples

---

[27] Formal statistical tests may then be used to assess whether any observed imbalances are consistent with chance variation.

of efforts to assess the quantitative implications of as-if random, using statistical tests.

Such examples lean rather less heavily on causal-process observations, however – for example, on whether key actors have the information, incentives, and capacity to subvert random assignment – to validate design and modeling assumptions. Certainly, one can find good examples of the use of qualitative methods by researchers to substantiate their own claims of as-if random. Iyer (2010), in an article in the *Review of Economics and Statistics*, uses extensive documentary and archival evidence on the Doctrine of Lapse during the reign of Governor Dalhousie, a central component of her effort to find as-if random variation in the presence of princely states in colonial India (as opposed to direct colonial rule by the British). Posner's (2004) article on interethnic relations in two African countries also makes very effective use of qualitative evidence, although it does so mostly to explore mechanisms more than to support the claim of as-if random placement of a colonial border between modern-day Zambia and Malawi. In the Argentine land-titling study and other settings, qualitative evidence also clearly plays a central role.

Yet, a review of the literature on natural experiments tends to suggest the *potential* utility of causal-process observations for interrogating design and modeling assumptions in multi-method work.[28] Critiques of as-if random have tended not to draw extensively on qualitative evidence – perhaps precisely because of the extensive case knowledge and detailed information required to do so. It therefore seems there is much opportunity for greater use of qualitative methods in natural-experimental research to probe design and modeling assumptions, yet one of the difficulties concerns how best to elicit and use varied qualitative information on processes of treatment assignment.

What sorts of research procedures might promote better use of CPOs, and particularly better validation of their evidentiary value? One possibility is to promote better cataloguing of qualitative data from fieldwork interviews, archival documents, and so forth. The new Qualitative Data Repository at Syracuse University is one effort to provide a platform for public posting of qualitative evidence.[29] There, researchers will be able to post field notes,

---

[28] Caughey and Sekhon (2011) also scour newspaper accounts from a random sample of close elections for qualitative evidence that could explain why Democrats win close races; however, here they are interested in evidence on mechanisms, so the qualitative evidence itself is not as central to evaluating violations of as-if random.

[29] The data repository has been established through a grant from the US National Science Foundation, with Colin Elman and Diana Kapiszewski as Principal Investigators.

transcripts of interviews, archival documents, and the like; the aim, inter alia, is to boost transparency and perhaps replicability in qualitative research.

There may be various forms of posting and accessing qualitative information. For instance, "active citation" allows references to archival documents or other sources in a publication or a research report to be hyperlinked to a partial or full virtual copy of the document (Moravcsik 2010). Other cataloguing procedures involve posting of entire interviews or transcripts – qualitative data *qua* data. Both sorts of information could be useful to researchers, within the adversarial tradition in which one scholar contests another's CPOs. For example, the suspicion that extracts from interviews may be cherry-picked to support particular propositions or interpretations might be mollified (or exacerbated) by review of an entire interview transcript.

Better use of such transparent research procedures would likely make for better process tracing by individual researchers in several ways. It would encourage them to think through whether they have "cast the net widely for alternative explanations" – in particular, for evidence that would undermine as well as support key assumptions – before the publication of their research. And it might also help researchers as well as their critics assess whether they are being "equally tough on the alternative explanations." And it may facilitate consideration of "the potential biases of evidentiary sources" – all best practices advanced by Bennett and Checkel in Chapter 1.

Consider the following concrete advantages of posting or registering interview transcripts or other qualitative materials.

- A careful reading of interview transcripts in which key issues of information, incentives, and capacity are broached might make claims of "evidence of absence" more compelling. For instance, the assertions in the Argentina land-titling study that Catholic Church organizers did not know abandoned land was not owned by the state, or that the legal owners of expropriated plots who challenged their taking in court did so for idiosyncratic reasons unrelated to the characteristics of squatters, may be made more credible by perusing transcripts of interviews with key actors.
- In contrast, the non-appearance of key interview questions, parenthetical remarks by informants, or other kinds of evidence might weaken the credibility of such claims. For example, we might expect researchers to probe informants' incentives, information, and capacities as they relate to the assertion of as-if random. The expectation of preparing qualitative materials for public posting might thus make individual researchers more self-conscious about the use of such tools.

- Individual researchers might be more prone to use various cognitive tricks to avoid confirmation bias – for instance, by assuming that they are wrong in their conclusions, or that their design assumptions such as as-if random are incorrect – and then asking how the evidence they have catalogued might support such alternative interpretations.
- Such documentation may also facilitate direct appeals to the expertise of communities of scholars. For instance, individual researchers might run key portions of their texts or even primary materials by area experts, historians, or key actors and informants who may be in a position to judge whether the scholars have misread key evidence bearing on issues such as as-if random.

To be sure, such documentation will not fully solve the problem of "missing CPOs" – that is, the problem that absence of evidence may not constitute evidence of absence. However, more complete recording of qualitative evidence – as laborious as that can be to provide – would surely improve on the current state of affairs. Researchers suspicious of an assertion such as as-if random would have a place to start looking for nuggets of information on context, process, or mechanism that would help to subvert such claims. And individual researchers adhering to such a transparent protocol could stake a more credible claim to have followed Bennett and Checkel's ten criteria for good process tracing.

Of course, the provision of more extensive documentation of qualitative evidence is probably only part of the solution to the challenges of validation. Like lawyers and judges, researchers have various incentives. Using CPOs culled from such documentation to probe the plausibility of as-if random involves substantial costs in time and effort, a point also recognized by Bennett and Checkel when they counsel scholars not to "give up" when confronting their ten best practices (this volume, Chapter 1, p. 22). Moreover, the intellectual reward may be uncertain and the professional returns meager – especially since, for better or worse, professional attention and credit seems likely to go to the discoverer of the design and less likely to accrue to the eager critic.

Finally, the deep and specialized substantive knowledge that is often required to identify potentially falsifying CPOs may also limit the utility of peer review. And those with the basis to know whether the full record of CPOs supports a claim of as-if random, or a particular modeling assumption like non-interference, might well have other incentives to attack or undermine another researcher's use of CPOs. This could leave the outside observer on shaky ground to determine what is true.

These caveats notwithstanding, greater provision of supporting qualitative documentation does seem likely to aid efforts to improve process tracing and thus to turn it from metaphor to analytic tool. Like the posting of quantitative data sets and replication files for published articles (which is by no means a universal practice, but certainly one backed by emerging norms), this effort can lend readers a reasonable expectation that contrary CPOs (i.e. those that contradict a main claim or hypothesis) would stand a decent chance of coming to light. Of course, there can be many practical or ethical issues that arise in posting qualitative data (such as protecting subject confidentiality), so the feasibility of providing supporting documentation may vary by project, or by type of evidence within projects.[30]

For multi-method research in the design-based tradition, this is good news. The assumptions of strong research designs often have sharper testable implications than conventional quantitative methods. For example, as noted above, as-if random assignment suggests that comparison (treatment) groups should be balanced on covariates and that policymakers or the units themselves should not have the information, incentives, and capacity to select into treatment groups in a way that may be correlated with potential outcomes. Each of these implications can be tested through a range of quantitative and qualitative evidence.

Conclusion: improving process tracing in multi-method research

The importance of multi-method work – in particular, of leveraging both qualitative and quantitative tools for causal inference – is increasingly recognized. With strong research designs, quantitative analysis can provide social scientists with powerful tools for assessing causation. Yet, analysis of data sets is rarely sufficient. To develop strong designs, validate causal models, and interpret effects, analysts typically require fragments of information that give crucial insights into causal processes of interest. Process tracing is a label for a set of techniques and methods designed to generate such insights. As such, it plays an important role in social-science research.

However, it is critical to assess the quality and probative value of particular instances of process tracing. The standards put forth by Bennett and Checkel in Chapter 1 are useful in this regard. Yet, it can be difficult for researchers to

---

[30] The Qualitative Data Repository is working actively with researchers on how to address such issues.

demonstrate – and for the scholarly community thus to certify – that they have indeed "cast the net widely for alternative explanations," been "equally tough on alternative[s]," "considered the potential biases of evidentiary sources," and so forth. One major difficulty is that the value of a particular causal-process observation presented by a researcher must be set in the context of other information, including possibly disconfirming evidence. Such information can be hard to find – and unless it is elicited and presented by researchers, the research community cannot assess its relative import.

Overcoming these challenges, if only partially, may involve: (1) the adoption of more transparent cataloguing practices for qualitative data, for instance, the posting of transcribed interviews and archival documents, and the use of active citations; and (2) facilitation of scholarly contestation of process-tracing claims, which will in turn be aided by transparent cataloguing. Thus, scholars could use comprehensive qualitative information – including the data provided by individual researchers under point 1 – to interrogate and perhaps contest specific claims about the information, incentives, and capacities of key decision-makers. Cataloguing interview transcripts and other sources would allow critics to focus on questions *not* asked, or answers *not* reported – which might allow some assessment of evidence of absence, as well as absence of evidence. To the extent that such information substantiates or undercuts researchers' design or modeling assumptions, it would be particularly useful for multi-method work, such as natural experiments. Thus, while standards for "good" process tracing may be difficult to implement, research *procedures* that boost transparency in qualitative research may help substantially to close this implementation gap. The result will be to advance this volume's central goal – i.e. improving process tracing. For individual researchers, the adoption of such procedures could facilitate credible and transparent claims about the probative value of process-tracing evidence.

In this chapter, I have illustrated these points with respect to natural experiments, but similar arguments are likely applicable to other forms of multi-method research – such as those combining formal theoretical models or cross-national regressions with case studies. Of course, the specific inferential issues may vary in those contexts: with more complicated models and less plausible design assumptions, the challenges of validation may be even greater. But in principle, the major challenges – of (i) understanding *selection processes* that assign cases to alternative causal conditions or categories of a treatment variable; and (ii) validating key modeling assumptions – also apply to these forms of research. Thus, "treatment-assignment" and "model-validation" causal-process observations also apply in these other settings.

In the end, however, there is unlikely to be a silver bullet. Social science is difficult, and causal inference is especially challenging. Discomfortingly, Gerber and Green (2012: 415) may have it right when they state: "Experiments are sometimes heralded as the gold standard of causal inference . . . a more apt metaphor would be gold prospecting, which is slow and laborious but when conditions are right, gradually extracts flecks of gold from tons of sediment." In a similar way, Freedman avers: "Scientific inquiry is a long and tortuous process, with many false starts and blind alleys. Combining qualitative insights and quantitative analysis – and a healthy dose of skepticism – may provide the most secure results" (2010). For mixed-method research, good process tracing can thus play a central role, together with many other techniques, but there are likely to be many failures along with the successes.

9 Practice tracing

Vincent Pouliot

The relationship between interpretivists and process tracers is one of mutual neglect, if not outright suspicion and even contempt. This is arguably puzzling given that on the face of it, these two groups of scholars would seem to have quite a few things in common. For instance, many process tracers and interpretivists share an inductive commitment to fine-grained case studies. They focus on processes and flows as opposed to static structures or entities (see also Checkel, this volume, Chapter 3). They are critical of explanations based on correlational logic, and generally skeptical of law-like statements. Process tracers and interpretivists like to narrate the unfolding of history and disaggregate it in smaller bits of time. They generally agree that despite the contingency and messiness of the social world, there exist scholarly standards thanks to which some analytical accounts fare better than others. Finally, both groups of scholars tend to espouse a humanistic bias in favor of agency and the micro-dynamics of social life. And yet, despite these many substantive commonalities, there is unfortunately little to no conversation, let alone cross-fertilization, currently occurring between process tracing and interpretivist bodies of literature.

This chapter seeks to chart a new path in order to tap into the many synergies between interpretive methodology and process tracing. What I call "practice tracing" is a hybrid methodological form that rests on two relatively simple tenets: social causality is to be established locally, but with an eye to producing analytically general insights. The first tenet, drawn primarily from interpretivism, posits the singularity of causal accounts: it is meaningful contexts that give practices their social effectiveness and generative power in and on the world. The second tenet, in tune with process analytics, holds that no social relationships and practices are so unique as to foreclose the possibility of theorization and categorization. Practice tracing seeks to occupy

For thoughtful comments on an earlier version of this chapter, I am grateful to the editors as well as to Stefano Guzzini, Patrick Jackson, Peter Katzenstein, Dan Nexon, Ed Schatz, and Srdjan Vucetic.

a methodological middle ground where patterns of meaningful action may be abstracted away from local contexts in the form of social mechanisms that can travel across cases. The added value of practice tracing, in terms of allowing for dialogue between process tracing and interpretivism, lies in simultaneously upholding singular causality and analytical generality.

As a conceptual meeting point for process tracers and interpretivists, I suggest the notion of practice (Adler and Pouliot 2011a). As I argue below, the key feature of practices that renders them particularly useful for this methodological engagement is that they are both particular (as contextually embedded actions) and general (as patterns of actions). My contention is *not* that all process tracers, or all interpretivists for that matter, should espouse practice tracing. Intellectual pluralism is a productive state of affairs and there is no methodological panacea on offer in this chapter (see also Checkel and Bennett, this volume, Chapter 10). Clearly, practices exhaust neither the array of processes one may trace, nor the universe of meanings social scientists may interpret. For example, speech acts are crucial social dynamics that may be captured otherwise than through practice tracing (see Guzzini 2011). Likewise, there are different ways to study practices than the specific methodology advocated here. My claim, which stems from the editors' invitation to look at process tracing from an interpretive point of view, rather is that practice tracing is a useful methodology for this kind of conversation because the concept of practice offers a common ground where concerns for contextual specificity and analytical generality can be equally met.

In the chapter I distinguish between practices and mechanisms. Both notions describe social processes, but in my view they operate on different planes. Practices describe ways of doing things that are known to practitioners. As contested and polysemic as they may be, practices are part of the social environment. While it is true that social scientists can only aspire to produce analytical re-descriptions of practices, this does not imply epistemic subjectivity at the level of action. By contrast, I reserve the concept of mechanisms for the theoretical abstractions that social scientists coin in order to classify practices, usually across cases. Mechanisms are analytical constructs whose objective is not to match actual social instances, but to draw useful connections between them. Admittedly, in making this distinction, I depart from Bennett and Checkel's scientific realist assertion that social mechanisms are out there, as ontological entities in the world (this volume, Chapter 1, p. 12). I am willing to argue that practices *are*, in some sense, out there, as epistemically objective patterns of actions that confront agents as external realities with which to grapple. But mechanisms, to the extent that they are part of the theorizing, follow a logic of abstraction that is very different from that of practice. In other words, practice tracing combines an inductive (and interpretive) sensibility with a commitment to analytical generality.

The deeper issue here has to do with the fundamental purpose of social scientific analysis. In Bennett and Checkel's rendition, a main objective of process tracing is theory development and testing (although see Evangelista, this volume, Chapter 6). The goal is to confront hypothesized links between variables with empirical data. Generalizations are inferred from deductive models; thanks to process tracing, hypotheses are either substantiated or falsified. This positivist view of the social scientific undertaking is quite different from the purpose that I think practice tracing should serve. We can certainly agree that the defining feature of the social scientific ethos is to look beyond specific cases and ask: what is this an instance of? But the search for analytical generality is not the same as testing empirical generalizations (see Jackson 2011: chapter 5). Theorization, in the former enterprise, means abstracting away from empirics in order to reach a conceptual level that makes cross-case comparison not only possible, but also useful. In this endeavor, there is no point in trying to match theory and reality, as per positivism. The whole idea is precisely to depart from data. As a result, the analytical generality that practice tracing aspires to cannot be validated through empirical testing, as if holding a mirror between models and data (i.e. the correspondence theory of truth). Just like typologies, practice theories are neither true nor false, but useful (or not) in making sense of messy arrays of practices.

I suggest that a successful practice-tracing account should accomplish two basic things: (1) demonstrate local causality; and (2) produce analytically general insights. First, using a broad understanding of causality, I argue that successful practice tracing should capture the generative links between various social processes. As physicist Bohm once put it: "everything comes from other things and gives rise to other things" (quoted in Kurki 2008: 16). In the social world, practices elicit practices elicit practices, etc. As I argue below, the task of tracing the stream of practice necessarily involves the interpretive grasp of local contexts. Second, a convincing account should locate specific instances of relationships as part of larger classes of social processes. In other words, as contextualized as the study of practice may be, the social scientific gaze must always look beyond specific cases, toward cross-case generality. Induction, interpretation, and abstraction are not competing objectives, but mutually reinforcing operations in practice tracing – a point the editors acknowledge in Chapter 1. However, as Jackson (2011: 115) aptly puts it, "what researchers do is to order analytically the empirical data in accord with a model the worth of which lies *not* in its correspondence to the world, but in its pragmatic consequences for ordering the facts of the world."

Fittingly, these two objectives of practice tracing work quite well with the ten criteria for good process tracing listed by Bennett and Checkel in the introductory chapter (this volume, pp. 20–31). Those four criteria that espouse an inductive spirit are particularly germane. In particular, good practice tracing should: evaluate context and authorship in making sense of evidence (criterion 3); justify the bounds of study based on the puzzle (criterion 5); aspire to in-depth but realistic empirical research, with a focus on probative evidence from diverse streams (criterion 6); and of course be open to inductive insights (criterion 8).

With the remaining six standards, I reinterpret them through a pragmatist lens. Thus, as regards alternative explanations (criteria 1 and 2), deduced implications (criterion 9), and conclusiveness (criterion 10), good practice tracing should aspire not to (dis)confirm theories. Rather, it should explain, first, why practice X (as opposed to Y and Z) is considered to lie behind an object of interest and, second, how X may fit within different theoretical categories. Similarly, convincing practice-tracing accounts should analyze how particular cases compare to others (criterias 4 and 7) – not to test theories, but to develop and fine-tune the analytical mechanisms thanks to which multiple social instances come to speak to one another.

The chapter contains three sections. First, I explain what practices are and why they are relevant to any discussion of process tracing. Not only are practices a fundamental category of social processes, they are also causal, in the sense that they make things social happen. The next two sections use examples from international relations (IR) literature to illustrate how one may go about grasping both the particularity and generality of practices. In the second section, I argue that causal analysis requires that practices be embedded in their social context through the interpretation of meanings. What renders a pattern of action causal, that is, what makes it produce social effects, are the practical logics that are bound up in it and intersubjectively negotiated. As such, meaningful causality is by necessity local (i.e. context-bound) and it must be reconstructed from within. In the third section, I contend that because practices are by nature repeated and patterned, one may heuristically abstract them away from context in the form of various social mechanisms. These mechanisms, however, are not causes per se, but theoretical constructs that allow for cross-case (i.e. analytically general) insights. I conclude on the need to move beyond meta-theoretical divides – which are by nature irresolvable – and let social scientific practices guide our methodological debates.

Why trace practices?

In this first section, I explain what practices are and why they are relevant to a book about process tracing (see also Gross 2009). Practices are socially meaningful and organized patterns of activities; in lay parlance, they are ways of doing things.[1] One can think of myriad practices, from handshaking to war making through grading, voting, and many more. Practices are distinct from both behavior and action. The notion of behavior captures the material aspect of doing. The concept of action adds on a layer of meaningfulness, at both the subjective (intentions, beliefs) and inter-subjective (norms, identities) levels. Practices, however, are not only behavioral and meaningful, but also organized and patterned. And because they are regular forms of action within a given social context, practices tend to become mutually recognizable for communities of practitioners. As Cook and Brown illustrate:

In the simplest case, if Vance's knee jerks, that is behavior. When Vance raps his knee with a physician's hammer to check his reflexes, it is behavior that has meaning, and thus is what we call action. If his physician raps his knee as part of an exam, it is practice. This is because the meaning of her action comes from the organized contexts of her training and ongoing work in medicine (where it can draw on, contribute to, and be evaluated in the work of others in her field). (Cook and Brown 1999: 387)

In a nutshell, anything that people do in a contextually typical and minimally recognizable way counts as a practice.

Practices are relevant to process tracing not only because they are processes, but also because they have causal power. First, practices are performances, which unfold in time and over time. In effect, practice X, that is, X-ing, is essentially the process of doing X; it is a fundamentally dynamic activity. In that sense, practices form a basic constitutive process of social life and politics, being a concrete, social flow of energy giving shape to history. Second and related, practices have causal power in the sense that they make other things happen. Practices are the generative force thanks to which society and politics take shape; they produce very concrete effects in and on the world. This is the

---

[1] With Adler I supply a slightly more complex definition, conceiving of practices as "socially meaningful patterns of action which, in being performed more or less competently, simultaneously embody, act out and possibly reify background knowledge and discourse in and on the material world" (Adler and Pouliot 2011a: 6). This paragraph borrows from this article. For applications to various practices in world politics, see the contributions in Adler and Pouliot 2011b.

performative or productive side of practices: under proper conditions, practicing X causes various other practices to follow. For example, in the field of international security, the practice of military exercise – which usually involves simulating an attack, setting in motion a chain of command, moving forces around, and delivering a response – produces various social effects. Depending on the political context at hand, the same practice will generate distinctive practices – indeed, in world politics practices such as military exercises are often intended to mean different things to different people. Between close partners, military exercising will likely produce communications sharing, officer exchanges, and follow-up meetings. When it comes to rivals, however, this practice may generate harsh diplomatic reactions, military deployments, and countermeasures. But whatever its effects, the military exercise, just like any other practice, will surely cause other practices in its wake.

The generative power of practices stems from the meaningful context within which they are enacted, which instructs actors about what is going on. At the level of action, the meaning of the practice of interest gets negotiated, in a more or less articulate fashion, between practitioners: what is happening here? Most of the time, rich interpretive clues are supplied by the existing intersubjective context, which renders the negotiation process not all that elastic. For instance, in our societies there is little chance that extending a hand forward (i.e. the practice of handshaking) will be interpreted as an act of aggression, given the thickness of background knowledge that surrounds social encounter. That said, many practices take place in ambiguous contexts, rendering meaning-making processes much more open and contested. Military exercising, to return to our example, may be interpreted in many contradictory ways and cause various kinds of responses, sometimes tragic. But the general rule remains the same: based on existing practical knowledge, whether thick or thin, practitioners react to what a given set of actions *count as*, in the current situation, with related practices that structure the interaction and *cause* practitioners to do a number of things which they may not have done otherwise. Similarly, in order to decipher the causal effects of the practice of military exercising, the analyst must grasp the prior background that structures a given political relationship.

If the causal efficacy of practices rests on the meanings that are bound up in them, then any account of causality must go through the interpretation of social contexts and practical logics (see also Falleti and Lynch 2009). As we have seen, the act of simulating a military attack does not, in and of itself, cause social patterns of, say, officer exchanges or counter deployments. It is the particular context in which the behavior is performed that turns it so – a collective defense organization versus an entrenched rivalry. Geertz (1973) made a similar argument, decades ago, about twitches and winks: the social effects that follow from the movement of an eyelid are determined by the inter-subjective background at hand: a love affair, a game of murderer and detective, or more simply a meaningless reflex. The main methodological implication, which the next section explores further, is that causal accounts cannot escape the interpretivist moment.

Meaningful causality: embedding practices in their social context

In terms of methods, how does one embed practices in their social context so as to interpret their bound-up meanings? In order to account for the causal effects of a practice, I argue, one has to grasp, interpretively, the constitutive relationship that makes it such. This renders causality inherently local.[2]

For the social scientist, the basic objective is to understand what the practice under study *counts as* in the situation at hand (Ruggie 1998: 31). Recall Searle's (1995) formula: X counts as Y in context C. In his famous example, worn bits of paper with certain engravings count as money in our banking system. There is no doubt that once constituted as such, money causes myriad effects in our society, from stock exchange to grocery purchase through economic depressions. By adding a gerund form to Searle's formula, we may apply the constitutive logic to any practice: X-ing counts as Y-ing in context C. For example, simulating an attack counts as allied military exercising in a collective defense alliance. This example is relatively settled because it rests on a thick background of intersubjectivity. In more ambiguous contexts, however, the exact constitutive logic that makes action X count as practice Y is far from obvious, even to practitioners. At the level of observation, the meaning has to be inferred from the close, interpretive study of the local interaction setting.

Methodologically speaking, this means that practices must be understood from within the community of practitioners so as to restore the inter-subjective meanings that are bound up in them. This is not to say that we need to get inside people's minds in order to probe their intentions and motives – a seemingly impossible endeavor given the tools that are currently at our disposal (see Krebs and Jackson 2007; and Jacobs, this volume,

---

[2] Compare with Lin (1998), who argues instead that in bridging positivism and interpretivism, the former should be in charge of (constant) causality, while the latter deals with (local) description.

Chapter 2, for a different view). The empathetic reconstruction of subjective beliefs (as in a certain kind of hermeneutics) is not what meaning-making processes are primarily about. Instead, the task is to reconstruct the "logic of practicality" (Pouliot 2008a), that is, the stock of intersubjective and largely tacit know-how that crystallizes the social meaning(s) of a pattern of action. Thanks to practicality, practitioners strive to figure out what other people's actions count as (i.e. what they are, mean, and do in the situation), and how to act and react on that basis.

For the researcher, the idea is to grasp practices as they unfold locally, that is, in a specific context.[3] Confronted with practice X, the researcher asks: what would one have to know – as inarticulate as that knowledge may remain – in order to feel or grasp the meaning of a given gesture, especially in terms of what it does in and on the world? To use Taylor's (1993: 45) example, in order to figure out how to follow a direction, one has to know that it is the arrow's point, and not the feathers, that shows the right way. This tacit know-how, which we all embody "naturally" thanks to past technological developments (the bow), is usually very inarticulate. In reconstructing practical knowledge, the objective is to understand the insider meanings that agents attribute to their reality. Thanks to induction, the researcher refrains as much as possible from imposing scientific categories, to instead recover practical meanings and locally enacted common sense (Hopf 2002).

From an interpretive point of view, making sense of practices raises a particularly thorny predicament, which Turner calls the "Mauss problem" (1994: 19–24). In order to decipher the meaning of a practice, its practicality must be both alien *and* native to the interpreter's own system of meanings. If, on the one hand, the meaning of a practice is too deeply embodied by the interpreter, chances are that it will remain invisible as a second nature. If, on the other hand, the logic of practicality is completely alien to the interpreter, then it may not be properly understood within its context. My own solution to this problem – one among many other valid ones – is to devise a "sobjective" methodology (Pouliot 2007) that develops not only "experience-distant," but also "experience-near" knowledge about social life and politics (using Geertz's (1987) terms). Epistemically speaking, the researcher is sitting on the fence between the community of practitioners and that of researchers, a position that generates a form of knowledge that is at once native and foreign.

A number of methods allow social researchers to embed practices in their social context, that is, to conduct practice tracing. The first and arguably the

---

[3] The following paragraphs draw on Pouliot 2012.

best method is ethnographic participant observation, which involves the researcher's direct and sustained participation inside of a social setting and its everyday dynamics (Schatz 2009). The unique value added of this method, on top of allowing direct observation of practices, is that it usually takes place within the "natural habitat" of practitioners, with limited disturbance from the outside.

In IR, Barnett's (2002) ethnographical stint inside the American Mission to the United Nations eloquently shows that practices of peacekeeping, Security Council deliberations, and many others had a distinctly *local* meaning, in the headquarters of the early 1990s, which caused multilateral inaction. He writes: "The culture within the UN generated an understanding of the organization's unique contribution to world politics. It produced rules that signaled when peacekeeping was 'the right tool for the job.' It contained orienting concepts such as neutrality, impartiality, and consent, which governed how peacekeepers were supposed to operate in the field" (Barnett 2002: xi). To understand the *causes* of UN failure, the interpretive reconstruction of context, which Barnett labels bureaucratic culture, is absolutely necessary. Admittedly, the exact work of interpretation performed by the analyst is not always easy to specify in ethnographic studies. The onus is on the researcher to be as transparent as possible about the scholarly meaning-making processes that go into the analysis.

Another compelling example of participant observation in the study of world politics is Neumann's ethnography of diplomacy (2012). Based on prolonged participant observation at the Norwegian Ministry of Foreign Affairs, the author reconstructs the discourse and practices that animate the everyday life of the diplomat. Posted at home, he observes, diplomats mainly engage in "text-producing practices," such as speech-writing, which generate two fundamental effects in the conduct of foreign policy: first, they produce the corporate identity of the ministry (and by extension of the state) by communicating a certain point of view to the external world; and, second, they reproduce these discursive structures through consensus-building processes and the tuning of multiple voices, which overwhelmingly favor stability over change.

As is often the case with ethnography, Neumann's analysis is not completely systematic, in that the causal arguments he is able to make are primarily determined by his lived ethnographic experiences in the field. As a result, alternative explanations are not explored at depth and the possible biases in evidentiary sources are given limited attention. Yet, despite these drawbacks and thanks to deep interpretive immersion, the author is able to document the generative effects of myriad diplomatic practices on international politics – going as far as to argue that "diplomacy is what states do [and] states are what diplomacy does" (Neumann 2012: 3). In other words, the book suggests, at least in a provisional way, that what *causes* states, along with war and trade, is the practice of diplomacy. This is no small claim and its substantiation depends on deep contextual interpretation.

In the actual practice of research, though, participant observation is often not feasible, whether for financial, organizational, legal, geographical, historical, or, even, ethical/personal-safety reasons (on the latter, see Lyall, this volume, Chapter 7). In his study of nuclear laboratory facilities in California, for instance, political anthropologist Gusterson realized early on that he would not be granted access to the premises because of secrecy. He consequently had to "rethink the notion of fieldwork [he] had acquired as a graduate student so as to subordinate participant observation, conventionally the bedrock of field-work, to formal interviewing and to the reading of newspapers and official documents" (Gusterson 1993: 63–64). In the study of practices, such is the tough reality of fieldwork. Whatever the reason, most of the time researchers need to be creative and look for proxies to direct observation. This often puts a limit on the diversity and relevance of the evidence that one is able to gather.

The good news is that, even when practices cannot be *seen*, they may be *talked about* through interviews or *read* thanks to textual analysis. Practice tracing can thus be done in a variety of additional ways. For instance, where practitioners are alive and willing to talk, qualitative interviews are particularly suited for reconstructing the practitioners' point of view. As conversations generative of situated, insider knowledge, interviews provide researchers with an efficient means to penetrate more or less alien life-worlds.

The main challenge, however, is that contrary to representational knowledge, which is verbalized and can be brandished, practical knowledge is generally unsaid and mostly tacit. "As soon as he reflects on his practice, adopting a quasi-theoretical posture," Bourdieu reminds us, "the agent loses any chance of expressing the truth of his practice, and especially the truth of the practical relation to the practice" (1990: 91). To use Rubin and Rubin's (1995: 20) analogy, gaining knowledge about background knowledge is often like asking fish, if they could speak, to describe the water in which they swim. The solution is to focus less on what interviewees talk *about* than what they talk *from* – the stock of unspoken assumptions and tacit know-how that ought to be presumed in order to say what is being said (see also Fujii 2010). That way, one is able to not only trace practices, but also interpret the context in which they are performed.

In my book (Pouliot 2010), I have used interviews as a proxy for participant observation, performing some sixty interviews with diplomats and experts located in Brussels, Moscow, Washington, London, Berlin, and Ottawa. I devised my semi-directed questionnaire so as to indirectly explore the background knowledge of NATO–Russia relations (see Pouliot 2012 for more on this). For instance, I would submit various scenarios to interviewees and ask them how they would react to such a situation. From their answers, I could often infer tacit assumptions and practical logics, which I would probe from one practitioner to the next. Alternatively, I would ask questions that specifically sought to examine the presence of taken-for-granted knowledge by unsettling it. As in Garfinkel's ethnomethodology, asking questions about things that are entirely taken for granted tends to destabilize (and render visible) practical knowledge. Finally, I would devote much attention to the practical activities performed on an everyday basis by my interviewees. I would subtly prompt detailed descriptions of daily interactions with Russian or Atlantic counterparts, diplomatic negotiations, military-to-military cooperation, and all sorts of innocuous activities that fill their daily lives as security practitioners.

This way, I was able to learn a great deal about what NATO and Russian practitioners do in and through practice, even though I could not attend meetings per se. Tracing diplomatic practices and interpreting their context allowed me to explain how and why recurring symbolic power politics grip NATO–Russia relations, curbing security community development. That being said, the interview method is only a second-best to reconstruct practicality. As reflexive as one may be about authorship, performance, and positionality, using interviews exposes one to rationalized renditions of practicality.

Another example of a study that builds on qualitative interviews in order to embed practices in their social context is Gheciu's (2005). Focusing on the practices enacted by NATO in Central and Eastern Europe after the end of the Cold War, the author casts them as part of a larger struggle over the meaning of security, democracy and liberalism in a new era. NATO's enlargement was not just a "natural" expansion of the democratic zone of peace; instead, Gheciu demonstrates how Alliance practices, ranging from human rights protection to civilian control of the military, were determinant in the power struggle to redefine the field of European security as a liberal zone of peace. To construct this causal account, the book locates diplomatic interactions in their specific context, largely thanks to interviews with involved practitioners. As far as local causality is concerned, Gheciu's account – just like most studies based on interviews – would be even stronger had she better spelled out the exact interpretive work that went into the interview process and its analysis: how were questions selected and framed, what was made of discrepant or contradictory points of view, how was tacit meaning inferred from specific utterances, etc. Again, establishing meaningful causality requires as much transparency as possible on the researcher's part – an injunction that both good practice tracing and good process tracing share (Checkel and Bennett, this volume, Chapter 1, pp. 64–74). That said, there are obvious and justifiable limits to this introspective exercise: reflexivity should not come at the expense of substance.

When practitioners are not available to talk, textual analysis can be put to work in order to trace practices and interpret the context in which they are performed. For instance, in his study of historical practices of governance, Reus-Smit looks into "the *justificatory frameworks* that sanction prevailing forms of political organization and repertoires of institutional action" (1999: 10 [emphasis in the original]). The objective of his discourse analysis, he continues, is to "reconstruct the shared meanings that historical agents attach to the sovereign state." What are the patterned ways of performing sovereignty? In various historical configurations, sets of practices evolved, from third-party arbitration in Ancient Greece or oratorical diplomacy in Renaissance Italy, to today's contractual international law and multilateral diplomacy. Reus-Smit uses textual accounts from various eras to embed practices in their local, historical context and explain their effects on evolving international societies. On a more critical note, it is not entirely clear which texts exactly served the analysis, how they were selected (or discarded), and what specific tools were applied to infer and assemble meanings out of them.

A more structured research design may be found in Hopf (2002), who interprets habitual practices through popular narratives of Russian identity. Based on a close reading of dozens of novels, magazines, and related sources – whose selection is carefully justified – Hopf maps various notions of we-ness in order to contextualize Russian foreign policy practices. He explicitly documents his text selection and also explains the interpretive steps that are built into the analysis. Hopf demonstrates that the causes of Russia's Great Power aspirations, for example, can be traced in peculiar practices of identity construction around the trope of "liberal essentialism."

Both Reus-Smit and Hopf select particular textual genres in order to open up a window onto practicality: respectively, political treatises and popular literary pieces. In sociology, Vaughn's historical ethnography – "an attempt to reconstruct structure and culture from archival documents and interviews to see how people in a different time and place made sense of things" (2008: 71) – is equally useful in reconstructing background knowledge out of practices that were never observed directly by the researcher. In order to explain what caused the Challenger disaster, she reconstructs practicality out of written traces of practices: reports, memoranda, minutes, etc.

As a general rule, certain textual genres offer particularly useful insights into enacted practices, from memoirs to court cases through handbooks. Other useful genres include annual reports, diplomatic cables, meeting minutes, personal diaries, recordings and transcripts, written correspondence, etc. In IR, poststructuralists such as Hansen (2006) have gone a long way in elaborating various models of intertextuality, casting increasingly wider nets of genre. Although one may question the methodological choice of sticking to texts in order to grasp the generative effects of practices (see also Hopf 2002: chapter 1), in any event the human propensity to inscribe meanings in writing makes for an inexhaustible archive of discursive traces.

For example, Doty (1996) looks into "practices of representation" and the ways in which they structure North–South relations. She focuses on asymmetrical encounters in which policymakers from the North were able to define the South with huge political effects in the following decades. She writes: "The Northern narratives that accompanied its encounters with various regions of the South are imbued with unquestioned presumptions regarding freedom, democracy, and self-determination as well as the identities of the subjects who are entitled to enjoy these things" (Doty 1996: 3). For example, she embeds foreign policy actions in their discursive context to show that US troops marching into Grenada could count as various – and often contradictory – practices, from an invasion to a rescue mission. What followed from such practices, she argues, was largely structured by the discursive practicality at work in specific instances. Admittedly, Doty's account would probably benefit from taking more seriously all those aspects of the practices under study that are less evidently discursive. North–South domination, after all, rests on a thick inter-subjective background, but also on material inequalities and organizational biases.

Despite their differences, these various works have one important thing in common: they all use various streams of evidence to deeply interpret the context in which various given political practices are enacted. By taking this step, the authors reviewed not only document-patterned ways of doing things; they also make causal claims (often left implicit), showing how one set of practices led to another. So defined, this practice tracing clearly qualifies as a form of the process tracing central to this volume. At the same time, the interpretive step of embedding practices in their social context does depart from the cross-case variation of intermediate variables, going into constitutive theorization instead. In order for a practice to deliver social effects (i.e. to have causal power), it must be constituted as such through interpretive dynamics of meaning making and intersubjective negotiation. Why does NATO's double enlargement cause intense symbolic power struggles with Russia? It is because this set of practices counts as a new form of containment for Russian foreign policy elites in the framework of NATO–Russia diplomacy (Pouliot 2010). Certainly, the causal scope of this claim is by necessity local or context-bound. The next section seeks to deal with this interpretive limitation.

To conclude, it must be borne in mind that any scholarly rendition of practices and of their performativity is by nature an analytical re-description. It aims, to paraphrase Ringmar (1997: 277), not at inscribing what practices really are, but what they resemble. Put differently, as inductively derived as it may be, a social scientific account of practices necessarily remains meta-phorical (Pouliot 2008b). Even with best efforts, it consists of a scholarly interpretation that inevitably departs from the practical interpretive logics on the ground (Hopf 2002).

As such, one may say that practices have, so to speak, a double existence: as social processes (at the level of action) and as reconstructed objects of analysis (at the level of observation). Accounts of practices are interpretations of interpretations; they are fundamentally reconstructive (and, thus, potentially reifying). As ethnographic or inductive as one may go, studying practices implies ordering, dissecting, and organizing them in a way that ultimately constructs them as units of analysis within an analytical narrative. In that sense, there is no point in trying to show that the practices discussed in a scholarly account correspond exactly to what practitioners do. The more humble aim should be to capture practical logics so as to explain their social effects, bearing in mind the reconstructive process that the interpretation of meanings necessarily entails.

Cross-case generality: abstracting mechanisms away from context

In this section, I argue that there is much value in abstracting practices away from their local context in order to attain a higher level of analytical generality (see also Bennett and Checkel, this volume, Chapters 1, 10, on generalization). Once the interpretive boundaries of context have been established, it is possible to move beyond singular causality toward cross-case insights – perhaps the most distinctive feature of the social scientific ethos. For clarity's sake, from now on, I shall use the term *mechanism* to describe the analytical constructs that result from abstracting practices away from their context. As already noted, this move departs from the editors' scientific realist lens, by which mechanisms denote "pieces of furniture" (Bunge 2004) out there in the world. In line with Hernes, I rather conceive of mechanisms as "the virtual reality of social scientists" (1998: 78). Mechanisms are analytical constructs that help organize empirics; they make sense of history, but do not drive it.

In this meaning, mechanisms are analytically general, but they do not necessarily rest on empirical generalization (Jackson 2011). Certainly, the interpretive study of practices may generate contingent generalizations and even local predictions because practices are typical ways of doing things in a given context. Practices are patterned and they are repeated; there is no such thing as a practice that occurs only once. Within a given context, practices exhibit regularities; otherwise there would be no structure to social interactions. The performance of practices in socially recognizable ways is the source of ontological stability in social life.[4] As Price and Reus-Smit correctly point out, "rejecting the pursuit of law-like generalizations does not entail a simultaneous rejection of more contingent generalizations" (1998: 275). Practices do exhibit a degree of regularity within the boundaries of a local context.

The crucial point when drawing contingent generalizations is to be explicit about their boundaries of applicability (Hopf 2002: 30). Within a local setting, I agree with Hopf (2007: 66) that prediction may even be possible, although "very narrow, confined within a case to a limited period of time." Put differently, generalizations and predictions are always limited in scope to a specific context and they often do not travel very well across cases or classes of cases. As such, there is little point in *testing* them, because they are inherently tied to a particular locale. When it comes to generalizability, thus, defining "scope conditions" does matter (see also Checkel, this volume, Chapter 3), but in the thick, interpretive, and endogenous sense of capturing the boundaries of the symbolic systems that allow practices to generate effects.[5]

For its part, analytical generality is achieved through a different kind of reasoning – essentially, by abstracting practices away from specific contexts. Herein occurs a fundamental shift at the level of validity. The validity of

---

[4] Of course, this is not to deny the political struggles and power relations that always lie beneath the veneer of social stability and common sense (Hansen 2011). Patterns of practice should be interrogated, not simply observed. That said, at the level of practice, regularities do occur and it is often useful to trace them.

[5] I thank Stefano Guzzini for drawing this point to my attention. For an application, see Guzzini 2012.

a generalization rests with its holding true across empirical occurrences, whereas the validity of analytical generality lies in its being useful to explain various cases. By implication, analytical generality cannot be true or false; only useful or not (Jackson 2011: chapter 5; see also Waltz 1979: chapter 1). Ultimately, this usefulness (in helping understand connections between practices) is intimately tied to contextualization, because a causal account is always local. The logic of generality serves the purpose of highlighting the contextual peculiarities that grant given practices certain generative powers. In this scheme, it would not make sense to test (allegedly) deductive hypotheses against mechanisms, hoping for empirical confirmation or falsification. For one thing, local causality is inferred through the interpretation of contextual data, not from some sort of predetermined or a-contextual logic. Practice tracing is thus an abductive methodology, based on the joining together of empirics and analytics. By implication, claims about empirical regularities do not precede process tracing, but *follow from* interpretive analysis. For another thing, social mechanisms are abstracted away from context: their whole point is to depart from reality, not to match it. As such, the mechanisms coined by researchers do not have empirical referents that would make them true or false. Instead of testing theoretical constructs, then, one should show their heuristic usefulness in explaining social phenomena across cases or even classes of cases.

Cross-case concepts and mechanisms are bought at the price of abstracting practices away from their context. Moving up the "ladder of abstraction" helps jump from the particular to the general. The "basic rule of transformation," as Sartori puts it, is "upward aggregation and, conversely, downward specification" (1991: 254). For a conceptualization of practice to travel across cases, one must separate it from its specific occurrences. This is hardly a novel insight in social science methodology. The added value of practice tracing, however, is that practices are perfect units of analysis to travel up and down the ladder of abstraction. As I explained earlier, this is because practices are particular to various social contexts, but general across cases. Once the interpretive boundaries of context have been set, patterns become easier to grasp. To use an example from world politics, the practice of "holding a bracket" – that is, deferring agreement on a particular language in a formal text – makes no sense outside of the socially organized environment of diplomacy, and yet, for the diplomat, it is a common, or typical, practice, whose causal effects are fairly regularized. The fact that practices are both general and specific is the main reason why it can serve as a meeting point for process tracers and interpretivists. One can cash out generality by abstracting regularities away from specific contexts and allowing them to travel across cases. At that comparative stage, the analyst plots the explanation around analytically general mechanisms, which retain what is typical in social processes while omitting contextual particularities.

The drawback, however, is that we cannot know what, exactly, the mechanisms cause, because mechanisms do not cause anything in and of themselves. Recall that mechanisms are sets of practices taken out of their context for the sake of theorization. Mechanisms refer to analytical classes of ways of doing things that the analyst deems worthwhile to group together in view of cross-case analysis. Interestingly, this understanding is quite consistent with that of Jon Elster, who defines mechanisms as "frequently occurring and easily recognizable causal patterns that are triggered under generally unknown conditions or with indeterminate consequences" (1998: 45). Mechanisms, short of contextualization, cannot establish causality. What they can do, instead, is allow different explanatory accounts to speak to one another in spite of their being rooted in fundamentally heterogeneous contexts.

How does one go about abstracting mechanisms away from local causal accounts? Examples from the IR literature may help illustrate the process. Let us begin with Jackson's (2006a) study of the processes of legitimation that underpinned the policy of German reconstruction in the wake of World War II. His historical narrative traces patterns of deployment of a key rhetorical commonplace by German, American, and other European statesmen at the time: the notion of "the West." As American liberals and German conservatives tied Western civilization to specific commonplaces – "preserving liberty," "fighting communism" – a political community across the Atlantic was created, justifying the German reconstruction effort. Jackson draws a "topography" of the rhetorical resources available at different points in time and proceeds genealogically to trace their deployment and uses.

Beyond his particular study, Jackson identifies three key mechanisms at work in any legitimation rhetorical contest: specifying ("the attempt to define a commonplace and its implications in a relatively precise way in the course of a debate"); breaking ("the use of a specified commonplace to disrupt the bond between commonplaces simultaneously held by an opponent"); and joining ("the use of a specified commonplace to help to 'lock down' the meaning of another one") (Jackson 2006b: 276). These are classes of rhetorical practices that reshape the meaning of commonplaces in ways specified by political and social context. It is worth noting that on the ladder of abstraction, Jackson's mechanisms are located particularly high, which allows for very wide generality, but more limited specificity (at least short of interpretive contextualization).[6]

In her book about the Anglo-American "special relationship" during the Suez crisis, Mattern (2005) reaches a similar result. She wants to explain why, despite the breakdown of collective identity that occurred during the crisis, the relationship between Washington and London remained peaceful. Mattern is interested in "representational force," a linguistic narrative that threatens subjectivity in order to obtain compliance. For example, during the crisis the Americans threatened the British identity as "Lion" in order to cast US Secretary of State Dulles's actions as friendly. The British, unwilling to appear "out of date with the demands of the contemporary international system" (Mattern 2005: 202), were forced into compliance with American demands for withdrawal.

At a higher level of generality, Mattern identifies two key mechanisms at work in representational force: *terror*, which is a type of discursive practice that issues a threat to the subjectivity of the dissident by playing on internal contradictions; and *exile*, which is another type of discursive practice that silences dissent. These narrative forms, Mattern argues, explain the power of language in politics. The key advantage of her conceptual categories (or mechanisms) is their portability: any linguistic exchange may, in theory at least, conform to one type or another. One drawback, however, is that one may lose analytical traction by focusing solely on language-based mechanisms to explain why certain discursive practices work (i.e. why they deliver their performative effects), but not others.

Despite their differences, Neumann (1999) and Hansen (2006) focus on similar processes of identity formation to explain foreign policy practices. Neumann seeks to explain how European identity has historically remained relatively coherent in opposition to its Eastern neighbors. He documents various discursive practices by which the Turks and the Russians were represented as Europe's Other. While the research design that informs the study remains unclear, the analysis rests on a particularly deep immersion in a vast amount of texts. Coining the mechanism of "othering," Neumann concludes that "[t]he use of 'the East' as the other is a general practice in European identity formation" (Neumann 1999: 207). Hansen, for her part, reconstructs key discourses about the Balkans in order to explain Western foreign policy

---

[6] Contrast Jackson's rhetorical practices with the concept of "rhetorical action" (Schimmelfennig, this volume, Chapter 4). Both scholars accord language a central role, agree that it generates a process to be followed, but disagree crucially over generalization – what it is and how it is to be accomplished.

during the Bosnian War. Thanks to a particularly rigorous and transparent framework, she shows that by depicting Bosnia as a radical and threatening Other, the discourse of "Balkanization" that prevailed in the early 1990s ruled out any Western responsibility with regard to the conflict. Then, the rise of a civilizational discourse portraying Bosnia as different, but transformable, eventually paved the way to military intervention. Hansen envisions two main mechanisms in the mutual constitution of identity and foreign policy: linking and differentiation. As she puts it: "meaning and identity are constructed through a series of signs that are linked to each other to constitute relations of sameness as well as through a differentiation to another series of juxtaposed signs" (Hansen 2006: 42). These analytically general mechanisms travel well across cases. That said, given how convincingly Hansen demonstrates the generative effects of discursive practices on both identity and foreign policy, one wonders why she also asserts "the impossibility of causality" (ibid.: 25). As Vucetic (2011) suggests, genealogical methods are compatible with causal analysis, broadly construed.

Jackson, Mattern, Neumann, and Hansen all start from context-specific discursive practices and abstract them away in order to devise general mechanisms that can travel from case to case: breaking, terror, linking, othering, yoking, etc. In these cases, meaning making, often in the form of textual practices, is the primary object of interest. As important as they may be, though, "semiotic mechanisms" (Wight 2004) do not exhaust the array of social processes that one may map through practice tracing. In fact, I agree with Nexon (2005) that inherent in interpretive methodology is the danger of "cultural reductionism," whereby non-discursive forms of social mechanisms risk getting overlooked. Beyond meaning making, a number of other social processes – ranging from relational ties to positional logics through organizational settings and material potentialities – also enable and constrain practices. One key advantage of practice tracing over more narrowly interpretive methodologies, I would argue, precisely is to capture social mechanisms beyond the realm of semiotics *stricto sensu*.

Nexon (2009) illustrates particularly well how thinking in terms of semiotic *and* relational mechanisms may enlarge – and enrich – the scope of analysis. Nexon is primarily inspired by Tilly's insight that "[r]elational mechanisms alter connections among people, groups, and interpersonal networks" (2001: 24). In his book, he wants to explain "why the Protestant Reformations produced a crisis of sufficient magnitude to alter the European balance of power" (ibid.: 3). By carefully tracing various episodes of contention in early modern Europe, the book shows how resistance and rebellion could spread through the reconfiguration of institutional ties across the political groups that comprised major composite states. For example, heterodox religious movements made political alliances between elites and ordinary people more likely, while also increasing the chances of foreign intervention.

Nexon identifies two key mechanisms, yoking and brokerage, underpinning changes in patterns of interactions and attendant identities (2009: 46). As analytically general as these mechanisms may be, Nexon is very careful to preserve the historical contingency of his case. As he puts it: "significant aspects of causation in social and political life inhere in transactions themselves. Many important causal mechanisms and processes, in particular, stem from the *formal* properties of specific relational structures in which actors operate ... How these dynamics resolve into specific outcomes, however, depends upon a number of contextual factors" (2009: 27). Striking this balance between contingency and generality goes to the heart of practice tracing – and, indeed, is central to process tracing more generally (Checkel and Bennett, this volume, Chapter 10). The next challenge is to specify how, exactly, content (meaning) and form (relational structure) come together in generating social outcomes.

In my own book, I also attempt to capture the local flow of practices with an eye toward more general social mechanisms. Throughout the empirical chapters, I pay close attention to everyday diplomatic practices in order to explain the limited pacification between Russia and NATO in the post-Cold War era. I reconstruct the flow of practices through interviews with diplomats, but also thanks to an in-depth, minute search of news outlets, policy documents, and meeting timetables. I map various diplomatic patterns to show how their contested meanings often challenged what each side construed as the new rules of the game in the field of international security. For instance, NATO's double enlargement practices defeated cooperative security in Moscow's eyes, while Russia's Great Power management had no resonance for the Alliance. This larger pattern of contestation and dissonance can be traced through the detailed interpretive analysis of diplomatic encounters and daily routines in NATO–Russia diplomacy. I then take these inductively recovered materials to a more analytical level, so as to draw theoretical lessons that travel beyond my case study.

My account hinges on the notion of "hysteresis," which is the mismatch that sometimes occurs between the dispositional and positional logics of a given practice. I argue that hysteresis stymies pacification because it sparks symbolic power struggles that push against self-evident diplomacy. For instance, so long as Russia's "junior partner" practices of the early 1990s (for example, supporting sanctions against Serbia) fitted well with its weak position in the field of international security (as defined by dominant powers), security community development proceeded smoothly. As hysteresis kept rising, however, symbolic power struggles gripped the NATO–Russia relationship, causing various practices (for example, Russia's military occupation of Pristina airport in June 1999) that challenged the new security order. The mechanism of hysteresis helps to understand why, in various contexts, diplomatic practices whose intersubjective dynamics do not fit with the positional structure of interaction often fail to generate political integration. On a self-critical note, though, my account does not go far enough into positional analysis. For the mechanism of hysteresis to truly combine relational and interpretive modes of analysis, a more systematic mapping of the distribution of resources in the field of international security would be required.

Let me conclude with a note on the relationship between induction and analytical generality in practice tracing. Most "analyticists" argue that theorizing is an activity firmly distinct from empirical research (Jackson 2011). As Waltz famously put it: "Induction is used at the level of hypotheses and laws rather than at the level of theories" (1979: 7). According to this view, theories – and analytically general mechanisms – are arrived at "creatively," through some kind of eureka intuition.

I think this glosses over the actual practice of theorizing. I would rather argue that to be able to reach a proper level of analytical generality, one must first delve deeply into data. Through induction, one gains the necessary background and experience to eventually manage to convert messy patterns of practices into neat theoretical categories. There is no direct connection from data to theory, of course; but the notion of purely deductive theory is a contradiction in terms (Schimmelfennig, this volume, Chapter 4, for a contrasting view). I could have never thought of hysteresis had I not spent years researching everyday diplomatic practices between NATO and Russia. Analytically general mechanisms do depart from practices – but in order to do so, practices (the departure point) must first be recovered thanks to inductive, interpretive empirical research. Creativity does not come out of thin air; it is rooted in research experience. As a form of inductive analyticism, practice tracing is an invitation to dissolve the conventional yet deeply misleading dichotomy between the empirical and the theoretical.

Conclusion

This chapter has sought to show that an interpretive form of process tracing is not only possible; it is also an effective and "do-able" research strategy. The study of practices, which are fundamental social processes with causal effectiveness, requires interpretation and allows for cross-case insights. It is often argued that interpretivists are interested in singular events, while many process tracers strive for the general. This dichotomy does not have to be so clear-cut. I, for one (see also Wedeen 2010), believe that no explanatory account is complete without close attention to local dynamics of meaning making; yet I also think that no practice is so unique as to foreclose some degree of generality. Practices are both particular (as contextually embedded actions) and general (as patterns of actions). It would be folly to sacrifice either of these insights on the altar of meta-theoretical orthodoxy.

A key added value of this book is that it engages with process tracing *in practice*, leaving meta-theoretical discussions behind in order to deal with concrete applications of the methodology. As a result, the issue of evaluative standards becomes front and center: "how would we recognize good process tracing if it were to walk through the door?" ask the editors (Bennett and Checkel, this volume, Chapter 1, p. 20). In this chapter, I suggested that a good practice-tracing account should, first, explain the social effects that practices of interest generate at the level of action (local causality); and, second, abstract mechanisms away from context to gain cross-case leverage (analytical generality).

Fittingly, these tasks are compatible with the "three-part standard" put forward by Bennett and Checkel (this volume, Chapter 1, p. 21). First, good process tracing should use a plurality of methods. As the above makes clear, this is a standard which I wholeheartedly embrace. A social ontology of practice is so multifaceted and complex that it is plainly impossible to capture it based on one single method (see Pouliot 2012). Practice tracing requires combining various tools, from statistics to discourse analysis through interviews, etc. At all times, though, methods must be attentive to context and meaning making in order to establish causality. Second, good process tracing must keep sight of both context and structure. This is easily done in practice tracing: after all, practices are "suspended" between structure and agency (they are structured agency, so to speak) and they have no meaning outside of the context of their enactment.

Third, good process tracing should account for alternative explanations and equifinality. The causal chains traced in a study are never the sole possible ones and attention should be paid to other scenarios. A practice analysis is always provisional and must remain open to contestation and revision because configurations of practices are so complex and shifting that one can never claim to have found the one causal practice. Equifinality, taken to mean that various practices may be implicated in causing the outcome of interest, is something that must be entertained at all times in social analysis.

Of course, at the epistemological level, practice tracing is not some kind of neutral middle ground where everybody happily lives in harmony. By emphasizing meaningful causality and analytical generality, practice tracing moves away from not only the nomological understanding of social science, but also the hypothesis-testing model espoused by many process tracers. That said, by emphasizing cross-case insights, practice tracing also runs counter to phenomenology and the singular causality emphasized by interpretivists.

The risk, thus, is that practice tracing will leave both groups equally dissatisfied. I believe it is a risk worth taking, however, to the extent that the meta-theoretical quarrels that currently divide interpretivists and process tracers will not be resolved any time soon. There is no denial that, philosophically speaking, the two approaches are somewhat incompatible; yet, they often look into similar problems and they even share certain methods. Why, then, should we let meta-theoretical rifts constrain dialogue? As Checkel observes, process tracers "are well placed to move us beyond unproductive 'either/or' meta-theoretical debates to empirical applications ... these scholars must be epistemologically plural – employing *both* positivist and post-positivist methodological lenses" (2008: 114). In this chapter, I have suggested one way to do just that.

In the absence of a philosophical Archimedean point, meta-theoretical issues cannot be resolved for good. This is what centuries of philosophical controversies confirm: there are no secure, metaphysical foundations upon which to build social scientific foundations. In fact, I would argue that the particularly pervasive notion that the validity of social science should rest on philosophical debates is fundamentally misguided. As Gunnell correctly points out, "philosophy is no more the basis of science than social science is the basis of society" (2011: 1467). Instead, in a pragmatist spirit we should ground social science in research strategies and let their empirical applications compete with one another. How useful are they, in demonstrating local causality and generating analytically general insights? Let research practice, not philosophy, be the judge of social scientific validity.

10 Beyond metaphors
Standards, theory, and the "where next" for process tracing

Jeffrey T. Checkel and Andrew Bennett

In this concluding chapter, we make three arguments. First, there is a strong consensus among this volume's contributors on the need for a clear understanding of what counts as "an instance of good process tracing." We document this fact by assessing the fit between the ten criteria advanced in Chapter 1 and their subsequent application by the contributors, arguing that future work utilizing process-tracing techniques must explicitly address all ten of these best practices.

Second, proponents of process tracing need to remember that method is not an end in itself; rather, it is a tool helping us to build and test theory. The development of cumulable social science theory and the theoretical explanation of individual cases are – or, rather, should be – the central goals of process tracing. We advance several design and theory specification suggestions to maximize the likelihood that the process tracing/theory relation is marked by cumulative theoretical progress.

Finally, process tracing is only one way to capture mechanisms in action. Quantitative and experimental methods clearly have roles to play, as do other techniques that can contribute to assessing mechanisms, their scope conditions, and their effects. We make this argument in a final section that highlights three additional challenges for the continuing development and use of process tracing: determining the proper degree of formalization in particular applications of it; raising and implementing standards of transparency; and keeping its application open to the inductive discovery of new theoretical connections, as well as the deductive testing of extant theories and explanations.

From best practices to standards?

At the outset, we proposed ten criteria as a starting point for assessing applications of process tracing and asked our contributors to apply, modify, and adapt them as necessary to their particular fields of study or research

Table 10.1 Process tracing best practices

1. Cast the net widely for alternative explanations
2. Be equally tough on the alternative explanations
3. Consider the potential biases of evidentiary sources
4. Take into account whether the case is most or least likely for alternative explanations
5. Make a justifiable decision on when to start
6. Be relentless in gathering diverse and relevant evidence, but make a justifiable decision on when to stop
7. Combine process tracing with case comparisons when useful for the research goal and feasible
8. Be open to inductive insights
9. Use deduction to ask "if my explanation is true, what will be the specific process leading to the outcome?"
10. Remember that conclusive process tracing is good, but not all good process tracing is conclusive

programs. We construed these fields and programs broadly, including particular research puzzles, common field research conditions, and the state of theory development, as well as our contributors' epistemological stances. Contributors did indeed take up the opportunity to modify our criteria, although not in all cases.

Instead of giving a chapter-by-chapter overview of the proposed modifications, we group them, and argue that the differences are best understood as a consequence of a preference for inductive or deductive forms of process tracing, as well as a search for best practices employed by process tracers versus external evaluative standards applied to assess individual instances of process tracing.[1]

For reference, we reproduce in Table 10.1 above the table from Chapter 1 of our ten process-tracing best practices.

Three chapters – Jacobs on ideational theory; Checkel on the study of international institutions; and Evangelista on explaining the Cold War's end – hew closely to our ten criteria, demonstrating their key role in identifying high-quality applications of process tracing. Jacobs, in precisely the spirit we intended, demonstrates that researchers utilizing process tracing in an ideational study need to build upon but further operationalize the ten criteria given in Chapter 1. For example, where we argue a need for process tracers explicitly to justify and establish starting and stopping

---

[1] We thank an anonymous reviewer at Cambridge University Press for highlighting this distinction.

points, he goes an additional step, showing a need for "expansive empirical scope," both temporally and across levels of analysis. This elaboration of our criteria is not pulled out of thin air, but grounded in specific inferential challenges that face ideational arguments.

More than any other contributor, Evangelista shows the value of our ten best-practice criteria. His task is to link the main theories on the Cold War's end to specific political, social, and psychological causal mechanisms that must come into play for these accounts to explain key events that constituted its end. Employing the criteria from Chapter 1, Evangelista evaluates these explanations on the basis of their process-tracing evidence. This systematic assessment does more to establish the validity of the differing theoretical arguments than the by-now hundreds of treatises devoted to explaining the end of the Cold War. As contributors to these debates in our past writings, we have a stake in them; however, our assessment of Evangelista's accomplishment is theory neutral. He demonstrates how largely unresolvable ontological assumptions – does the world we study have a material or ideational base – can be translated into specific hypothesized causal mechanisms whose presence and measureable impact *can* be evaluated on the basis of carefully executed process tracing.

Checkel's chapter, which again closely follows the ten criteria from Chapter 1, shows that their application can – somewhat paradoxically – have negative effects at the level of theory development. Specifically, he argues that the causal mechanisms at the heart of process-tracing accounts are not readily integrated into broader, more generalizable theories; the theoretical take-away of carefully executed process tracing is often little more than "endless lists of case-specific causal mechanisms" (Checkel, this volume, Chapter 3, p. 97). Thus, with process tracing and its systematic execution, there can (almost) be too much of a good thing: the existence of too many (methodological) best practices and standards can lead scholars to take their eyes off the (theoretical) ball – an issue to which we return in the next section.[2]

In contrast to the foregoing, three other chapters adopt a "ten criteria plus" approach, where important amendments are required to what we lay out in Chapter 1. This group includes Schimmelfennig and his notion of efficient process tracing; Lyall on civil war and conflict studies; and Dunning on mixed-method designs. For the former two, their additional best practices are largely the result of an explicit focus on deductive forms of process tracing. Schimmelfennig, for example, argues that process tracing need not be time

---

[2] Focusing on quantitative techniques, Mearsheimer and Walt (2013) make essentially the same argument.

intensive, especially if done "efficiently" through the testing of deductively generated causal mechanisms. This leads him to emphasize design issues over the actual conduct of process tracing – our focus in Chapter 1.

Deduction, for Schimmelfennig, is the key. It helps researchers make a (better) justified decision on when to start and how to specify causal mechanisms; it also allows them to design more decisive and focused tests. This is excellent and sound advice for process tracers, and we largely concur with it. At the same time, an important scope condition for its use is that relevant theories in an area be sufficiently well developed to allow for such a deductive strategy.[3]

Moreover, doing process tracing efficiently requires not only a sense of what kind of evidence would prove most probative and of how different kinds of evidence might cumulate (see also Bennett, this volume, Appendix), but also judgments on what evidence is accessible and how difficult or costly it is to obtain. The latter kind of knowledge is practical rather than theoretical, and it can benefit from advice from those with expertise on what archives are available, which potential respondents are likely to grant interviews, and how difficult it is to do research in different field settings.

In his chapter on process tracing and civil war, Lyall takes our criteria from Chapter 1 as a "springboard for a discussion of how to identify and conduct rigorous process tracing in settings marked by poor (or no) data, security concerns, and fluid events" (Lyall, this volume, Chapter 7, p. 186). Yet, more is needed – he claims – especially if one is utilizing process tracing to test theories. Indeed, those theories should be "elaborate," which is to say they should articulate multiple measures for the mechanism(s) at work, and these should be specified before moving to empirical testing. Moreover, the latter should involve an explicit commitment to counterfactual reasoning and to designs that incorporate out-of-sample tests. The goal here is to minimize reliance on induction and the curve fitting that Lyall claims often accompanies it. His language and subject matter may be different, but this is a set of process tracing "best practices plus" that bear striking resemblance to Schimmelfennig's.

With Dunning, the motivation to go beyond the ten best practices outlined in Chapter 1 is driven not by a choice in favor of deductive or inductive process tracing. Rather, the concern is more practical: to elaborate research procedures that will increase the likelihood that our ten best practices are actually

---

[3] Schimmelfennig thus benefits by focusing on European integration, where the theories – after four decades of debate and testing – are well developed.

implemented. Dunning argues that one such procedure is transparency – for example, requiring scholars publicly to catalogue their process-tracing evidence from fieldwork interviews, archival documents, and the like (Dunning, this volume, Chapter 8, p. 228).[4]

While not explicitly listed as one of our ten best practices, we do emphasize the importance of transparency throughout Chapter 1 (e.g. p. 9), and thus fully support Dunning on this point. However, he goes an important step further, embedding his discussion of transparency in a broader research procedure he calls legal adversarialism, where "transparent procedures ... should assist scholars with relevant subject-matter expertise in debating the evidentiary weight to accord to specific observations on causal process" (p. 229). The central goal is to facilitate open scholarly contestation about the probative value of qualitative evidence.

Finally, two chapters – Waldner, Chapter 5, on comparative politics; and Pouliot, Chapter 9, on practice tracing – argue for a sharper break with our ten best practices. In Waldner's case, the break is a consequence of his move from internally derived best practices to logically generated standards. For Pouliot, it is his careful, empirically grounded effort to bridge differing epistemological starting points that creates tension with our arguments.

In his chapter, Waldner explicitly favors deductive forms of process tracing and argues they must be evaluated against a completeness standard. The latter requires a "complete causal graph, a complete set of descriptive inferences from particular historical settings to the graph, and a complete set of inferences about the causal mechanisms that generate realizations of the causal graph" (p. 128). In his stress on deduction, Waldner's approach has a family resemblance to the arguments advanced by Schimmelfennig and Lyall. Yet, he differs in grounding his arguments in conceptual and logical analysis.

Indeed, Waldner is moving from the realm of the best practices advanced in Chapter 1 – rules followed from within, by those actually carrying out process tracing – to standards – evaluative criteria applied from without. This is seen in the way in which he deconstructs and then logically reconstructs the term "process tracing." Waldner first clarifies the concept of a process, invoking and elaborating what he calls the "continuity criteria." He then builds on this conceptual discussion to articulate a logical procedure for tracing a causal process, which involves the formalized graphs mentioned above (pp. 130–132).

---

[4] Such procedures are fully consistent with an emerging discussion on data access and research transparency in political science; Symposium 2014.

This is a valuable move, articulating clear and explicit standards for what constitutes a good application of process tracing. Waldner uses his completeness standard to show that prominent research examples are incomplete in theorizing and in providing evidence on major steps in their causal explanations, steps for which the theoretical literature provides obvious potential explanations and for which relevant empirical evidence is available.

At the same time, a narrow adherence to Waldner's completeness standard has costs and limitations. For one, it may inadvertently demoralize aspiring process tracers. It sets the bar so high that it is not clear how anyone can reach it – including the prominent comparativists whose work Waldner assesses in Chapter 5. It is very ambitious to expect a theory or explanation to be fully complete, as there will always be steps in an explanation that involve variables exogenous to a theory, steps for which strong empirical evidence is not available, and steps that are at a more micro level of analysis than a researcher chooses to explore. Thus, not every step in a theoretical explanation of a process will fully determine the next step in it. In addition, Waldner's approach strongly implies that induction should play little or no role in process tracing. Finally – and similar to Schimmelfennig's efficient process tracing – the use of Waldner's standard is limited to areas where the relevant theories are sufficiently well developed to allow for such a deductive strategy.[5]

If Waldner suggests that our best practices do not go far enough, then Pouliot's chapter argues nearly the opposite. Given his interpretive starting point, where induction has pride of place, it is not surprising that he embraces those four of our ten best practices that "espouse an inductive spirit." Yet, in an indication of the constructive spirit that pervades the chapter, Pouliot does not simply reject our remaining six criteria, but re-assesses them through an interpretive lens. This allows him to articulate a set of modified best practices that "convincing practice-tracing accounts" should follow (p. 240). Such community understandings will be invaluable for the growing number of interpretive scholars explicitly invoking process tracing in their empirical studies.[6]

Where does this leave us? Collectively, Chapter 1 and the eight that follow deliver on the volume's subtitle – to move process tracing from the realm of metaphor to analytic tool. Yet, as the foregoing suggests, the concept of "analytic tool" is operationalized in a number of different ways. Our take on

---

[5] As Waldner notes, the work he reviews had its "origins in long-standing theoretical disputes" (Waldner, this volume, Chapter 5, p. 127).

[6] Beyond the works cited in Pouliot's chapter, see also Guzzini 2012: ch. 11; and Norman 2013.

this diversity occupies a middle position between "my way or the highway" and "let a thousand flowers bloom."

Most foundationally, we argue that any work utilizing process-tracing techniques must explicitly address all ten best-practice criteria advanced in Chapter 1. "Explicitly address" need not mean blindly implement; as the contributors demonstrate, our best practices should be viewed as a baseline and starting point. Depending upon the type of process tracing (inductive or deductive) or epistemological stance, they may be amended, reformulated, or modified. These modifications in no sense lead to a watering down or to lowest-common-denominator thinking; indeed, in all cases, they led to tighter and more stringent requirements – say, on research design or theory specification.

Even with Pouliot's chapter, where slippage might have been expected due to different epistemological starting points, this does not occur. Instead, he starts with our ten criteria and, where necessary, modifies them, maintaining stringency, but now viewed through interpretive eyes. Thus, where we talk of the importance of testing empirical generalizations, he reformulates this as using process/practice tracing as a tool seeking "analytical generality." The latter "cannot be validated through empirical testing, as if holding a mirror between models and data ... Just like typologies, practice theories are neither true nor false, but useful (or not) in making sense of messy arrays of practices" (p. 239).

To put the foregoing bluntly, our bottom line is that systematization of the technique and transparency in its execution should be the hallmark of all future process-tracing studies. The ten best practices advanced in Chapter 1 have withstood the test of application. At the same time, we recognize and "view these ten practices as a starting point, and not the final word" (Bennett and Checkel, this volume, Chapter 1, p. 22). This leads to four summary observations.

First, we welcome future efforts that build upon the ten best practices that are the core take-away of this volume. This may involve further best practices that emerge from work by other process tracers. However, it may equally involve a (partial) move away from internally generated practices to logically derived external standards. A shift to the latter is precisely how one should read Waldner's chapter. And he is certainly not alone. Bennett's Appendix is a formalization of the Bayesian logic that undergirds much of the process-tracing analysis in this book and elsewhere (Beach and Pedersen 2013a); it concludes by noting and endorsing calls for more explicit application of such logic. Mahoney (2012) draws upon recent efforts by methodologists working on criteria for assessing the relative importance of necessary and sufficient conditions to think more systematically about the probative value of particular pieces of process-tracing evidence. This further refines our discussion of hoop and smoking-gun tests in Chapter 1 (which, in turn, drew upon Van Evera 1997).

More formal application of the logics of Bayesianism, set theory, or causal directed graphs in work using process tracing may be a tough sell in a qualitative research community which has always prized fluid narratives and concepts that are difficult to quantify. Yet, a powerful argument for greater formalization is that it only asks researchers to do systematically and explicitly what they already had to be doing implicitly if their process tracing could legitimately claim to have reached justifiable inferences. One need not formalize every inference for every piece of evidence in a given application of process tracing. At the same time, the transparency of one's inferences will markedly improve if, at a minimum, researchers identify their priors and likelihood ratios for alternative hypotheses with respect to the evidence they consider to be the most probative to their key inferences.[7]

Second, we view the choice between best practices and standards as a false one. As best practices are operationalized, used, and debated by a community of scholars, they take on more the quality of externally generated and given standards. In five years' time, some – or even all! – of the Bennett and Checkel best practices may experience such an evolution. In the end, the goal should be collectively agreed community standards – note the plural – where what counts as good process tracing respects and builds from the challenges that characterize various research traditions and epistemological starting points.[8]

Third, the systematization of process-tracing best practices must not lead to a denigration of inductive, "soaking and poking" applications. This is all the more important given that efforts at formalizing the method invariably privilege deductive variants (Schimmelfennig (Chapter 4), Waldner (Chapter 5), Bennett (Appendix), all this volume). By placing the researcher in close proximity to his or her data, process tracing can capture the serendipitous, unexpected reality of the social world we inhabit and study. In some instances – depending upon the question asked or the state of theory development – an inductive approach may be essential for capturing this serendipity and advancing the knowledge frontier (see also Hall 2013: 27).

---

[7] Bennett's discussion in the Appendix of Nina Tannenwald's (2007) work on the "nuclear taboo" shows how this might be done.

[8] This builds in part on the "community standards approach" that the American Political Science Association has adopted in its work on data access and research transparency; Lupia and Elman 2014: 20.

Induction is not a license to say anything goes. In fact, it is far from it, as demonstrated by systematic applications of inductive process tracing by both interpretive scholars (Pouliot, this volume, Chapter 9, and the literature reviewed therein) and positivists/scientific-realists (Wood 2003). Moreover, to reiterate a point made in Chapter 1, many studies proceed via a staged research design, where inductive discovery is followed by deductive process tracing. The latter is applied to new or "out of sample" empirical material, which could still be taken from the same case from which the theory was generated so long as it involves evidence independent of that which gave rise to the theory.

Finally, rigorous and transparent process tracing is and should be compatible with lively, interesting, and well-written case studies. Operationally, this means researchers should avoid two extremes. One is the "method-data disconnect," where a prior discussion of process tracing is followed by case studies in which the method's application is at best implicit (see also Elman and Kapiszewski 2014: 44). Systematic use of our ten best practices will minimize the likelihood of this occurring.

On the other hand, a transparent application of process tracing should not lead to a second extreme: dry, hard-to-read empirics, where the analyst spends less time relating his or her account and more explaining this or that feature of the method. Systematic use of process tracing need not lead to this outcome. A researcher, at the beginning of his or her empirical chapter or section, can remind readers of its purpose – to provide process tracing evidence of one or more causal mechanisms at work. This "holding of the reader's hand," as it were, then allows for a straightforward presentation of empirics not burdened by excessive methodological discussions. This is the strategy followed by Schimmelfennig (2003) in his process tracing of the multiple mechanisms that led to the European Union's enlargement in the early 2000s (see also Checkel, this volume, Chapter 3). Readers can thus see his process tracing in action – in a rich, readable account.

In addition and in a fashion similar to many quantitative studies, it is possible to place in an appendix the details of the Bayesian, set theoretic, causal graph logics or mathematics that lie behind specific process-tracing inferences. For example, in a study of taxation policy in Latin America, Fairfield operationalizes her process tracing in a commendably detailed and transparent manner. Then and before presenting her case studies, she notes the following:

Appendix A not only reviews the key ideas in this methodological literature, but also explicitly guides the reader through the multiple process tracing tests that form the basis for my analysis of Chile's 2005 tax reform; process-tracing practitioners usually leave these tests informal and implicit for the sake of presenting readable analytical narratives. The same logic described in Appendix A underpins the analysis of each case study presented below. (Fairfield 2013: 47)

This is an excellent example of how to deal with the methodological under-pinning of one's study in a clear way that still allows for a straightforward recounting of the empirics. A similar strategy might be useful for integrating empirics with the process-tracing causal graphs advocated by Waldner (this volume, Chapter 5). An appendix could also be used to address the threefold transparency challenge that Elman and Kapiszewski (2014: 45) see as confronting process tracers: to be more explicit on how observations are drawn and data generated; to more precisely explain how process tracing is used to reach conclusions; and to share more of the data.

Method and theory

This volume has highlighted method, arguing that practitioners of process tracing need to invest both more time and more training in the technique. Yet, this systematization should not lead to a theory-light approach, where theory building and testing is subordinated to methodological technique, and there is a "triumph of methods over theory" (Mearsheimer and Walt 2013: 429).

Process tracing can and should be a tool that helps push forward major bodies of theory – from those seeking to explain the Cold War's unexpected and peaceful end to the choice made in favor of democracy over authoritarianism. In all too many cases, however, this does not happen. Students of process tracing seem to have more modest theoretical objectives – from developing a theoretically coherent account of a particularly important case to building theories with localized, partial generalizability.

Neither effort is immune to criticism. With the first, the danger is that the resulting theory may be little more than lists of non-cumulable causal mechanisms – a development that Checkel argues marks much contemporary, process-based work on international institutions and organizations (Checkel, this volume, Chapter 3).

With the second – partial generalizability – one enters the analytic realm of middle-range theory. Typically, this brings together several variables to explain an outcome; the ideal is that the resulting framework will have some degree of generalizability – in a particular region or during a particular period of time, say (Glaser and Strauss 1967; George 1993). Specifically:

Middle-range theory is principally used ... to guide empirical inquiry. It is intermediate to general theories of social systems which are too remote from particular classes of social behavior, organization, and change to account for what is observed and to those detailed orderly descriptions of particulars that are not generalized at all. Middle-range theory involves abstractions, of course, but they are close enough to observed data to be incorporated in propositions that permit empirical testing. Middle-range theories deal with delimited aspects of social phenomena, as is indicated by their labels. (Merton 1949: 39–40)

More recently, prominent scholars have endorsed such thinking as the way forward for contemporary political science, arguing that it is particularly well suited for building theory based on causal mechanisms (Katzenstein and Sil 2010; Lake 2011) – precisely what process tracing seeks to attain. Indeed, the vast majority of the literature reviewed by our contributors – Jacobs (Chapter 2) on ideational approaches, Checkel (Chapter 3) on international institutions, Schimmelfennig (Chapter 4) on European integration, Evangelista (Chapter 6) on theorizing the Cold War's end, Lyall (Chapter 7) on conflict studies, and Pouliot (Chapter 9) on practice tracing – clearly occupies this theoretical middle ground.

So, middle-range theory is popular among process tracers, has a historical pedigree in the social sciences stretching back to the early years after World War II, and is thus apparently good. Yet, we need to move from a general claim that such theory is good to a realistic assessment of its strengths and weaknesses, and how the latter can be addressed. In particular, to insure a productive relation between process tracing and (middle-range) theory development, we highlight two key issues and strategies to pursue. Attention to them will increase the likelihood that the process tracing/theory relation is marked by "cumulative theoretical progress, [open] scholarly discourse, and effective pedagogy" (Bennett 2013b: 472).

First, at the risk of sounding like scolding advisors, prior, up-front attention to research design matters crucially (see also Schimmelfennig, this volume, Chapter 4; Checkel, this volume, Chapter 3, p. 92; and Checkel 2013a). Theory development will be difficult if individual efforts are over-determined, where – with several independent variables or mechanisms in play – it is not possible to isolate the causal impact of any single factor. One way to minimize this problem is by emphasizing research design at early stages of a project, carefully choosing cases for process tracing that allow the isolation of particular theorized mechanisms. There are, of course, various ways to improve designs, from Lyall's (this volume, Chapter 7) stress on identifying counterfactual (control) observations to help isolate causal processes and effects, and out-of-sample testing; to Dunning's (this volume, Chapter 8) advice on utilizing, as natural experiments, observational studies in which causal variables are assigned at random or as-if at random, thereby leveraging the power of causal inferences derived from process tracing.

Whatever the design choices, the point is to be thinking about them at early stages in a project. This may sound like Grad Seminar 101 advice, but failure to heed it is a common problem in the articles we have reviewed for possible publication in refereed journals. In our experience, many of those most attracted to process tracing as method are problem-driven scholars who want – simply and admirably – "to get on with it," explaining better the world around us. However, if we move too fast in "getting on with it," our explanations will be limited and, in the worst case, undermined.

Second, students of process tracing should, whenever possible, scale up, locating their particular mechanism(s) within broader families of theories on mechanisms – agent to structure, structure to agent, agent to agent, structure to structure mechanisms, for example. They should also – following on from Mahoney (2000) – explore whether their mechanisms relate to processes involving material power, institutional efficiency, or social legitimacy.

When combined, these two dimensions create a taxonomy of social mechanisms that can be visualized in a 4 × 3 table (Bennett 2013a: 215; 2013b: 473). Such a taxonomy is invaluable for students of process tracing as they seek to develop and test their mid-range theories. For one – and echoing a key best practice advanced in Chapter 1 – it provides a checklist to insure that one is not leaving out important potential alternative explanations of a phenomenon. As Dunning correctly notes (this volume, Chapter 8, p. 228), our advice on alternative explanations – "to cast the net widely" – is easier to say than to operationalize; utilizing the taxonomy as a starting point begins to address this implementation issue.

More important, the taxonomy can be used to develop middle-range, typological theories about how combinations of mechanisms interact in shaping outcomes for specified cases or populations (Bennett 2013a: 221–228). A typological theory is a theory that not only defines individual independent variables and the hypothesized causal mechanisms that shape their effects, but provides "contingent generalizations on how and under what conditions they [these variables] behave in specified conjunctions or configurations to produce effects on specified dependent variables" (George and Bennett 2005: 235).

The taxonomy thus encompasses the building blocks of theorized mechanisms that can be brought together in different conjunctions to develop typological theories on how combinations of variables behave. Typological theories allow for cumulative theorizing as scholars can add variables or re-conceptualize them to higher or lower levels of abstraction (Elman 2005), and such theories can be fruitfully and cumulatively modified as they encounter anomalous cases or expand to encompass new types of cases.

In summary, the challenge at this level of mid-range theory is the same as we have identified for process tracing – to move from metaphor to analytic tool. While the epistemological underpinnings and specific details of typological theory may be a step too far for interpretive variants of process tracing, we nonetheless share with the latter a commitment to utilizing the method to generate cumulative knowledge that extrapolates beyond the bounds of particular instances or cases – to what Pouliot in Chapter 9 calls analytic generality. As he argues, a "convincing [practice-tracing] account should locate specific instances of relationships as part of larger classes of social processes. In other words, as contextualized as the study of practice may be, the social scientific gaze must always look beyond specific cases, toward cross-case generality" (Pouliot, this volume, Chapter 9, p. 239).

Building upon the Pouliot quote, we conclude this section with a comment not on theory and process tracing, but on meta-theory. The meta-theory of process tracing – as we argued in Chapter 1 – departs from both strict forms of positivism and strong versions of interpretivism. This creates a meta-theoretical space, as demonstrated by the contributions to this volume, where proponents of Bayesian-inspired process tracing and interpretive practice tracing (see also Guzzini 2012: chapter 11) can productively meet. They are anything but "ships passing in the night."

Process tracing – where next?

Reflecting on the findings of this volume and other recent work on process tracing (Collier 2011; Mahoney 2012; Rohlfing 2012; 2013a; 2013b; Humphreys and Jacobs 2013; Symposium 2013; Beach and Pedersen 2013a; 2013b), we see four cutting-edge challenges.

The first challenge is that process tracing, while an important tool for measuring causal mechanisms and their observable implications, is not the only way to capture mechanisms in action. The challenge is thus to combine process tracing with quantitative and other techniques through mixed-method designs. Statistical analysis, for example, can be used to establish a relation or correlation that hints at causal mechanisms, whose validation in particular cases then requires process tracing (see also Dunning, this volume, Chapter 8). Here, quantitative analysis indirectly contributes to the measuring task by suggesting there is some relation worthy of measurement.

Other such quantitative/process-tracing pairings come readily to mind. Game theory can be used to generate deductive, stylized representations of the real world and the hypothesized relations of interest, which are then empirically tested via process tracing (Kuehn 2013). In a similar fashion, process tracing "provides an attractive method for evaluating formal models," especially given that the latter often seek to go beyond covariation "to learn about the mechanisms leading to an outcome" (Lorentzen *et al.* 2013: 10).

Quantitative methods can also make a more direct contribution to measurement, however, now within a single qualitative case study. Surveys, for example, may prove invaluable in generating additional observable implications of hypothesized causal mechanisms, as Lyall argues elsewhere in this volume. In a similar manner, agent-based modeling – which is a form of computer simulation – can be used to explore the logic and hypothesized scope conditions of particular causal mechanisms whose presence has first been established using process tracing. In recent work on civil war, such a modeling exercise provided important confirmation of social learning mechanisms originally measured through process tracing (Nome and Weidmann 2013).[9]

Thus, while process tracing is fundamentally a technique used by qualitative scholars, future work would do wise to heed Gerring's (2007a: 36) more general injunction that quantitative methods can often play an important role in their research (see also Bennett 2013b: 471–472).

These pairings with quantitative methods certainly do not exhaust the ways in which process tracing can be supplemented. From an interpretive perspective, discourse and other forms of textual analysis may be required to generate additional data for the execution of what Pouliot (this volume, Chapter 9) calls practice tracing. More ambitiously – because it involves moving across epistemological boundaries – we might imagine the following staged design. One begins interpretively, using textual methods inductively to recover the properties of a particular factor, country, or political system. Then, in a second, positivist/scientific-realist step, the inductively generated data creates observable implications whose presence is measured by process tracing.

---

[9] In a similar fashion, Wood (2003: Appendix) presents a formal model that further explores the logic of the causal mechanisms uncovered through her process tracing.

This type of epistemologically plural design has been used by Hopf to good effect. In a study of identity and its causal impact on Soviet/Russian foreign policy, he first inductively and interpretively recovered Russians' self-understandings of who they were. These identities created discursive scripts whose presence and causal impact he then sought to measure in several process-tracing case studies of Soviet/Russian alliance choice (Hopf 2002; see also Hopf 2012). In a plural, empirically grounded spirit similar to that evoked by Pouliot in this volume (Chapter 9), Hopf argues that the supposed (epistemological) divisions separating interpretive analysis and standard case studies quickly shrink when one operationalizes arguments and applies them to real-world puzzles (Hopf 2007; see also Price and Reus-Smit 1998).

A second challenge concerns the move – already underway (see above) – to formalize more fully the logic and intuitions that underlay process tracing. To date, this has focused on explicating the Bayesian logic that is consistent with deductive forms of process tracing, as Bennett shows in this volume's Appendix (see also Beach and Pedersen 2013b; Humphreys and Jacobs 2013; Rohlfing 2013a; 2013b), and articulating the logic of causal graphs (Waldner, this volume, Chapter 5) and set theory (Mahoney 2012) as they apply to process tracing. While somewhat technical and specific – involving, in the case of Bayesianism, the quantification of priors and likelihood ratios and the sorting out of multiple tests in sequence using uncertain evidence – further work on Bayesianism and other formal approaches holds the promise of making even more explicit and clear the logic of process-tracing tests.

A third, less formal, but nonetheless important challenge for all process tracers – inductive, deductive, scientific realist, and interpretive – is to enhance the transparency of their process-tracing tests. This is relatively straightforward to execute and – earlier above – we suggested several strategies in this regard. The real difficulty here is a stylistic one: to integrate enhanced transparency and explicit attention to method with the well-written prose and lively narratives that exemplify case research at its best. With so much political science writing already in the category of "not easy bedtime reading," we have no desire to further that tendency.

The last point leads to a final challenge for process tracing. As we further systematize and operationalize, and, to some degree, formalize it, the method must maintain its openness to inductive discovery, soaking and poking, and the element of surprise that often mark the study of the social world. In the opening pages of Chapter 1, we referred to the volume as "an applied methods book ... where the aim is to show how process tracing works in practice." That formulation was no accident. Our goal was to capture process tracing in all its diversity and to begin a conversation over its best practices and community standards. As we and our contributors have argued and shown, it is decisively not anything goes. Nor, however, should it be or is it a case of one size fits all.

Appendix: Disciplining our conjectures
Systematizing process tracing with Bayesian analysis

Andrew Bennett

One of the attractions of process tracing is that it does not require technical training to be able to use the method. Just as one can be a decent cook with only a recipe and an intuitive understanding of chemistry, it is possible to do process tracing well by following the prescriptive advice in Chapter 1 and having an intuitive understanding of its logic. Yet, sometimes our intuitive understandings lead us astray. Just as a cook who understands chemistry will be better able to develop new recipes, adapt to different kitchens and ingredients, and teach cooking to others, researchers who understand the underlying logic of process tracing are likely to be better able to do it, teach it, and defend their applications of it.

This appendix thus outlines the mathematical logic of process tracing. Although technical, it should be accessible to readers with modest exposure to algebra, probability theory, and formal logic. The Appendix focuses on Bayesian reasoning as one way of illuminating the logic that underlies deductive process tracing. An important caveat here is that although the logic of process tracing and that of Bayesianism have much in common, they are not entirely coterminous. In particular, the use of process tracing to generate theories by "soaking and poking" in the evidence does not (yet) have a place in Bayesian epistemology. Also, the logic underlying process tracing can be explicated in terms of set theory and directed acyclic graphs as well as Bayesianism.[1] Yet, Bayesianism is the inferential logic that has been developed the furthest in the context of process

I would like to thank Derek Beach, Jeff Checkel, David Collier, Colin Elman, Macartan Humphreys, Alan Jacobs, James Mahoney, Ingo Rohlfing, and David Waldner for their insightful comments on an earlier draft of this appendix. Any remaining errors are my own.

[1] For an explication of process tracing that draws on set theory, see Mahoney 2012: 570–597; for one in terms of directed acyclic graphs (DAGs), see David Waldner's chapter (this volume, Chapter 5). It is not yet clear whether there are methodologically consequential differences among these approaches, and there are many ways in which these three logics are compatible and translatable; on this point, see Pawlak 2001; Abell 2009: 45–58.

tracing.[2] Accordingly, this appendix first outlines the fundamentals of Bayesianism and then advances six important implications for process tracing. The underlying premise here is that more rigorous and explicit use of inferential logic in process tracing, whether Bayesianism, directed acyclic graphs, set theory, or some other logic, will contribute to better process tracing.

Fundamentals of Bayesian analysis

Consider an excellent example of process tracing: in her book *The Nuclear Taboo*, Nina Tannenwald takes up the question of why nuclear weapons have not been used since 1945.[3] She considers several possible explanations that at first glance seem equally plausible: the use of nuclear weapons may have been deterred by the threat of nuclear retaliation; nuclear weapons may have lacked military utility in the particular crises and wars that nuclear-armed states have faced since 1945; or a normative taboo may have arisen against the use of nuclear weapons.[4]

Next, Tannenwald considers the observable implications that should be true, if one alternative explanation or another were true, about the *process* through which the use of nuclear weapons should have been considered and rejected. Finally, she examines the evidence on these observable implications in cases in which American leaders considered the possibility of using nuclear weapons, paying particular attention to evidence that undercuts one explanation or another and to evidence that fits one explanation but does not fit the others. She concludes that a nuclear taboo did not exist in the United States in 1945, but that such a taboo arose after reports of the effects of radiation on victims in Hiroshima and Nagasaki. This taboo, she argues, inhibited the use of nuclear weapons by American leaders after 1945 even in situations where these weapons could have had military utility against adversaries who lacked the ability to retaliate with nuclear weapons of their own or those of an ally.

---

[2] Particularly useful contributions to this literature include: Abell 2009; Beach and Pedersen 2013a; 2013b; Collier 2011; Humphreys and Jacobs 2013; Mahoney 2012; and Rohlfing 2012; 2013a; 2013b.

[3] Beach and Pedersen (2013a: 22–23) similarly identify Tannenwald's work as an example of good process tracing that nicely illustrates the use of Bayesian logic. For further discussion of this and other examples of process tracing that make excellent class exercises, see Collier (2011) and the online exercises associated with this article at the Social Science Research Network website at http://papers.ssrn.com/sol3/papers.cfm?abstract_id=1944646.

[4] Tannenwald 2007: 30–43. Tannenwald considers additional possible explanations, but I limit the present discussion to these three for purposes of illustration.

Each of these steps can be given a Bayesian reading, following the logic first systematized by Thomas Bayes in the mid 1700s. Bayes focused on the question of how we should update our confidence in an explanation in the light of new evidence. This updated confidence in the likely truth of a theory is referred to as the posterior probability, or the likelihood of a theory conditional on the evidence.

In Bayes's approach, we need three key pieces of information, in addition to the evidence itself, to calculate this posterior probability. First, we need to start with a "prior" probability, or a probability that expresses our initial confidence that a theory is true even before looking at the new evidence. Second, we need information on the likelihood that, if a theory is true in a case, we will find a particular kind of evidence in that case. This is referred to as the evidence conditional on the theory. Third, we need to know the likelihood that we would find the same evidence even if the explanation of interest is false. This is often referred to as the false positive rate, or the likelihood that evidence or a diagnostic test will show up positive even when a theory is false.

For illustrative purposes, let us consider each of these three probabilities in the Tannenwald example. Tannenwald does not identify a specific prior for her alternative explanations, but for our illustration let us assume that the prior probability that the taboo explanation is true in any given case is 40 percent. Let us further assume for the sake of simplicity that the three explanations considered by Tannenwald are mutually exclusive, so the probability that a taboo does *not* explain a particular case is 1 minus 40 percent, or 60 percent.[5]

Second, we need an estimate of the likelihood, assuming the taboo theory is true, that we would find evidence in a case that is consistent with the taboo theory. In the terminology used in medical testing, this is the likelihood of a "true positive" test result, where the theory is true and the test result indicates that the theory is true. Consider here two kinds of tests of Tannenwald's theory, a "hoop test" and a "smoking-gun" test. These tests are defined more precisely below, but essentially, a hoop test is one where a hypothesis must "jump through a hoop" by fitting the evidence. If the

---

[5] One complication here is that theories or explanations can be mutually exclusive, that is, only one could be true, or they can be complementary. My example, like many pedagogical presentations of Bayesianism, simplifies this point by considering only whether one theory is true or false, so the probability that it is false is one minus the probability that it is true. Here, the probability that the taboo theory is false subsumes all of the alternative hypotheses to this theory (see also Rohlfing 2012: ch. 8). In social science research, often researchers face the more complex question of hypotheses that are partly complementary and partly competing, or competing in some cases and complementary in others (on this challenge, see Rohlfing 2013a).

hypothesis fails a hoop test, it is strongly undercut, but passing such a test does not strongly affirm the hypothesis. A smoking-gun test is the converse: passing this kind of test greatly raises the likelihood that a hypothesis is true, but failing such a test does not strongly impugn a hypothesis.

Regarding Tannenwald's work, we might pose a hoop test as follows: if the taboo theory is true, we would expect to see decision-makers considering the possible use of nuclear weapons, but deciding against using these weapons because individuals within the decision group raised normative arguments against nuclear weapons. This constitutes a hoop test because it would be hard to sustain the taboo interpretation if there was no evidence that normative concerns were even raised, unless the taboo was so strong that the use of nuclear weapons could not even be discussed. For our illustration let us assign this hoop test a probability of 90 percent; that is, we are 90 percent likely to find evidence that normative constraints were discussed if the taboo argument correctly explains a case and if we have access to evidence on the decision meetings. Indeed, Tannenwald does find evidence to this effect (Tannenwald 2007: 206–211).

As for a smoking-gun test for the nuclear taboo theory, we might expect that decision-makers who favored the use of nuclear weapons would complain that normative constraints undercut their arguments and prevented the use of nuclear weapons. This would constitute smoking-gun evidence for at least some level of taboo because finding such criticism would strongly support the taboo hypothesis. We would not necessarily expect advocates of nuclear use to risk social or political opprobrium by openly criticizing norms against nuclear use, however, so even if those who advocated using nuclear weapons felt that normative arguments unduly undermined their advice, they might not want to acknowledge this. So let us assign a probability of 20 percent to the likelihood of finding evidence of criticism of non-use norms. Here, again, Tannenwald finds evidence that such criticism took place (Tannenwald 2007: 135–139, 144–145, 149).

Third, we need to estimate the likelihood of finding these same kinds of evidence – invocation of normative constraints, and complaints against normative constraints – even if the nuclear taboo explanation were false. In medical terminology, this is the "false positive" rate, or the instances where a test indicates a disease, but the patient does not in fact have that disease. In the Tannenwald example of a hoop test, if there were instrumental political reasons that actors would attribute the non-use of nuclear weapons to normative restraints even if this was not the real reason nuclear weapons were not used, evidence that normative concerns were raised would not prove that they were decisive or even relevant. A leader might cite his or her "principled" restraint in not using nuclear weapons, for example, when in fact he or she was deterred by the threat of retaliation. Also, leaders might discuss normative constraints, but not make them the deciding factor if the military utility of nuclear weapons is in doubt. Regarding the hoop test, let us therefore assign a probability of 70 percent to the discussion of normative constraints even in cases where they were not decisive regarding nuclear non-use.[6]

As for the smoking-gun test, it is harder to think of an instrumental reason that actors would criticize norms against the use of nuclear weapons, and state that these norms unduly limited their policy options, even if such norms did not exist or did not in fact constrain the decision process. So let us assign a probability of only 5 percent that this would happen.

It is important to note that ideally these three estimated probabilities – the prior likelihood the theory is true, the likelihood of finding certain evidence if the theory is true, and the likelihood of finding that same evidence even if the theory is false – would be either empirically based on studies of many prior cases, or based on strong and well-validated theories or experiments. This is true in the medical research examples that are common in textbook discussions of Bayesianism. Unfortunately, in the social sciences we often lack such data and must begin with more subjective guesses on these probabilities. Moreover, even when estimates of probabilities are based on large populations of prior cases and well-validated experimental results, there can still be considerable uncertainty as to what the probabilities should be for the particular individual or case at hand. An individual or a case may come from a distinctive sub-population for which data on priors is sparse, and the individual or case may differ from previous cases on variables or interaction effects that are relevant, but that have not been measured or included in previous models or data. The reliance on subjective expectations of probabilities, and differences in individuals' estimates of these probabilities, is an important challenge for Bayesianism. Researchers who start with different priors for alternative theories, and who give different estimates for the likelihood of finding certain kinds of evidence if theories are true or false, may continue to disagree on how, and how much, to update their confidence in different theories in the light of new evidence. I return below to the

---

[6] For a test to be a hoop test, the likelihood of passing the test if the theory is true has to be higher than the likelihood of passing the test if the theory is false. For a test to be a smoking-gun test, the likelihood of a theory passing the test must be much lower if the theory is false than if the theory is true.

question of how much and when different subjective estimates of prior and conditional probabilities matter, and when they disappear or "wash out" in the light of evidence. For present illustrative purposes, let us simply posit these probabilities while keeping firmly in mind the fact that their subjectivism poses important limitations for Bayesianism.[7]

We now have illustrative examples for all the three estimated probabilities necessary for Bayesian updating of the taboo hypothesis via the hoop test and smoking-gun test. Using P for the taboo proposition, $pr(P)$ for the prior probability that P is true, and k for the evidence, we have:

Hoop test (were norms raised?)

Prior likelihood P is true, or $pr(P) = 0.40$
Probability of hoop evidence k, if P is true $= 0.90$
Probability of hoop evidence k, if P is false $= 0.70$

Smoking-gun test (did advocates of using nuclear weapons criticize non-use norms?)

Prior likelihood P is true, or $pr(P) = 0.40$
Probability of smoking-gun evidence k, if P is true $= 0.20$
Probability of smoking-gun evidence k, if P is false $= 0.05$

We can now address the question: given that Tannenwald found evidence consistent with the hoop and smoking-gun tests, what should be the updated probability, for each test considered by itself, that the taboo explanation is true? The Bayesian math on this is simple, but it can take some time to sort out for those coming to the topic for the first time, and it can produce results that are counterintuitive. Newcomers to Bayesian analysis may find it easiest, before reading the math below, to check first a website that uses Venn diagrams to illustrate the intuition behind Bayes's Theorem.[8]

In a common form of Bayes's Theorem, the updated probability that a proposition P is true in light of evidence k, or $Pr(P|k)$, is as follows:

$$Pr(P|k) = \frac{pr(P)\,pr(k|P)}{pr(P)\,pr(k|P) + pr(\neg P)\,pr(k|\neg P)}$$

[7] There is a long-running debate between "objective" and "subjective" versions of Bayesianism that is beyond the scope of this appendix. For a recent contribution on this topic, see Berger 2006. For an overview, see the Stanford Encyclopedia of Philosophy web page on Bayesian epistemology at http://plato.stanford.edu/entries/epistemology-bayesian/.

[8] See, e.g. the site created by Oscar Bonilla at http://oscarbonilla.com/2009/05/visualizing-bayes-theorem/.

Notation:

> *Pr* (P|k) is the posterior or updated probability of P given (or conditional on) evidence k;
> *pr*(P) is the prior probability that proposition P is true;
> *pr*(k|P) is the likelihood of evidence k if P is true (or conditional on P);
> *pr*(¬P) is the prior probability that proposition P is false; and
> *pr*(k|¬P) is the likelihood of evidence k if proposition P is false (or conditional on ¬P).

In words, the updated or posterior probability that proposition P is true, given new evidence k, is equal to the right side of the equation, where the numerator is the prior probability accorded to P multiplied by the likelihood of the evidence k if P is true. The denominator on the right-hand side is the *sum* of this same numerator *pr*(P)*pr*(k|P) *plus* the prior likelihood that P is not true, or *pr*(¬P), multiplied by the likelihood of finding the evidence k even if P is false, or *pr*(k|¬P).

If we put the illustrative numbers from the Tannenwald hoop and the smoking-gun tests into this equation, the updated probability of the taboo theory for each test considered independently, given that Tannenwald did indeed find the evidence predicted by the taboo theory for both tests, is 0.46 for the hoop test and 0.73 for the smoking-gun test:

Probability taboo is true for passed hoop test:

$$\frac{(0.4)(0.9)}{(0.4)(0.9)+(0.6)(0.7)} = \frac{0.36}{0.36+0.42} = \frac{0.36}{0.78} = 0.46$$

Probability taboo is true for passed smoking-gun test:

$$\frac{(0.4)(0.2)}{(0.4)(0.2)+(0.6)(0.05)} = \frac{0.08}{0.08+0.03} = \frac{0.08}{0.11} = 0.73$$

We can use Bayes's Theorem to calculate the posterior probability of a failed hoop test – in the current example, plugging the numbers into the equation gives us a posterior probability of 0.18. Thus, as the name of the hoop test implies, passing the test only slightly raises the likelihood that the theory is true, from 0.4 to 0.46, while failing the test sharply reduces our confidence that the theory is true, from 0.4 to 0.18. The posterior probability that the taboo theory is true even if it fails the smoking-gun test is 0.36, so passing the test raises the theory's probability far more (from 0.4 to 0.73) than failing it would slightly lower this probability (from 0.4 to 0.36).

Some readers may be surprised that the passing of the smoking-gun test increases the likelihood of the theory's truth far more than the passing of the hoop test, since the probability of finding smoking-gun test evidence if the taboo was true was only 20 percent and that for the hoop test was 90 percent.[9] Yet, this illustrates a key feature of Bayesianism: the extent of updating is driven by the prior probability of the theory *and* the ratio of true positives (the probability that the evidence is consistent with the theory when the theory is indeed true) to false positives (the probability that the evidence is consistent with the theory when the theory is false) (Rohlfing 2013b). This is called the *likelihood ratio*. Here, the likelihood ratio for positive evidence on the hoop test is 0.9/0.7 or 1.29, and the likelihood ratio for the smoking-gun test is 0.2/0.05 or 4.[10] Thus, passing the smoking-gun test in this example raises the likelihood that the theory is true far more than passing the hoop test, because it is extremely unlikely that we would find smoking-gun evidence even if the taboo theory were false, but it is fairly likely we would find hoop test evidence even if the theory were false.

The likelihood ratio provides a useful measure of the diagnostic power of a test or piece of evidence. The *sensitivity* of a diagnostic test is defined as the probability that the test or the evidence will be positive when the theory is true. The *specificity* of a piece of evidence is the probability that the evidence will be negative when the theory is false. The likelihood ratio of a positive test (designated LR+) is thus:

$$LR+ = \frac{\text{Probability evidence positive when P true}}{\text{Probability evidence positive when P false}} = \frac{\text{Sensitivity}}{(1 - \text{Specificity})}$$

There is also a separate likelihood ratio for a negative test result (LR–). This is the ratio of false negatives to true negatives:

$$LR- = \frac{\text{Probability evidence negative when P true}}{\text{Probability evidence negative when P false}} = \frac{(1 - \text{Sensitivity})}{\text{Specificity}}$$

The LR+ is typically greater than 1, and the LR– typically has values between 0 and 1.[11] The farther the LR is from 1, the more powerful or discriminating the

---

[9] Indeed, even doctors, who make evidence-based diagnoses and who are usually trained in Bayesian analysis to do so, often give intuitive analyses that violate Bayesian logic (Casscells *et al.* 1978: 999–1001).

[10] For arguments that the likelihood ratio, or more specifically the log of the likelihood ratio, is the best measure of the evidential or confirmatory support of evidence, see Fitelson 2001; and Eels and Fitelson 2002.

[11] In medical diagnostic tests, if the LR+ is less than 1, or the LR– is greater than 1, then the interpretation of what is a "positive" test result is simply reversed, as a "positive" test result is defined as one that indicates the suspected underlying disease is more likely given a positive test result than a negative one (Spitalnic

evidence: finding positive evidence when the LR was 4, as in the smoking-gun test example, greatly increases the likelihood that Tannenwald's proposition is true. Finding positive evidence in the hoop test, where the LR is 1.29 (i.e. closer to 1 than the LR for the smoking-gun test) is less definitive. Failing the hoop test, where the LR– can be calculated to be 0.33, is more definitive evidence against the taboo proposition than failing the smoking-gun test, where the LR– is 0.84, or closer to 1. When the LR is equal to 1, evidence has no discriminatory power: the posterior is the same as the prior.

An alternative formulation that expresses Bayes's Theorem in odds form, known as Bayes's rule, uses the likelihood ratio directly:

$$\frac{\Pr(P|k)}{\Pr(\neg P|k)} = \frac{pr(P)}{pr(\neg P)} \cdot \frac{pr(k|P)}{pr(k|\neg P)}$$

Here, the second term on the right-hand side of the equation, $pr(k|P)/pr(k|\neg P)$, is the likelihood ratio. Note that this formulation yields the same result as that above. To illustrate this using probabilities from the hoop test of the taboo hypothesis:

$$\frac{\Pr(P|k)}{\Pr(\neg P|k)} = \frac{0.4}{0.6} \cdot \frac{0.9}{0.7} = 0.857$$

This result is the same as the 0.46 answer in the hoop test calculation above, since the 0.857 result is expressed as an odds ratio, and converting an odds ratio to a probability uses the formula:

$$\text{Probability} = \frac{\text{Odds}}{(1+\text{Odds})}$$

Thus, in this case:

$$\frac{0.857}{1.857} = 0.46$$

Macartan Humphreys and Alan Jacobs have devised a very nice graphical illustration of how the likelihood ratio determines the strength of evidentiary tests, reprinted here as Figure A.1 with these authors' generous permission

2004: 56). In tests of the observable implications of hypothesized causal mechanisms, however, researchers do not necessarily flip the meaning of a "positive result"; here, evidence that is consistent with a theory might be even more confirmatory of the null hypothesis that the theory is false, a point I return to below.

(Humphreys and Jacobs 2013: 17). Figure A.1 illustrates straw-in-the-wind tests (tests that only slightly update in either direction when passed or failed) and doubly decisive tests (tests that strongly raise the posterior if passed and sharply lower it if failed), as well as smoking-gun and hoop tests. Humphreys and Jacobs's figure shows how these evidentiary tests relate to one another. The figure also shows how these tests relate to the two measures that comprise the likelihood ratio: the probability of observing evidence when a proposition P is true (labeled q_1 on the y-axis of the figure) and the probability of observing positive evidence even when the proposition P is false (labeled q_0 on the x-axis of the figure; in the figure, ¬P is used to denote "P is False"):

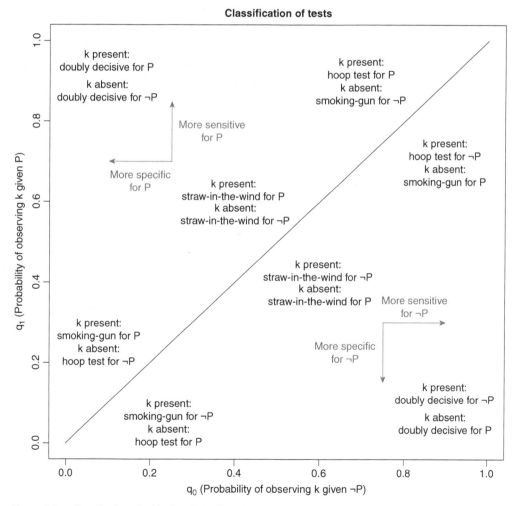

Figure A.1   Classification of evidentiary tests (Humphreys and Jacobs 2013)

The figure also illustrates several other properties of Bayesian tests. As Humphreys and Jacobs point out, the type of test involved depends on both the relative and the absolute values of q_0 and q_1 (Humphreys and Jacobs 2013: 16). Also, the 45-degree diagonal line shows where $q_0 = q_1$, so along this line the likelihood ratio is 1 and all tests exactly on this line are uninformative, that is, they do not update the prior probabilities. The arrows in the figure indicate the directions in which the sensitivity and specificity increase for tests of P and ¬P.

The figure also shows that there are several mirror-image relations among tests depending on whether evidence k is present or absent. This can be seen by comparing the areas in the lower-left and upper-right corners just above and below the 45-degree line: a test that provides smoking-gun evidence for P when k is present constitutes hoop test evidence for ¬P when k is absent, and vice versa. This is because P and ¬P are inversely proportional – their probabilities add up to 1 – so a smoking-gun test whose passing greatly raises the likelihood of P and whose failing only slightly reduces the likelihood of P will have the opposite effects on the probability of ¬P and will thus constitute a hoop test for ¬P. Similarly, a hoop test for P is a smoking-gun test for ¬P.

Humphreys and Jacobs also introduce a set of figures that further illustrate the properties of different evidentiary tests, again reproduced here as Figures A.2 to A.5 with their kind permission.[12] These figures show how different prior probabilities map onto posterior probabilities for the illustrative likelihood ratio used in each graph. Examples are shown for likelihood ratios representing hoop, smoking-gun, doubly decisive, and straw-in-the-wind tests. Because q_0 and q_1 can vary continuously between 0 and 1, in addition to the examples in Figures A.2 to A.5, one could draw any number of curves for tests of different discriminatory power within each family of tests using different combinations of q_0 and q_1. In other words, tests within the same family are not equally powerful.[13] For example, the test "was there a smoking gun in the hand of the accused when the victim was shot" is not as definitive when the murder was committed at a shooting range.

These graphs nicely illustrate the point that the extent to which we should update our prior depends on the values of both the prior and the likelihood ratio. As Humphreys and Jacobs point out, we will not lose as much confidence in a hypothesis that has achieved a high prior through repeated earlier testing, even in the face of a failed hoop test (visually, in Figure A.3 the vertical

---

[12] Humphreys and Jacobs 2013: 19; see also Rohlfing 2013b: 20–29.
[13] On this point, see Mahoney 2012; and Rohlfing 2013a.

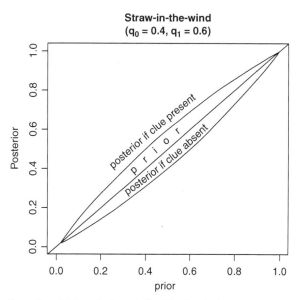

Figure A.2   Properties of "straw-in-the-wind" evidentiary test

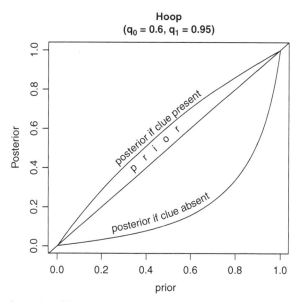

Figure A.3   Properties of "hoop" evidentiary test

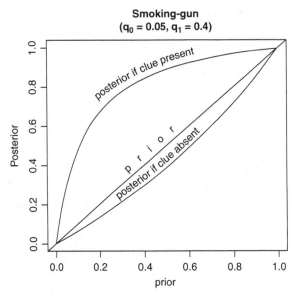

Figure A.4   Properties of "smoking-gun" evidentiary test

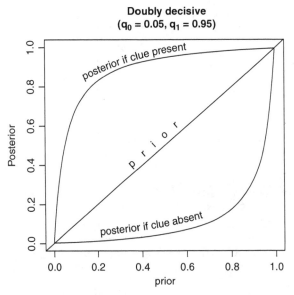

Figure A.5   Properties of "doubly decisive" evidentiary test

distance from the 45-degree diagonal to the curved line for the failed hoop test, which shows how much lower the posterior is than the prior, is less when the prior is close to 1.0 than it is when the prior is between 0.4 and 0.8). Even so, if the likelihood ratio for a hoop test is even more extreme than that in the hoop test shown in Figure A.3, a theory with a very high prior will be sharply updated if it fails the test. Moreover, the likelihood of a theory with a low prior can be greatly updated if the theory passes a very demanding smoking-gun test or a doubly decisive test.

Humphreys and Jacobs also make another crucial point in this context. Many discussions of Bayesianism focus on the problem of trying to justify the prior probabilities attached by researchers to hypotheses. When researchers lack sufficient evidence on earlier instances of a phenomenon to establish reliable or relatively "objective" priors, they may have to use more subjective estimates or priors, or they might arbitrarily adopt priors that are relatively equal for alternative hypotheses. Critics often point to the reliance on partly subjective priors as a weakness of Bayesianism. Defenders of Bayesianism typically reply, correctly, that with enough strongly discriminating evidence from the case or cases being studied, differences in researchers' subjective priors should "wash out," and researchers' posteriors should converge to similar values even if they started with different subjective priors.

An example helps to illustrate this point. Consider two individuals: Itchy, who has never seen a coin with two heads, and Scratchy, who has. A no-nonsense judge shows them a coin and asks them to guess the likelihood that the coin has two heads: Itchy assigns this a prior probability that is 0.01, and Scratchy, suspecting something is up, estimates 0.5 as the prior. After one coin flip comes up heads, Itchy uses Bayes's Theorem and updates her posterior to 0.0198, and Scratchy moves to 0.67 as her updated posterior. After ten coin flips in a row come up heads, Itchy's updated posterior is 0.91, and Scratchy's is 0.999, so the posteriors have come closer together. With repeated flips that turn up heads, both posteriors will eventually converge to very close to a probability of 1.0 that the coin is two-headed.

If highly probative evidence is not available, however, observers may continue to diverge in their estimates of the likelihood that alternative hypotheses are true. Moreover, as Humphreys and Jacobs note, researchers may differ not just in their prior estimates that theories are true in particular cases, but also in their estimates of the conditional probabilities of finding certain kinds of evidence if a theory is true or if it is false. These estimates build upon researchers' potentially different expectations on how the hypothesized mechanisms work. These expectations may also converge as new evidence on processes becomes known, but if strongly discriminating evidence on mechanisms is not available, researchers may continue to disagree on how hypothesized mechanisms work, and on how much or even in which direction to update the likelihood of theories in the light of new evidence.[14]

An interesting question, and one which could be studied through experiments, is whether scholars find it easier to agree on the conditional probabilities of finding certain kinds of evidence, if alternative theories are true, than to agree on probabilistic priors regarding the likely truth of theories. It might be easiest of all to get intersubjective agreement that certain evidence, if found, would favor one theory over another, without necessarily agreeing on theoretical priors or on the precise likelihood ratio bearing on how much a piece of evidence would favor one theory. Even this limited level of agreement can lead to some convergence on priors once the evidence is uncovered. In the Tannenwald case, for example, one can imagine that scholars with different theoretical priors could have agreed, in advance of looking at the evidence, that the likelihood of the taboo theory should be raised if participants stated to contemporaries that they felt a taboo prevented them from advocating nuclear use as strongly or successfully as they would have liked. This kind of agreement by itself would have been sufficient for some convergence once Tannenwald's evidence on this came to light, even if scholars continued to disagree on precisely how much convergence was warranted.

Yet, if strongly discriminating evidence on outcomes and processes is not available, researchers who start with different priors and/or different conditional probabilities may continue to differ substantially in their views on which theories are likely to be true and how theories work (Humphreys and Jacobs 2013: 20). Bayesians acknowledge this as one of the many reasons that we should never be 100 percent confident in any theory.

Implications of Bayesian analysis for process tracing

The foregoing sections outline the basic mechanics of Bayesian updating. The remainder of the appendix briefly summarizes six sometimes counterintuitive implications of Bayesian mathematics for process tracing.

---

[14] It is also possible that researchers could agree that a variable could have affected outcomes through any one of several different mechanisms, so finding evidence of any of these mechanisms in operation would raise the likelihood that the variable had a causal effect. Yet, researchers might still disagree on the relative likelihood of the different mechanisms, and the conditional likelihood of finding evidence on them. I thank Alan Jacobs for pointing this out.

1. Evidence consistent with a theory can actually lower its posterior and evidence that does not fit a theory can raise its posterior

These counter-intuitive outcomes arise when the likelihood ratio is less than 1.[15] Figures A.2 to A.5 all have likelihood ratios where q_1 is greater than q_0; that is, they are all drawn from above the 45-degree diagonal in Figure A.1. When q_0 is greater than q_1, the likelihood ratio is less than 1 (as in the area below the 45-degree diagonal of Figure A.1). When this happens, evidence consistent with P actually reduces the likelihood that P is true, while evidence that is not consistent with P actually raises the likelihood that P is true. One way to see this is to note that Bayesian updating works by both affirmative evidence and eliminative induction. In other words, evidence has discriminating power not only by fitting or contradicting the theory of interest, but also by fitting or contradicting the alternative explanations. Sometimes, the latter effect is stronger than the former.

Consider an example in which two people, a trained killer and a jealous lover, are the main suspects in a murder case. A detective considers these suspects to be equally likely to have committed a murder. The trained killer has ten weapons, including a gun, with which they could have committed the murder, and is equally likely to have used any of them. The jealous lover could only have committed the murder with a gun or a knife, and is equally likely to have used either one. If the detective finds evidence that the victim was killed by a gun, this is consistent with the hypothesis that the trained assassin is the killer, but it actually reduces the odds of this from one in two to one in six, because the jealous lover is five times as likely to have used a gun than the trained killer.

As noted above (in footnote 11), in medical tests, when a test result has a likelihood ratio of less than 1, then the meaning of a "positive" and "negative" test result is simply flipped, as a positive result is defined as the test result that makes more likely the possibility that the patient has the disease or condition in question.[16] When evidence instead bears on whether a particular social mechanism is in operation, however, we do not necessarily flip the interpretation of positive and negative test results. Thus, evidence consistent with the operation of one hypothesized mechanism might make it even more likely that the outcome is explained by another theory that entails the same evidence. Researchers are likely to realize this if they have already conceived of the alternative theory and considered how likely it would be to generate the

---

[15] See Rohlfing 2013b: 5, 19, 20.

[16] It may still be possible, however, that interactions among physiological variables could make a test result indicative of a higher likelihood of a disease or condition in some sub-populations and a lower likelihood in others.

same evidence. If a researcher is unaware of the alternative explanation or fails to consider whether the same evidence is likely in view of this explanation, he or she might fail to realize that evidence consistent with the explanation they did consider may in fact make that explanation less likely to be true.

2. Bayesianism provides a logical rationale for the methodological prescription that independence and diversity of evidence is good in process tracing

A common intuition consistent with Bayesianism is that evidentiary tests that are independent of one another, and diverse in the sense that they bear on different alternative hypotheses, are desirable (see Bennett and Checkel, this volume, Chapter 1). Regarding independence, if one piece of evidence is wholly determined by another, it has zero additional power to update prior probabilities. Put another way, if two pieces of evidence are perfectly correlated, the joint probability of seeing them both if a theory is right is the same as the probability of seeing only one of them if the theory is right, so there is no additional updating from seeing the second piece of evidence. In practice, one piece of evidence can be fully dependent on another, fully independent, or anywhere in-between. To the extent that it is dependent, it is less probative once the other evidence on which it is dependent is known.

With regard to diversity of evidence, as we accumulate more and more pieces of evidence that bear on only one alternative explanation, each new bit of this evidence has less power to update further our confidence in a theory. This is true, even if the evidentiary tests are independent, because we have already incorporated the information of the earlier, similar evidence. Consider the coin-tossing example above: if the coin were presented by a magician rather than a no-nonsense judge, repeated flips that turned up heads would soon lose their ability to update the posteriors. These repeated flips would rule out the possibility of a fair coin, fairly tossed. Yet, they would not rule out the possibility that the magician was either switching coins or had practiced how to toss exact numbers of rotations. Itchy and Scratchy would want to have evidence other than the toss results, such as slow motion video, to address these hypotheses.

The most precise Bayesian statement on this issue is that researchers should prioritize evidence whose confirmation power, derived from likelihood ratios, is maximal when added to the evidence they have already used to determine and update their prior probabilities.[17] In practice, this often

---

[17] This suggestion comes from Fitelson (2001: S131).

will be evidence that is both independent of and different in kind from that already collected.[18]

3. Multiple weak tests, if independent from one another, can sometimes cumulate to strongly update priors, but uncertainties regarding the evidence can complicate this process

Straw-in-the-wind tests, and weak smoking-gun and hoop tests, are the kinds of tests that might be called "circumstantial evidence" in a court case. Many such weak tests can cumulate to strongly update priors if these tests are independent and if all or even most of them point in the same direction. It is highly unlikely that all, or a high proportion, of independent weak tests would point in the same direction unless a theory is true. This is analogous to the low likelihood that a coin is fair, or equally weighted in the likelihood of heads or tails, if that coin comes up heads in any proportion that is significantly different from 50 percent in a large number of fair tosses.

When there is uncertainty regarding the interpretation of the evidence, or on the instruments through which evidence is observed or measured, however, the question of how to update on the basis of multiple tests becomes more complex. The challenge here is that new evidence can push us to update not only the likelihood that a theory is true, but also the likelihood that our instruments of observation and measurement are reliable. The coin toss example is a simple one in which the determination of heads or tails is unambiguous. In contrast, when the reading of the evidence is uncertain and observers represent their understandings of the evidence as either degrees of certainty or confidence intervals, it becomes more difficult to update priors in a logically coherent way.

In particular, we should expect Bayesian updating to achieve two goals that can come into conflict when there is uncertainty regarding the reading of evidence: (1) updating on the basis of evidence should be *commutative*, that is, it should not depend on the order in which evidence is received; and (2) updating should be *holistic*, that is, the probative power of evidence should be sensitive to our less-than-certain background assumptions about how to read evidence, and these assumptions should change on the basis of earlier

---

[18] A related issue is the "old evidence" problem: can evidence or facts already known still update the likelihood of hypotheses? For a summary of debates on this and other issues regarding Bayesianism, see the Stanford Encyclopedia of Philosophy web page on Bayesian epistemology at http://plato.stanford.edu/entries/epistemology-bayesian/.

evidence (Weisberg 2009). Yet, some efforts to allow for uncertain evidence lead to sharply different results when evidence cumulates, depending on the order in which evidence is considered.[19] Alternatively, one could update on the basis of new evidence in ways that are commutative, or independent of order, but that do not take advantage of opportunities to update prior understandings of how to read and interpret evidence.

The classical Bayesian updating discussed above essentially applies only in the special case when evidence is certain. This form of updating does not insure both commutativity and holism when the reading of the evidence is uncertain. Scholars have proposed various solutions to this problem in the last four decades, but these subsequently proved unable to insure either commutativity or holism.[20]

Most recently, Dmitri Gallow has proposed an approach to conditionalization that offers both holism and commutativity even in the face of uncertain evidence (Gallow 2014). The mathematical justification of Gallow's approach is too complex to recount for present purposes, and the approach is too new to have undergone and withstood the kind of scrutiny that has pointed out flaws in earlier attempts to resolve this issue. Gallow's approach looks promising, however, so its general outlines are worth noting. Gallow begins by noting that alternative theories involve different background assumptions on things like the instruments of measurement and observation, and hence the accuracy or certitude of evidence. At times, these background theories will agree that one kind of evidence is credible and that it validates some background theories more than others. Gallow's central insight is that when theories agree that a piece of evidence was learned, and that it makes one theory more likely than the other, the likelihood accorded to these theories can be updated in light of this evidence. If theories do not agree on whether the evidence was learned or is accurate, then there is no updating between those theories (Gallow 2014: 24–25).

As Gallow's approach to conditionalization is very new as of this writing, there are of course no applications of process tracing that explicitly use it. Analogous kinds of reasoning have long been evident in arguments over the interpretation of evidence in process tracing, however, as Gallow's insight

---

[19] For an example, see Hawthorne 2004: 97–98. Hawthorne also discusses approaches that achieve commutativity.

[20] Richard Jeffrey proposed an approach in 1965, termed "Jeffrey Conditionalization," that allows for uncertainty regarding evidence during updating, but his method has been criticized for failing to achieve either commutativity (Hawthorne 2004) or holism (Weisberg 2009: 806), and Jeffrey himself recognized that his 1965 approach was not sufficient (Jeffrey 1965). Hartry Field proposed another approach in 2009 that is commutative (Field 2009: 361–367), but this solution proved non-holistic (Weisberg 2009: 802–803).

arguably applies to disagreements between theorists as well as those between theories. The discussion above, for example, noted that researchers who differed in their degrees of belief in Tannenwald's theory could converge in their views if they agreed that certain evidence, if found, would make one theory more or less likely to be true. Here, we can take up Gallow's argument and extend the earlier discussion to allow for potentially different readings of the evidence. Convergence would still occur in the Tannenwald example if the contending researchers agreed in their reading of the evidence, as this would be equivalent to the special case of certain evidence. Yet, if the researchers could not agree on the certainty of the evidence – for example, if one of them thought the respondent who provided the evidence in an interview was telling the truth and the other thought the respondent was misinformed or lying – then the researchers could not narrow their disagreement on the basis of evidence from this respondent. In other words, intersubjective convergence, or sequential updating, is more powerful when contending theorists, or alternative theories, agree in their reading of the evidence.

4. Bayesian logic helps determine whether absence of evidence is evidence of absence

Absence of evidence is a much bigger challenge for the social sciences than for the physical sciences that are often used as textbook examples of Bayesian logic. Social scientists study thinking agents who may try to hide evidence. Interpreting the absence of evidence regarding social behavior thus involves judgments on social actors' ability and incentives to hide evidence, or to simply fail to record and keep it and make it available, versus the incentives for actors to make evidence public. For example, it was not entirely unreasonable to assume in 2003 that Saddam Hussein was hiding evidence that he was pursuing or already had weapons of mass destruction (WMD), as he had strong incentives and capabilities to hide any such evidence, but it became unreasonable to maintain this hypothesis after the US Army occupied Iraq and still failed to find evidence of WMD despite scouring the country for months.

It can be useful to think of the conditional probability of finding evidence if a theory is true as reflecting: (1) the probability that a process happened and that observable evidence on that process will be generated if the theory is true; (2) the probability that those with evidence on the process will preserve it and make it available rather than destroying, hiding, or simply mis-remembering it; and (3) the level and kind of effort invested by the researcher in trying to obtain or uncover evidence (see also Bennett and Checkel, this volume,

Chapter 1).[21] Jointly, these enter into the likelihood of finding evidence should a theory be true, and they thereby help to determine the degree to which the absence of evidence is evidence of absence.[22] In the Tannenwald example, one reason there is a low probability of finding evidence that actors criticized a nuclear taboo for having unduly constrained their options, even if a taboo did in fact limit policy choices, is that we might expect actors to be circumspect in arguing against a taboo in settings where such criticism would be recorded and could be made public.

5. Bayesian logic has implications for which cases to select for the purpose of process tracing

Several recent discussions of case selection in small-n research have moved in the direction of favoring the selection of cases, at least for some research purposes, which are positive on the main independent variable of interest and the dependent variable.[23] Others have argued for selection of cases that are extremely high or extremely low on the value of the main independent variable of interest, as well as deviant cases.[24] These cases can indeed be valuable as tests of hypothesized mechanisms since we would expect to find evidence of these mechanisms in such cases. Positive-positive cases, extreme value cases, and deviant cases can also facilitate inductive process tracing to develop or refine theories, as the operation of unexpected as well as hypothesized mechanisms may be more evident in such cases.

At the same time, Bayesian logic suggests that different kinds of cases – representing different combinations of positive and negative values on the independent variable of interest, the independent variables of alternative explanations, and the outcome – can be informative choices for process tracing as well, depending on the likelihood ratios for such cases in the view of the contesting theories. Whether particular cases, and the evidence within them, is probative is not just a question of whether the evidence in the case fits or contravenes the theory of interest, but also whether it is probative for the alternative theories that may or may not be rendered less likely.[25] Put another

---

[21] Conversely, we should also consider the likelihood that other actors would have the means, motive, and opportunity to manufacture and make public evidence suggesting a theory is true, even when the theory is false. This enters into the likelihood ratio of false positives. Most textbook discussions of Bayesianism overlook the possibility of planted evidence because they focus on examples where there is no incentive for such behavior.

[22] For Bayesian discussions of this issue, see Stephens 2011; and Sober 2009.

[23] Schneider and Rohlfing 2013; Goertz and Mahoney 2012.   [24] Seawright 2012.

[25] For a detailed discussion on this issue, see Rohlfing (2013a).

way, likelihood ratios are determined by the hypothesized mechanisms of both the theory of interest and the alternative explanations.

6. Explicitly assigning priors and likelihood ratios and using Bayesian mathematics can make process tracing more rigorous and transparent

Earlier discussions treated Bayesianism as a useful metaphor for process tracing (McKeown 1999) or a way of clarifying its logic (Bennett 2008), without arguing that Bayesian mathematics should be used explicitly in process tracing. More recently, a number of scholars (Abell 2009; Humphreys and Jacobs 2013; Rohlfing 2013a; 2013b) have suggested that researchers should implement Bayesianism more concretely, explicitly identifying their priors and likelihood ratios and using Bayes's Theorem to determine posterior probabilities. This need not involve point estimates of probabilities, as researchers can use confidence intervals to convey their degrees of uncertainty regarding evidence and its interpretation. Other researchers argue that more explicit use of Bayesian mathematics in process tracing is impractical and would convey a false sense of precision (Beach and Pedersen 2013a; although Beach and Pedersen 2013b urge more explicit and transparent use of Bayesian logic, if not specific use of mathematical probability estimates).

A powerful argument for using Bayesian mathematics more explicitly in process tracing is that this only asks researchers to make specific and public the assumptions that they must make implicitly for process tracing to work. The process of clearly specifying the likelihood of finding a certain kind of evidence, not only conditional on the truth of a theory, but also conditional on the falsity of the theory, can push researchers to clarify their own thinking. It also makes this thinking more transparent and subject to challenge by other scholars, eliminating the considerable ambiguity in many verbal phrases used to convey probabilities.

Using Bayesian mathematics explicitly to update priors and likelihood ratios can also push researchers to be more consistent in their logic as they update their confidence in alternative theories and explanations. Evidence is mixed on whether trained scholars, or people in general, are typically good (Gigerenzer and Hoffrage 1995) or poor (Casscells *et al.* 1978) at intuitively approximating Bayesian logic. Further research is warranted on whether scholars proceed differently or reach different conclusions when they use Bayesian mathematics explicitly rather than implicitly, and whether explicit use of Bayesianism helps to counteract the cognitive biases identified in lab experiments (see also Checkel and Bennett, this volume, Chapter 10).

There are examples of process tracing where scholars have been exceptionally careful and explicit in the evidence they used and the type of tests (hoop tests, smoking-gun tests, etc.) they applied in making inferences (Fairfield 2013). There are as yet no full-fledged examples where scholars have done process tracing with explicit priors and numerical Bayesian updating, however, so this remains an area where the advice of at least some methodologists diverges from the practices of working researchers.[26] Whether one prefers to use Bayesian logic implicitly or explicitly, understanding this logic helps to clarify the logic of process tracing.

---

[26] Abell (2009: 59–61) provides a brief illustrative example of explicit Bayesian updating in process tracing. In this example, he uses a panel of trained researchers, rather than an individual researcher, to estimate likelihood ratios based on shared evidence from the case.

References

Abadie, Alberto. 2006. "Poverty, Political Freedom, and the Roots of Terrorism." *American Economic Review* 96/2: 50–56.

Abell, Peter. 2009. "A Case for Cases: Comparative Narratives in Sociological Research." *Sociological Methods and Research* 38/1: 38–70.

Acemoglu, Daron, Simon Johnson, and James A. Robinson. 2001. "The Colonial Origins of Comparative Development: An Empirical Investigation." *American Economic Review* 91/5: 1369–1401.

Acharya, Amitav and Alastair Iain Johnston (eds.). 2007. *Crafting Cooperation: Regional International Institutions in Comparative Perspective.* Cambridge University Press.

Adler, Emanuel. 1997. "Seizing the Middle Ground: Constructivism in World Politics." *European Journal of International Relations* 3/3: 319–363.

2013. "Constructivism and International Relations: Sources, Contributions and Debates," in Walter Carlsnaes, Thomas Risse, and Beth Simmons (eds.). *Handbook of International Relations,* 2nd edn. London: Sage Publications.

Adler, Emanuel and Vincent Pouliot. 2011a. "International Practices." *International Theory* 3/1: 1–36.

(eds.). 2011b. *International Practices.* Cambridge University Press.

Akhromeev, S. F. and G. Kornienko. 1992. *Glazami marshala i diplomata.* Moscow: Mezhdunarodnye otnosheniia.

Akhromeeva, Tamara Vasil'evna. 1995. "Ia nikogda ne poveriu, chto on ukhodil na smert' . . ." *Sovershenno sekretno* 7: 16–17.

Albouy, David. 2012. "The Colonial Origins of Comparative Development: An Empirical Investigation: Comment." *American Economic Review* 102/6: 3059–3076.

Alexander, Gerard. 2002. *The Sources of Democratic Consolidation.* Ithaca, NY: Cornell University Press.

Angrist, Joshua D. and Alan Krueger. 2001. "Instrumental Variables and the Search for Identification: From Supply and Demand to Natural Experiments." *Journal of Economic Perspectives* 15/4: 69–85.

Angrist, Joshua D. and Jörn-Steffen Pischke. 2008. *Mostly Harmless Econometrics: An Empiricist's Companion.* Princeton University Press.

Arbatov, Georgii. 1990. "Armiia dlia strany ili strana dlia armii?" *Ogonek* 5: 4.

Autesserre, Severine. 2009. "Hobbes and the Congo: Frames, Local Violence and International Intervention." *International Organization* 63/2: 249–280.

2010. *The Trouble with the Congo: Local Violence and the Failure of International Peacebuilding.* Cambridge University Press.

Bakke, Kristin. 2013. "Copying and Learning from Outsiders? Assessing Diffusion from Transnational Insurgents in the Chechen Wars," in Jeffrey T. Checkel (ed.). *Transnational Dynamics of Civil War*. Cambridge University Press.

Baklanov, Oleg. 1991a. "Ob itogakh obsuzhdeniya v komissii TsK KPSS po voennoi politiki partii khoda razrabotki kontseptsii voennoi reformy i perspektiv razvitiia Vooruzhennykh Sil SSSR. 8 ianvariia (memorandum reporting on a meeting of 12 December 1990)," in Rossiiskii Gosudarstvennyi Arkhiv Noveishei Istorii (RGANI), Fond 89, Opis' 21, Delo 63.

1991b. "Ob itogakh obsuzhdeniia v komissii TsK KPSS po voennoi politiki khoda peregovorov po sokrashcheniiu vooruzhenii. 6 fevral'iia," in Rossiiskii Gosudarstvennyi Arkhiv Noveishei Istorii (RGANI), Fond 89, Opis' 21, Delo 63.

Barnett, Michael. 2002. *Eyewitness to a Genocide: The United Nations and Rwanda*. Ithaca, NY: Cornell University Press.

Barnett, Michael and Raymond Duvall. 2005. "Power in International Politics." *International Organization* 59/1: 39–75.

Barnett, Michael and Martha Finnemore. 2004. *Rules for the World: International Organizations in Global Politics*. Ithaca, NY: Cornell University Press.

Bates, Robert, Barry Weingast, Avner Greif, Margaret Levi, and Jean-Laurent Rosenthal. 1998. *Analytic Narratives*. Princeton University Press.

Bazzi, Samuel and Christopher Blattman. 2011. "Economic Shocks and Conflict: The (Absence of?) Evidence from Commodity Prices." Unpublished manuscript.

Beach, Derek and Rasmus Brun Pedersen. 2013a. *Process-Tracing Methods: Foundations and Guidelines*. Ann Arbor, MI: University of Michigan Press.

2013b. "Turning Observations into Evidence: Using Bayesian Logic to Evaluate What Inferences Are Possible without Evidence." Paper presented at the Annual Meeting of the American Political Science Association. Chicago, IL (September).

Bendor, J., A. Glazer, and T. Hammond. 2001. "Theories of Delegation." *Annual Review of Political Science* 4: 235–269.

Bennett, Andrew. 1999. *Condemned to Repetition?: The Rise, Fall, and Reprise of Soviet-Russian Military Interventionism, 1973–1996*. Cambridge, MA: MIT Press.

2003. "Trust Bursting Out All Over: The Soviet Side of German Unification," in William C. Wohlforth (ed.). *Cold War Endgame: Oral History, Analysis, Debates*. University Park, PA: Pennsylvania State University Press.

2007. "Multimethod Work: Dispatches from the Front Lines." *Qualitative Methods: Newsletter of the Qualitative Methods Section of the American Political Science Association* 5/1: 9–11.

2008. "Process Tracing: A Bayesian Approach," in Janet Box-Steffensmeier, Henry Brady, and David Collier (eds.). *Oxford Handbook of Political Methodology*. Oxford University Press, pp. 702–721.

2010. "Process Tracing and Causal Inference," in Henry Brady and David Collier (eds.). *Rethinking Social Inquiry: Diverse Tools, Shared Standards*, 2nd edn. Lanham, MD: Rowman & Littlefield.

2013a. "Causal Mechanisms and Typological Theories in the Study of Civil Conflict," in Jeffrey T. Checkel (ed.). *Transnational Dynamics of Civil War*. Cambridge University Press.

2013b. "The Mother of All Isms: Causal Mechanisms and Structured Pluralism in International Relations Theory." *European Journal of International Relations* 19/3: 459–481.

Bennett, Andrew and Colin Elman. 2007. "Case Study Methods in the International Relations Subfield." *Comparative Political Studies*. 40/2: 170–195.

Berger, James. 2006. "The Case for Objective Bayesian Analysis." *Bayesian Analysis* 1/3: 385–402.

Berman, Nicholas and Mathieu Couttenier. 2013. "External Shocks, Internal Shots: The Geography of Civil Conflicts." Unpublished manuscript.

Berman, Sheri. 1998. *The Social Democratic Moment: Ideas and Politics in the Making of Interwar Europe*. Cambridge, MA: Harvard University Press.

Beschloss, Michael R. and Strobe Talbott. 1993. *At the Highest Levels: The Inside Story of the End of the Cold War*. Boston: Little Brown & Co.

Blanton, Thomas. 2010. "US Policy and the Revolutions of 1989," in Svetlana Savranskaya, Thomas Blanton, and Vladislav Zubok (eds). *Masterpieces of History: The Peaceful End of the Cold War in Europe, 1989*. Budapest: Central European University Press.

Blattman, Chris. 2009. "From Violence to Voting: War and Political Participation in Uganda." *American Political Science Review* 103/2: 231–247.

Bleich, Erik. 2003. *Race Politics in Britain and France: Ideas and Policymaking since the 1960s*. Cambridge University Press.

Blyth, Mark. 2002. *Great Transformations: Economic Ideas and Institutional Change in the Twentieth Century*. Cambridge University Press.

Bourdieu, Pierre. 1990. *The Logic of Practice*. Stanford University Press.

Brady, Henry and David Collier (eds.). 2010. *Rethinking Social Inquiry: Diverse Tools, Shared Standards*, 2nd edn. Lanham, MD: Rowman & Littlefield.

Brooks, Stephen G. 1997. "Dueling Realisms (Realism in International Relations)." *International Organization* 51/3: 445–477.

2005. *Producing Security: Multinational Corporations, Globalization, and the Changing Calculus of Conflict*. Princeton University Press.

Brooks, Stephen G. and William C. Wohlforth. 2002. "From Old Thinking to New Thinking in Qualitative Research." *International Security* 26/4 (Spring): 93–111.

2003. "Economic Constraints and the End of the Cold War," in William C. Wohlforth (ed.). *Cold War Endgame: Oral History, Analysis, Debates*. University Park, PA: Pennsylvania State University Press.

2000. "Power, Globalization and the End of the Cold War: Reevaluating a Landmark Case for Ideas." *International Security* 25/3: 5–53.

Brown, Archie. 1996. *The Gorbachev Factor*. Oxford University Press.

2007. *Seven Years that Changed the World: Perestroika in Perspective*. Oxford University Press.

Buhaug, Halvard, Lars-Erik Cederman, and Jan Ketil Rod. 2008. "Disaggregating Ethno-Nationalist Civil Wars: A Dyadic Test of Exclusion Theory." *International Organization* 62/3: 531–551.

Bunge, Mario. 1997. "Mechanism and Explanation." *Philosophy of the Social Sciences* 27/4: 410–465.

2004. "How Does It Work? The Search for Explanatory Mechanisms." *Philosophy of the Social Sciences* 34/2: 182–210.

Capoccia, Giovanni and R. Daniel Kelemen. 2007. "The Study of Critical Junctures: Theory, Narrative, and Counterfactuals in Historical Institutionalism." *World Politics* 59/3: 341–369.

Caporaso, James, Jeffrey T. Checkel, and Joseph Jupille. 2003. "Integrating Institutions: Rationalism, Constructivism and the Study of the European Union – Introduction." *Comparative Political Studies* 36/1–2: 7–41.

Cartwright, Nancy and Jeremy Hardie. 2012. *Evidence-Based Policy: A Practical Guide to Doing It Better*. Oxford University Press.

Casscells, W., A. Schoenberger, and T. B. Graboys. 1978. "Interpretation by Physicians of Clinical Laboratory Results." *New England Journal of Medicine* 299: 999–1001.

Caughey, Devin M. and Jasjeet S. Sekhon. 2011. "Elections and the Regression-Discontinuity Design: Lessons from Close U.S. House Races, 1942–2008." *Political Analysis* 19: 385–408.

Cederman, Lars-Erik and Luc Girardin. 2007. "Beyond Fractionalization: Mapping Ethnicity onto Nationalist Insurgencies." *American Political Science Review* 101/1: 173–186.

Cederman, Lars-Erik, Andreas Wimmer, and Brian Min. 2010. "Why Do Ethnic Groups Rebel? New Data and Analysis." *World Politics* 62/1: 87–119.

Checkel, Jeffrey T. 1997. *Ideas and International Political Change: Soviet/Russian Behavior and the End of the Cold War*. New Haven, CT: Yale University Press.

2003. "'Going Native' in Europe? Theorizing Social Interaction in European Institutions." *Comparative Political Studies* 36/1–2: 209–231.

(ed.). 2007. *International Institutions and Socialization in Europe*. Cambridge University Press.

2008. "Process Tracing," in Audie Klotz and Deepa Prakash (eds.). *Qualitative Methods in International Relations: A Pluralist Guide*. New York: Palgrave Macmillan.

2013a. "Theoretical Pluralism in IR: Possibilities and Limits," in Walter Carlsnaes, Thomas Risse, and Beth Simmons (eds.). *Handbook of International Relations*, 2nd edn. London: Sage Publications.

(ed.). 2013b. *Transnational Dynamics of Civil War*. Cambridge University Press.

Chernoff, Fred. 2002. "Scientific Realism as a Meta-Theory of International Relations." *International Studies Quarterly* 46/2: 189–207.

Coleman, James. 1986. *Foundations of Social Theory*. Cambridge, MA: Harvard University Press.

Collier, David. 1999. "Data, Field Work, and Extracting New Ideas at Close Range." *Newsletter of the Organized Section in Comparative Politics of the American Political Science Association* 10/1.

2011. "Understanding Process Tracing." *PS: Political Science and Politics* 44/3: 823–830.

Collier, David, Henry E. Brady, and Jason Seawright. 2004. "Toward an Alternative View of Methodology: Sources of Leverage in Causal Inference," in Henry E. Brady and David Collier (eds.). *Rethinking Social Inquiry: Diverse Tools, Shared Standards*. Lanham, MD: Rowman & Littlefield.

2010. "Sources of Leverage in Causal Inference: Towards an Alternative View of Methodology," in Henry E. Brady and David Collier (eds.). *Rethinking Social Inquiry: Diverse Tools, Shared Standards*, 2nd edn. Lanham, MD: Rowman & Littlefield.

Collier, Paul and Nicholas Sambanis (eds.). 2005. *Understanding Civil War: Evidence and Analysis*. New York: World Bank Publications.

Condra, Luke and Jacob Shapiro. 2012. "Who Takes the Blame? The Strategic Effects of Collateral Damage." *American Journal of Political Science* 56/1: 167–187.

Cook, S. D. N. and J. S. Brown. 1999. "Bridging Epistemologies: The Generative Dance between Organizational Knowledge and Organizational Knowing." *Organization Science* 10/4: 381–400.

Cox, Michael. 1990. "Whatever Happened to the 'Second' Cold War? Soviet–American Relations: 1980–1988." *Review of International Studies* 16/2: 155–172.

Culpepper, Pepper D. 2008. "The Politics of Common Knowledge: Ideas and Institutional Change in Wage Bargaining." *International Organization* 62/1: 1–33.

Cusack, Thomas R., Torben Iverson, and David Soskice. 2007. "Economic Interests and the Origins of Electoral Systems." *American Political Science Review* 101/3: 373–391.

De Soto, Hernando. 2000. *The Mystery of Capital: Why Capitalism Triumphs in the West and Fails Everywhere Else.* New York: Basic Books.

Dessler, David. 1999. "Constructivism within a Positivist Social Science." *Review of International Studies* 25/1: 123–137.

Deudney, Daniel and G. John Ikenberry. 2011a. "The End of the Cold War after 20 years: Reconsiderations, Retrospectives and Revisions." *International Politics* 48/4–5: 435–440.

2011b. "Pushing and Pulling: The Western System, Nuclear Weapons and Soviet Change." *International Politics* 48/4–5: 496–544.

De Vreese, Leen. 2008. "Causal (Mis)understanding and the Search for Scientific Explanations: A Case Study from the History of Medicine." *Studies in History and Philosophy of Biological and Biomedical Sciences* 39: 14–24.

Dobrynin, Anatoly. 1995. *In Confidence: Moscow's Ambassador to Six Cold War Presidents.* New York: Crown.

Doty, Roxanne Lynn. 1996. *Imperial Encounters: The Politics of Representation in North–South Relations.* Minneapolis, MN: University of Minnesota Press.

Doyle, Sir Arthur Conan. 1930. "The Adventure of the Blanched Soldier," in Doyle, *The Case-Book of Sherlock Holmes.* Published in *The Complete Sherlock Holmes.* Vol. 2. New York: Barnes and Noble Classics, 2003, pp. 528–529.

Drozdiak, William. 1990. "East and West Declare the End of Cold War at Paris Conference." *International Herald Tribune.* 20 November.

Dunning, Thad. 2008a. "Improving Causal Inference: Strengths and Limitations of Natural Experiments." *Political Research Quarterly* 61/2: 282–293.

2008b. "Natural and Field Experiments: The Role of Qualitative Methods." *Qualitative Methods: Newsletter of the American Political Science Association Organized Section for Qualitative and Multi-Method Research* 6/2: 17–22.

2008c. "Model Specification in Instrumental-Variables Regression." *Political Analysis* 16/3: 290–302.

2010. "Design-Based Inference: Beyond the Pitfalls of Regression Analysis?" in Henry Brady and David Collier (eds.). *Rethinking Social Inquiry: Diverse Tools, Shared Standards,* 2nd edn. Lanham, MD: Rowman & Littlefield.

2012. *Natural Experiments in the Social Sciences: A Design-Based Approach.* Cambridge University Press.

Earman, John. 1992. *Bayes or Bust: A Critical Examination of Bayesian Confirmation Theory.* Cambridge, MA: MIT Press.

Eels, Ellery and Branden Fitelson. 2002. "Symmetries and Asymmetries in Evidential Support." *Philosophical Studies* 107: 129–142.

Elman, Colin. 2005. "Explanatory Typologies in Qualitative Studies of International Politics." *International Organization* 59/2: 293–326.

Elman, Colin and Diana Kapiszewski. 2014. "Data Access and Research Transparency in the Qualitative Tradition." *PS: Political Science & Politics* 47/1: 43–47.

Elster, Jon. 1989. *Nuts and Bolts for the Social Sciences*. Cambridge University Press.

1998. "A Plea for Mechanisms," in Peter Hedstroem and Richard Swedberg (eds.). *Social Mechanisms: An Analytical Approach to Social Theory*. Cambridge University Press, pp. 45–73.

English, Robert D. 2000. *Russia and the Idea of the West: Gorbachev, Intellectuals, and the End of the Cold War*. New York: Columbia University Press.

2002. "Power, Ideas, and New Evidence on the Cold War's End: A Reply to Brooks and Wohlforth." *International Security* 26/4: 70–92.

2003. "The Road(s) Not Taken: Causality and Contingency in Analysis of the Cold War's End," in William C. Wohlforth (ed.). *Cold War Endgame: Oral History, Analysis, Debates*. University Park, PA: Pennsylvania State University Press.

Evangelista, Matthew. 1986. "The New Soviet Approach to Security." *World Policy Journal* 3/4.

1991. "Sources of Moderation in Soviet Security Policy," in Philip Tetlock, Robert Jervis, Jo Husbands, Paul Stern, and Charles Tilly (eds.). *Behavior, Society, and Nuclear War 2*. Oxford University Press.

1993. "Internal and External Constraints on Grand Strategy: The Soviet Case," in Richard Rosecrance and Arthur Stein (eds.). *The Domestic Bases of Grand Strategy*. Ithaca, NY: Cornell University Press.

1999. *Unarmed Forces: The Transnational Movement to End the Cold War*. Ithaca, NY: Cornell University Press.

Fairfield, Tasha. 2013. "Going Where the Money Is: Strategies for Taxing Economic Elites in Unequal Democracies." *World Development* 47: 42–57.

Falkenrath, Richard A. 1995. *Shaping Europe's Military Order: The Origins and Consequences of the CFE Treaty*. Cambridge, MA: MIT Press.

Falleti, Tulia G. and Julia F. Lynch. 2009. "Context and Causal Mechanisms in Political Analysis." *Comparative Political Studies* 42/9: 1143–1166.

Fearon, James and Alexander Wendt. 2002. "Rationalism v. Constructivism: A Skeptical View," in Walter Carlsnaes, Thomas Risse, and Beth Simmons (eds.). *Handbook of International Relations*. London: Sage Publications.

Fearon, James and David Laitin. 2003. "Ethnicity, Insurgency, and Civil War." *American Political Science Review* 97/1: 75–90.

Field, Hartry. 2009. "A Note on Jeffrey Conditionalization." *Philosophy of Science* 45: 361–367.

Finnemore, Martha. 1996. *National Interests in International Society*. Ithaca, NY: Cornell University Press.

Finnemore, Martha and Kathryn Sikkink. 1998. "International Norm Dynamics and Political Change." *International Organization* 52/4: 887–917.

Fitelson, Branden. 2001. "A Bayesian Account of Independent Evidence with Applications." *Philosophy of Science* 68/3: S123–S140.

FitzGerald, Mary. 1989. "The Dilemma in Moscow's Defensive Force Posture." *Arms Control Today* 19/9.

Forsberg, Randall. 1981a. "The Prospects for Arms Control and Disarmament: A View from Moscow." Brookline, MA: Institute for Defense and Disarmament Studies.

1981b. "Randall Forsberg Visit to Moscow, 8–18 December 1981: List of Organizations and People Visited." Brookline, MA: Institute for Defense and Disarmament Studies.

1985. "Parallel Cuts in Nuclear and Conventional Forces." *Bulletin of the Atomic Scientists* (August): 152–156.

1987. "Alternative Defense in the Soviet Union: A Discussion with Alexei Arbatov." Transcript. November 4. Brookline, MA: Institute for Defense and Disarmament Studies.

1989. "Report on Moscow IGCC Conference, 2–8 October 1988." *Defense and Disarmament Alternatives* 2/1.

Freedman, David A. 1999. "From Association to Causation: Some Remarks on the History of Statistics." *Statistical Science* 14: 243–258.

2008a. "On Regression Adjustments to Experimental Data." *Advances in Applied Mathematics* 40: 180–193.

2008b. "On Regression Adjustments in Experiments with Several Treatments." *Annals of Applied Statistics* 2: 176–196.

2009. *Statistical Models: Theory and Practice*, 2nd edn. Cambridge University Press.

2010. "On Types of Scientific Inquiry: The Role of Qualitative Reasoning," in David Collier, Jasjeet S. Sekhon, and Philip B. Stark (eds.). *Statistical Models and Causal Inference: A Dialogue with the Social Sciences*. Cambridge University Press, pp. 337–356.

Friedrichs, Joerg and Friedrich Kratochwil. 2009. "On Acting and Knowing: How Pragmatism Can Advance International Relations Research and Methodology." *International Organization* 63/4: 701–731.

Fujii, Lee Ann. 2010. "Shades of Truth and Lies: Interpreting Testimonies of War and Violence." *Journal of Peace Research* 47/2: 231–241.

Galiani, Sebastian and Ernesto Schargrodsky. 2004. "The Health Effects of Land Titling." *Economics and Human Biology* 2: 353–372.

2010. "Property Rights for the Poor: Effects of Land Titling." *Journal of Public Economics* 94: 700–729.

Gallow, J. Dmitri. 2014. "How to Learn from Theory-Dependent Evidence; or Commutativity and Holism: A Solution for Conditionalizers." *British Journal for the Philosophy of Science* 65: 493–519.

Gates, Robert. 2010. "Gorbachev's Gameplan: The Long View." Memorandum, November 24, 1987, in Svetlana Savranskaya, Thomas Blanton, and Vladislav Zubok (eds.). *Masterpieces of History: The Peaceful End of the Cold War in Europe, 1989*. Budapest: Central European University Press.

Gates, Scott. 2008. "Mixing It Up: The Role of Theory in Mixed-Methods Research." *Qualitative Methods: Newsletter of the American Political Science Association Organized Section for Qualitative and Multi-Method Research* 6/1: 27–29.

Geddes, Barbara. 2003. *Paradigms and Sand Castles: Theory Building and Research Design in Comparative Politics*. Ann Arbor, MI: University of Michigan Press.

Gerber, Alan S. and Donald P. Green. 2012. *Field Experiments: Design, Analysis, and Interpretation*. New York: W. W. Norton & Co.

Geertz, Clifford. 1973. *The Interpretation of Cultures*. New York: Basic Books.

1987. "'From the Native's Point of View': On the Nature of Anthropological Understanding," in Michael. T. Gibbons (ed.). *Interpreting Politics*. Oxford: Blackwell, pp. 133–147.

Gelman, Harry. 1992. *The Rise and Fall of National Security Decisionmaking in the Former USSR*. RAND Report R-4200-A. Santa Monica, CA.

George, Alexander L. 1979. "Case Studies and Theory Development: The Method of Structured, Focused Comparison," in Paul Gordon Lauren (ed.). *Diplomatic History: New Approaches*. New York: Free Press.

  1993. *Bridging the Gap: Theory and Practice in Foreign Policy*. Washington, DC: US Institute of Peace Press.

George, Alexander L. and Andrew Bennett. 2005. *Case Studies and Theory Development in the Social Sciences*. Cambridge, MA: MIT Press.

Gerring, John 2007a. *Case Study Research. Principles and Practices*. Cambridge University Press.

  2007b. "Review Article: The Mechanismic Worldview: Thinking Inside the Box." *British Journal of Political Science* 38/1: 161–179.

Gheciu, Alexandra. 2005. *NATO in the "New Europe": The Politics of International Socialization after the Cold War*. Stanford University Press.

Gigerenzer, Gerd and Ulrich Hoffrage. 1995. "How to Improve Bayesian Reasoning without Instruction: Frequency Formats." *Psychological Review* 102/4: 684–704.

Glaser, Barney G. and Anselm Strauss. 1967. *The Discovery of Grounded Theory: Strategies for Qualitative Research*. Chicago, IL: Aldine Publishing Co.

Goertz, Gary and James Mahoney. 2012. *A Tale of Two Cultures: Qualitative and Quantitative Research in the Social Sciences*. Princeton University Press.

Goldstein, Judith. 1993. *Ideas, Interests, and American Trade Policy*. Ithaca, NY: Cornell University Press.

Goodwin, Jeff. 2001. *No Other Way Out: States and Revolutionary Movements, 1945–1991*. Cambridge University Press.

Gorbachev, Mikhail. 1988a. Letter to Frank von Hippel. November 16, 1987, in *F.A.S. Public Interest Report* 41/2 (February).

  1988b. Address to 43rd United Nations General Assembly Session. December 7.

  1995a. *Zhizn' i reformy* 1. Moscow: Novosti.

  1995b. *Zhizn' i reformy* 2. Moscow: Novosti.

Gorski, Philip S. 2003. *The Disciplinary Revolution: Calvinism and the Rise of the State in Early Modern Europe*. University of Chicago Press.

Grieco, Joseph. 1997. "Realist International Theory and the Study of World Politics," in Michael Doyle and G. John Ikenberry (eds.). *New Thinking in International Relations*. New York: Westview Press.

Gross, Neil. 2009. "A Pragmatist Theory of Social Mechanisms." *American Sociological Review* 74/2: 358–379.

Gunnell, John G. 2011. "Social Scientific Inquiry and Meta-Theoretical Fantasy: The Case of International Relations." *Review of International Studies* 37/4: 1447–1469.

Gusterson, Hugh. 1993. "Exploding Anthropology's Canon in the World of the Bomb: Ethnographic Writing on Militarism." *Journal of Contemporary Ethnography* 22/1: 59–79.

  2008. "Ethnographic Research," in Audie Klotz and Deepa Prakash (eds.). *Qualitative Methods in International Relations: A Pluralist Guide*. New York: Palgrave Macmillan.

Guzzini, Stefano. 2011. "Securitization as a Causal Mechanism." *Security Dialogue* 42/4–5: 329–341.

(ed.). 2012. *The Return of Geopolitics in Europe? Social Mechanisms and Foreign Policy Identity Crises*. Cambridge University Press.

Haas, Peter. 2010. "Practicing Analytic Eclecticism." *Qualitative & Multi-Method Research: Newsletter of the American Political Science Association Organized Section for Qualitative and Multi-Method Research* 8/2: 9–14.

Hacker, Jacob S. and Paul Pierson. 2005. *Off Center: The Republican Revolution and the Erosion of American Democracy*. New Haven, CT: Yale University Press.

Hall, Peter A. 1993. "Policy Paradigms, Social Learning, and the State." *Comparative Politics* 25/3: 275–296.

2003. "Aligning Ontology and Methodology in Comparative Politics," in J. Mahoney and D. Rueschemeyer (eds.). *Comparative Historical Analysis in the Social Sciences*. Cambridge University Press.

2013. "Tracing the Progress of Process Tracing." *European Political Science* 12/1: 20–30.

Halliday, Fred. 1983. *The Making of the Second Cold War*. London: Verso.

Hansen, Lene. 2006. *Security as Practice: Discourse Analysis and the Bosnian War*. London; New York: Routledge.

2011. "Performing Practices: A Poststructuralist Analysis of the Muhammad Cartoon Crisis," in Emanuel Adler and Vincent Pouliot (eds.). *International Practices*. Cambridge University Press, pp. 280–309.

Hawkins, Darren, David Lake, Daniel Nielson, and Michael Tierney (eds.). 2006. *Delegation and Agency in International Organizations*. Cambridge University Press.

Hawthorne, James. 2004. "Three Models of Sequential Belief Updating on Uncertain Evidence." *Journal of Philosophical Logic* 33: 97–98.

Heckman, James. 2000. "Causal Parameters and Policy Analysis in Economics: A Twentieth Century Retrospective." *Quarterly Journal of Economics* 115/1: 45–97.

Hedström, Peter and Richard Swedberg (eds.). 1998. *Social Mechanisms. An Analytical Approach to Social Theory*. Cambridge University Press.

Hedström, Peter and Petri Ylikoski. 2010. "Causal Mechanisms in the Social Sciences." *Annual Review of Sociology* 36: 49–67.

Hellman, Geoffrey. 1997. "Bayes and Beyond." *Philosophy of Science* 64/2: 191–221.

Héritier, Adrienne. 2007. *Explaining Institutional Change in Europe*. Oxford University Press.

Hernes, Gudmund. 1998. "Real Virtuality," in Peter Hedström and Richard Swedberg (eds.). *Social Mechanisms: An Analytical Approach to Social Theory*. Cambridge University Press, pp. 74–101.

Herspring, Dale. 1990. *The Soviet High Command, 1967–1989: Personalities and Politics*. Princeton University Press.

Ho, Daniel, Kosuke Imai, Gary King, and Elizabeth Stuart. 2007. "Matching as Nonparametric Preprocessing for Reducing Model Dependence in Parametric Causal Inference." *Political Analysis* 15/3: 199–236.

Hobarth, Robin. 1972. "Process Tracing in Clinical Judgment: An Analytical Approach." Ph.D. Thesis. University of Chicago.

Hoffmann, Matthew. 2008. "Agent-Based Modeling," in Audie Klotz and Deepa Prakash (eds.). *Qualitative Methods in International Relations: A Pluralist Guide*. New York: Palgrave Macmillan.

Holzscheiter, Anna. 2010. *Children's Rights in International Politics: The Transformative Power of Discourse*. London: Palgrave Macmillan.

Hooghe, Liesbet and Gary Marks. 2009. "A Postfunctionalist Theory of European Integration: From Permissive Consensus to Constraining Dissensus." *British Journal of Political Science* 39/1: 1–23.

Hopf, Ted. 2002. *Social Construction of International Politics: Identities and Foreign Policies, Moscow, 1955 and 1999*. Ithaca, NY: Cornell University Press.

   2007. "The Limits of Interpreting Evidence," in Richard Ned Lebow and Mark Irving Lichbach (eds.). *Theory and Evidence in Comparative Politics and International Relations*. London: Palgrave Macmillan, pp. 55–84.

   2012. *Reconstructing the Cold War*. Oxford University Press.

Horiuchi, Yusaka and Jun Saito. 2009. "Rain, Elections and Money: The Impact of Voter Turnout on Distributive Policy Outcomes in Japan." ASIA Pacific Economic Paper No. 379.

Hoxby, Caroline M. 2000. "Does Competition Among Public Schools Benefit Students and Taxpayers?" *American Economic Review* 90/5: 1209–1238.

Humphreys, Macartan and Alan Jacobs. 2013. "Mixing Methods: A Bayesian Unification of Qualitative and Quantitative Approaches." Paper presented at the Annual Meeting of the American Political Science Association. Chicago, IL (September).

Humphreys, Macartan and Jeremy Weinstein. 2008. "Who Fights? The Determinants of Participation in Civil War." *American Journal of Political Science* 52/2: 436–455.

Independent Commission on Disarmament and Security Issues. 1982. *Common Security: A Blueprint for Survival*. New York: Simon & Schuster.

Institut mirovoi ekonomiki i mezhdunarodnykh otnoshenii (IMEMO). 1987. *Disarmament and Security 1986*. Vol. 1. Moscow: Akademiia Nauk SSSR.

Iyer, Lakshmi. 2010. "Direct vs. Indirect Colonial Rule in India: Long-Term Consequences." *Review of Economics and Statistics* 92/4: 693–713.

Istochnik. 1993. 5–6: 130–147.

Jackson, Patrick Thaddeus. 2006a. *Civilizing the Enemy: German Reconstruction and the Invention of the West*. Ann Arbor, MI: University of Michigan Press.

   2006b. "Making Sense of Making Sense: Configurational Analysis and the Double Hermeneutic," in Dvora Yanow and Peregrine Schwartz-Shea (eds.). *Interpretation and Method: Empirical Research Methods and the Interpretive Turn*. New York: M. E. Sharpe, pp. 264–280.

   2011. *The Conduct of Inquiry in International Relations*. London: Routledge.

Jacobs, Alan M. 2011. *Governing for the Long Term: Democracy and the Politics of Investment*. Cambridge University Press.

Jaeger, David and M. Daniele Paserman. 2008. "The Cycle of Violence? An Empirical Analysis of Fatalities in the Palestinian–Israeli Conflict." *American Economic Review* 98/4: 1591–1604.

Jeffrey, R. 1965. *The Logic of Decision*. New York: McGraw-Hill.

Johnson, James. 2006. "Consequences of Positivism: A Pragmatist Assessment." *Comparative Political Studies* 39/2: 224–252.

Johnston, Alastair Iain. 1996. "Learning Versus Adaptation: Explaining Change in Chinese Arms Control Policy in the 1980s and 1990s." *China Journal* 35: 27–61.

   2008. *Social States: China in International Institutions, 1980–2000*. Princeton University Press.

Kalyvas, Stathis. 2006. *The Logic of Violence in Civil War*. Cambridge University Press.

Kalyvas, Stathis and Matthew Kocher. 2007. "How 'Free' is Free-Riding in Civil War? Violence, Insurgency, and the Collective Action Problem." *World Politics* 59/2: 177–216.

Katzenstein, Peter and Rudra Sil. 2010. *Beyond Paradigms: Analytic Eclecticism in World Politics*. New York: Palgrave Macmillan.

Katzenstein, Peter, Robert Keohane, and Stephen Krasner. 1998. "International Organization and the Study of World Politics." *International Organization* 52/4: 645–686.

Kelley, Judith. 2004a. *Ethnic Politics in Europe: The Power of Norms and Incentives*. Princeton University Press.

2004b. "International Actors on the Domestic Scene: Membership Conditionality and Socialization by International Institutions." *International Organization* 58/3: 425–457.

Kennan, George F. (X). 1947. "The Sources of Soviet Conduct." *Foreign Affairs* (July): 566–582.

Keohane, Robert. 1984. *After Hegemony: Cooperation and Discord in the World Political Economy*. Princeton University Press.

Khong, Yuen Foong. 1992. *Analogies at War: Korea, Munich, Dien Bien Phu, and the Vietnam Decisions of 1965*. Princeton University Press.

King, Gary, Robert Keohane, and Sidney Verba. 1994. *Designing Social Inquiry. Scientific Inference in Qualitative Research*. Princeton University Press.

Kirilenko, G. 1990. "Legko li byt' oborone dostatochnoi?" *Krasnaia zvezda*. March 21.

Kocher, Matthew, Thomas Pepinsky, and Stathis Kalyvas. 2011. "Aerial Bombing and Counterinsurgency in the Vietnam War." *American Journal of Political Science* 55/2: 201–218.

Kokoshin, Andrei. 1988. "Alexander Svechin: On War and Politics." *International Affairs* (November).

Kokoshin, Andrei and Valentin V. Larionov. 1987. "Kurskaia bitva v svete sovremennoi oboronitel'noi doktriny." *Mirovaia ekonomika i mezhdunarodnye otnosheniia* 8: 32–40.

Kokoshin, Andrei and V. N. Lobov. 1990. "Prevideniia (Svechin ob evoliutsii voennogo iskusstva)." *Znamia* 2: 170–182.

Kramer, Mark. 2001. "Realism, Ideology, and the End of the Cold War: A Reply to William Wohlforth." *Review of International Studies* 27/1: 119–130.

Krasner, Stephen D. 1978. *Defending the National Interest: Raw Materials Investments and US Foreign Policy*. Princeton University Press.

Krebs, Ronald R. and Patrick Thaddeus Jackson. 2007. "Twisting Tongues and Twisting Arms: The Power of Political Rhetoric." *European Journal of International Relations* 13/1: 35–66.

Kreuzer, Marcus. 2010. "Historical Knowledge and Quantitative Analysis: The Case of the Origins of Proportional Representation." *American Political Science Review* 104/2: 369–392.

Kuehn, David. 2013. "Combining Game Theory Models and Process Tracing: Potential and Limits." *European Political Science* 12/1: 52–63.

Kuehn, David and Ingo Rohlfing. 2009. "Does It, Really? Measurement Error and Omitted Variables in Multi-Method Research." *Qualitative Methods: Newsletter of the American Political Science Association Organized Section for Qualitative and Multi-Method Research* 7/2: 18–22.

Kurki, Mlija. 2008. *Causation in International Relations: Reclaiming Causal Analysis*. Cambridge University Press.

Kurth, James. 1971. "A Widening Gyre: The Logic of American Weapons Procurement." *Public Policy* 19/3: 373–404.

Ladbury, Sarah. 2009. "Testing Hypotheses on Radicalisation in Afghanistan: Why Do Men Join the Taliban and Hizb-i Islami? How Much Do Local Communities Support Them?" Technical report, Department for International Development (DFID). London.

Laitin, David. 1998. *Identity in Formation: The Russian-speaking Populations in the Near Abroad*. Ithaca, NY: Cornell University Press.

Lakatos, Imre. 1970. "Falsification and the Methodology of Scientific Research Programs," in Imre Lakatos and A. Musgrave (eds.). *Criticism and the Growth of Knowledge*. Cambridge University Press.

Lake, David. 2010. "Two Cheers for Bargaining Theory: Assessing Rationalist Explanations for the Iraq War." *International Security* 35/3: 7–52.

    2011. "Why 'Isms' are Evil: Theory, Epistemology, and Academic Sects as Impediments to Understanding and Progress." *International Studies Quarterly* 55/2: 465–480.

Layne, Christopher. 1994. "Kant or Cant: The Myth of the Democratic Peace." *International Security* 19/2: 5–49.

Lebow, Richard Ned. 1985. "The Soviet Offensive in Europe: The Schlieffen Plan Revisited?" *International Security* 9/4: 44–78.

    1994. "The Long Peace, the End of the Cold War, and the Failure of Realism." *International Organization* 48/2: 249–277.

Lebow, Richard Ned and Thomas Risse-Kappen (eds.). 1995. *International Relations Theory and the End of the Cold War*. New York: Columbia University Press.

Lee, David S. 2008. "Randomized Experiments from Non-Random Selection in U.S. House Elections." *Journal of Econometrics* 142: 675–697.

Leibfried, Stephan and Paul Pierson. 1995. *European Social Policy. Between Fragmentation and Integration*. Washington, DC: Brookings.

Lévesque, Jacques. 1997. *The Enigma of 1989: The USSR and the Liberation of Eastern Europe*. Berkeley, CA: University of California Press.

Levy, Jack S. 1994. "Learning and Foreign Policy: Sweeping a Conceptual Minefield." *International Organization* 48/2: 279–312.

Lieberman, Evan. 2005. "Nested Analysis as a Mixed-Method Strategy for Comparative Research." *American Political Science Review* 99/3: 435–452.

    2009. *Boundaries of Contagion: How Ethnic Politics Have Shaped Government Responses to AIDS*. Princeton University Press.

Lin, Ann Chih. 1998. "Bridging Positivist and Interpretivist Approaches to Qualitative Methods." *Policy Studies Journal* 26/1: 162–180.

Liubimov, Iu. 1989. "O dostatochnosti oborony i nedostatke kompetentnosti." *Kommunist vooruzhennykh sil* 16: 21–26.

Lorentzen, Peter, M. Taylor Fravel, and Jack Paine. 2013. "Bridging the Gap: Using Qualitative Evidence to Evaluate Formal Models." Mimeo. Berkeley, CA and Cambridge, MA: University of California, Berkeley and Massachusetts Institute of Technology (August 5).

Lubkemann, Stephen. 2008. *Culture in Chaos: An Anthropology of the Social Condition in War*. University of Chicago Press.

Lupia, Arthur and Colin Elman. 2014. "Symposium – Openness in Political Science: Data Access and Research Transparency – Introduction." *PS: Political Science & Politics* 47/1: 19–42.

Lustick, Ian. 1996. "History, Historiography, and Political Science: Multiple Historical Records and the Problem of Selection Bias." *American Political Science Review* 90/3: 605–618.

Lyall, Jason. 2009. "Does Indiscriminate Repression Incite Insurgent Attacks? Evidence from Chechnya." *Journal of Conflict Resolution* 53/3: 331–362.

2013. "Bombing to Lose? Airpower and the Dynamics of Coercion in Counterinsurgency Wars." Unpublished manuscript.

Lyall, Jason, Graeme Blair, and Kosuke Imai. 2013. "Explaining Support for Combatants in Wartime: A Survey Experiment in Afghanistan." *American Political Science Review* 107/4: 679–705.

Lyall, Jason, Kosuke Imai, and Yuki Shiraito. 2013. "Coethnic Bias and Wartime Informing." Unpublished Manuscript.

MacCoun, Robert J. 1998. "Biases in the Interpretation and Use of Research Results." *Annual Review of Psychology* 49: 259–287.

McKeown, Timothy. 1999. "Case Studies and the Statistical World View." *International Organization* 53/1: 161–190.

Mahoney, James. 2000. "Path Dependence in Historical Sociology." *Theory and Society* 29/4: 507–548.

2001. "Review – Beyond Correlational Analysis: Recent Innovations in Theory and Method." *Sociological Forum* 16/3: 575–593.

2010. "After KKV: The New Methodology of Qualitative Research." *World Politics* 62/1: 120–147.

2012. "The Logic of Process Tracing Tests in the Social Sciences." *Sociological Methods and Research* 41/4: 570–597.

Martin, Lisa. 2000. *Democratic Commitments: Legislatures and International Cooperation*. Princeton University Press.

Martin, Lisa and Beth Simmons. 1998. "Theories and Empirical Studies of International Institutions." *International Organization* 52/4: 729–757.

2002. "International Organizations and Institutions," in Walter Carlsnaes, Thomas Risse, and Beth Simmons (eds.). *Handbook of International Relations*. London: Sage Publications, chapter 10.

2013. "International Organizations and Institutions," in Walter Carlsnaes, Thomas Risse, and Beth Simmons (eds.). *Handbook of International Relations*, 2nd edn. London: Sage Publications, chapter 13.

Mason, T. David and Dale Krane. 1989. "The Political Economy of Death Squads: Toward a Theory of the Impact of State-Sanctioned Terror." *International Studies Quarterly* 33/2: 175–198.

Mattern, Janice Bially. 2005. *Ordering International Politics: Identity, Crisis, and Representational Force*. London: Routledge.

Mayntz, Renate. 2004. "Mechanisms in the Analysis of Macro-Social Phenomena." *Philosophy of the Social Sciences* 34/2: 237–259.

Mearsheimer, John and Stephen Walt. 2013. "Leaving Theory Behind: Why Simplistic Hypothesis Testing is Bad for International Relations." *European Journal of International Relations* 19/3: 427–457.

Mendelson, Sarah. 1998. *Changing Course: Ideas, Politics, and the Soviet Withdrawal from Afghanistan*. Princeton University Press.

Merton, Robert K. 1949. "On Sociological Theories of the Middle Range," in Robert K. Merton. *Social Theory and Social Structure*. New York: Simon & Schuster / The Free Press, pp. 39–53.

1973. *The Sociology of Science*. University of Chicago Press.

Miguel, Edward, Shanker Satyanath, and Ernest Sergenti. 2004. "Economic Shocks and Civil Conflict: An Instrumental Variables Approach." *Journal of Political Economy* 112/4: 725–753.

Mill, John Stuart. 1868. *A System of Logic*. London: Longmans.

Mitchell, Ron. 1994. "Regime Design Matters: Intentional Oil Pollution and Treaty Compliance." *International Organization* 48/3: 425–458.

Moiseev, M. A. 1989. "Eshche raz o prestizhe armii." *Kommunist vooruzhennykh sil* 13: 3–14.

Moore Jr., Barrington. 1966. *Social Origins of Dictatorship and Democracy: Lord and Peasant in the Making of the Modern World*. Boston, MA: Beacon Press.

1978. *Injustice: The Social Bases of Obedience and Revolt*. New York: M. E. Sharpe.

Moravcsik, Andrew. 1993. "Preferences and Power in the European Community: A Liberal Intergovernmentalist Approach." *Journal of Common Market Studies* 31/4: 473–524.

1998. *The Choice for Europe. Social Purpose and State Power from Messina to Maastricht*. Ithaca, NY: Cornell University Press.

2010. "Active Citation: A Precondition for Replicable Qualitative Research." *PS: Political Science and Policy* 43/1: 29–35.

Nau, Henry. 2011. "No Alternative to 'Isms'." *International Studies Quarterly* 55/2: 487–491.

Neumann, Iver B. 1999. *Uses of the Other: "The East" in European Identity Formation*. Minneapolis, MN: University of Minnesota Press.

2002. "Returning Practice to the Linguistic Turn: The Case of Diplomacy." *Millennium – Journal of International Studies* 31/3: 627–651.

2008. "Discourse Analysis," in Audie Klotz and Deepa Prakash (eds.). *Qualitative Methods in International Relations: A Pluralist Guide*. New York: Palgrave Macmillan.

2012. *At Home with the Diplomats: Inside a European Foreign Ministry*. Ithaca, NY: Cornell University Press.

Nexon, Daniel. 2005. "Zeitgeist? The New Idealism in the Study of International Change." *Review of International Political Economy* 12/4: 700–719.

2009. *The Struggle for Power in Early Modern Europe: Religious Conflict, Dynastic Empires and International Change*. Princeton University Press.

Nickerson, Raymond S. 1998. "Confirmation Bias: A Ubiquitous Phenomenon in Many Guises." *Review of General Psychology* 2/2: 175–220.

Nome, Martin and Nils Weidmann. 2013. "Conflict Diffusion via Social Identities: Entrepreneurship and Adaptation," in Jeffrey T. Checkel (ed.). *Transnational Dynamics of Civil War*. Cambridge University Press, chapter 7.

Norkus, Zenonas. 2005. "Mechanisms as Miracle Makers? The Rise and Inconsistencies of the 'Mechanismic Approach' in Social Science and History." *History and Theory* 44/3: 348–372.

Norman, Ludvig. 2013. "From Friends to Foes: Institutional Conflict and Supranational Influence in the European Union." Skrifter utgivna av Statsvetenskapliga föreningen i Uppsala 186 (Ph.D. Thesis). Uppsala, Sweden: Uppsala University, Acta Universitatis Upsaliensis.

Oatley, Thomas. 2011. "The Reductionist Gamble: Open Economy Politics in the Global Economy." *International Organization* 65/2: 311–341.

Oberdorfer, Don. 1992. *The Turn: From the Cold War to a New Era*. New York: Poseidon Press.

Odom, William E. 1998. *The Collapse of the Soviet Military*. New Haven, CT: Yale University Press.

Ogarkov, Nikolai. 1985. *Istoriia uchit bditel'nosti*. Moscow: Voenizdat.

Olson, Mancur. 1965. *The Logic of Collective Action*. Cambridge, MA: Harvard University Press.

Oye, Kenneth A. 1995. "Explaining the End of the Cold War: Morphological and Behavioral Adaptations to the Nuclear Peace?" in Richard Ned Lebow and Thomas Risse-Kappen (eds.). *International Relations Theory and the End of the Cold War*. New York: Columbia University Press.

Parrott, Bruce. 1985. "Soviet Foreign Policy, Internal Politics, and Trade with the West," in Bruce Parrott (ed.). *Trade, Technology, and Soviet–American Relations*. Washington, DC: Center for Strategic and International Studies.

1988. "Soviet National Security under Gorbachev." *Problems of Communism* 37/6: 1–36.

Parsons, Craig. 2002. "Showing Ideas as Causes: The Origins of the European Union." *International Organization* 56/1: 47–84.

2003. *A Certain Idea of Europe*. Ithaca, NY: Cornell University Press.

Pawlak, Zdzisław. 2001. "Bayes' Theorem – the Rough Set Perspective." Available at http://bcpw.bg.pw.edu.pl/Content/1935/btrsp_or.pdf.

Phillips, R. Hyland and Jeffrey I. Sands. 1988. "Reasonable Sufficiency and Soviet Conventional Defense: A Research Note." *International Security* 13/2: 164–178.

Pierson, Paul. 1996. "The Path to European Integration: A Historical Institutionalist Perspective." *Comparative Political Studies* 29/2: 123–163.

2000. "Increasing Returns, Path Dependence, and the Study of Politics." *American Political Science Review* 94/2: 251–267.

Pollack, Mark. 2003. *The Engines of European Integration: Delegation, Agency, and Agenda Setting in the EU*. Oxford University Press.

Popkin, Samuel. 1979. *The Rational Peasant: The Political Economy of Rural Society in Vietnam*. Berkeley, CA: University of California Press.

Popper, Karl. 1959. *The Logic of Scientific Discovery*. New York: Basic Books.

1963. *Conjectures and Refutations. The Growth of Scientific Knowledge*. London: Routledge and Kegan Paul.

Posner, Daniel N. 2004. "The Political Salience of Cultural Difference: Why Chewas and Tumbukas Are Allies in Zambia and Adversaries in Malawi." *American Political Science Review* 98/4: 529–545.

Pouliot, Vincent. 2007. "'Sobjectivism': Toward a Constructivist Methodology." *International Studies Quarterly* 51/2: 257–288.

2008a. "The Logic of Practicality: A Theory of Practice of Security Communities." *International Organization* 62/2: 257–288.

2008b. "Reflexive Mirror: Everything Takes Place as if Threats Were Going Global," in Markus Kornprobst, Vincent Pouliot, Nisha Shah, and Ruben Zaiotti (eds.). *Metaphors of Globalization: Mirrors, Magicians and Mutinies*. London: Palgrave Macmillan, pp. 34–49.

2010. *International Security in Practice: The Politics of NATO–Russia Diplomacy*. Cambridge University Press.

2012. "Methodology: Putting Practice Theory in Practice," in Rebecca Adler-Nissen (ed.). *Pierre Bourdieu and International Relations*. London: Routledge, pp. 46–59.

Price, Richard. 1997. *The Chemical Weapons Taboo*. Ithaca, NY: Cornell University Press.

Price, Richard and Christian Reus-Smit. 1998. "Dangerous Liaisons? Critical International Theory and Constructivism." *European Journal of International Relations* 4/3: 259–294.

Prokhanov, Aleksandr. 1990. "Tragediia." *Literaturnaia Rossiia.* January 5.

Putnam, Robert. 1988. "Diplomacy and Domestic Politics: The Logic of Two–Level Games." *International Organization* 41/3: 427–460.

Putnam, Robert, with Robert Leonardi and Raffaella Nanetti. 1993. *Making Democracy Work: Civic Traditions in Modern Italy.* Princeton University Press.

Ragin, Charles. 1987. *The Comparative Method: Moving beyond Qualitative and Quantitative Strategies.* Berkeley, CA: University of California Press.

Reagan, Ronald. 1983. Address to the Nation on National Security. March 23.

   1992. *An American Life.* New York: Simon & Schuster.

Reus-Smit, Christian. 1999. *The Moral Purpose of the State: Culture, Social Identity, and Institutional Rationality in International Relations.* Princeton University Press.

Richards, Paul. 2011. "A Systematic Approach to Cultural Explanations of War: Tracing Causal Processes in Two West African Insurgencies." *World Development* 39/2: 212–220.

Richardson, Benjamin Ward. 1887 [1936]. "John Snow, M.D." *The Asclepiad.* Vol. 4. London: pp. 274–300. Reprinted in *Snow on Cholera.* London: Humphrey Milford/Oxford University Press.

Ringmar, Erik. 1997. "Alexander Wendt: A Social Scientist Struggling with History," in Iver B. Neumann and Ole Waever (eds.). *The Future of International Relations: Masters in the Making?* London: Routledge, pp. 269–289.

Risse, Thomas. 2000. "'Let's Argue!': Communicative Action in World Politics." *International Organization* 54/1: 1–39.

   2011. "Ideas, Discourse, Power and the End of the Cold War: 20 Years On." *International Politics* 48/4–5: 591–606.

   (ed.). 2014. *European Public Spheres: Bringing Politics Back In.* Cambridge University Press.

Risse, Thomas, Stephen Ropp, and Kathryn Sikkink (eds.). 1999. *The Power of Human Rights: International Norms and Domestic Change.* Cambridge University Press.

   2013. *The Persistent Power of Human Rights: From Commitment to Compliance.* Cambridge University Press.

Risse-Kappen, Thomas. 1994. "Ideas do not Float Freely: Transnational Coalitions, Domestic Structures, and the End of the Cold War." *International Organization* 48/2: 185–214.

Roberts, Clayton. 1996. *The Logic of Historical Explanation.* University Park, PA: Pennsylvania State University Press.

Roberts, Geoffrey. 2007. *Stalin's Wars: From World War to Cold War, 1939–1953.* New Haven, CT: Yale University Press.

Roessler, Philip. 2011. "The Enemy within: Personal Rule, Coups and Civil War in Africa." *World Politics* 63/2: 300–346.

Rohlfing, Ingo. 2012. *Case Studies and Causal Inference.* New York: Palgrave Macmillan.

   2013a. "Comparative Hypothesis Testing via Process Tracing." *Sociological Methods and Research* (pre-published online, October 15; DOI: 10.1177/0049124113503142).

   2013b. "Bayesian Causal Inference in Process Tracing: The Importance of Being Probably Wrong." Paper presented at the Annual Meeting of the American Political Science Association. Chicago, IL (September).

Rosenbaum, Paul. 2010. *Design of Observational Studies.* New York: Springer.

Rothstein, Jesse. 2007. "Does Competition among Public Schools Benefit Students and Taxpayers? A Comment on Hoxby (2000)." *American Economic Review* 97/5: 2026–2037.

Rubbi, Antonio. 1990. *Incontri con Gorbaciov: i colloqui di Natta e Occhetto con il leader sovietico*. Rome: Editori Riuniti.

Rubin, Donald B. 1978. "Bayesian Inference for Causal Effects: The Role of Randomization." *Annals of Statistics* 6/1: 34–58.

2006. *Matched Sampling for Causal Effects*. Cambridge University Press.

Rubin, Herbert J. and Irene S. Rubin. 1995. *Qualitative Interviewing: The Art of Hearing Data*. Thousand Oaks, CA: Sage Publications.

Rueschemeyer, Dietrich, Evelyne Huber Stephens, and John D. Stephens. 1992. *Capitalist Development and Democracy*. University of Chicago Press.

Ruggie, John Gerard. 1998. *Constructing the World Polity: Essays on International Institutionalization*. London: Routledge.

Salmon, Wesley. 1990. *Four Decades of Scientific Explanation*. University of Pittsburgh Press.

Sambanis, Nicholas. 2004. "Using Case Studies to Expand Economic Models of Civil War." *Perspectives on Politics* 2/2: 259–279.

Sapir, Jacques and Thierry Malleret. 1990. "La politique militaire soviétique: de la restructuration à la réforme." Paper presented to the 4th World Congress for Soviet and East European Studies. Harrogate. July 21–26.

Sarotte, Mary Elise. 2009. *1989: The Struggle to Create Post-Cold War Europe*. Princeton University Press.

Sartori, Giovanni. 1991. "Comparing and Miscomparing." *Journal of Theoretical Politics* 3/3: 243–257.

Savranskaya, Svetlana. 2010. "The Logic of 1989: The Soviet Peaceful Withdrawal from Eastern Europe," in Svetlana Savranskaya, Thomas Blanton, and Vladislav Zubok (eds.). *Masterpieces of History: The Peaceful End of the Cold War in Europe, 1989*. Budapest: Central European University Press.

Savranskaya, Svetlana, Thomas Blanton, and Vladislav Zubok (eds.). 2010. *Masterpieces of History: The Peaceful End of the Cold War in Europe, 1989*. Budapest: Central European University Press.

Schatz, Edward (ed.). 2009. *Political Ethnography: What Immersion Contributes to the Study of Power*. University of Chicago Press.

Schimmelfennig, Frank. 2003. *The EU, NATO and the Integration of Europe. Rules and Rhetoric*. Cambridge University Press.

2005. "Strategic Calculation and International Socialization: Membership Incentives, Party Constellations, and Sustained Compliance in Central and Eastern Europe." *International Organization* 59/4: 827–860.

2012. "Constructivist Perspectives," in Erik Jones, Anand Menon, and Stephen Weatherill (eds.). *The Oxford Handbook of the European Union*. Oxford University Press, pp. 34–47.

Schneider, Carsten Q. and Ingo Rohlfing. 2013. "Combining QCA and Process Tracing in Set-Theoretic Multi-Method Research." *Sociological Methods & Research* 42/4: 559–597.

Schneider, Gerald and Margit Bussmann. 2013. "Accounting for the Dynamics of One-Sided Violence." *Journal of Peace Research* 50/5: 635–644.

Schultz, Kenneth. 2001. *Democracy and Coercive Diplomacy*. Cambridge University Press.

2013. "Domestic Politics and International Relations," in Walter Carlsnaes, Thomas Risse, and Beth Simmons (eds.). *Handbook of International Relations*, 2nd edn. London: Sage Publications, chapter 19.

Scott, James. 1976. *The Moral Economy of the Peasant: Rebellion and Subsistence in South-East Asia.* New Haven, CT: Yale University Press.

Scriven, Michael. 1976. "Maximizing the Power of Causal Investigation: The Modus Operandi Method." *Evaluation Studies Review Annual* 1.

Searle, John R. 1995. *The Construction of Social Reality.* New York: Basic Books.

Seawright, Jason. 2012. "The Case for Selecting Cases that Are Deviant or Extreme on the Independent Variable." Presentation at the Institute for Qualitative and Multimethod Research, Syracuse University, June.

Seawright, Jason and Gerring, John. 2008. "Case Selection Techniques in Case Study Research: A Menu of Qualitative and Quantitative Options." *Political Research Quarterly* 61/2: 294–308.

Sekhon, Jasjeet S. 2009. "Opiates for the Matches: Matching Methods for Causal Inference." *Annual Review of Political Science* 12: 487–508.

Shadish, William R., Thomas D. Cook, and Donald T. Campbell. 2002. *Experimental and Quasi-Experimental Designs for Generalized Causal Inference.* Boston, MA: Houghton-Mifflin Co.

Shenfield, Stephen. 1984a. "The USSR: Viktor Girshfeld and the Concept of 'Sufficient Defense.'" *ADIU Report* 6/1: 10.

1984b. "Colonel X's Warning: Our Mistakes Plus Your Hysteria." *Détente* 1: 2–3.

1985. "Colonel X's Peace Proposals." *Détente* 2: 2–4.

Shepsle, Kenneth A. 1985. "Comment," in R. Noll (ed.). *Regulatory Policy and the Social Sciences.* Berkeley, CA: University of California Press.

Shevardnadze, Eduard. 1991. "Eduard Shevardnadze's Choice." *International Affairs* 11: 4–11.

Shultz, George P. 2007. "A Perspective from Washington," in Kiron K. Skinner (ed.). *Turning Points in Ending the Cold War.* Stanford, CA: Hoover Institution Press.

Simmons, Beth. 1994. *Who Adjusts? Domestic Sources of Foreign Economic Policy during the Interwar Years.* Princeton University Press.

2009. *Mobilizing for Human Rights: International Law in Domestic Politics.* Cambridge University Press.

Snow, John. (1855) 1965. *On the Mode of Communication of Cholera*, 2nd edn. London: John Churchill. Reprinted in *Snow on Cholera.* London: Humphrey Milford/Oxford University Press.

Snyder, Jack. 1987. "The Gorbachev Revolution: A Waning of Soviet Expansionism?" *International Security* 12/3: 93–131.

1991. *Myths of Empire: Domestic Politics and International Ambition.* Ithaca, NY: Cornell University Press.

2011. "The Domestic Political Logic of Gorbachev's New Thinking in Foreign Policy." *International Politics* 48/4–5: 562–574.

Snyder, Jack and Andrei Kortunov. 1989. "French Syndrome on Soviet Soil?" *New Times* 44: 18–20.

Sober, Elliott. 2009. "Absence of Evidence and Evidence of Absence: Evidential Transitivity in Connection with Fossils, Fishing, Fine-Tuning, and Firing Squads." *Philosophical Studies* 143/1: 63–90.

Sovey, Allison and Donald Green. 2011. "Instrumental Variables Estimation in Political Science: A Reader's Guide." *American Journal of Political Science* 55/1: 188–200.

Spitalnic, Stuart. 2004. "Test Properties 2: Likelihood Ratios, Bayes' Formula, and Receiver Operating Characteristic Curves." *Hospital Physician*, October, pp. 53–58.

Spruyt, Hendrik. 1994. *The Sovereign State and Its Competitors*. Princeton University Press.

Steel, Ronald. 1981. *Walter Lippmann and the American Century*. New York: Vintage Books.

Stein, Janice Gross. 1994. "Political Learning by Doing: Gorbachev as Uncommitted Thinker and Motivated Learner." *International Organization* 48/2: 155–183.

Stephens, Christopher Lee. 2011. "A Bayesian Approach to Absent Evidence." *Informal Logic: Reasoning and Argumentation in Theory and Practice* 31/1: 56–65.

Stone, Jeremy J. 1999. *"Everyman Should Try": Adventures of a Public Interest Activist*. New York: Public Affairs.

Stone Sweet, Alec and Wayne Sandholtz. 1997. "European Integration and Supranational Governance." *Journal of European Public Policy* 4/3: 297–317.

Ströber-Fassbender, Ralph. 1988. *Die Studiengruppe Alternative Sicherheitspolitik: Eine Dokumentation*. Bonn: Dietz.

Symposium. 2007. "Symposium: Multi–Method Work – Dispatches from the Front Lines." *Qualitative Methods: Newsletter of the American Political Science Association Organized Section on Qualitative Methods* 5/1: 9–27.

2013. "Symposium: Process Tracing." *European Political Science* 12/1: 1–85.

2014. "Symposium: Openness in Political Science: Data Access and Research Transparency." *PS: Political Science & Politics* 47/1: 19–83.

Tannenwald, Nina. 2007. *The Nuclear Taboo: The United States and the Non-Use of Nuclear Weapons since 1945*. Cambridge University Press.

Tarrow, Sidney. 1996. "Making Social Science Work across Space and Time: A Critical Reflection on Robert Putnam's Making Democracy Work." *American Political Science Review* 90/2: 389–397.

Taylor, Brian D. 2003. *Politics and the Russian Army: Civil–Military Relations, 1689–2000*. Cambridge University Press.

Taylor, Charles. 1993. "To follow a Rule," in Craig Calhoun, Edward LiPuma, and Moishe Postone (eds.). *Bourdieu: Critical Perspectives*. Cambridge: Polity Press, pp. 45–59.

Thomas, Daniel. 2001. *The Helsinki Effect: International Norms, Human Rights, and the Demise of Communism*. Princeton University Press.

Tiedtke, Jutta. 1985. *Abrüstung in der Sowjetunion: Wirtschaftliche Bedingungen und soziale Folgen der Truppenreduzierung von 1960*. Frankfurt am Main: Campus Verlag.

Tilly, Charles. 1990. *Coercion, Capital and European States, AD 990–1992*. Oxford: Blackwell Publishing.

2001. "Mechanisms in Political Processes." *Annual Review of Political Science* 4: 21–41.

Trachtenberg, Marc. 2006. *The Craft of International History*. Princeton University Press.

Tsentral'noe statisticheskoe upravlenie SSSR. 1968. *Narodnoe khoziastvo SSSR v 1967 g.: Statisticheskii ezhegodnik*. Moscow: Gosstatizdat.

Turner, Stephen. 1994. *The Social Theory of Practices: Tradition, Tacit Knowledge, and Presuppositions*. University of Chicago Press.

US Army. 2007. *US Army Field Manual No. 3-24*. University of Chicago Press.

Van Evera, Stephen. 1997. *Guide to Methods for Students of Political Science*. Ithaca, NY: Cornell University Press.

Vaughn, Diane. 2008. "Bourdieu and Organizations: The Empirical Challenge." *Theory and Society* 37/1: 65–81.

Volkov, E. 1989. "Ne raz'iasniaet, a zatumanivaet." *Krasnaia zvezda*. September 28.

Voors, Maarten, Eleonora Nillesen, Philip Verwimp, Erwin Bulte, Robert Lensink, and Daan van Souest. 2012. "Violent Conflict and Behavior: A Field Experiment in Burundi." *American Economic Review* 102/2: 941–964.

Vorotnikov, V. I. 1995. *A bylo tak . . . Iz dnevnika chlena Poltiburo Tsk KPSS*. Moscow: Sovet veteranov knigoizdaniia.

Vucetic, Srdjan. 2011. "Genealogy as a Research Tool in International Relations." *Review of International Studies* 37/3: 1295–1312.

Wagner, R. Harrison. 1993. "What was Bipolarity?" *International Organization* 47/1 (Winter): 77–106.

Waldner, David. 2007. "Transforming Inferences into Explanations: Lessons from the Study of Mass Extinctions," in Richard Ned Lebow and Mark Lichbach (eds.). *Theory and Evidence in Comparative Politics and International Relations*. New York: Palgrave Macmillan.

 2011. "Process Tracing, Its Promise, and Its Problems." Paper presented at the Research Group on Qualitative and Multi-Method Analysis, Syracuse University, Syracuse, NY (June).

 2012. "Process Tracing and Causal Mechanisms," in Harold Kincaid (ed.). *The Oxford Handbook of the Philosophy of Social Science*. Oxford University Press, pp. 65–84.

 2014. "Aspirin, Aeschylus, and the Foundations of Qualitative Causal Inference." Unpublished paper, University of Virginia, June.

Wallace, William 1983. "Less than a Federation, More than a Regime: The Community as a Political System," in Helen Wallace, William Wallace, and C. Webb (eds.). *Policy-Making in the European Community*. Chichester: Wiley & Sons, pp. 403–436.

Wallander, Celeste. 1999. *Mortal Friends, Best Enemies: German–Russian Cooperation after the Cold War*. Ithaca, NY: Cornell University Press.

Waltz, Kenneth N. (1979), *Theory of International Politics*. New York: McGraw-Hill.

Wedeen, Lisa. 2010. "Reflections on Ethnographic Work in Political Science." *Annual Review of Political Science* 13: 255–272.

Weinstein, Jeremy. 2007. *Inside Rebellion: The Politics of Insurgent Violence*. Cambridge University Press.

Weir, Margaret. 1989. "Ideas and Politics: The Acceptance of Keynesianism in Britain and the United States," in P. A. Hall (ed.). *The Political Power of Economic Ideas: Keynesianism across Nations*. Princeton University Press.

Weisberg, Jacob. 2009. "Commutativity or Holism: A Dilemma for Conditionalizers." *British Journal for the Philosophy of Science* 60/4: 793–812.

Wendt, Alexander. 1987. "The Agent-Structure Problem in International Relations Theory." *International Organization* 41/3: 335–370.

 1999. *Social Theory of International Politics*. Cambridge University Press.

Wight, Colin. 2002. "Philosophy of Science and International Relations," in Walter Carlsnaes, Thomas Risse, and Beth Simmons (eds.). *Handbook of International Relations*. London: Sage Publications.

2004. "Theorizing the Mechanisms of Conceptual and Semiotic Space." *Philosophy of the Social Sciences* 34/2: 283–299.

2006. *Agents, Structures and International Relations: Politics as Ontology.* Cambridge University Press.

Wohlforth, William C. 2003. *Cold War Endgame: Oral History, Analysis, Debates.* University Park, PA: Pennsylvania State University Press.

2011. "No One Loves a Realist Explanation." *International Politics* 48/4–5: 441–459.

Wood, Elisabeth Jean. 2000. *Forging Democracy from Below: Insurgent Transitions in South Africa and El Salvador.* Cambridge University Press.

2003. *Insurgent Collective Action and Civil War in El Salvador.* Cambridge University Press.

2006. "The Ethical Challenges of Field Research in Conflict Zones." *Qualitative Sociology* 29/3: 373–386.

Zaks, Sherry. 2011. "Relationships Among Rivals: Analyzing Contending Hypotheses with a New Logic of Process Tracing." Manuscript. Berkeley, CA: University of California.

Zubok, Vladislav. 2003. "Gorbachev and the End of the Cold War: Different Perspectives on the Historical Personality," in William C. Wohlforth (ed.). *Cold War Endgame: Oral History, Analysis, Debates.* University Park, PA: Pennsylvania State University Press.

Index